RINGS

RINGS

On the Life and Family of
a Southern Fighter

RANDOLPH BATES

Farrar, Straus & Giroux

NEW YORK

Library of Congress Cataloging-in-Publication Data
Bates, Randolph.
    Rings : on the life and family of a Southern fighter. — 1st ed.
    p.   cm.
    1. Phillips, Collis.   2. Boxers (Sports)—United States—
Biography.   I. Title.
GV1132.P48B38   1992   796.83'092—dc20   [B]   91-27875   CIP

In
Memory
of
EVA THURBER BATES
and
ULMER FORTINBERRY *and* MARVIN BATES

Contents

The things that I used to do
Lord, I won't do no more
—EDDIE JONES
(Guitar Slim), 1953

ONE

The Gym

□

1

☐

March 15, 1979

The first time I stepped into the gym on Magazine, I saw no one in the shadowed spaces of the old building. I had ducked in off the congested street to find myself, half blind from the glare outside, in a narrow passing space between the ring and a brick wall. Scrap wood protruded from below the ring's apron near my ankles. I was so intent on not stumbling that, before I noticed him, I had walked up to an old man who sat between the heavy bags in a broken school desk. He was eating from something gathered in tinfoil. I took a breath and asked to see Willie Pastrano.

A week before, while running the levee on a false-spring morning, I had come up on a youth who punched the air as he jogged. When he bragged about the police department's boxing program and said Willie Pastrano was in charge, I remembered being ten or eleven and reading about Willie Pastrano in *Ring* magazine. After I thanked the young boxer and drew away, I wondered if, now that I had finished graduate school, this might not be a last chance to try my hands at a fantasy I'd had since adolescence. Since I was between things, hack-teaching at several universities, I could think of no excuse—once I reasoned down my fears of being disgraced or hurt.

"Wh-who . . . ? W-Willie . . . ?" The old man acted confused. He blinked and flinched, then brushed his fingers over his stereotypically cauliflowered ear. "Sometimes I misremembers. Y-you sees how it is." He smiled and flinched again. "Wh-what you want?"

Also stammering, I told him I wanted to box.

He laughed. "You shoulda *tol'* me that! Cain' tell who go'n walk in here, aksin' things . . . Willie gone. For today . . . How many fights you had?"

When I told him what I felt certain he could see, that I had had none, he surprised me again by smiling.

"How old is you?"

To be doing this at my age—thirty-four—seemed to invite ridicule. I had prepared a lie, one made plausible by my boyish face and years of exercise. "Twenty-nine."

He scowled.

"Too old?" The moment I asked him that, I realized I'd as soon he say yes.

He answered solemnly, speaking with exaggerated care. "Normally . . . ? Course. Any man already growed up is late comin' to this game. I'd be lyin' if I was to tell y' any different."

Then he grinned as if we shared a secret. "But, *shit!* You don' know. You might be a damn natural . . ."

"C'mon," he said brusquely, thrusting himself up out of the desk with his hands. "Lemme show y' whatcha go'n need."

I noticed that his arms and shoulders were still roped with muscle before I realized the man couldn't walk.

"Reach me them crutches. Against that bag behind y'."

His useless left foot made a slick, scraping sound as he swung himself across the concrete. Flourishing keys, he opened a flimsy tin locker that was tilted against the wall next to a pile of trash. "C'mon."

I watched him lay strips of stained cloth along the training table. "Don't you come here with no cheap wraps. You go to Malcolm Faber's. Git you some good ones. Like these here. An' a mouthpiece. I'll show you how to boil it an' set it, an', you know"—he touched his fly—"a cup. To stick down in y' jockey strap."

He frowned at my expensive leather handball shoes. "Them tenneys is all right . . . for now. You can use my gloves an' this other. Till you wants to have y' own." Then he asked if I knew where Faber's was. "Malcolm, all of 'em, they knows me. You tell 'em you's one a Collis's fighters. Git y'self a discount."

One of Collis's fighters. I couldn't help liking the sound of it. Even though I sensed his premature willingness to take me seriously was largely a hustle, it seemed so transparent that I didn't really mind. Though I needed to prepare to teach a night class, I stayed around and helped him pick up litter from around the bags, piling it onto the trash heap and under the ring.

The building was originally a firehouse, but I didn't know that then. I assumed families had once lived there. Toward the rear, dusty stairs led to a second floor. In the small room next to them were kitchen counters, cabinets, and the mounts for speed bags. A metal garage door formed the back wall. I rolled it up into the ceiling for him and looked out on an open space, a paved courtyard banked with junk and closed off by the backs of neighboring buildings.

He grumbled when I told him I had a night job and couldn't come in on Tuesdays and Thursdays. "Well, a man gotta do what he gotta do. But you oughta be in the gym just as much as you can. Days you ain' comin' in, you sho better take the road."

I started to leave, but he called after me. "Reach in that wall box by the do', screw in them fuses."

When I did as he said, exposed light bulbs flashed on, giving the gym a hard, gold cast.

"Now reach round them chairs there, plug in the bell."

A brace of old theater seats faced the ring just inside the doorway. As I groped behind them, I thought about how it must have been for him to do that. Then I walked back around the ring to ask him a last question, one that turned out to be stupid. "W-will I need Willie's permission? You know, to train here?"

He looked away.

"I likes Willie," he said slowly. "The city made Willie the boss. An' they shoulda. Willie was a champ sho' 'nuff."

He looked at me.

"But I runs the gym."

The bell didn't ring; it made a flat, tinking sound. As I stepped out into the hot, late-winter afternoon and unchained my bicycle from a drainpipe, I could hear the faint, scraping sounds of Collis moving about. The bell tinked again—terminal, utterly without echo. With a surge of unseasonal energy I swung onto the bike, which was already rolling, and a raucous group of signifying young fighters swung past me and into the gym.

2

□

March 15, 1988

It took me little more than a month to satisfy myself that I was no natural, and not much longer than that to confirm that I didn't have it in me to find pleasure in fighting. It was only after I tried to end my flirtation with boxing that I discovered how strong a hold my brief time in the gym had on me. I'm not speaking now of my moments of queasy exhilaration while sparring or of how the place stamped itself on my imagination. I'm referring to what, in looking back, I recognized as most important about the experience: Collis Phillips, the way he treated me, and the things I learned about him and his family.

Almost before I was aware of doing it, I began mentally to record fragments of the story that I encountered on Magazine Street in New Orleans. It was this story, his and his family's, that was the natural—or it would be, if I could find a way of ordering it that would falsify neither its facts nor my distance from them. After anguishing for too long about this distance, I decided it had its own advantages, which were natural enough.

Yet something more was needed. Because every impression to follow will be filtered through my fatherless, blue, Mississippian's eyes and because my personal circumstances subsequently suffered a large change that involved race, my narration must take intermittent account of me—and, briefly, of my family too. My way toward ordering the full story begins with the gym and those afternoons nine years ago when I first glimpsed how it was to have lived Collis's life.

3

□

March 16, 1979

As he had told me to be, I was back on Magazine Street at the same time the next day. But, to my dismay, the plyboard-buttressed door to the gym was padlocked. Feeling conspicuous in my workout clothes, I moved over to stand before the secondhand shop on the uptown side of the gym. Slanting sunlight flashed from passing cars and buses. I squinted and shallowly inhaled the fumes.

Soon a young man about my weight turned the corner down by the fish market. He seemed to lean against his shoulder bag as he sauntered up the sidewalk with one arm swinging in slow circles away from his body. With the fingers of that hand, he unwrapped a stick of gum. The wrapper floated behind him as he folded the gum into his mouth in stages that went with the hitch in his walk. He stopped before the gym and dipped his shoulder. The bag fell, he hiked his jeans, squatted, then sat exactly on the lip of the doorway, where he stayed hunched forward, plucking the untied laces of his high-topped basketball shoes until they gathered like ribbon. Then he slumped audibly against the door and scanned the street through half-closed eyes, his gaze crossing me and moving away before coming back to follow a woman who was passing between us. I had begun to hope Collis wouldn't come when a gold Buick with dented fenders swerved into the no-parking space in front of the gym.

Willie Pastrano slid from under the wheel in mid-conversation and hustled around the car still talking to the two men inside. He was only slightly heavier than he had been in the photographs I remembered from *Ring*, and he wore flashy black clothes in an offhand way that suited the subtly blurred features of his dark Italian face.

The other two appeared to have come straight from sleeping. The Buick rocked as a heavyweight lurched from the back seat, cradling clothes and equipment. He was shirtless and wore his shoes slipper-style, with walked-over backs.

Willie Pastrano snapped open the padlock and chattered at his protégé, the name middleweight in the front. "C'mon, Tony. C'mon, babe. Work time."

Tony Licata kicked the car door closed with his bare foot and scuffed across the hot concrete bow-legged to keep up his unsnapped jeans. He carried a bundle of clothes and a fluttering sports page.

The fighter who had been waiting in front of the gym stepped in behind the heavyweight and Licata, and Willie Pastrano spoke to him—"Aw right, Cheetah! Whatcha say!"—as he waved the three of them through the door with a torn pack of Luckies.

I could see this was business, no place for me. I waited a while longer, then walked to the door to take a last look around before I left. There, blinking in the doorway, I found myself an arm's length from Willie Pastrano, who was jiggling the fuse box.

"What say, babe? What can I do for you?"

Witless, I blurted to him what I had told Collis, simply that I wanted to box.

"Sure, babe. You can start here." His tone expressed only polite interest, but he clapped me on the shoulder with his famous left hand. "You got wraps? C'mon."

The fighters seemed to be dreaming. They moved languidly in their ring shoes and cut-off training sweats, rolling their shoulders and shaking down their arms. There was little talk. A rotating fan beat the air, and the bell tinked at three- and one-minute intervals.

When they began wrapping their hands, I turned my back and tried to do the same.

"No, babe! Not like that."

I thought it strange that Willie Pastrano would notice me. I didn't understand then that he had nothing else to do while he waited for them.

"Left hand first, spread your fingers, keep 'em stiff. You married? Still gotta take that ring off. I'll hold it for you. Keep 'em stiff, now."

I watched him put the band on his little finger and begin turning my hand between his, quickly winding the spotless wraps. "Now these bag gloves. Always the left on first." He winked. "For luck."

Broken pigment splotched his cheeks and the slightly crooked bridge of his nose, and his eyes seemed independent of the rest of his face. But there was no trace that I could detect of the period of heroin addiction that had followed his two years as world light heavyweight champion.

"Now go on up. Get the feel of the ring."

The canvas was almost spongy, much softer than I imagined. He followed me through the ropes, working his hands into flat vinyl pads about the size of my son's catcher's mitt.

"You a lefty, babe? That's good. I love to turn lefties around."

He made me lead with my left and, explaining simply and clearly, showed me how to throw a jab ("Don't pull it back, the punch comes direct out from the shoulder"), then a jab-cross-hook combination ("Elbow in, hips and legs drive a hook"). I hit the pads.

"Now try it." Holding the pads still, he began to glide. I missed. I missed again. Then he let me connect. "That's it. Now shadowbox in the ring. Two rounds."

That was the last attention he paid me. Tony Licata and the one he called Cheetah had come in between the ropes, and he turned to watch them. Cheetah kept to himself in a far corner, but Licata began circling the ring in a prancing backpedal, shooting punches straight overhead with both hands. The ropes vibrated, and the flooring buckled and thundered. It felt like being on a carelessly built boat. Keeping sight of Licata in the mirrors level with the ring's apron, I took care to stay out of his way as he spun about, bobbing, weaving, and breathing out, as if in caught sneezes, with each half-withheld punch. When, circling, he looked at me in passing, I saw a lean boyish torso, a sparse stubble on his square chin, and neither hostility nor recognition in his Asian eyes. From this angle, it seemed absurd that local sportswriters had hinted he was washed up.

"*Two-* . . . *gun* . . . Tony Li*c*ata, ladies an' gentlemen! The middleweight champ . . . of the *South!*"

Licata answered without looking around. "Aw right, Mister Collis. How ya feelin'?"

He stood propped on his crutches in the doorway, the tilt of his head disclosing the underside of his cocked hat brim. Cheetah juked toward him in an abbreviated ring bow. I tried to look busy.

"Naw, naw, *naw!*" At once I knew he was talking to me. "You jus' *push*in' that jab. Gotta *snap* it. Look here."

He shifted his weight to one crutch, his fist shooting straight from the shoulder. "Bing, *bing!* Then . . . you step in with the right. *Bam!*"

I started to practice in the mirror, but he stopped me. "That's y' rest bell." He waved me toward him and out of the ring. "C'mon."

"You listens pretty good," he told me later, after I had hit one of the heavy canvas bags exclusively with jabs until I could no longer hold up my left arm. Now, after I had finished using his leather skip rope, sweat puddled beneath me as he leaned on my shins and I did tension sit-ups on the padless wooden stomach bench. He plucked at his pant cuff as if it were a sling and lifted his paralyzed left leg out

of his way when he sat down. Straining, I concentrated
alternately on his huge hands and on his short-brimmed hat;
when the hat fell off, I focused on his cropped silver temples
and bald beige crown.

"You sho *strong* in the belly," he commented as if it were
a marvel. I didn't mention I had done sit-ups for years, and
went to towel myself off next to the ring.

By then the gym had begun to fill up. Fighters continued
to come in, and white men in ties stood against the apron
watching Tony Licata work with a third sparring partner.
"Women in the gym!" someone shouted; a group of black
schoolgirls giggled in the theater seats by the door. One of
them whooped when the speedy dark-skinned fighter in with
Licata landed a flurry and then veered out of range.

"He was *hit*tin' you, Tony!" I heard Willie Pastrano whisper
after the round ended and they moved down the steps and
over to Licata's special locker. "Why you let him hit you?"

Collis now pulled himself, hand over hand, up the steps
and then the turnbuckles. Supporting himself against one
of the corner posts, he took charge of the rest of the sparring
and half jokingly announced each fighter.

"An' now, ladies and gentlemen! Wearin' a stylish new
sweat suit! The number-three-ranked middleweight . . . in
the world!" He grinned down at Willie Pastrano. "Soon to
be seen against the highly regarded Tony Li*ca*ta, here he is,
ladies an' gentlemen: Freddie . . . *John* . . . son!

"An' his first opponent. From right here in this city.
Wearin' no shirt. A ten-round fighter . . ."

The sparring went on. Before long I noticed that the light
outside had changed and that Tony Licata's personalized
leather heavy bag had been taken down and he and Willie
Pastrano were gone.

A boxer poked a red training glove near my chest and
curtly asked me to tie its laces. Because he looked to be at
least as old as I was, I took special notice. Coarse hair stood
out around his headgear, but his skin was as light as mine
and his flattened nose seemed wrong for the rest of his thin
features. He wore two pairs of wrinkled, satiny old match

trunks, red over green, a grayed T-shirt, and dusty, cracked boxing shoes.

When he asked if I was new to the city, I mistakenly tried to talk to him. I sensed he could tell me if I should expect to box that night. To my question, he simply gazed past me into the ring until the rest bell.

"Keep comin' in," he said, starting up the steps, "hit the bags, skip the rope, it'll happen." Then, like biting an apple, he took in his mouthpiece off the heel of his glove.

Freddie Johnson, who was still holding the ring, rested in a corner with his arms on the ropes. When the work bell tinked, the fighter who had spoken to me dipped through the ropes and put up his guard. Collis, who had been trying to solicit a fresh sparring partner for Johnson, seemed surprised. He hesitated before making another of his announcements.

"Wha . . . ? Looka here, ladies and gentlemen. Wearin' the red trunks an' red headgear, it's . . . *Terrell* . . . the tornada from Texas!

"That Terrell's . . . aw right now," he added just before Johnson bulled the smaller man into the ropes and banged hooks to his arms and kidneys. Late in the round, Terrell's legs straightened when Johnson's right split the crook in his left arm and drilled him over the heart.

Johnson shoved him aside. "Goddammit, shit, Mista Collis! We gotta fight comin' up. Ain' no time for this mess!"

Collis appeared somehow embarrassed. "You aw right, Terrell?"

The old fighter nodded doggedly, dabbed at his headgear, and reassumed his stance.

Collis spoke to his fighter. "Go on now, Freddie. Round's 'bout over. *Box* with the man!"

Johnson said "Shit," walked through Terrell's jab, pinned him on the ropes, and ripped to the body.

"Time!"

It was Collis who had shouted.

The rest bell tinked several seconds after Johnson leaped down from the ring, faintly cursing.

"I thought I'd just done heard that bell," Collis said and made a show of laughing at himself.

But Freddie Johnson wouldn't look at him.

After all the sparring was done, Collis sat down on the apron and nudged his paralyzed leg over the edge; then, still seated, he lowered himself down the steps, crablike, with one foot and his hands. I held out his crutches, and he looked around at me as if we were strangers. "What you doin' still here?" When I said I didn't know whether I was supposed to stay and box, his voice softened. "Oh, naw . . . You's always done when you finishes calisthenics." Then he shook his finger at me. "An' if you ain' comin' in but ev'ry other day, you sho better take the road tomorra."

As I started for the door, he shook his finger again, but this time he was smiling. "An' you stay away from that *cat* now," he said, airing an old belief about athletic conditioning and sex. "That *cat* takes y' strength . . . Don't you be lookin' back at me like that. You knows what I means. I sees you do. Terrell too!"

Terrell had been sullenly off to himself since his round with Freddie Johnson, but Collis kept at it until everyone was laughing.

"Don't you grin! Look at Terrell grinnin'. Terrell *knows!*"

It was a sweet night. Traffic had lulled, and bullbats soared low, screaking near the old buildings. I turned my bike at the Winn-Dixie on the nearest uptown corner of Magazine. Evening bells began as I pedaled past the church on Camp. Eight o'clock. At home, they would already have eaten. On Valence, streetlamps splashed shadows and gold shapes in the thick branches overhead. I pedaled slowly with no hands, hot-dogging, taking my time.

4

Spring 1979

"Wrap up. You go'n box the other white boy."

Before Collis spoke, I had sensed that the boxer I saw in the ring was waiting for me. He rolled his dark, curly head in warm-up and swayed from side to side, holding his hands in training gloves away from his body in an inverted, swaggering V. I hadn't seen him before.

Although I had been in the gym only a few times, I had already asked Collis to let me spar. It wasn't so much that I was eager as that I wanted to appear to be eager. Now, as I rummaged in my bag for my wraps, nausea swirled in my stomach and bowels.

The phone rang while I was wrapping my hands. Collis ended up having to take the call and give someone a dizzy explanation of why Willie Pastrano couldn't be reached just then. In the meantime, Cheetah went up into the ring already laced into his own gloves. The young white amateur shook his head and turned away. Cheetah kept stepping around in front of him, and finally the amateur nodded. At the work bell, they touched gloves and squared off.

By the time Collis had hung up the phone, Cheetah, boxing with his hands below his waistband, had walked the amateur into a corner and begun stinging him with rising lefts and rights. Collis shouted, but he had to swing himself all the way over to the apron before Cheetah seemed able to hear him. Cheetah backed off, and the amateur began backpedaling about the ring with his gloves high, almost to his hairline. Collis shouted again, angrily, at Cheetah, then paused and called to the amateur. "Stop *run*nin', Whatcha-callit! Stick with y' left!"

The amateur slowed a beat and circled to his left, for the first time almost toward Cheetah. Cheetah took two quick skipping steps and sealed him into another corner, then slipped a jab with his head and feinted with his right. The amateur shifted to block the right, and Cheetah rocked low and to the left. Collis had shouted "Time!" before Cheetah came in and up, his sable torso twisting rapidly back to the right. The hook, a blur, clipped the amateur below the ear just as the punch was level with the plane of Cheetah's shoulder.

Cheetah walked away with no expression on his face. The amateur, who had flinched to the right just in time to keep from being knocked down, sagged against the turnbuckle, his head lower than the top rope, gloves still against his face, thighs visibly shaking.

Collis muttered wearily. "*Man* . . . Cheetah . . . That ain' no way to do." He gestured to the amateur. "C'mere, Whatchacallit!"

After Cheetah shrugged and stepped through the ropes, the amateur made his way over to us, walking with a float-footed, sheepish step. "Shee!" he said, letting out breath. "That Cheetah, he's . . . *fast!*"

"Yeh? Well, you bet' listen at me, an' not Cheetah." Collis drew me toward him. "This'n's the one I want f' you. Say, Cheetah, let us use y' gloves a few. Freddie gittin' mine stitched."

Reluctantly, Cheetah allowed him to untie his training gloves and hold them open for me.

"Push."

Inside, the gloves were hot and wet. It felt like a handicap to have their overstuffing laced midway to my elbows. As I climbed the steps, I heard Collis tell the amateur to take it easy on me. The work bell had already tinked, so we both hustled through the ropes and he bobbed toward me right away.

Our punches—and many misses—now are less clear in memory than are other sensations: adrenaline and an almost immediate and near-total fatigue; the smothering smell of sweat and the taste of my mouthpiece as I plodded forward across the increasing resistance of the ring's spongy surface; the faces and objects around the apron that seemed to tilt in, in a tightening circle, around me; the slick, alien feel of the retreating young amateur's wet skin; and my spent confusion when, even before the rest bell, he coughed his mouthpiece into his glove and gasped that he couldn't go on because Cheetah had used him up. It was a confusion followed by distrust, then relief . . . then also something like pity.

Collis waved us out of the ring and took him aside. As I went down the steps, my knees trembled with tension. I felt as if they would give way. Cheetah snatched at my wrists, anxious to have back his gloves. As he seized the laces, I could hear Collis berating the amateur. "My fighters runs on the road, not in the ring. If you loves y'self, you in the wrong game."

Later, he came over to hold the heavy bag I was hitting. "That's it, snap it, *bing!* Then right back with the right, *bam!* Now the hook, *bang!*" At the rest bell, he turned to a tall fighter who had been working the other heavy bag. "Lamont, shake hands with y' new stablemate." Lamont looked non-committally past my ear as he extended sheathed knuckles to knock against mine.

5

□

Rusted gutters out back streamed with rain, and a cool mist blew into the kitchen. I had finished my fifth round on the speed bag, pleased that I had begun to catch its rhythm. It was dark outside and only two fighters remained, but Collis had told me to train as long as I wanted.

"I don' never stop a man when he *wants* to work."

The fighters, Cheetah and an amateur heavyweight, were dressed to leave, but they continued to stand around, talking to Collis, who had just pointed at me. "Wadn't that y' work bell? Take the rope."

The others watched idly. After the round, the heavyweight came over and gave me a tip about timing the rope. Tournament patches covered his windbreaker.

I found no sign of ridicule in his face, and at the work bell, I tried to do as he said.

"See, Mista Collis," I heard him say, interrupting their talk of something else. "He doin' better already."

"You boys don' know *nothin'*," Collis said to them later as he finished holding my shins down for the tension sit-ups. "You go round woofin' 'bout things is now—C'mere, show him a jackknife."

Cheetah slid alongside me on the narrow stomach bench without touching my body and snapped out three perfect jackknifes.

"Like that," Collis told me and went on talking to them. "You thinks you has it hard. When I was breakin' in, open spots on the black cards was scarce. An' you couldn' git in the ring with no white boy! So you know that was some heat." He jerked his thumb toward his chest. "But I always got work. An' you know why . . . ? It's 'cause I kep' in shape, an' always give a good show.

"An' 'cause I knew how to git along with people. You hear me, Cheetah?"

At the top of a jackknife, I glanced at Cheetah, who was looking at me. Then he blinked, and when he opened his eyes, he was looking somewhere else.

Collis spoke to him again. "What's that, Cheetah? Say."

The young fighter mumbled something I think none of us understood before answering clearly. "You know I always hears *you*, Mista Collins." Then he grinned and feinted at the heavyweight.

Since Collis rode three buses to return home from the gym and since I had the car that night, I volunteered to drive him. The heavyweight's ride came, and though I felt awkward asking him, I offered to drive Cheetah home too.

"Oh, naw . . . Un-unh." He ducked his head and mumbled about having to wait for someone there.

While he helped Collis close up the gym, I brought the car around, for once just as happy it was beat up and old. Collis handed his crutches and two paper sacks with his things in them across the seat. Then he lifted his limp leg in with his hands and let his body fall into the car after it. Cheetah shut the door and stepped back under the awning of the bar on the downtown side of the gym.

As we pulled away, Collis snapped his fingers and grimaced. "Neb' min'," he said when I turned to him. "Ain' nothin'. I jus' meant to git one a them boys to run to the sto' f' me."

"Lord, Mister Collis. I don't mind. I'm still wet from the gym."

He shook his head, but I was able to coast into a rare parking space in front of the Magazine Street Winn-Dixie.

His manner becoming formal, he took out a rubber coin purse and fished a bill from it. "Just a loaf a white bread, a bottle a orange juice—the good kind—an' two newspapers. If you please."

"Two?"

"Aw, there's a old man stays by me. He don' git out."

As I ran for the store, I saw Cheetah turn down Camp and stride beyond the streetlight, head tucked against the rain.

"Nar*cot*ics."

He came down hard on the middle of the word, just as he did in "Li*ca*ta." He had been talking about one of his sons, the son who, I just then realized, was the same Phillips I remembered from sports pages in the late sixties and early seventies. This Phillips, Alvin, had been a popular local headliner. He was reported to be on the verge of a shot at the world middleweight title, but finally it never happened.

"I sees him whenever I takes amateurs up to the penitentiary for a show."

Much later, I would learn that he had last taken boxers to the state penitentiary at Angola in the 1950s, that he had never visited his son Alvin there, and that it had been six years since they had seen each other.

"E'body up at Angola treat me real nice. Always tryin' to buy me sumpum to eat. They all know I'm Alvin's father. Never got in trouble myself. 'Less you wanna count a coupla times when I was a young man an' didn' know nothin'. Let m'self git mad. But jus' li'l things, hardly enough to even worry my wife . . . She didn' git over Alvin, though. She wasn't strong. Was ailin' since Alvin was a chil'. An' him a nice boy, one a the nicest of my chil'ren . . . She gone now. Been three years since I buried her."

We rode farther down Broad in silence. Then, to hearten the conversation, I asked about the celebrated controversial draw between Alvin and Tony Licata at the Rivergate.

"You mean the first fight? Whoo! Alvin was goin' good then. Had the Southern title all to hisself, jus' like I usta. We was shakin' an' rollin' that night! Whupped the *shit* outta Tony! Tony know."

"I read Tony had to sweat off weight the day of the fight."

"I read that too."

I didn't mention the rematch, which reportedly commenced Alvin's slide, and he changed the subject with a kind of a yawn. "Yeh . . . a smart white boy can move up quick in this game. Way up. Look at Tony."

"So, Mister Collis . . ." I couldn't wait any longer to ask about what was most on my mind. "When do you think you'll put me in again?"

"Lef'," he said. "Turn left at the light. What's that now?"

I repeated the question.

He seemed to think it over, then answered slowly. "Well, far as that goes, if you in a hurry, you can go back up in that ring any time you want. Not many blow in off the street in the kinda shape you's in." He snapped his finger on my arm. "But don' go gittin' cocked up 'bout that. They's some smart boys come in that gym. They'll *knock* yo' *dick* off! Jus' to be doin' it. *Then* whatcha go'n do . . . ?

"You bet' not grin! I ain' playin'. They'll do it in a minute! You b'lieve it?"

"Yes!"

"You better. Nothin' worse'n a fighter don' feel no respec'."

His tone changed. "But you stick in the gym. Keep listenin' an' workin' nice like you's doin'. I got a few more boys in mind. They'll be comin' in. I might letcha step a few rounds with some a them. Next week maybe. Might could find you a spot on a show pretty soon. You got a family?"

I told him I did.

"Yeh?! Chil'ren? . . . Two! You don' mean it! It was the same with me when I was fightin'. If y' wife's like mine, she go'n fuss . . . Specially after I got this ear. She say sixty fights was enough an' she couldn' git no rest till I give up the ring."

He shrugged.

"What I'm go'n do? That's right, *re*tire, let her have her way."

He thumped my arm again and winked.

"But I still ain' give it up . . . Slow down. We here."

The St. Bernard housing project dripped in the rain's aftermath. Phosphorescent light from the few functioning streetlamps silvered some of the façades of the brown brick apartments. He told me to pull up over the curb and pointed to a concrete porchway that, to me, looked like all the others.

"Been stayin' here thirty years. Woncha come in?"

Surprised, I automatically shook my head and said something about needing to be home.

"Oh, yeh! Course. Y' family. I was f'gittin'."

As he gathered his crutches and sacks, he began talking about his career. To smooth over the awkwardness, I guessed. He couldn't find the door handle, and I cut the engine. Also to smooth over awkwardness, I asked him to name some of the best boxers he had met in the ring.

"What's that boy's name?" he answered. "Cheetah! That's it. You know him? *Dark* skin. Sorta chunky. A low-weight fighter. Now, he moves pretty good. Ain' too slow neither."

"No," I said. "Not fighters you train—I meant some of the best you *fought*."

"You shoulda said that, then. The best? You wouldn' know of him. Fella name Coffee. We was matched once down here and a coupla times more in Chicago. I won the last one, but it didn' feel like it. God . . . *dam*, he could hit!" He looked around as if a related idea had just come to him. "Y' know, I got clippin's, an' there's plenty a this juice. Sure you won't . . . ?"

I hesitated. I had thought his mannerliness toward me had been basically a form of cunning, a way of somehow getting over. Now I wondered if, under the pressure of hosting, he might prove to be what some of the fighters in the gym seemed to think he truly was: a Tom. I knew I didn't want any part of that. Still, his invitation might just have been a matter of generosity. Or loneliness. I see now that another possibility was a mild interest on his part in having his neighbors see him accompanied by a white person who was quite willing to carry his bundles and hold the door. But, whatever his motive, I knew I wanted to go in, and I was about to say so when he popped open the car door.

"Naw," he said as he pulled, then rocked himself to his foot. "Don' listen at me. *Go home.* You right to put y' family first. You should always do that."

A city bus stopped at the curb in front of us. He cocked his hat, settled himself on his crutches, a sack clutched around a wooden grip in each hand, and peered down into the car.

"Take the road tomorra."

After he shut the door, he scanned the people who had stepped down from the bus. I started the car, then looked back around before pulling away. He had reached the sidewalk. Someone from the bus, a pretty young woman, stepped up and kissed his cheek.

I made a U-turn, and when I passed again, he was standing at ease on his crutches. Several other people were gathered about him.

Now it occurred to me with a near visceral force that I had just missed an opportunity, one that might have meant more than any I would have in the gym. Miserably, I promised myself not to hold back if he ever asked me again.

6

□

Preoccupied with how I would soon do against the white amateur, I was in the gym early, but he didn't come. After Tony Licata worked, Collis replaced Willie Pastrano on the corner of the apron in order to handle Freddie Johnson during his rounds. I learned that Licata and Johnson would soon meet as headliners of the undercard of the Mike Rossman–Victor Galindez rematch. In one of New Orleans's biggest boxing events, Rossman had taken Galindez's light heavyweight title some seven months before on the same bill in which Muhammad Ali had achieved sports legend by regaining his crown for a third time in a decision over Leon Spinks. These next Superdome fights were only a short while away, and Collis had no time for me while Freddie Johnson worked. But between rounds, he glanced down and said, "Shadow, but don' git tired."

"What's Collis been tellin' you?" I had hardly broken a sweat before being snapped at. I shrugged and regarded the speaker, an old Jewish ex-fighter and trainer they called Mister Arthur, who often talked about a featherweight title shot he had been promised, then deviously denied. He had one or two fighters in the gym on Magazine, but he spent most of his time there, wandering in and out, picking up things and moving them around. He rarely sat and always seemed angry, muttering profanely about the training habits of fighters "nowdays" and sometimes describing them as "monkeys!" when they were possibly within earshot. When

I continued shadowboxing, he answered himself. "Nothin',
probably." He fumbled with a scrap of rope. "You know
why the only beginners who last in this sport are kids?" I
hooked off my jab. "You know, don't you, that unless he's
grown into it, an older guy's body can't adjust to the
punishment?" Jab, hook: bing, bang. "That Collis!" Moving
on, he spoke sourly—and at the same time with concern—
back over his shoulder. "You *know* . . . you're droppin' your
left?"

When amateurs and lesser pros took over the ring, Collis
came down and sat near me. A pro welter named Joe Weber
leaned over him and dropped his arm familiarly around his
shoulders. "What say, Mista Collis? How 'bout me steppin' a
few witcha new white boy?"

Collis appeared to ignore him before eventually answering
almost inaudibly. "When he's ready."

"Aw, Mist' Collis!" Weber's front teeth were framed in
gold. "I ain' go'n—"

Collis batted the arm from his shoulder. "Git on, Joe
Weber!"

Weber staggered away, mugging, as if he had been hit.
Collis looked past him. "Here's somebody," he said. "Git
ready."

Terrell came through the doorway in his street clothes—
dusty jeans, boots, and a brakeman's cap—but he carried his
gym bag.

"An' now, ladies an' gentlemen! Wearin' the red-an'-red
headgear, the Texas tornada . . . ! An' his opponent, in the
gray shawts an' gray T-shirt, a undefeated new
prospec' . . . !"

At the bell, we touched gloves and Terrell circled me,
bouncing coltishly. I stepped forward and to the left behind
two jabs, both meeting leather, the second smacking his
headgear. He started as if to move away, and I moved with
him, when suddenly I was stopped in mid-step. My head
had popped back, whatever punch he hit me with I didn't
see, and my nose felt prickly and moist. Just as I realized I
had to stop blinking and move, I saw his right, on its way.

Son of a bitch, it seemed an outrage that so soon he meant to hit me again. I flinched just quickly enough so the punch only fanned my face with its breeze. I lashed back, missing, but this made him circle backwards, giving me a moment to breathe. Faces and things around the ring bulged in toward us. I could hear Collis shouting from the corner, but I had no time to make sense of it. My years of running and other exercise were suddenly like nothing: the round had scarcely started, and already it seemed I was slogging through water. Sparring sessions with the amateur had been deceptive. I moved toward the old fighter with new caution.

He peered at me over his gloves and bobbed from side to side, pausing to jab. I couldn't elude these punches, but because I saw them coming, they didn't hurt as much as the punch I hadn't seen. Then he jolted me with a right-hand lead that had me blinking again. I grabbed at him, feeling I had to be closer so I could smother his gloves. As if granting my intention, he retreated to the ropes. I leaned into him, already seeing how I would hook to his body and head. He froze my left glove in his armpit, but I thought I was about to reach him with my right one when I discovered I couldn't pull it back. He had caught me behind the elbow, and as if handing me through a door, he slid to the side and guided me firmly past him into the space he had vacated on the ropes.

Feeling tricked and foolish, I turned around, expecting to square off again and start over. Then my heart raced in alarm, and what I saw from the corner of my eye made me feel more foolish still. It was a demonstration of protect-yourself-at-all-times that I wouldn't forget. His fist, launched from behind me, whistled toward my head, and I was turning straight into it. The blow crashed against my ear, and I didn't hear Collis or anything except ringing for the rest of the round.

Deafened, I was even more conscious of the taste of my mouthpiece and the smells of the ring. He hit me again, then backed into the adjacent ropes. I moved after him into the smothering odor, and even though I thought I was ready for it, he turned me around by the elbow again. But this time I whirled with my hands up, and he held his punch and made a stand in the middle of the ring. When I closed with him, he shocked me again. This time, instead of trying to evade me with a turn, he gave me a hard shove, his face for the first time turning violent. Momentarily intimidated by his expression, I took my first step back. He moved after me, but the rest bell tinked, and he pivoted aside.

"You workin' nice together," Collis told us as we stood in the corner. He gave Terrell water from a gin bottle not wrapped in adhesive tape, then poured more on his mouthpiece, rinsing it over the bucket by the corner post. When it was my turn to spit, I was surprised to see blood, which must have been draining into my throat from high in my nose, fall into the bucket. Collis took no notice. "Now, in this next round . . ." The rest bell had been so welcome that I had momentarily forgotten another round would follow. It was a horrible prospect. He dabbed Vaseline on my cheekbones and eyebrows, clapped in my mouthpiece, and repeated instructions to make use of my left.

As we waited for the bell, I took deep breaths and looked at Terrell on the other side of the ring. He ignored me and shuffled about, his expression perfectly neutral.

In this round I tried to move more, but not so directly toward him, and found that I tired less quickly. We bobbed back and forth, truly sparring, flicking out jabs and feinting with rights. Toward the end of the round, we bumped together, and I tried to clinch, to throw a short jolting body punch such as I had seen Freddie Johnson and others do. Again he prevented me from setting myself and pushed me roughly away. As I recoiled from the shove, I must have broken concentration and dropped my guard, for he then stung me with a long face-numbing combination. My mouthpiece flew out, and Collis immediately called time. He waved me to him to have the retrieved mouthpiece rinsed over the bucket.

"That's go'n happen long as you fights wit' y' mouth open."

"It was *open?*"

"Like a *trapdo'!*" He clapped my chest and back between his hands and staggered with laughter. "Boy, you a knockout! That's y' rest bell. I'll letcha go one more."

As uneasy as I was, I couldn't help laughing too. Then I moved to stand off by myself.

Once we had resumed, Terrell tried to turn me into the ropes again, but this time I caught hold of him. As we stumbled sideways toward a corner, I felt him tense himself to shove me, so I shoved first, following it with a full swing. But I had shoved too hard, sending him out of range. He lunged back to counter, and we hit each other at the same time and spatted together at the shoulder. Glimpsing his unprotected midsection, I hooked. Then I was helpless.

There had been a clear popping thump, and I grunted loudly enough for him to hear as my wind rushed out. His hook, a quicker one than mine, had caught me flush in the ribs. My knees locked, and I couldn't move except to cover up with my gloves and elbows. He pulled away, hesitated, then leaned back against me, propping me up and tapping me with gentle punches along the shoulders and arms until I regained my breath and began tapping back. When I had recovered just enough to be able to defend myself, he pushed me away. I was more than content to jab and feint, as he wished, for the rest of the round.

"Le's give 'em a hand, ladies an' gentlemen!" Collis smiled widely and held out his hands for our mouthpieces. We bumped together moving toward him, and Terrell cuffed me across the shoulder and chest, something I had seen other fighters do after acceptable sparring. I was exhausted, but also so relieved and pleased that it took further effort not to smile or to cry.

7

☐

Again to the gym. Again early. The wet heat on Magazine was like late summer. Up ahead in his brakeman's cap and boots, Terrell appeared to ripple along the sidewalk. Had this happened before? I followed him into the gym and suddenly felt certain I was, in fact, dreaming. I blinked and waited for my eyes to adjust. But it wasn't a dream. The ring was gone.

And so was everyone except Collis and an out-of-shape heavyweight I had seen cutting grass in university neighborhoods. They were arguing as we came in.

"C'mon!" Collis snapped at me, slashing the air with his forearm. "You go'n work the bags."

As he wrapped my hands, he seemed to have to gather himself for the tedium of explaining that the promoters of the Rossman-Galindez fight needed an extra training ring. "Sent them boys from the jail up here yesterday. They taken it down, moved it to the Dome. Out-a-town fighters be checkin' in, tomorra maybe. I has to close up the gym an' be down to the Dome till after the fight. Turn y' hand over. Them big shots wants me to work with Roslan, the champ. We worked wit' him before the first fight, me an' Freddie."

"Well," I told him, feeling relaxed. "I'll keep running."

"You sho will. An' you be down to that Dome too an' keep trainin' right along."

"Is that allowed? I mean, you know, somebody green like me . . . Will the fighters on the card mind?"

"Why should they? Doncha wear britches same as them? Course, if you *plan*nin' to git in the way . . ."

"Well, no. But won't I need some kind of special permission?"

His voice took on further resonance. "You lookin' at it. You think I don' know people? Shit. I got author'ty to take anybody down there I want." He looked around at the heavyweight. "An' I ain' takin' no bums . . .

"But see?" he said confidentially. "I'm watchin' out f' you. 'Cause you's new to this game. An' 'cause you listens."

He tied off the wrap and released my wrist with a toss, then backhanded me sharply on the diaphragm. I pretended it hadn't hurt, hadn't caused a knifing cold catch in my breath.

"So listen at this: a smart fighter protects his gut. Ain' that right, Terrell? Now git the bag gloves. That's y' work bell."

I had almost finished my rounds on the heavy bag when a ruckus interrupted me. I looked around to see him up on his crutches shouting at the heavyweight, who was backing away, grinning, with his palms held out. Collis seemed about to let it go. Then the big man murmured something else and ducked behind the other heavy bag. Collis snatched up the untaped gin bottle and, with deceptive speed, swung himself across the concrete. Terrell, who had been working the rope in the courtyard, moved inside, still skipping. When Collis reached the bag he smacked the bottle against the canvas where the heavyweight's hand had been. The glass didn't break, but tepid water spattered all of us.

The whir of Terrell's rope was the only sound. Then the heavyweight wilted. "C'mon, Mista Collis. What's wrong you cain't take a li'l joke? I watn't talkin' 'bout *yo'* family."

Collis cocked the bottle. "You the joke, you bigmouth bastard! All you is! Lotta talk! I'll *bust* the *piss* out you. How long you been comin' in this gym? Year? Two? An' you still ain' had no fights! This time you step out that do', you can f'git comin' back."

When Collis finally turned away, Terrell skipped the rope back out into the courtyard. The heavyweight began working the bag bare-handed, grunting earnestly with each punch as if nothing had happened.

Later, he tried to smooth things over. "Mista Collis . . . ?" Collis turned his back. "Aw right, Mista Collis, jus' to make you happy, I'm own go. Mista Collis?"

Collis reached for the bottle.

The heavyweight left.

Joe Weber, who had just walked in with several other fighters, grinned toward the doorway, then back at Collis. "Where he now, Mista Collis? Say, Mista Collis. Where?"

Collis shrugged, but didn't look at him. "Jus' gone, I reck'n."

Weber hooted, and some of the others broke into soundless snicker-laughter. Collis wouldn't join them.

That night on the way home, he was subdued, just as he had been in the gym for the rest of the afternoon and evening. I decided it was best to let him alone. But halfway down Broad, he began to speak as if I had asked him a question. "Ain' no secret."

"What's no secret?"

"How I got this way."

"What way?"

"Crippled."

"Oh."

"I done tol' y' 'bout my daughter."

"The one you wanted to go to college, the one who lives in New York?"

"Yeh, the one shot me. Ain' no secret."

I put both hands on the wheel. "No, you didn't tell me about that."

"Wadn't nothin'. She was growin' up fast. Wantin' to do things her way, 'steada mine. Chil'ren's like that, you'll find out.

"Then the riffraff come. It was a grown man. I knew he was no-'count, but I loved her, you can see how it was, an' I tried not to mix in it. Then Junior come to me one day an' say, 'Daddy, that man's married, he got chil'ren same name as him.' "

He gazed past me at buildings drifting past. "After I run him off, I was standin' in the hall. I didn' know she'd got my pistol out the dresser, not even when I heard it behind me. Some a them little guns can be loudest. Knocked me down, but I still didn' know what happened, till my wife commenced screamin', from the bed."

I pulled up as closely as I could to his apartment and cut the lights and the engine. As much to myself as to him, I murmured something about not being able to imagine the pain of that event.

"Aw, man, they was times I'd a almost been happy to die. I think I told y', my wife wasn't strong."

He looked away, his eyes following some of the traffic. When he looked back at me, he was grinning. "That hospital room *stayed* full a flowers an' food. I wish you coulda seed all the people that come to me. An' not jus' fighters. There was so many white folks that one a them doctors looked at me funny an' said, 'Phillips! What line a work you in?' "

He laughed and slapped my leg. "You see what he was thinkin', doncha? Took me for some kind a big-shot crook!" He pushed my arm. "Can you see me, mixed up with nar*cot*ics an' all a that?"

I said no, and he opened the door. "No, indeed. My game's right there in that gym, for anybody to see. An' right now I gotta help that boy Roslan keep his title. Then, you keep listenin' an' comin' 'long nice like you's doin', I'm go'n gitcha a few fights. You'll win 'em too, I don' never take a man to a show 'less I know he go'n win. Then we be ready to make us some money. You wouldn' mind some money, would ya?"

He had hoisted himself up out of the car before leaning back in and pointing at me. I had taken the key out of the ignition.

"Now go home. Be wit' y' family."

8

□

In the carpeted assembly room at the Superdome, the sweat-stained training ring from Magazine Street seemed shoddy and out of place, foreign to the static refrigerated air and purring fluorescent light. Five days before, a Sunday, I had brought my seven-year-old son, Richard, to watch Victor Galindez train. I envisioned myself as introducing Richard to masculine mysteries, providing the kind of guidance I had missed as the only child of a lone mother.

Richard showed interest in the private corridors of the Superdome and in the training area teeming with busy fighters and fight people. But once the session had settled into its arduous patterns, his attention wandered.

When twenty-two-year-old Mike Rossman and Freddie Johnson entered the ring, an older man, some sort of minor official or official's crony, made introductions in an ingratiating voice. "Well, c'mon, folks," he called, drawing out his duties. "Give 'em some noise! Fighters like noise!"

Testy under the pressure of the rematch, Rossman spoke out like a shot. "You ever been a fighter?"

The man acted as if the champ had made a joke, but an awkward quiet remained until after Rossman finished sparring and began skipping rope to a Bruce Springsteen cassette. As soon as he left, ex-champion Galindez arrived. Wearing a black groin protector stamped with an arching red scorpion, Galindez executed a flamboyant demonstration of energy and power against three sparring partners. In his last round, his third opponent, local contender Jerry Celestine, had to put all his effort into avoiding trouble. When Galindez knocked Celestine along the ropes with a hook to the elbow, Galindez's trainer cut the round short. "¡Perfecto! ¡Bastante!"

On the chair next to mine, Richard suddenly stiffened. A second had scissored the wraps from Galindez's hands, and the fighter had tossed one of them up for older boys to fight over. He laid the other on Richard's still knee. Then he ruffled Richard's white-blond hair.

After Galindez had autographed picture postcards of himself and given kisses and roses to young and old women who waited in a line, he and his entourage ambled toward the assembly room's exit. Since Collis wasn't there that Sunday, Richard and I also headed out. Noticing Richard, as I was picking a path for us through his boisterous Argentine camp members, Galindez stopped near the doorway. His people stopped around him. Squeezing by, I wished him well. He ignored me and bent over Richard. Speaking in labored English, he offered his dark hand. "How are you, my friend?"

Richard hesitated before gripping Galindez's hand firmly and, as I had made a point of teaching him to do, meeting his eyes. "Hello."

"Are you my friend?"

"Fine."

Afterwards, as we stood together on the descending escalator, Richard looked at what he held in his hands. The gauze was still damp, but the tape had already begun browning. "What am I supposed to do with this?"

Now it was Good Friday, the day before the fight. All the fighters on the card were gone, except for Galindez. He was in the ring alone, sweating off the last, hardest pounds. His trainer held a watch and, in Spanish, counted cadence for the brutal calisthenics. When Galindez finally jumped down and headed for the exit, someone off to the side—I think it was either Collis or Willie Pastrano—began to clap, softly at first, then louder as other ex-fighters joined in. Galindez—who within twenty-four hours would regain his title in savagely dramatic fashion—paused in the doorway and raised his hands.

After everyone else had left, I worked Galindez's big bag, a fine leather one that, unlike canvas bags, popped rather than thudded when you hit it; and Collis moved among the plastic spectator chairs, daydreaming and poking idly through the litter with the tips of his crutches. The metal-framed chairs clicked together as his crutch swiped them aside. There were several clicks at once, then an urgent scuffling sound. I stopped hitting the bag. In the horrible instant of silence that followed, I whirled only in time to see him going over forward, crutch snagged in a chair frame, hands frozen on the grips. He glanced off the chairs and fell limply the rest of the way.

When I reached him, he smiled as if stupidly, eyes glazed and blinking. His body lay chest-down on the thin carpet. It was deadweight. We almost toppled when I lifted him. A skein of spit twirled from his lip. Jelled blood plugged one of his nostrils.

"Naw," he said, settling onto his crutches. "I don' need to set down. They's a towel in the sack. Le's go."

I gathered the rest of our things while he stood there cleaning his face and angling the brim of his hat over his eyes. "Jus' blacked out," was the only answer he gave to my fretful questions.

I was still shaky when we reached the escalator. He put both crutches under his left shoulder and reached to grip the rubber runner with his right hand. "You goin'?"

Other evenings, leaving, I had insisted on standing below him. I put my foot on the sharp, vibrating step, which was grooved like hair clippers.

"No!" I told him, all at once oddly enraged. "And neither are you. You don't have any business on this *god*dam thing."

He tipped back his head and gazed at me across his cheekbone. "Man gotta do what he gotta do."

"Not this. I'll find an elevator."

"Soun' like you think you tellin' me."

"Whatever. C'mon."

He looked skeptical. But he pushed himself away from the lip of the steps. "Aw right, champ. Suit y'self."

We had to circle a vast concessions area before I found an elevator in service. He scraped steadily along beside me, and we criticized the construction of the place as if it were ours. At each of the ramps leading into the cavernous arena, we glimpsed media gear, technicians, and the floodlit blue ring.

9

□

Joe Weber was screaming.

It was the first day the ring was back up, and the gym was overcrowded. Not with headliners such as Tony Licata—who, after three listless rounds, had lost to Freddie Johnson on a freak cut—but with would-bes and has-beens stimulated by the recent show. When I arrived to find bikes and teenagers blocking the door, I had gone around the corner to wrap my hands in privacy under the shadow of the church on Camp Street. As I edged in past the teenagers, Collis motioned urgently from the apron. "You ready? C'mon."

The white amateur was working with Terrell. Many waited to use the ring. I clapped in my mouthpiece and ran up the steps, a surge of queasiness rising toward my throat: if he put me in with the amateur, I would be evenly matched and therefore have more to lose. The amateur was missing determined swings at Terrell as I thrust my hands into the gloves Collis held open. Then Joe Weber had run out along the apron and stood against my back.

"Goddammit, *shit*, Mista Collis! The man jus' come in here! How come he ain' gotta wait like ev'body else?"

Collis tilted his head at the sparring and drew the laces snug. " 'Cause I needs to work him with this here."

Weber flung away. "Man, you *color*-blind!"

Collis answered calmly. "You the one cain' see. If you was a pro sho' 'nuff, you wouldn' be gittin' hot 'bout sumpum like this. Count up the colors in here. Then think about it."

He took hold of me at the rest bell. "You go'n box the older fella. The other one tired." Glancing toward the fighters Weber sat among on the stomach bench, he added, "I cain' letcha go but one round." Then he waved the amateur over to him. "C'mere, Whatchacallit. You's doin' better but . . ."

I turned quickly from the two of them and also avoided looking in Weber's direction. Terrell stood in the opposite corner shaking down his arms and staring vacantly toward the courtyard. More teenagers had pushed in and now lined the brick wall, and the theater seats were taken by schoolgirls and a pregnant young woman in house shoes.

Moving to meet Terrell, I was conscious of crowd noise and the voices of Collis and Joe Weber. The faces around the ring took on their usual skewed proportions, as if reflected in a convex surface. Collis shouted "Stick!," Weber heckled, my jab and Terrell's landed at the same time, pain lodging in my sore jaw hinge, and the round began.

It stretched into two, and afterwards I waited for Collis's approval, but he didn't say much while he took off my gloves in the crowd next to the ring. Above us, Joe Weber and Cheetah had already started. Behind me someone spoke to Collis in a muffled voice.

"Who?" Collis said. "This here?" He laughed and smacked the sweaty gloves together. "Why, this here's my protégé. You wanna piece a his contrac'?"

The one who had questioned him said nothing.

"Say. You wanna buy into him?"

I looked at the person he was speaking to, at a low hat brim and the smudged tattoo on his cheek. He looked past me without expression as I stepped over to spit out pink phlegm, wondering what the joke was and whom it was on.

Saturday. In the morning. Few fighters had come in—not the white amateur, not Terrell—but gangs of children roamed the gym. Except when he took off his outer shirt, propped his crutches behind him, and held the heavy bag for me, Collis spent most of the time making up errands they could do. He grew stern only when they loitered near his locker.

"Le's git sumpum to eat," he said when I had finished calisthenics.

I remembered I had only coins in my bag. "For me just something to drink. But I have the car today. I can drive us."

After I helped him close up the gym, he directed me down Magazine to a pool hall that served po-boy sandwiches. We entered a cool, shady room. It was an off-hour. We were the only customers. He made me tuck a towel under the damp neck of my sweatshirt to guard against chill from the slow fan overhead. Then he arranged himself and his crutches at the counter across two of the stools. "They has good fish samiches here. Whatcha want?"

I insisted I was only thirsty.

"Naw, naw. I got money."

The waitress leaned against the counter and studied her slender brown fingers.

"How's the prettiest young lady on Magazine Street?"

She smiled absently.

"Bring us two large fish sanwiches—dressed—an' two large root beers. If you please."

She tore the pad and pushed away in the same tossing motion, gold hoops swinging from her earlobes.

While we waited, he told stories about boxing. "They's things 'bout this game don' nobody know." And about other gyms he had run. "Usta be one in this joint rightchere, upstairs . . ."

We left after he had tipped the waitress and teased her into a haughty good humor. On the sidewalk he turned away from my old car.

"That's aw right. I'll jus' catch the bus. On Sat'days I makes some stops."

It was then I understood that, of course, he preferred the

bus—the independence and the very difficulty of it—and that where we had eaten was a part of his weekly pattern. I thanked him for the meal.

"Ain' nothin'. Take the road tomorra. I'll see y' Monday evenin'."

Days of rain followed. I biked to Magazine in a poncho, expecting to spar with the white amateur, only to find the place almost empty, curtains of rain and runoff at the windows and doors. No one came in but Terrell. We boxed painful, spiritless rounds.

Later at the Winn-Dixie for Collis, I saw Terrell again. He was up ahead in the line at the checkout, buying oranges and a TV dinner. His heavy boots and the discs on his cap and on the seams of his jeans seemed better suited to some kind of pretender than to the disciplined veteran who regularly beat me to the punch. When he was called back for his change, we acted as if we hadn't noticed one another. He stomped out into the rain.

I telephoned Collis as he had asked me to. It involved putting my name and number in a book he kept at home. "Gotta git my stable straight," he had said.

On the phone his voice sounded faint. Even though Richard and Julia, my three-year-old daughter, sat with me on the sofa waiting to read, it was hard to break away. He began to cast back over his life.

Trying to ease out of it tactfully, I diverted him with a question. "Did you get headaches when you were first training?"

"Shoo-wee!" he said. "Sometimes I come away from them smart boys head throbbin' like a drum."

After Richard and Julia were in bed, I examined my face in the mirror. The bridge of my nose was swollen, but not very noticeably. There were no visible lumps on the sore places in front of my ears. I pulled down my lower lip and looked at the purple, zipperlike teeth marks inside. Not much damage. Yet I felt more foolish now than I had at first. Now that it was this hard, and becoming harder each time.

Insomniac, late on a weekend, I stole down the back flight of steps and soon was on the bike. Pedaling fast, I sailed past blocks of wharves and warehouses down deserted Tchoupitoulas. Below Napoleon I turned away from the river and circled back.

Beyond the fish market, Magazine was quiet. Even the rickety old bar had closed for the night. With its bricked front pitched in shadow, the gym looked clean, and abandoned.

I turned again and passed through neighborhoods, watching shapes melt in the branches overhead, meeting no traffic, surprising cats. On St. Charles I coasted toward a man standing by the streetcar tracks. He took metal from his pocket. I veered to the side. "Hey, bruh," he said, and waved me on with a comb.

Ravenous, I entered our still apartment and found scraps from various meals in the refrigerator. I ate standing. Then I compounded these excesses by settling down to an old escape: ice cream and the sports page. In the front room I put the TV on without volume but paid it little mind.

The sports section was a letdown: few new box scores, no running. On the last page I found a filler about boxing surrounded by ads:

KNOXVILLE, TENN. (AP) — Arnauldo Maura, 19, an Army private from Ft. Bragg, N.C., died in East Tennessee Baptist Hospital following his loss Thursday night to Johnny Bumphus of Nashville, Tenn., in the first round of the Southern Golden Gloves Tournament. Jerry "Ace" Miller, the tournament's director, said . . .

The television station had signed off, and snow now filled the tiny screen. I regretted my lapse into overeating. Moist wind swept in from the porch and twirled the rat guards on the wires outside. I looked around the room and tried to appraise what I saw: the sofa we had saved for, friends' paintings, Julia's shoes, the books.

10

□

Cheetah wore a red rag on his head. Waiting in the ring, I watched him pass through the glare from the doorway and come along the wall, training gloves slung across his shoulder, walking close to the bricks. He laid a neat bundle of boxing clothes on the stomach bench and, using the tips of his fingers, lifted the bandanna away from his hair. It had been freshly hot-ironed and pomaded and combed straight back to lie flat on his head. The look was bizarrely old-fashioned, yet no one teased him.

Collis had agreed to put me in with the white amateur as soon as he came, but a few minutes earlier he had said, "Look like a slow day. If you don' wanna keep waitin', you can go on finish y' workout an' box another time." He was by the heavy bags, working with a very young black teenager who was new to the gym. Poignantly, the teenager wore his school PE uniform. He pawed at the bag.

Willie Pastrano was there for the first time since Tony Licata lost to Freddie Johnson. He sat in the school desk making phone calls. Between calls he seemed to be looking at nothing. Out back, a fit heavyweight I had never seen before was wrapping his hands and limbering his muscles.

I had been jittery all day—from my waking moments when I lay watching the sky lighten to pearl. In bed, hearing the birds so very clearly, I formulated the logic I used to drive myself to the gym: if I conclusively bested the white amateur,

I could quit. On my bike ride from home, I had stopped to buy lemonade from children selling it on the sidewalk. When I bought a second oversweet cupful and tried to keep them talking, I realized I was procrastinating.

Now I walked in the ring and shook down my arms. I had shadowboxed enough. In the kitchen, Cheetah fussed with his hair before a blade of mirror. Still the amateur didn't come.

At last I glimpsed another shadow on the bricks. My stomach lurched with anticipation, which began to subside as soon as I saw the brakeman's cap.

"I guess Whatchacallit ain' comin'." Collis swung himself toward his locker. "But here's somebody." He tossed me the training gloves and started up the steps to lace them on.

"Cheetah's already asked me," Terrell said when he came from the kitchen in his two pairs of trunks and Collis pointed to me. "Let me and Cheetah go a few and then I will."

I stood next to Collis on the apron as they began to box. Between rounds Cheetah paced close to us, dabbing at his silky new black match trunks. Terrell rolled his head and forced a smile. "Something must have happened to my neck."

What had happened was that Cheetah had walked him into the ropes and hit him with a flurry that snapped his chin from one shoulder to the other.

I had expected the second round to be their last, but they stayed in the ring to start a third. I looked into the open locker below us at the old headgears and flaking foul protectors. Although, following the example of many of the nonheadliners in the Magazine gym, I had never sparred in any of this before, I asked Collis if I could wear it now. "Wha—? Sho'!" he said. "You shoulda tol' me you wanted them things. Bring 'em on up." He tied the bulky equipment on me, and I stood there with him through one, two, three more rounds. After each round, I thought my turn was next. During each rest period, Terrell tried to grin as if cockily cheerful. In each round, Cheetah punished him more. After the fifth, Collis said he thought that was probably enough. Terrell looked at Cheetah and waited. Cheetah kept pacing and said nothing. "One more," Terrell told Collis.

Increasingly, I felt pity for Terrell. As Cheetah worked him back into the ropes and banged away, I winced, amazed that he didn't fall and that Cheetah had the stomach to keep hitting him. Near the end of the round, I looked up at Collis from under the loose headgear.

"Whatsa matter?" he said.

The rest bell tinked, and Cheetah came toward us with his arm around Terrell. "This here Terrell's aw right now!" He chucked Terrell on the back of his head. Terrell tried to smile.

Collis looked away from me and gave Terrell the bottle. "I mean to tell y' Terrell's aw right!" he said, echoing Cheetah.

Cheetah chucked Terrell again, then turned to duck through the ropes. I wish I could say I motioned with my glove. If I had, he would have stayed in the ring.

As things were, having had a crisp workout, he exited the ring quickly, thinking about what I can only guess. It was Terrell with whom Collis said I should work—as I knew too well, I still wasn't ready for Cheetah or the other black pros from whom Collis sheltered me. As I waited on the apron with him, watching Terrell absorb increasing punishment in each round, I grasped more surely than I had before that improving as a boxer meant enduring a series of such beatings. If I was successful in besting the white amateur or even Terrell, behind them stood Cheetah, and behind him someone else.

After witnessing what Cheetah had done to him, I intensely did not want to hit Terrell. Or, just then, to hit anyone. And I wanted even less to have anyone hit me.

Terrell *was* all right. He may have been over the hill as a fighter. But he was one. Still. He looked forward to rounds with Cheetah and Freddie Johnson, for instance, as an opportunity—even if it meant he would suffer—because he *liked* to fight, the one quality Collis almost daily repeated as being most essential: *You cain' make a man want it. Fighters is bawn!*

"An' now, ladies an' gentlemen . . . !"

Terrell amazed me, and he hurt me. After his six rounds with Cheetah, he should at least have been tired. But the punishment he had withstood seemed to have given him fresh life and made him fight all the harder. He was less forgiving of my greenness than ever before, and I had to box backing away—something I wasn't used to, and I did it clumsily. Yet, to Collis's credit, I managed to keep fighting him off me and to last the round.

At the rest bell, Collis rinsed my mouthpiece over the bucket, then drew me in close. "I wancha to do like I've showed y'." I could smell his breath.

I wanted to please him. But, for the moment, like the pink saliva falling away into the bucket, my nerve was about gone.

Terrell bumped my shoulder as he stepped up and tipped his head back for water. Collis held the bottle for him but continued speaking to me. "Now, in this next one—"

They both looked around at me. How did they know the exact instant my heart left?

"It's up to you now. You don' have to."

When he finished his instructions, I moved to the opposite corner to wait by myself.

At the work bell, Terrell bobbed within range. I swung desperately, missed, and he was on me. His first punch popped on a sore place, and I thought about going down as I hit back into his gloves. I could hear Collis calling for me to work my left, to stick and to move, but I couldn't escape from the ropes. Blows began landing before I could set myself to take them, and it was an effort to remember to punch. I could feel him tentatively hooking into my arms and gloves, probing for an opening, as I tried to cover my diaphragm and chin. The headgear had slipped low on my brow, and the loose foul protector, knocked askew, must have flapped ludicrously as we slammed together and jumped. But none of that seemed important compared with catching my breath. I dimly sensed I was about to be knocked out and felt myself submitting to it just as Collis shouted "Time!" and an uppercut smashed through my gloves. Terrell held me for a moment, and I understood that he would have kept me from crumpling if I had needed him. Then he was walking diagonally away and I was weaving toward the corner, blinking back tears.

"It ain' broke," Collis said as he toweled the blood from my nose. "But, see? You stopped listenin'. You didn' stay busy an' keep movin'. An' he ain't as strong a man as you is. Whatcha think woulda happened if he'd a been pressin' you harder?"

When I denied nothing and stared steadily at the canvas, he held up his hands. "Lemme see that left. C'mon! Lemme see you snap it . . ." The punch, thrown short, popped faintly against his palm, and he held on to it. "See?" he said. "You hits hard."

Then he caught at the laces and stripped off his gloves.

"Second month or third?"

The heavyweight who had been in the courtyard now stood on the apron, waiting to come in the ring. "Man, you shoulda seen me at first." He stretched the ropes apart for me. "I was worse than you."

Willie Pastrano had just hung up the receiver and still had the look of a man listening to a voice on the phone. As, to keep from toppling, I went carefully down the steps, he gave me a distant wink. "What say, babe?"

"Don't you want some a this juice? You can have some." Holding the bottle in a paper sack, Collis poured orange juice into a row of paper cups he and Mister Arthur had set out on the stomach bench. For a second time I declined.

Calisthenics done, I slowly rolled up my wraps and put them in my bag. It had grown dark out. Except for heavyweights, all the fighters had gone. The white businessmen who owned the heavyweights had come in to watch them work. The ring buckled and creaked. The heavyweight who had spoken kindly to me was in with a former amateur champion. Collis had a huge new prospect, a young pro, who had boxed with both and was now blurring the speed bag. Collis leaned against the doorframe of the kitchen and sipped his juice. I gathered my things and went over to him.

He looked around and smiled. "Whatsa matter?"

"I don't know. Maybe I can tell you later."

"Aw right, champ. It's left to you."

Moving by him, I patted at his shoulder. He reached around and caught my left hand in his before turning back to his heavyweight. The rest bell tinked, the owners applauded their fighters, and I left the gym on Magazine.

11

□

Summer 1979–July 1981

After I stopped going there, my time in the gym seemed increasingly unreal. I didn't like thinking of how Collis probably had shrugged and said "Jus' gone" to anyone who happened to ask about his new white boy. I was even less comfortable knowing that, unlike most of the others, I was privileged simply to walk away.

But I couldn't put the gym out of my thoughts—or my dreams. There was also the evolving recognition that I had begun to experience in the gym: Collis's complex human worth. To share in more of that, to improve myself, and not to let him go: these were my reasons for beginning to try, not long after I left Magazine Street, to build the courage to go back.

Meanwhile there was the usual living to make. While Sally, my wife, went to nursing school, I met our expenses by taking a two-year teaching job at the state university up the river in Baton Rouge. She had done library work to help me through graduate school, and her turn to prepare for a career was long overdue. I commuted on the Greyhound and Trailways, taught composition classes, and wrote the scholarly articles and reviews that I hoped would ensure a better future. In a way, I was willing enough to defer the matter of the gym. The older I became, the more natural it would be if I failed when I tried again. If I had ever truly burned to be in there mixing it up, things might have been

different. As it was, I never had experienced that particular
desire.

Like admonitions to me, sports-page briefs announcing
imminent fight cards made clear that it was business as usual
on Magazine Street, and one day a photo sketch by G. Andrew Boyd in "The Eye," a feature series of *The Times-
Picayune*, brought Collis and the gym into sudden rectangular
focus. It was a thoughtful piece called "The Dream Trainer"
and one that must have pleased him. Boyd's grainy photographs showed him working with rough kids who evoked
the streets in their chopped-off jean shorts and worn basketball shoes. One picture caught his most affecting smile as,
at the end of a training day, he unscrewed his speed bag
from one of the mounts in the kitchen. In another, he has
just arrived on the Magazine bus and stands poised to
disembark and swing down to the curb on his crutches;
posed in the foreground, a small boy waits for him on the
sidewalk under shoulder-slung training gloves as long as his
torso. The brief text portrayed its subject as a colorful shaper
of the vigor and improbable dreams of young males with
little else to hope for. While reading and clipping the piece,
I experienced the feeling that something privately mine had
been trespassed on.

Not long after "The Dream Trainer," the term of my job
in Baton Rouge ended, professionally having led nowhere.
Again with only the prospect of temporary work before me,
I had no easy justification for staying away from the gym
and Collis. Then something happened that simplified my
problem.

It was steaming, July in New Orleans, and I was running
in the park, working on my wind and thinking about my
fluctuating resolve to start back on Magazine Street as soon
as the heat unclenched. Up ahead, I noticed a teenager
glistening with sweat and trudging along in a pleasureless
way that made me guess he was doing roadwork. I looked
at his feet. Of all things to have to run in: flat, slick-soled
ring shoes. As I often did when I happened on a fighter
while running, I drew alongside and asked about his boxing,

then if he was acquainted with Collis. It was a small way of keeping up.

He was a member of an amateur team from another parish that would box on a show uptown within the next few days. Yes, he said, his team had done some of its training in the gym on Magazine. But, no, he wasn't familiar with anyone named Collis. Glum and puzzled, I wished him a win.

"Hold on," he said, breathing heavily. "You say a old man? On a crutch?" It was someone he had heard about from gym regulars. "He's sick. He fell out in the gym. They said, on the floor."

From the young boxer's point of view, I must have become like an interrogator. He looked at me suspiciously before making any response to my several sudden questions. "Me, I don' know. Said mighta been his heart."

I ran home at a near sprint. I don't know which I felt more strongly: concern about Collis's condition or relief that now I might not have to return to the gym.

I dumped out my dusty gym bag on the bed and took up the torn box top he had used to give me his phone number. The blue ink had bled, but the scrawled digits were still legible.

I tried to compose my words. A hoarse male voice answered after several rings. It was younger than his, and harsher.

"Who *is* this?" the man snapped when I asked for "Mr. Collis Phillips."

I told him my name.

"And who is *that?*"

What to say to such a question?

He cut into my pause. "You a fighter?"

"Yes," I said, grabbing at it. "One of his fighters."

"You sure 'bout it?"

I bluffed into the receiver, affecting a phrasing and tone I had heard in the gym. "*Course* I'm sure! Know it for a *fact.*"

"Hold on," he said, apparently laying the phone quickly aside on a hard surface.

A minute or so later he was back. "He don' stay here no more. You gotta pencil?"

After I dialed the number the man gave me, I let the phone ring much longer than normal. I held on numbly, starting to feel a kind of relief about this too—at least I had tried. Then someone picked up. There was a muffled pause. I could hear the receiver being bumped around.

"Y-yeh." He sounded feeble. Also annoyed.

I told him who it was, then went directly into a physical description of myself in case he had forgotten me.

He interrupted, his voice suddenly animated. But also noncommittal. "Yeh! I know y'!"

He scolded me for having left the gym, but there was nothing particular in it. He could have been addressing any of the many novices he had seen come and go through the years.

Then we spoke of his health. As near as I could tell, a combination of high blood pressure and hardening arteries caused him to lose consciousness when he exerted himself. The punches he took in the 1930s may also have had something to do with it. He told me about collapsing, first in the gym and, on another day while on his way there, at the St. Bernard bus stop. He said a doctor had forbidden him to continue to train fighters, so that part of his life, for the time being, was over.

After this it appeared there was nothing more to say. We had started repeating ourselves and begun clichéd leave-takings before finally I was inspired by the obvious: just ask.

Interrupting my own goodbye, I blurted that his life interested me. Would he be willing to let me write about it?

He laughed. "Well, sho'! 'S aw right wi' me. I been writ up befo'."

I said this might be different; I was also interested in his family. "It probably wouldn't be only about boxing."

"Well, that's left to you. You the one gotta write it."

"I'd need background. I might have to ask a lot of questions."

"Whatsonever you say. I'm rightchere. If you wanna pass

this way . . ." He gave me an address, which he described as "on the end." This was several courtyards beyond his old apartment, which had been located on St. Bernard Avenue in the front of the project.

I asked him to name a time that would be best for him.

"Anytime you want. The opportunity is yours."

"Well . . . like this afternoon? Now?"

"Anytime you want, just *any*time at all. The opportunity is yours."

"If it's all right, I can be there in twenty minutes."

"C'mon."

I waited for him to finish, then realized that that was it. He was hanging up. I could hear him fumbling with the receiver. Then I heard a woman's voice in the distance ask who he had been talking to. He grumbled, not answering her. Her voice came closer; insistent, she asked again. I heard him mutter wearily an instant before the receiver fell deafeningly into its cradle.

"Aw, jus' some white boy."

12

□

July 1981

"Riverside, Io-*way!*" I thought he said he had been born there. Another time he seemed to be telling me it was "New Avery, *Tex*as!*"

It took me several trips to determine that neither was correct, and months passed before I felt I better understood the ambiguous elements of his life. By then I had been places that otherwise would have remained unknown to me.

That first afternoon that I went to see him, it was dark, almost like night, in his new apartment. A stout middle-aged woman answered my knock on the screen door, which on the inside was draped with a bedspread.

"Hello-o!" she sang out, but in an anonymous way.

When I told her my name, she didn't mention hers but brushed aside the folds of her large shift and spoke in a high breathless voice, her other hand involuntarily rising as if to obscure her face. "C'mon in, you can just come right on in! He's up! He's waitin' on you! Right here in the front."

As I passed her, I noticed that her right eye (which years later I would learn had been defective from birth) listed to the side. Then she covered it with her hand. Although she smiled, her other hand rose to conceal her teeth.

Hangings shrouded each window against the heat radiating from the bricks outside, and no lamps burned.

"That's my daughter: Gloria." I recognized his voice before

I made out where it came from—a slip-covered chair in the corner of the room. As I went farther into the dimness and moved around the furniture to take his hand, I felt as if I were displacing a settled layer of heat.

"Yaa-h! There you is!" His voice and gestures signified a fondness I couldn't entirely believe.

He flashed his familiar smile, slapped at my shoulder, half knocking me down on the sofa next to his chair, and opened with some of his flattery. "You's a slick one! Fooled me! Thought you was go'n make a fighter. Come to find out you was up to sumpum else all along."

He had, as he would have phrased it, evidently made up his mind not to "handle" me "just any kinda way," and I could look forward to more of his unusual mixture of bluntness and tact.

His fringe of hair—whiter and much longer than I remembered—now curled in patches around his ears and down his neck. Hospital identification tapes circled his wrists. A jar of tap water from the Mississippi stood at his elbow next to cylinders of pills and the plastic urinal he spat in. As our conversation ranged, he downplayed his poor health and went on to speak confusingly of Iowa and Texas. I noticed that he moved less than I did in the heat, hardly seeming to breathe, and that his T-shirt and baggy suit pants remained dry after my clothes had begun to soak through.

I was beaded over with sweat by the time a shapely young woman in shorts and house shoes walked through from the kitchen toward the draped screen in the front.

He spoke harshly. "Where's y' manners, girl? This here's Mista—"

She had pushed open the screen. Now she turned back toward us in the blinding crack of light. "Good evenin'," she said tonelessly, her pretty face solemn, eyes unmistakably hostile. Then she passed on through the doorway.

"That's my granddaughter, Gloria's youngest child: Trina."

Eventually I asked how Trina came to be given that name. When I became more organized in what I was doing, this was a question I would find it worthwhile to ask about many others in his family.

"Glor*ia!*" The word rumbled from deep in his chest and ended in a resonance that must have carried to both floors of the apartment. "Gloria Mae!"

After she shouted back from the kitchen and he knew he had her attention, he spoke in a level tone as if she and not I were sitting next to him. "Who Trina was named for?"

"*What?* What's that, Daddy? What?"

This made me so uneasy I wanted to leap from the sofa and through the screen—I had no idea who else was in the apartment or otherwise within earshot—but I had reached out my hand too late to shush him. Their exchange followed a pattern that over time I would become used to—with Gloria calling out from another part of the apartment and him questioning her in an impatient, uninterested tone.

"*Trina?!*" she shouted. "Her *name?!* What you mean?"

"I *said*, who was your daughter named for?"

I learned nothing specific about Trina's name that day—not even that, as I discovered later, she was the second of his granddaughters to be named Trina. As they called and spoke back and forth, I wondered, looking around the small room, if Gloria was the daughter who had shot him.

With the sofa, chair, console color TV and stereo, there was little space for other furniture. But the room also held a coffee table, a rocker, and, in the corner next to the entranceway to the kitchen, a ladder of shelves lined with trophies. Family photographs were grouped on the coffee table and on top of the stereo, and a trio of velveteen portraits—John and Robert Kennedy flanking Martin Luther King, Jr.—dominated the longest wall. Across from this wall, a cement stairway led to the two bedrooms and bath on the second floor. On the wall enclosing the stairway, next to another picture of JFK, a small plaque proclaimed:

In Appreciation to Collis Phillips
For Devoted Services to Amateur Boxing
Delta Boxing Club
1978

A tall trophy stood by itself on the highest of the shelves in the corner. I could see that it was Alvin's, a token of the Southern middleweight title he won only a few years before being sent away to the penitentiary at Angola. When Collis and Gloria ended their exchange about Trina's name, hoping he wouldn't summon her about this too, I ventured a question concerning the smaller, unmarked trophies on the lower shelves.

Without pause, he said they were bowling trophies, won by a younger son of his, Jerry. Then he added, "Yeh . . . Jerry. The one hung hisself in New Yawk."

I didn't know what to say in response to this further personal catastrophe, but he seemed to pay that no mind and went on as if I were sitting there at my ease.

"Y'see, when my daughter shot me, he took it more to his heart than the rest a my chil'ren. He *stayed* at that hospital."

He suddenly spoke louder, at a level Gloria could hear. "Not like some of 'em."

Just as abruptly the edge went out of his voice, and I had to strain to hear him. "He was there with me *ev*'ry night. In that chair by the bed. I couldn't turn in my sleep without I'd hear a li'l whisper out the dark: '*Dad*dy! Whatsa matter? You want sumpum?'

"When I come to in the mornin', there he'd be. 'Sleep, in that chair. His head down on the sheet, next to mine."

He brusquely crossed his wrists and dipped his forehead toward them. "Like that."

"How old was he?"

"At that time? Aw, he watn't no more'n thirteen, fo'teen maybe." He smiled. "Come daylight I'd look over, an' there he'd be. 'Sleep." He pressed his brow to his wrists, again showing how it was. "That li'l head."

Thinking he was about to cry, I looked away. When I glanced back, he was watching me alertly, features placid.

"Lemme tell you sumpum. You might not understan' this—I couldn't say—but I know what I'm talkin' about: when somebody shows you he's like *in love* wit' you, you cain' help but feel close to 'em. Cain' *help* it!"

I said I felt I could understand that, though probably not as well as he could. He shrugged.

"I tol' him not to go back to New Yawk. But he wouldn' listen. Worried me for a week for the money to go."

He shrugged again. "Once they grown an' got they minds made up, whatcha go'n do?" His fingers pantomimed digging into his pocket and offering out its contents on an opened palm. "I give'm the hunerd dollars. That was my son, you understan'.

"His sister Connie, the one lives up there, she wrote us about it. He took his own life between Chris'mas an' New Year's." His chin trembled, and his words trailed off. ". . . that li'l head . . ."

I looked down—though I didn't yet grasp that the holidays he referred to were those most recently past.

"Glor*ia!*" Again the startling resonance. "Where Connie's letter?"

"What!?"

"The letter. Connie's letter. About Jerry."

But I cut him off, and this time I was firm. I felt my intentions were all right, but I also felt I had to spend longer with this and do more to earn his family's trust. Otherwise, such confidences were too much like theft.

At some point in our conversation that afternoon, I suggested that, in whatever I wrote, it might be best to change some or all of the names. He spoke up quickly and almost hotly about that.

"The writin's yo' department. But I never been ashamed a my name. I always tell my chil'ren, 'A name means more to you than anything you got!' "

When I asked if there was something in particular that he

would like to read about himself, he made a joke of it and shouted, "Jus' don' put too much polish on me!"

Then, in seriousness, he added, "They is one thing. But it's on you, an' not me. If you could put in somewhere along in there that you's a family man." (Earlier, I had shown him and Gloria billfold snapshots of Sally and Richard and Julia.) "An' not jus' some guy off the street."

I left that afternoon, as I intended, about an hour after I had come, making as certain as I could not to tire him or overstay my welcome. I took a welter of impressions with me but little information of any depth. I had learned that by his wife, Dorothy (deceased), he had fathered six children in New Orleans, but I remained ignorant of the ones who had died in infancy or were born and still lived in Texas. Gloria, his oldest in New Orleans, was also a parent of six. Then came Collis Jr., father of Collis III and four other children from two marriages. Then Alvin: six children. Then Jerry. The baby, Farris, I would find out, was in the same maximum-security disciplinary camp at Angola as Alvin, but, unlike Alvin, he was due to come home soon.

Collis had answered my question about Farris's charge by saying he didn't know much about it but he had heard it involved "a stickup at a Time-Saver, sumpum like that."

Immediately Gloria came through the curtain that partitioned off the kitchen and stood with her fists on her hips. She didn't look at me, but I could see she wasn't talking to him. "Farris was railroaded. Umn-humn. I know *that* for a fact."

As I drove away, carefully nosing the car the long length of the project, trophies were the images most prominent in my mind. Not Alvin's, but the ones beneath it. For bowling. Those most of all deepened my desire to gather the whole story.

13

□

Just about anyone who diligently read the New Orleans newspaper could, at that time, have known almost as much about Collis and his family as I did. Certainly anyone could have had more information about Alvin, the member of the family whose name had most often appeared in print.

On June 14, for example, *The Times-Picayune* had run a feature article by Alan Citron, a news reporter who had won awards for his writing about state institutions. With the cooperation of prison officials Citron had been studying the penal system in Louisiana, and on this Sunday his subject was Alvin. I had been out of town that weekend and might not have learned of the article if, in July, I hadn't mentioned the project I had undertaken to a friend who had read his paper that Sunday in June. The next day I was in the library rifling back issues.

Alan Citron's article summarized Alvin's boxing career, his drug addiction, and his imprisonment for selling a small amount of heroin to an undercover agent. All of this I knew from sports pages and from conversations in passing with Collis. I hadn't known—and Citron reported it—that Alvin was serving a life sentence. Nor did I then know—and the report hadn't mentioned this—that the sentence was for "natural life," which meant Alvin was ineligible for parole. Nor that this sentence was based on his only adult conviction.

The article included other startling information, though: that Alvin refused to perform required work in Angola; that in his five years there, he had been written up for sixty-eight violations of prison rules; that for an indeterminate stretch of time, apparently as a disciplinary measure, he had been confined to a solitary cell for twenty-three hours of each day; and that he had mutilated himself twice with a razor and once, more recently, by pouring laundry bleach into his eyes.

Citron also wrote, in suggesting Alvin's isolation and abandonment, that his wife and children had moved to New York shortly after his conviction and that his mother was dead and his father, "a crippled ex-fighter, is too ill to make the trip to Angola." Too ill? The article evidently had been prepared before the recent deterioration of Collis's health. Even back when I had been in the gym, I had perceived hints of a resentment between Collis and Alvin, a resentment in some way connected to Mike Cusimano, an ex-fighter, prominent businessman, and recent boxing commissioner, who had managed most of the pros Collis had trained over the years, including Alvin from the start of his career on into his prime. This resentment might more accurately have explained why Collis chose not to visit his son in prison.

For me the most intriguing passage in Alan Citron's report was rendered in Alvin's own words: " 'Me, I don't know anything. I was just a lot of front street action. I got disgusted with the pressure of life. Working, fighting, kids. What are you going to do about anything? Drugs were escapism. I thought it was smarter to sell than to buy. Now I've turned myself off. I could really turn myself on, you know, with booze and all that, but that's no good. My hook stinks now, but goddam. Other fighters keep themselves mad. I couldn't keep myself mad.' "

I paused in rereading the article, grateful for Citron's work but also wondering about one of its captions—"The final bell has not been sounded, but this man's fight ended years ago"—and about its conclusion that Alvin had been "defeated" by Angola's "tense inner world of streetwise urban convicts." Facts that contradicted this view already seemed relevant: for instance, how closely that tense prison world approximated some of the conditions of Alvin's past life and, when he chose, how capably he could function in those conditions. Yet Citron had recounted that when Alvin entered Angola, prison officials said he told them "he feared for his life."

14

□

September 25, 1981

Because of the potential for exploitation in our agreement, I was glad the matter of formalizing things came up right away. Not that the remote chance of making money played much of a part in my projections, but—given the suspicions I knew I would soon meet—it was a relief to have someone else arrange the opportunity for me to commit myself, in a public and binding way, to my belief that Collis and his family deserved as much of any profits as I did. It was Mike Cusimano who suggested we have something official on paper. Collis probably checked with Mike as soon as he saw I was serious.

Mike's son Sal, a lawyer, drew up a contract for us. It stung the jealous part of my nature to learn from Sal Cusimano that he too knew Collis from the gym and that Collis had brought him successfully from a green beginner through his first and only amateur fight, which he won. Collis eventually told me several times of the "swell blowout," a dinner party and dance, that followed and how he, as one of the guests of honor, had been "treated real white, tops," and "kep' out till three." When I asked Sal Cusimano to bill me for his services, he laughed and said, "Just chalk it up to Collis!"

The most common boxing contract is a 66/33 split, the larger share to the fighter, expenses off the top. Before sending our draft to Sal for translation into legal language, Collis and I joked about which of us in this project corresponded to the athlete, each acting as if he thought the other should have the 66. Then we settled things simply, cutting our imaginary riches down the middle and writing it up grandly, to include movie rights, TV, any kind of profit at all, 50/50 between us, or between his heirs and mine.

The evening I took him the contract, I found him evidently feeling better than he had at any time since he had left the gym. He, Gloria (as witness), and I were upstairs in his bedroom for the signatures. Such legalistic doings seemed to appeal to him, probably because they recalled the fight game. He had often told me, "When you git a fighter on paper, you got him where you want him." Although he again hadn't left his bed all day, his eyes snapped with luster as he sat up against the headboard, clinic bracelets jumping on his wrists, and demonstrated combinations: "Bing! Bang! Then come back wi' th' hook, *bam!*" Outside, dusk deepened. From the back stoops and alleyway below his window, TVs and ratchety cassettes competed with each other and the goosed clatter of a tinkered-on engine.

Before we signed the contracts, I had been cautioning him about the odds against publication and the likelihood that, even if what I wrote saw print, it might not earn anything because my first and most selfish concern was with a different kind of worth. He hooted and fell away, then jabbed his open palm into my shoulder, almost pushing me off the chair next to his bed. "Man, you a knockout! Talkin' 'bout the book *'might not be of interest'!*" His fingers closed around my shoulder, and he broke into a spell of laughter. "Look. If this don' make a dime, what can you do"—he shrugged, at the same time tucking his chin behind his left shoulder in an old fighting move—" 'cept use what you got the best way you know? We jus' seein' how far we can go. If we don' go nowhere . . . ?"

He shrugged again, turned his hands palm-up at the level of his hips on the mattress, and continued to smile. "Glor*ia!* Reach me that pen."

Never, outside the gym, had I seen him so exalted, and I enjoyed it and was reluctant to alter his mood. I was also anxious to beat nightfall and be on my way before the project came fully awake. The only object on the walls of his room was the yellowed cover of a boxing program—Alvin, squared off alone—taped high above his bed. I tried to imagine him balanced on his good leg on the mattress, torn strips of adhesive on the tips of his fingers, the program in his other hand. I wanted to know exactly what he was thinking as he smoothed on the strips of tape. It was the kind of seemingly trivial question that interested me most, the kind I often couldn't bring myself to ask. That night was no exception. Instead, we ended up talking for a while about his segregated fights at the Coliseum and about Jim Crow. Just before I left, I gathered he was telling me about more than boxing. He had been describing his style in the ring and how he would gladly trade with an opponent, take two or three blows to land one.

"I was always willin' to gamble," he said, his hand jostling my shoulder. " 'Cause I knew what I had."

Either I'm mistaken or he was also trying to help me trust in things and myself—not just on my way out to the car or on a trip across town, but now. Right now. This moment as I write.

TWO

The Coliseum

□

1

☐

September 26, 1981

The tall, acne-blistered guard made small talk. His black uniform rustled synthetically as he showed me along the outdoor walkway toward Cuda tier, an isolated one-story compound at the far end of the yard in Camp J, Angola's specialized outpost for problem prisoners. The guard seemed to have the mistaken idea that I was someone officially important, possibly a journalist, and he asked deferential, countrified questions that vaguely pertained to documentary reporting and to publishing a book. I looked at his pale, suffering skin and answered in a way that didn't directly correct his false impression of me. My omission probably led him to pass on the same mistake to the caretaker at Cuda, who eventually peered out from behind the steel door that the guard rapped on. The caretaker, who I guessed was a trusty, wore deeply wrinkled street clothes, and he looked groggy—either drugged or as if we had roused him. They conferred for a moment, the caretaker nodding vacantly. Then, to my surprise, the guard obligingly waved me inside, and walked away.

From the glare of the open walkway, I stepped uncertainly into a dim, barren room. The only light was a wrenched gooseneck lamp. Beneath it, drawn up to a metal desk littered with the remains of a meal, stood a grimy stuffed chair. It was like a nest—crammed with newsprint and copies of *Penthouse*, mashed pillows, and a visibly greasy transistor radio.

After the caretaker finished locking himself and me in, he straightened slowly as if he had back trouble and asked without interest "which of 'em" I was supposed to see. I had just noticed, next to the desk, a door with a barred window in it. When I told him who I had come to visit, he scuffed over to this door and shouted an order I couldn't understand through the bars. Then, groping among the flaps of keys on his ring, he set about opening the lock beneath the window.

Beyond the windowed door was a second door, all bars. These yielded a full view of a corridor and a young man partly wrapped in a towel. He wore a shower cap and, taking short, precise steps, came toward us from the latrine entrance at the far end of the corridor. Cement block enclosed the corridor to the right; ventilation slats near the ceiling let in fanlike stripes of light. To the left, I made out a row of about a dozen cells. The caretaker shouted impatiently at the man in the towel while working a switch that caused the door to the prisoner's cell to slide open, then to shut behind him. The caretaker swiped at another switch with the edge of his hand. The bars before us shuddered, and snicked open.

"He down there. About on the end."

I waited for the man to lead the way. When he didn't move, it struck me in a rush that he assumed I had clearance to be anywhere in the prison.

On crepe soles, I stepped silently into the corridor, trying to move with a confidence I've never felt.

The prisoners were sleeping. Or seemed to be. Numbly I moved through the striped light, and through a sodden moist smell I'll never be able to name, or forget. In each toilet-dominated cell, a man's prone form lay on a steel bunk suspended on two chains. Not one of the prisoners was white, and all lay turned away to the wall, each drawn in to himself—except for the one who had come from the shower. He stood, penis semi-erect, clenching the balled-up hems of the towel now yoked across the back of his neck.

The prisoner in the next cell snored. I saw dingy under-shorts and a huge man's massive bulk.

Then the next cell and I saw Alvin.

It wasn't the posters or the snapshots and sports-page photographs I had pored over that made me know him at once: he didn't look like *them* anymore. He lay, unlike the other prisoners in Cuda, with his head at the foot of his bunk, facing the bars, jaw cradled in the crook of his arm. As I stepped silently into view, filling the space he had been gazing across, he peered up, big-eyed. Despite the scar tissue and his now permanently sagging right brow—caused, if family rumor could be believed, by spooked guards who had beaten him with bats—I saw Collis stamped unmistakably in the open expression in and around his eyes. It was a look in which curiosity replaced caution. When I stayed where I was, making it clear that he was why I was there, the look vanished and he recoiled toward the wall.

It was after I had begun to talk—about what, I don't recall—that he finally roused himself, rose deliberately, and took the single step from his bunk to the bars. It seemed to disturb and confuse him when, without my willing it, giddy nervous energy caused me to reach into his cell.

After pausing and looking at it squarely, he took my hand and, in odd social compliance, shook it: a fighter's limp grip, protective of his own knuckles.

For a moment I just looked at him.

After all I had read and heard about him, it was unusually hard to see him as simply real. Teeth missing in places and hair gone in the front, he wore baggy denims and a plain white T-shirt that fit him, except across his wide shoulders, the way a father's garment fits a young son.

When I asked if my letter (of self-introduction) had reached him, he began to speak, in soft-voiced, fast, repetitious, whispery riffs, as if only to himself. Frequently he paused, stuttering, to take issue with what he had just said, correcting himself in fragmented phrases. Yes, he allowed, staring in annoyed wonderment at the hand I had touched, he *had* received a letter, but he couldn't understand it. It was written funny, and his mind was "jammed up, too jammed up—jammed up, like in *J*, Camp *J*, this is *lock-down*, Camp *J*, where I live."

I tried to explain what I had written in the letter, my interest in his father and his family and the endeavor I had begun.

"Yeh, well," he interrupted, speaking louder, "a book can be *up*, a book can be *down*. Book can be a lift. Like my hand there. *You see my hand!?*" His slack left arm appeared to levitate, his ringless, tattooed fingers—L-O-V-E—drifting vertically along the bars. "Or a book can look like a lift and still be a jam. Bible's the only book I read now. The Bible's a lift, the Bible's a *jam*."

Hoping to put him at least somewhat at ease, I made the mistake of showing him the contract. He took it and held it on his side of the bars and looked at it for a long time, shaking his head. I tried to explain how well I understood the irony of this contract in relation to the other contracts in his past and how they had caused him problems. I labored to make him see that I was aware of all that. This one would be different. (I cringed at the lameness of my phrases.)

But he paid me little mind. More agitated than before, he spoke so quickly and softly I could scarcely follow him. It seemed he was talking about jewelry. At first this was all I could gather. I listened in nervous bafflement as the words "emerald" and "diamond" kept coming back.

"My wife was a diamond," he said, as if the transition were obvious. "That's what I always told her."

Then he was talking about one of his sons, the last child his wife, Diane, had had by him, a child who was the congenitally handicapped brother of a twin born dead.

The family used different names when speaking of this son, who—though Alvin didn't know it—was now, according to necessity, in a foster home somewhere in New York.

Jude: Gloria eventually told me that this was his last son's name. "After the saint," she said, "St. Jude, the one for trouble that's hopeless." But Farris's girlfriend would later tell me, no, this was wrong, the child was named Julius— after Alvin and Diane's close friend and former drug-selling "podnah," Pete, who would allow, when I met him the following spring, that this *was* possible, since his own given name was Junius Pierre Cole III. But on one point everyone agreed: Alvin had named the twins on his own. Diane said she had thought up enough names for babies. That was before she had left New Orleans, after a minor drug charge, for her present life in Harlem.

"Words will run," Alvin whispered now, looking down toward the base of the bars. "Names run, don't they?"

Though he continued to talk of "precious stones . . . jewels," I still didn't understand. It would be more than a year before, casting back over this part of this day as I often did, I suddenly would see it: "jewels," Jules! He had named his son Jules.

It was "like precious stones," he said again. The year Jules was born, the Beatles had that song, "Hey, Jude": "And that was like 'Lucy in the Sky.' You know, 'Lucy in the Sky . . . with Diamonds.' " And his ex-manager Mike Cusimano— whom Collis revered and Alvin now seemed to mistrust— Mike Cusimano had an address that appealed to him. "Mist' Cusimano stays in that big house on Emerald Street." He said it evenly, but also as if he were cursing. "'Bout big as this paper here." He handed back the contract and the letterhead envelope bearing the name of the law firm of Mike's son Sal. "You know Mist' Cusimano? You been to his house on Emerald Street? Maybe you work for him. I worked for him. I—"

He stepped back from the bars. Three guards had entered the corridor and, bickering and chuffing, now trotted toward us. I heard the tallest one tell the others to take me out quickly. They put their hands around my arms. They would have to move us, the tallest one said, to a regular visiting area. But first—and here he produced a document—Alvin would have to sign a publicity release. The guard stuck the form and a pen through the bars.

"Yes, suh. Yes, suh," Alvin said, in what sounded to me like a parody of slavishness.

When I said, no, he needn't agree against his will, he only shook his head.

"I signs all the papers," he said. "It's like a contract."

He scrawled his name, and, while the tallest guard opened the cell, he turned around like an obedient child and put the hairless sides of his wrists together behind his back, holding them away from his body so one of the other guards could more easily bracelet them with handcuffs.

Flanking each of his shoulders, the first two guards steered him out of the cell. The third guard and I waited for them to wheel by; then we fell in behind, lurched forward, and became a procession.

Every prisoner now lay so his opened eyes could track us the width of his cell. Alvin walked meekly between the guards, his ears about level with their shoulders. The heels of his shower thongs snapped at his overlong pant cuffs. It wasn't until we had all moved clumsily through the slowly opened sequence of doors and were outside that I was able to read the very small letters—R-O-C-K—written in nail polish across the back of his T-shirt.

I stepped to the side of him as we waited for the door to a visiting cell farther down the walk to be unlocked from within. It was a cloudless afternoon. Sunlight glinted on the chain-link fences beyond and shone beautifully on fertile fields rippling in the distance. In a gun tower between the fences, one of Angola's female sharpshooters appeared in silhouette through a window framed in print kitchen curtains. She chatted into a telephone receiver and stroked the underside of her puffed hive of hair.

The bright light disclosed the full extent of Alvin's newly receded hairline and the blurred margins of the greenish jailhouse-tattooed letters on his sallow brown arms: D-I-A-N-E and (his first two sons) A-L-V-I-N and K-E-V-I-N. It was easy to study him now because, as we waited, he paid no evident attention to the guards or to me. His eyes roamed the distant grass and sky. Breeze ruffled his denims and loose T-shirt. "Rock," the small word on the cotton across his shoulder blades, seemed a frail, if persistent, contradiction of Alan Citron's portrait of him as a frightened, broken man. Even when trained down into fighting shape, Alvin had been a full-bodied middleweight who, in gyms, had walked through large light heavies. Now he was smaller than I was, and weighed, at the most, maybe 140.

When the door at last opened, I glimpsed another cell-block. A prisoner walking there called out, "Say, Al-*vin!*" in an eager pleased way that made me think they hadn't seen each other in a long time. Alvin scarcely nodded, for at the first clatch of the tumblers in the lock, he had become attentive to the guards, and when one of them touched him, he at once stepped inside.

The tallest guard, the pale one with the acne, sullenly guided me to a second door and shut me in in a small, dim visiting room. The space was empty except for a straight chair. Doubled steel mesh formed a panel in one wall. Above me, its blades stalled, a shorted-out ventilator hummed. The door, which stood crooked on its hinges, grated on the gritty cement, then slammed behind me. A key turned the complaining tumblers back into place.

Beyond the panel was a space identical to mine and also furnished with a chair. Because of the motionless air and extreme heat, my shirt was soaked through by the time the door opened on Alvin's side. His wrists were now cuffed in front of him. He sat down at some distance from the screen and began speaking right away.

"Was married when I was seventeen. Have a wife and six children in New Orleans. I tell my children to stay in school and make between forty and a hundred on the cards. They don't do it, don't do it right, I whip 'em, tear 'em up! But they gotta eat. That's what I tell 'em. *Eat!*"

Misaligned gaps in the doubled mesh made his image waver before me. If I had still hoped our conversation might loosely follow the pattern of an interview, that hope now vanished. He spoke on, compulsively and insistently, in low whispers that I couldn't always clearly hear. It was obvious that he wouldn't be attentive to whatever it was I had thought I wanted to learn. He would talk, as he said, "till the time is gone," and I would strain forward in the chair opposite him, trying to catch the meaning that might lie in his words and in his alternately mocking and humble inflections.

"Down time," he said quickly, his head bowed toward his chest. "This is down time. Like a strip-down, a jam, all the things been jammed in my head—like they was jammed in backwards. Backwards and down. It all presses down to the feet, but can't go no further 'cause nothin's under there but concrete and rock. Yeh, concrete and rock, that's right. Well, a diamond's harder than a rock, but I still remember how to use my feet."

He paused for possibly a minute, then asked if I had seen Jimmy Carter in New Orleans. I said I had not.

He seemed agitated. "Wh-what? You mean the . . . the . . . the President didn't come to Louisiana?"

When I said I didn't think so, he accused me of misleading him. "You say the President didn't come to Louisiana? You must be playin' with my head. You could do it too, ex-fighter, ex-junkie's got a head easy to play with. But I know *Louisiana*, it's the bottom, and the shit's go'n fall on everybody!"

Not knowing how to answer his bitterness, I asked if I could ask him a question.

"*Shoot!*" he shouted immediately and in a way that made me think of the multiple implications, which seemed deliberate, in many of his phrases.

Supposing the memory might be more pleasant to him, I brought up his trip to the Riviera with his friend Johnny Powell, the trainer who worked for Malcolm Faber and who had replaced Collis after Alvin and his father had argued about Mike. I asked how it had been traveling and training in Europe before his last fight.

He whispered to himself for a few moments; then his voice gradually rose: "Monte Carlo, San Remo, the racetrack, casinos, that smelled pretty good, smelled better than Louisiana, better than New Orleans, better than Carter and the Kennedys, *all* a the Kennedys."

He raised his head to peer at me for the first time. Because of the doubled screen, I couldn't look at both of his eyes at once.

"If I was to tell you the moon is green—" He stopped himself and dropped his eyes.

As if finally stifled by the heat, we sat for a moment in silence except for the audible current in the broken ventilator.

"I'm not in my right head," he continued apologetically. "Been goin' through these changes, can't keep a thought straight, nuttin' up." Now he shouted: *"I'm nuttin' up!"*

After another silence, he mentioned headaches. These seemed to refer both to physical pain and, I inferred, to my visit's causing him problems with other convicts who might think that, through me, he was gaining something worth trying to take from him. I asked if he preferred for me just to let him alone. His response was incoherent, and abruptly he began talking about boxing.

"That ring," he said. "That's what you want to hear about, I know that's it, that must be it— What was we speakin' of now . . . ? Wait . . . here it come, here it come round again: That ring. That ring's cold as ice. Hot ice. Emile Griffith, Gil Clancy, Carlos Monzon, the Garden. That ring's a mystery, you got all types a rings around it. You got ten-round, eight-, six-, you got four-round fighters, two-round fighters—that's right, you b'lieve it, *two*-round—you got amateurs, got people whose daddies help 'em just put a foot in it, people who make a safe livin' off a makin' fights, other people who write about it . . . 'Scuse me, you hafta excuse me. My mind's not right."

I asked if he knew of a way I could help him.

"What do I need?" he snapped. "What I need? I need some eyeglasses, I need me some specs to talk about that ring."

He went on at a rushing pace I couldn't follow. Then I

made out one muttered phrase: "Fat butt!" I thought he was
referring to his last opponent, Jean-Claude Bouttier, the
European champion. But he said, no, that it was only like
Bouttier—"practically the same name as him"—and that he
was thinking about Joe Bordelon, a man who managed the
Circle Drugstore, which stood on St. Bernard Avenue across
from the project. Implying he had stolen from Bordelon's
store as a child, he spoke savagely and said the man "had a
fat butt and was never nice to kids!"

In futility I looked at the sheaf of sweat-smudged notes
and questions in my lap. He continued talking into his chest
too softly and too fast for me to make out the rest of his
words. Suddenly my eyes stung, and I kept my head down
so that, even if he looked at me, he wouldn't be able to tell
they had teared over. I had been wrong in thinking myself
prepared for this visit. "What's it *like?*" I blurted, as if angry,
interrupting his low, running murmur. "What do you *do*,
just in that cell twenty-three hours a day!?"

"Oh, I travel," he answered distinctly and at once. "At
night I drive all over New Orleans, my home. Been to New
York. Rome. London. But it all comes back home. Home to
the Seventh Ward, where I come up. Yeh, nights I drive up
on Canal Street. Then around on the Lakefront, Ponchartrain Park. Then back down St. Bernard." He whispered
confidentially. "I just leave a small flame burnin'. I cut across
the courtyard and watch for the broken step . . ."

As I would soon read in the transcript of his trial, the step
up to the entrance from the front porchway of his and
Diane's apartment in the project became a point of contention
in testimony against him.

"I watch for that broken last step," he said. "Then I go in
and check the stove to see that that small flame's still lit. I
turn it down if I have to. That's where I go at night. That's
where I live."

Current pulsed into the ventilator, then ceased.

I don't know how much later it was when someone rapped
on the door. Although I was wary of false hope—for either

of us—I quickly ventured that what I wrote might improve things for him and the rest of the family.

He sneered. "What you wanna play with my head for? Words run. Cain't no *book* do nothin'."

Standing, I said I didn't think his crime deserved its punishment and that, even if I was wrong, he still didn't belong in a place like Angola.

He looked up, the doubled mesh making the motion from his neck appear to have seams. "Yeh, well," he answered, "if I don't belong here, I guess they's maybe a thousand like me don't belong here either." He said something more, a gush of words, as the door was dredged open and a guard spoke to me sharply.

Moving toward the bright doorway, I raised my hand in a subdued wave. Beyond the screen, he mimicked my gesture exactly. On the walkway, I turned and looked back inside. He was a blurred silhouette on the panel. A tepid breeze felt cool on my wet clothes. I raised my hand again, and he did exactly the same as the guard lunged on the heavy door, slamming it between us.

All the guards now stared at me, and the pale one with the acne began to question why, earlier, I would complicate their jobs by entering a part of the prison I must have realized was forbidden me. Although I looked attentively up at him, at his poor ravaged skin, I was still hearing the last things Alvin had said.

"You see my wife and children back in New Orleans, you tell 'em you saw me, just say I'm still sittin' here, say 'Al's alive,' tell 'em I miss 'em, tell 'em I love 'em, words run, don't they, *my wife was a diamond*."

2

□

I'M 30 NOW I CAME IN HERE WHEN I JUST MADE 23. I FEEL GOOD MY MIND AND BODY. I DO 1000 PUSH UP'S 250 SAT UPS 3 TIME'S A WEEK I READ A LOT OF BOOK'S TO KEEP MY MIND TOGETHER I BEEN CONFINE TO THESE CELL'S SENCE 1977 LAST TIME I WAS IN THE OPEN YOU NO TO WALK OR PLAY BALL WAS 1976. I'M GETTING USE TO A CELL BUT I WOULD LIKE TO BE OUT SO I CAN WALK OR PLAY FOOTBALL BUT THEY DON'T WANT TO LET ME OUT THESE'S CELL I DON'T LET IT WORRY ME I LET NOTHING THEY DO WORRY ME. I WROTE ALVIN A LETTER HOPEING TO PULL HIM TOGETHER HE NOT STRONG AS I AM. IM WRITING ABOUT THIS "MAD" "HOUSE" THEY CALL "ANGOLA" AND THESE DOGS THAT RUN IT DON'T WANT ME TO DO IT.

The guards at the front gate had searched the car, then me, and after calling the warden they let me drive inside. It was the simplest entry to Angola I would have. I had written, then telephoned, the warden explaining my purpose and sending a tortuously scrawled note from Collis asking that I be allowed to visit his sons.

Beyond the entrance, a freckled driver climbed leisurely into a pickup and gestured for me to follow him. Keeping a careful distance between us, I drove slowly on the new asphalt road, which looked as if it had been swept, the purplish surface ribboning between neatly furrowed fields of vegetables and single-storied compounds ringed in chain link. Gun towers, painted the same drab green as all the other prison buildings, stood at the four corners of each compound.

We passed several clusters of trailers, the homes of resident staff. Around them were bikes, toys, domestic clutter. The warden lived on the highest of the few hills within the prison. The long driveway to his low brick house wound up through a stand of pines. As I waited outside before the carport while the driver went in for him, a distant chain saw broke the stillness of an afternoon reminiscent of listlessly warm fall Saturdays from my early youth in Mississippi.

The warden greeted me guardedly but cordially. His main concern seemed to be determining that I was the person who had written him and spoken to him several times on the phone. I laid my identification on the dusty hood of my car. He was almost apologetic about carefully reviewing these documents. "This *is* a prison, you know." I sensed genuine but restrained concern as he spoke briefly of his sketchy awareness of Alvin and then fatalistically of how "some men never adjust to prison life" and especially not to "the extended lock-down situation their maladjustment causes." He could specifically answer none of my questions and concerns about Alvin—"We have four thousand men here"—and he seemed mildly relieved, as someone might feel on parting with a door-to-door zealot, to have me be on my way driving behind the freckled driver toward Camp J. Still, he had given me more cooperation than I would receive from anyone else established in Louisiana's penal hierarchy.

The driver followed a winding fork through the cultivated fields. When the land became hilly and less sumptuous, the road dipped into a long grade, and a small lake rose into view. Camp J lay across the road from the gray water. To me, it appeared to be no different from the other olive-drab compounds we had passed.

After the driver climbed down from his truck, he stood on the paved parking area and lit a cigarette. Limber-kneed and perky, he fooled with his hard pack and disposable lighter as he joshed with a matronly woman who pressed buzzers that unlocked the entrance to Camp J. They made small talk as I wrote personal information on a battery of forms. Eventually, telling the woman he would see her later, he strolled out to the truck and drove off. About an hour after that, the inner doors to the compound slid open and a guard waved me inside the cyclone fencing, which I assumed was electrified. There, he put me in the charge of another guard, who waited on a slick cement walkway that intersected the yard at ground level.

This guard was the tall, acne-seared youth. With watchful politeness, he ushered me down the ceilinged walkway through several barred electronic archways. Small groups of prisoners in denim idled beyond the fencing that bounded either side of the walk. As if about to speak, they turned and looked at me openly.

Two other young guards joined us. Masking their interest, they asked roundabout questions concerning my reason for being there. When I answered them frankly, they fell silent and glanced down suspiciously as if trying to think of surer ways to gauge what my game really was.

The tall guard broke off for a different destination, leaving me with the other two, and the three of us turned down an adjacent walk that passed between facing rows of concrete blockhouses. This was Gar tier, the return address on the two letters written to me from Angola; I would visit here— and see Alvin's youngest brother—before my first visit to Alvin himself.

9/8/81

HELLO

I HAVE A SLIP FROM THE MAIL ROOM SAYING THEY SENT A LETTER BACK TO YOU. REASON YOU SENT 1 18 CENT STAMP IN YOUR LETTER THAT IS NOT "PERMITTED" I

DON'T HAVE KNOWLEGE OF WHO YOU ARE I DON'T NO YOUR FIRST NAME OR SHELL I PUT MR. OR MRS. ON THE ENVELOPE THEY JUST SENT ME A SLIP WITH YOUR LAST NAME AND YOUR ADDRESS. I BEEN THINKING AND THINK- ING. TRY TO MAKE MY MIND GO BACK TO JUNE 1974 THAT WHEN I WAS ON THE STREET "LAST" BUT I STILL CAN'T REMEMBER NO ONE AROUND YOUR ADDRESS IF YOU PLEASE WRITE TO ME AGAIN DON'T PUT ANYTHING IN SIDE OF THE ENVELOPE JUST THE LETTER NOTHING ELSE "OK" PLEASE WRITE "OK" ANSWER SOON.

9/21/81

I JUST GOT YOUR LETTER TODAY AND I WAS VERY GLAD TO HERE FROM YOU I FEEL A DEEP PAIN IN SIDE OF ME FOR MY DADDY. SO I WILL TALK TO YOU "OK" I NO A LOT ABOUT HIM AND HIS "PASS" I PRAY I SEE HIM BEFORE HE "DIE" I WAS "CONFINE" WHEN MY MOTHER "DIE" AND I AN'T SEEN MY MOTHER GET "BURY" I DON'T WANT THE SAME THING TO HAPPEN TO MY DADDY. I WILL TALK TO YOU SOON AS YOU CAN COME "UP" HERE "OK"

The guards put me in a visiting space very similar to the one I would occupy an hour or so later during the last part of my meeting with Alvin. I waited for a while in the narrow enclosure; then the door beyond the screen in the wall opened. Haltingly, his ankles and wrists shackled, Farris edged inside.

He wasn't tall, but his torso almost equaled the width of the doorframe. Following at a distance, a guard leaned in with a key.

Farris said he didn't care either way when the guard asked him if he wanted the manacles removed. The guard hesitated and said, well, he was supposed to be unshackled. Then, intently watching him, the guard reached into the locks with the long key. As the guard backed through the doorway, Farris remained facing him. He breathed "umn-un" when the guard asked if he wanted a chair. The guard said, well, he was entitled to a chair, but Farris shook his head. Only after the guard withdrew and locked the door did he turn and stare at me.

Muscled like a manic bodybuilder, he wore a stretched red T-shirt. A wild Afro fringed the maroon scarf tied around the crown of his head, giving him the look of a coarsened sixties militant. Other features—his pocked face, burn scars, and amateur tattoos—more accurately reflected what in a narrowly practical sense he was: a maximum-security convict.

Because he disdained to sit, I stood away from the chair on my side of the screen, and he appeared not to notice. He immediately asked to see the contract and interrogated me bluntly concerning my motives.

I answered him plainly and honestly. He seemed to understand me at once and to have no trouble accepting my interest in his family. Nor did he seem to find it unacceptable when—not without trepidation—I told him what I'd often thought but never before uttered: that my sense of lacking a real father deepened my attraction to his, and that our racial difference strengthened rather than weakened the attraction. I added that my upbringing in an unusually racist region and time was also a factor. When I finished, he nodded and said we could speak.

His family's happiest times, he felt, were when they all lived together in his parents' former apartment "in the front," one of the project's choice locations, directly on St. Bernard Avenue. Connie had a room to herself. When Collis Jr. wasn't traveling with one of the blues bands he played in, he shared the third bedroom with the boys, Jerry and Farris. Alvin lived just "across the driveway" on Jumonville with his young wife, Diane. Gloria, who was also newly married, had moved to another housing project—Desire— but her husband was "sick in the head, the kind to lock her out," and so she spent many nights in Connie's room.

This period, and Farris's sense of childhood, ended with the shooting—of which he said he had little memory. But he remembered that soon after it happened, Connie was gone, Alvin became "like the head" of the family, and more of the house chores fell to the boys. Their mother, Dorothy, had been confined to a wheelchair since Farris's birth: "I never saw my mother walk." In the year immediately following the shooting, Collis was a second invalid in the apartment. Jerry, who later became a professional cook, fixed meals and "made groceries." Farris did the heavy cleaning.

"My daddy wanted it *clean!* Umn-humn." He nodded with finality, sealing his lips. Appearing to ripple because of the doubled screen, he leaned close for emphasis. "I worked that wax cloth! You ever buffed a whole room with just these?" He raised his hands. "When I got finished, you could *skate* on them floors. See y'self too."

Gloria had asked me to give him a message, and this caused us to talk of her for a while. Although others had told me he deeply cared for his older sister, there was no sentiment in the way he recalled her now. "Man, Glo could be evil." Elaborating, he told me how, in her teens, Gloria had dropped a cat from a third-story window to see if it would land on its feet. He also described her once picking out the eye of a goldfish with a fork while "that fish was still flippin'," and I thought of her involuntary habit during conversation of using her hands to obscure her eye and her teeth. "And one time she shut that cat up in the oven too, and turned it on." He pressed his lips together in a mannerism expressing finality. "But that cat come *out* that oven. Um-hunh, that's right."

Later on he said that, as he grew older, he did still more of the housework, and there was little time to take part in the organized sports and the boxing that his father loved. Little time for school: "Le's don' talk about school. I was bad in school. Okay? But I would show any dude with weights or with football that I could do better than him."

He quit junior high because, before he was fifteen, he was "runnin'" with dropouts much older than himself: "These was dudes twenty-four, twenty-five. Can't impress them easy, so you know that had to be guns."

He would say little about his first armed-robbery conviction in New York—"I love that city!"—or about his second in New Orleans. It would be months—after I had reviewed police records and listened to other people's accounts—before I would have a clear sense of what happened. Rather than speak of these convictions, he was more interested in telling about the distant past or about conditions in Angola. "Alvin was tempered like our mother," he said, "he could get along with anybody. He wasn't mean" except in a fight, but then he was "like our daddy." His earliest recollections of school were of walking the short distance home and seeing crowds of boys in a field between the playground and the project. Alvin would be in the moving circle in their midst, fighting. In his youngest brother's memory, he never lost: "He'd knock guys down two, three times."

Farris's descriptions of the prison were so abusive that I caught myself uneasily scanning the walls for eavesdropping devices. He was eager for me to read what he had already written about Angola. He said a friend in a less restricted camp was typing this for him. Then, compulsively, he continued about life in Angola, how it was "cold, cold," how a "li'l podnah" of his had been stabbed to death by his enemy, "Duck." This, he said, was why he had been isolated in Camp J for almost a year—as mutual protection for himself and Duck. When they were both in population and the last time they had seen each other, he said he had told Duck, "Le's just *do* it!" They had slipped away for their hidden knives and later were circling toward each other across the yard when a troop of guards broke it up. "Man, it was a riot! Or close to it." Assuming the air of a knowing older person telling tales to a credulous youngster, he described other violence he had experienced behind bars, dwelling on an incident in which he was "jooged in the back" with an ice pick in Orleans Parish Prison. He gestured with his thumb toward his spine, but unlike what his father would have done, he didn't turn around, exposing his back, and roll up his shirt to display the scar. The man who stabbed him escaped through a door that had a screened window in it. "Like this screen here," he told me, extending his hand toward the panel between us, his mottled triceps hanging hugely slack from his raised arm. "He slammed the door on me, but I come through that screen. Umn-hunh. Like it was paper."

Later, when he was telling about some of the many "cross-plays" in the prison, he again raised his arm to point. "Take that shirt," he said, languidly waggling two fingers at the costly broadcloth now pasted by sweat to my ribs. "Somebody in here might take that shirt there, they might take it out your laundry bag and put it in somebody else's. Just to see what you'd do."

His voice had a similarly taunting edge when I asked why his father often seemed willing to give whites the benefit of the doubt. "You mean *white folks?*" I thought he would laugh, but after looking at me sidewise for a moment, he answered seriously. His daddy sometimes let whites take advantage of him, he said, shaking his head over it, just because he liked them. "He always been like that. And when he make up his mind, can't nothin' change it."

Hearing the key in the lock, I hurriedly asked him one of my prepared questions: the origin of his name. He moved his eyebrows in a way that suggested I was strange, but he answered, "It came from a doctor," the last name of the doctor who had delivered him.

"A white doctor?" There wasn't time to go into what Collis had told me: that Farris was the name of one of his favorite amateurs, a light-skinned welterweight he had trained in 1950 just before Farris was born.

"It would have to be, wouldn't it?" He spoke louder as a guard swung back the door and beckoned me out. "That was thirty years ago. Watn't no black doctors at Charity then. Watn't none the last time I was on the street neither." He gestured dismissively toward the screen. "That was seven years ago.

"But I feel *good* now," he added, nearly shouting. He seemed suddenly to be addressing the guards. "I feel strong!" Strength had been a refrain in his conversation. "Strong as a horse!" A key turned in the lock behind him, and wheeling to face the door, he moved away from the screen.

As I stepped out of the sweltering blockhouse, I could no longer see him. But I could hear him.

"I feel like I'm twenty-one! Twenty-one, and ready for any *fuck*in' thing!"

After my visit with Alvin and then the annoyed guards' lecturing of me, it was a long wait outside Camp J before the freckled driver appeared to escort me to the front gate. Another guard, who had just come on duty, was obliged to wait with me. At my prompting he talked about his Cajun ancestry, then about his work routine and driving from the southwest each day, approaching the Mississippi River (Angola's impermeable western boundary), and entering the prison by a crossing that only staff were allowed to use. When I questioned him pointedly about Alvin and possible risks to his life, he became testy. "Nah, don't believe everything you read, it ain't so dangerous here," he said in a bluff way transparently calculated to suggest the opposite. "Shoot, if it was, I wouldn't stay around. I like livin' too much."

He changed the subject, but I tried once more, wondering aloud if Alvin was in danger. I said it looked as if Farris could take care of himself there, but Alvin seemed "withered," and vulnerable.

"Looks is tricky," the young guard said, surveying the lake, which lay just across the road and had darkened beneath the onset of dusk. "I can't speak to you about official prison business, but I'll tell you this one thing, and that's all: Alvin is more man than Farris'll *ever* be. Next to Alvin, Farris is a baby."

3

□

December 28, 1981

Although for some white New Yorkers travel to and around uptown beyond Central Park is a routine matter, my first such trip felt anything but that. Though I was in New York ostensibly to attend the Modern Language Association convention, I had come primarily to meet Connie. In answer to my letter, she had written, "Sir, I will look forward to talking to you on one of the days that you are here just call me my number is above." Two days before Christmas, I had visited Alvin's son Alvin Jr. in Parish Prison. Alvin Jr. had lived intermittently with Connie and her family during his years in New York, and he gave me directions to her building. "Just take the A train," he said. "You ain't got nothin' to worry about."

But I had no luck with the A train. After I went down the steps to a midtown station for my first subway ride, I found I didn't know how to enter the turnstile. There was no one in sight except two large black men standing on the platform. They wore robes and turbans. One turned to look at me. He nudged his companion. The turnstile grated in my hand. How did one come by the tokens to work it? Now both men stared scornfully. I turned and went back up the steps. And since I had allowed myself plenty of time and since I was wearing running shoes anyway, I just *ran* to Harlem.

On this unseasonably mild afternoon, after I jogged beyond the park, then continued uptown walking briskly, I moved through throngs of people clotting littered, noisy sidewalks. Though I passed only a few whites, no one paid me the slightest attention.

I located Connie's building not far from a busy intersection but saw no one in the lobby. While I was looking for a stairwell, a man approached me from behind. My pulse increased, but he gestured at an elevator's closed doors, mashed a button, and stepped inside with a proprietorial air. Thinking he might be a custodian, I followed him. The elevator smelled of singed cloth and hot tin. Eventually it lurched to a stop, the doors stuttered open, and the man weaved away. The doors closed, leaving me feeling trapped, and the car shuddered and continued its ascent. Then I was there, on the eleventh floor, walking slowly past metal-framed doors. Light bulbs in cages lined the ceiling.

I expected to recognize Connie. Alvin's friend and last trainer, Johnny Powell, had given me a handful of snapshots. One of these, taken after a fight of Alvin's in Madison Square Garden, showed Connie in a crowded hotel room next to but leaning slightly away from Jerry, who had his right arm around her, each dressed in black leather pants and a matching jacket. Jerry's expression, as his father's usually was, was unguarded (his fingers bearing the same formulaic L-O-V-E as Alvin's). But Connie's hard features were forbidding, especially the furrow above her severely plucked eyebrows, and she wore a man's hat. Another of Johnny's photos showed her sitting thigh to thigh with Alvin—who sat hunched forward in bell-bottoms and platform heels, holding a cigarette and seeming about to nod out. In this one, she was smiling.

Near the far end of the hall I stopped before a door marked with the letter "I." A few moments after I knocked, a bolt shot back; then there were the clicks and metallic whisk of a night chain being freed from its sheath. The door swung slowly inward as the young woman behind it gained a fuller look at me. Her expression was so much softer and more vulnerable than the woman's in Johnny's pictures that I took her for the oldest of the four teenaged children Gloria told me Connie now had.

She insisted on helping me out of my jacket; then she showed me into the small shag-carpeted living room to the right of the door. Protective plastic covered the brocade sofa and matching easy chairs. The room also held a stereo cart and a console TV.

A man, who had been sitting on the sofa, rose unhurriedly as I came in. Connie's daughter introduced us. I have rarely shaken a larger hand.

I was about to ask for Connie when her daughter urged me to sit down. I took a seat opposite hers, and for an instant we looked at each other curiously. Then she read my mind. "*I'm* Connie," she said, by her tone taking responsibility for my mistake. "You didn't know that."

As I tried to explain about Johnny's photographs, I saw what I had failed to notice at the door: Collis's rounded forehead and long upper lip.

She remembered avoiding the camera when Johnny began taking pictures during the muted family gathering that followed Alvin's fight in the Garden. She also remembered the hard-faced woman I had expected her to be: this was Marguerite (this name is fictitious), Jerry's wife at the time. "And those *suits!*" she said in a way that made it clear she would never wear such a thing. Jerry and Marguerite had paired themselves in leather for the big night with Alvin. "They took a week to decide about those. You'd have thought I don't know what." I later learned that, following Jerry's suicide, Connie had beaten Marguerite into helplessness on a Harlem sidewalk.

Connie's daughters now brought us coffee on a tray. I wanted to take careful notice of them and to pay attention to Connie's concerned, articulate conversation about Alvin —there were few nuances of New Orleans and the South in her speech—but the man—she had introduced him as Philip—asserted his presence.

In the course of the afternoon I came to understand that Connie had asked Philip to be present to make certain I was on the level. He questioned me closely concerning my intentions. I answered each question truthfully and about as completely as I could, including those about my relatively privileged upbringing in Mississippi. I gathered that Philip was involved in cultural projects in Harlem, and it appeared that he devoted much of his time trying to provide positive guidance to boys in the neighborhood. It was through his efforts to keep Alvin's ten-year-old son Farris out of trouble that he had met Connie. Farris was then living with her, her husband, Walter, and their five children. Philip had taken special interest in Farris because of the athletics and imprisonment in Farris's family. Philip said he had played football on scholarship at Southern University in Baton Rouge, and he also alluded to having served time. He looked at me fixedly as he spoke.

The only one of his questions I think I answered to his entire satisfaction concerned football. He had asked skeptically if the name Marion Motley meant anything to me. I couldn't guess his purpose, but I answered that Marion Motley, number 76, played for the Cleveland Browns in the forties and fifties and was the first of the great black running backs to gain national acclaim. From childhood, my mind has been full of such information.

That was a question, he said, that too many people, especially too many black people, couldn't have answered. Then he told me Marion Motley was his father.

This fact, in which he showed profound pride, became the focus of much of the rest of our conversation, and he described having recently taken Farris and other boys from Harlem to the Football Hall of Fame in Canton, Ohio, where his father also lived. It was through his father that he was personally acquainted with Don King, the boxing entrepreneur, and he proposed publicity strategies involving King, strategies that he thought could be of practical benefit to Collis's family.

When the talk returned to Alvin, Connie told me he had lived in her apartment in 1974 after he had jumped bail in New Orleans and a few months before he was arrested on new charges and sent to Rikers Island. She said he kept to himself as much as possible during those months. He would

sit alcoved away from the rest of the apartment in the part
of the living room "where you're sitting now," and he would
read books, "a whole stack of books," and he would weep.
The children would come to her in the kitchen and say,
"Uncle Alvin's crying again." She felt helpless to comfort
him. She held a clerical job at that time, and on weekday
mornings she would leave him in the living room with the
books around him. Often, when she returned home, he
would still be where she had left him, either with his face
behind a book or uncontrollably grieving. To my question,
Connie said, no, she didn't remember the titles of any of the
books.

I wanted most of all to know her feeling about her father
and the shooting, but with Philip there it seemed better not
to bring it up. By the time she had finished talking about
Alvin's stay with her, the sun had gone down and the
afternoon was tilting into twilight. Even if I hadn't needed
to be at the convention that night, I would have wanted to
leave. Midtown seemed very distant, and I wasn't sure, even
in daylight, exactly how to reach it.

As I set about leaving, we made plans to see each other
the next day: Philip insisted on taking me to Don King's
offices, and Connie still had to introduce me to Alvin's wife,
Diane, who was supposed to have been at Connie's that
afternoon but hadn't come. We agreed to meet at the
convention hotel since Philip said King's offices were near
there. Looking up at me from the sofa, he asked if I intended
to return as I had come, on foot, or if I meant "to go
quick"—by subway. I said I supposed by subway. He gave
me directions to the nearest station; then, watching me
steadily, he asked if I had it "down." I said I thought so—
even though I actually had no clear idea of what he had
described. (I naïvely hoped to catch a cab.) He must have
sensed my uncertainty and ignorance, because he then said
it would probably be best to let Connie's children show me
to the bus.

So I left, walking down the corridor quickly in order to
keep a step or two behind little Farris and Connie's fourteen-

year-old son Donny. In the elevator I was struck by how closely Farris, with his close-cropped head and blocky stature, resembled Alvin as he appeared in childhood pictures. Donny stopped the car a few floors above the lobby, and we went down several flights of concrete exit stairs toward a fire door at the back of the building. I smelled urine and sweet wine. Just inside the open doorway, where the smells were strongest, half a dozen men slouched in a half circle, facing out. Donny and Farris dipped swiftly through a space between them. I followed like their shadow. Someone exclaimed in surprise as I passed. At a trot, we crossed a hilly playground. We cut between several similar buildings and suddenly were looking down on an avenue streaked with headlights. Donny pointed to a bus at an adjacent corner. "That's yours!" he said. "I'll hold it." Then he darted down the hill and, dodging cars, stutter-stepped diagonally across the intersection.

Farris was right behind his cousin, but I caught up to him at the curb. In the exertion, forgetting myself and speaking to him as I sometimes did to my son, I commanded that he stop and wait for the safety of the light. He did as I said, I think out of surprise. As a result of our stopping, a car screeched just in front of us. Farris reacted as if the screech were a charge. Instead of remaining on the curb, he bolted on toward the bus, picking a limber path through the traffic. I followed less gracefully.

The bus had nosed out from the stop. I sprang through the closing doors as Donny casually swung himself down from the first step to the street. The bus lurched into its route downtown, and when I turned to wave, we exchanged a look of mutual dismay.

December 29, 1981

They said they had waited two hours for Philip uptown; then we waited for him in the lobby. He didn't turn up, so we took the elevator to the eleventh floor, to the room that

I was sharing with my wife, Sally. I was grateful for her quiet presence, especially at this moment—she seemed to have a calming influence on both Connie and Diane, who I sensed wouldn't have been much more comfortable joining me in a hotel room than I had been in seeking them out in Harlem. Now we sat politely and regarded each other through air smoky from Diane's cigarettes as Connie talked to me about Jerry.

I knew he had died shortly after Christmas, but family members had spoken of his death with such control that it hadn't registered with me before that it had occurred so recently—December 27, 1980. This perhaps explained why Connie mentioned him immediately. I regretted that my visit coincided with so sad a first anniversary.

She said Jerry had married Marguerite although he knew she was pregnant by another man. It was "a big Baptist wedding." And he had "loved the baby like his own." Still, about three years after their marriage, Marguerite had left him. He went home to New Orleans, and when he returned to New York, he learned she had remarried.

I remembered Gloria describing Jerry's last visit home during the Christmas holidays a year before his death. For her it had been, at moments, an especially fine visit—at midnight on New Year's Eve she felt hopeful despite "the terrible things" the family had endured and she had persuaded Jerry and Collis Jr. to kneel with her and pray for the future. But there were other times when Jerry couldn't be roused from his depression. He might still "fix nice coffee and cakes" for the rest of them in the morning, but he took no pleasure in the music she often played to distract him and he told her bitterly that "we just come from dirt and go back to dirt."

Back in New York, Connie told me, Jerry became despondent and began talking to himself so loudly and so often that his landlord, who lived on the floor below, accused him of boarding someone in his apartment upstairs. In reply to my questions about Jerry, Farris had copied, in one of his letters to me, part of the last letter Jerry had written him:

"THOSE WHITE PEOPLE DOWN SOUTH GIVE ME ALL KIND
OF HELL DADDY WAS GOING THROUGH ALL KIND OF
PRESSUR MAN BUT GOD DONT LIKE UGLY AND IN THE
END YOU WILL SEE WHAT HAPPEN FARRIS I KNOW THAT
THERE IS ONLY ONE WAY TO BE FREE DEATH."

On Christmas Day in 1980 he swallowed a handful of
sleeping pills. Connie took him to Harlem Hospital, where
his stomach was pumped in time. He remained on the
psychiatric ward for observation. Next he tried unsuccessfully
to electrocute himself in the shower, and soon after, to
overdose on some heroin that had come into his possession.
Connie told me he fought with psychiatric aides who teased
him for " 'not being able to kill hisself right.' " On the 27th,
after he had gained permission to go into a bathroom alone,
a nurse reported she found him behind the door—hanged
with strips of cloth torn from his mattress liner.

Connie didn't mention that she pawned her rings to pay
for his burial, but she did say she wasn't fully satisfied his
death was a suicide. When she unzipped the shroud he had
been placed in, he looked "like he was asleep" with no mark
on his neck though it supposedly was broken.

I let the subject die, and Diane and I, primarily Diane,
talked about Alvin.

Then, it seemed suddenly, it was well past the time at
which they earlier had said they needed to leave. Outside
the hotel, Connie said she would keep in touch. She waved
as they merged with a crowd. I waved and turned to hurry
upstairs, by then certain to be late for the main event on
that evening's convention agenda, a reading by an author
celebrated in academic circles.

4

□

January 4, 1986

Scraps.

A cardboard drawer stands on the floor near my desk, in it the remains of a scrapbook: remnants of construction-paper pages disintegrating into flakes, their colors reversed with age, black pages faded to brown, white pages to yellow, all melding toward sepia. Torn bits of training tape gum the flakes to the corners of photographs, invitations, and newspaper clippings spanning four decades.

The pictures are of family and friends; of fighters; of some of the white people Collis worked for and of some of their children. Somewhere on the surface of each print, his large scrawl captions the photo.

"KING COLLIS & QUEAN": A tidy elementary school classroom and twenty small children in Mardi Gras costume (a cowboy, a clown, a fairy or ballerina) stand in a half circle and gaze diffidently toward the camera. The two figures seated in the exact center of the formation hold scepters and wear crowns and tinsel. The king's long white train has been draped to extend around him like a splash across the shining hardwood foreground. His trainless queen scowls primly straight ahead while his glance lists to the side, his little-boy mouth slightly open; he seems to me distracted by some impulse toward volatile play and heedless of everything about the moment except his place in it. The cabinet top above their heads is bare except for a pair of recently sprouted avocado plants that flank a goldfish in a tiny bowl.

Many of the invitations and some of the pictures also bear an ink stamp: "Dance Pass/C. B. Phillips." Most of the clippings concern fighters or other entertainers. Except for himself and Alvin, the fighter most frequently to appear is Joe Louis; but the articles concern Louis's earnings, not his fights.

Deeper in the drawer, my hand riffles letters, telegrams, scrolled fight contracts, and life-insurance forms; an almost daily sequence of canceled checks—most for very small sums—to Gloria Sornia (sic), the Circle Drugstore, the Independent Insurance Company, Malcolm Faber Sporting Goods & Trophy Manufacturers, and the Greater Asia Baptist Church; a thick packet of prescription receipts; the front cover of a red photograph album; tithing envelopes from a score of years; a single horrifically pornographic cartoon card exhibiting a donkey's explicit penetration of a naked woman whose arms and legs encircle its withers and back.

There is also a manuscript copy of an essay about the second Galindez-Rossman fight—2,500 words of mine that, judging by the recurrence of a penciled "stop" and notations of the time of night, he read in five sittings over several days. Columns of crooked figures deface the backs of many of the envelopes and the margins of the manuscript. Most of these tabulations involve his checking account and installment payments to the Housing Authority, to insurance companies, and, less frequently, to loan offices. Other slanted lines of numbers are useless pharmaceutical identifiers; others are dosages; and others are changing amounts of life-insurance coverage on each of his children and some of his grandchildren, coverage whose sole purpose was to guarantee funerals for those insured. Written alongside the figures on envelopes and pieces of documents are many, many notes to himself, reminders like the ones I often saw taped up around his bed, memos he could read from the pillow.

TAKE PILL 6:30

ATTI COLLIS GET A WRITING TABLET

LOANED TRINA $6.00 FOR LINEL

JERRY PHILLIPS JERRY

GLORIA FIND MY SHOE

ATTI COLLIS GET 2 SYMPTON CARDS

TRINA TOOK 2 SCREW DRIVER & THE HAMMER

CALL HOSPITAL IN JACKSON SWEATER TO DOROTHY

GLORIA SEE ABOUT JR

January 5, 1982

See about Jr.

Gloria sounded as if she were crying over the phone, telling me how her brother Collis Jr. "just won't let that liquor alone."

Farris had spoken of his oldest brother dismissively, stepping back from the steel screen and bringing his thumb to his lips. "Junior don't want to go out and *do* nothin'. Just have a li'l layout job and his li'l wine." He tipped back his thumb.

"I never could care for a man that ran behind drinkin'," his father usually said at some point when speaking of his namesake. "Behind drinkin' an' behind women that stays in the streets"—adding, "Type a women that's out there now, I wouldn' *piss* on."

I heard other such comments about Collis Jr. well before I met him. And I met him last among Collis's New Orleans children because he wasn't around the apartment during the first six months I visited there. During much of this period, Gloria had told me, he was in and out of the detoxification unit and other wards at Charity Hospital, recovering from various bouts of drinking. I gathered that he spent most of the rest of his time where he sometimes

worked, at the liquor store and pool hall that stood next to
the Star Lounge and faced the project across St. Bernard
Avenue.

On this clear, cool morning I found him next door to
Gloria's, in a recently vacated apartment the family had
rented before the Christmas holidays. He had sent word for
me to come early because he thought he might work that
day. I arrived at nine and woke him with knocks on his
door. He had been sleeping on the only piece of furniture
in the main room, the box springs and hardwood frame of
a once expensive sofa. Now he waved me inside, seeming in
a hurry to be off the cold concrete and back among the old
quilts and slipcover he had been wrapped in. As he rebolted
the lock, I noticed the back of the door was reinforced with
plyboard and covered with tacked-up snapshot portraits.
Scrolled like vegetation on the wood framing the photos
were numerous sexually explicit ballpoint drawings. He
scuttled back to the sofa and eased himself down on it. After
a spell of coughing, he took out a cigarette and, gazing
blankly between his socked feet, lighted it. I sat across from
him on a box and looked at the door, the dim apartment,
and him.

The smoke rose and turned a milky blue in a streak of
sunlight that knifed between the rags plastering the windows.
Partly in blue light, partly in shadow, an old studio photograph of an infant hung crookedly in an oval frame over
the sofa just above his head.

"You can probably see," he said, plucking at the sleeve of
the shirt he had slept in, "I got some miles on me."

Taller than his brothers, almost his father's height, he was
less bulky than any of them. His thin mustache and wispy
goatee failed to conceal the almost exact structural resem-
blance between his and his father's rounded faces. But there
was a hardness in the features of the son—plus a grainier,
darker complexion and more deeply etched lines—that was
absent in Collis's disarming countenance.

Following the direction of my glance, he gestured toward

the snapshots cluttering the back of the door. "That's some miles right there."

I stepped over and studied the pictures as he explained that they were of his five children from two marriages. They included a twenty-two-year-old daughter, very pretty, and a son, Collis III, nicknamed "Mookie," who reminded me of photos I had seen of Collis Jr. when he was a boy. I thought in particular of the one that had been taken of Collis Jr.'s elementary school class just before Mardi Gras. I mentioned that photograph now, and, flicking ashes on the floor, he recalled how his father sold bundles of carnival raffle tickets to better-paid employees who worked where he then did. He said these sales "put me on top," earning him the prize of royalty among his classmates for an hour.

"White folks always loved my daddy," he said, shaking his head over it. "But that man could work," he added. "He always took care of us." He looked up at me squarely. "We never went hungry. If he had five dollars and one of us needed it"—his fingers crawled at his waist to show his father reaching for money—"he was openhearted in that way."

When eventually I steered the subject toward his own energies, he volunteered, as if conclusively to eliminate the subject, that he had "tried" boxing. But he had given it up after two amateur fights. He stressed that it wasn't that he was "scary" about fighting—"I fights now, had a fight last week, I'll fight in a minute and hit first if I need to"—it was rather that he "just didn't like it," the training and rising early to run. He demonstrated throwing a short downward punch in the same brusque decisive way as his father did— "Bing!" One of Alvin's friends would tell me that Collis Jr. was actually the son who fought best in the family. Now I asked Collis Jr. what he thought of Alvin as a fighter in their youth, but he couldn't "remember Alvin having any street fights to speak of. It was always me. But Farris now, Farris would put some pain on you if he needed to." He laughed, remembering how, the last time Farris had been "out," they had argued over money and he "hit Farris in the mouth and

Farris threw me into them trees." He gestured toward the outside. "Yep, right into them trees." I wondered *what* trees. Every courtyard that I had seen in the project was barren. But he changed the subject by pitching his cigarette butt toward a corner and beginning to talk about music.

After he "gave up on boxin'," he said, he "took up the git-tar." This was when he was eighteen. His father wanted him "to blow a sax," but he "couldn't go that." For him it was "only the git-tar." He started his own band, the Rhythm Rockers, and "played the joints" in neighborhoods near the project. Then he went on the road as part of a larger band headed by a bass player named Bill Senegal. They traveled in Florida and Tennessee. He spoke proudly of meeting Bobby "Blue" Bland in Nashville and later backing up such headliners as Little Johnnie Taylor, Roscoe Shelton, and Mary Wells. He loved to play "tunes like 'Stormy Monday' and, you know, B. B. King's old song, what's it called?" He bent, almost double, over an imagined low-slung guitar. " 'The Things,' that's it." He was singing now. " 'The Things That I Used to Do . . .' "

For some moments he remained hunched forward, head cocked, as if in reverie. Then he told how he drove the bus for Senegal and led off the band: "One. Two. One, two, three . . . Yeh, smoked a lot a weed on the road, had plenty women, sometimes two, three in the bed, got my dick sucked plenty. Been around some a them bull-daggin' bitches too."

"Bull-what?"

"They's women fix things on their tongue long as your dick—I've seen some things—and they fuck each other with that. And if you didn' watch it, they'd *fuck* you too."

He looked up from his socks and peered at me through the still-blue beam of light. "I told you, I got some miles on me. Started drinkin' steady when I was sixteen. An' I drink now. 'Cause I'm go'n enjoy life while I'm here. Guys tell me if I talk to you, it'll come out I'm, like, a alcoholic. But I say tell the truth."

And I have no doubt that tell the truth was basically what he did that morning, for he spoke with the authority of someone who had given up hope of gain and whose only remaining possession was a certain independent pride. This pride showed when he stressed the fact that he had no criminal record—though his father always told his mother that Junior was the one of their children who would go to prison. He seemed to take pleasure in telling me that, despite his temper and his father's belief that " 'somebody go'n stick a knife' " in him, he was the only one of Dorothy and Collis's sons "still out here. Most a the boys I come up with," he added, "is dead now."

I must have shown surprise at his saying he had no record because he made a point of backtracking to emphasize that he was speaking then of no *criminal* record. "Far as that goes, I was four months last year in Parish." (Parish Prison.) This was for not keeping up alimony payments. When the family kept asking after him and if he wanted his father to see if Mike would help bail him out, he said they could just leave cigarette money. "Shit, I'm a man. It don't worry me to stay in no prison."

As if aware of the unappealingly swaggering sound of this last, he abruptly began talking of humor, of how—even though "Christmas ain't very mellow when other things ain't right"—funniness is always present. He remembered another Christmas season, a warmer one, and stifled a snort of laughter as he described his brother Jerry, who liked to read and had a fondness for using "big words to my daddy— somethin' about him not 'compre-*hend*ing the situation' and 'being ignorant of the meaning of things.' " His father mildly beckoned Jerry over as if he hadn't heard him clearly. Outwardly calm, he motioned for his son to bend toward his ear. Then "*Pow!* Put that crutch *on* Jerry. Knocked him *through* the screen. *Off* the porch!" He coughed with laughter. "I mean *all* the way off! We had to buy a new screen door.

"No disrespect for the dead intended," he said, referring to Jerry as his laughter subsided, "though they is guys out there"—he nodded toward the window—"plenty of 'em, who'll play about that." He raised a finger. "I know. I saw it when my mother died." The day before this happened, he had been in Charity recovering from a drinking seizure, "layin' up there with that bag a water drippin' in my arm." He had come home to his father's old apartment on St. Bernard only to be roused from a difficult sleep by Gloria screaming into the phone: " 'Junior! Come quick! Mama! Mama! Mama's gone!' " Alone in the apartment, he almost passed out putting on his pants. By the time he made his way across the courtyard, the crash truck had arrived. The two litter-bearers were "crippled up raggedy old men." He smiled, remembering the look they exchanged when, after laboriously climbing the narrow stairs to the bedroom, they glimpsed Dorothy Philips's body: "My momma was a big woman then. 'Bout two hundred pounds." She had been ailing for a long time—"She couldn't even catch a bus"— and in Gloria's indulgent care she had put on the excessive weight. He kissed his mother and helped zip her into a hospital shroud. He and the other two were so feeble that Gloria had to send for her son Theron, who was still a child. The four straining males tottered down the stairs with the load. Now he smiled again. "May she forgive me, we was a sight." Then, his voice hardening, he described a mishap on the stoop and the reason he had mentioned his mother in the first place. One of the old men neglected to set the brake on the rolling litter. When they reached the porch and, lunging, tried to set down their load, the litter scooted over the unenclosed edge, pitching its burden into the high weeds below.

He didn't smile now. "Just to show you how cold, there's people out there, behind my back, made a joke outta that. Somebody's mother, don't matter, we heard about how they'd be hangin' from the step posts, laughin' at the dead."

In the silence that followed, he lit another cigarette.

It was distracting to be sitting in the gutted apartment with the sounds of waking sleepers and a radio filtering down the stairwell. I had to visit him again the following afternoon for help in piecing out my memory of his recollections.

As Gloria had told me I would, I found him the next day

at the pool hall, Merlin's it was then called, on St. Bernard. Crosshatched bars and crusted grime made it impossible to see from the street through the glass front doors of the windowless cinder-block building. With a surge of adrenaline, I pulled open one of the doors and stepped in. About half a dozen men stood around the bar. They all turned to look at me and at once fell silent. The stocky bartender came forward, asking bluntly what I wanted. "I'm looking for Collis," I told him. His expression was sternly neutral. Then, off to the side, I saw Collis Jr. bent over a broom handle with his back to us, sweeping broken glass. He looked even frailer than the morning before, a near-derelict, and menial in the extreme. But his voice had familiar depth. "Well, you found him, Collis is right here." The bartender looked from him to me for a moment, then laughed and said, "Yeah, an' what if he had been a detective!" The others turned back to the bar, joking about how Collis had neglected to be careful. He dismissed them with a curse and came over and ostentatiously gave me his hand soul-style in a slap, I think to make it seem that our business together was some easily explainable street exchange such as one involving money.

When I had met him in the apartment he shared with several others, our conversation ended when one of the sleepers from above came down the stairs. This man stood insistently around, for some reason waiting for Collis Jr., and soon I made my way out. As I left, Collis and I shook hands conventionally, and my gaze traveled up past his pillow-mashed hair to the faded studio photograph. "That's me," he said, raising his cigarette toward the oval frame. "Five months old. I'd guess it's a antique now. Be cool."

5

□

January 19, 1982

If Dorothy Phillips and another patient happened to be
alone together long enough, Dorothy would steal up to her
and scream in her ear. Depending on the other patient's
reaction, Dorothy would then either run away or claw the
other patient's face. This was the main remembrance of the
counselor who was showing me around the East Louisiana
State Hospital for the mentally ill.

We were in Jackson, Louisiana—about thirty-five miles
from Angola—in a vacant ward, the ward in which conditions
had been most terrible in the years before the counselor first
came to Jackson in 1961. Because of my curiosity after
glimpsing its white sheen through a windowed door, she
had shown me into the unfurnished room that, with its
tilelike surfaces and drains in the floor, resembled a vast
showering area. "In the old days," she said, many of the
worst patients had been kept here, though a long-delayed
public investigation found others, equally ill, living at large
on the wooded grounds, their naked bodies caked with dirt
and excrement.

Taking advantage of the pause, I had asked pointedly
about Dorothy Phillips. The counselor had pondered the
name, searching her memory of the numberless people in
extremity she had observed over twenty-one years. Then,
her manner approximating that of the person she recalled,
she whispered seethingly that, yes, there had been a Dorothy
Phillips, a troublemaker. Moving closer to me, she explained

Dorothy Phillips's shock tactic as if I were about to be its victim. Breaking eye contact and walking on to dispel the little drama it seemed she might act out, I felt stunned that this could have been Collis's wife. I asked for physical details. Moving alongside me, our footsteps echoing, my guide described a small, quick woman in her early forties. I wondered aloud how to reconcile this profile with the fact that Dorothy was fifty when she was committed to Jackson and by then a heavy woman who for some years had been unable to walk without help.

"A walker?" the counselor asked. "She used a walker?" I said I believed she had. Her intensity diminishing, she then recalled another woman whose name might well have been Phillips, an older, larger woman who, except that she could walk only with a walker, gave no trouble and was so quiet she was easily forgotten.

Back in the administration building, where at Collis's written request I was allowed access to Dorothy's file, I learned she had been admitted on December 30, 1965— about four years after he was shot. A report accompanying her from Charity identified her as suffering from diabetes and high blood pressure. The report stated that "due to neurological problems she has not walked alone in two years. Screams a lot, hallucinates, and has ideas of persecution. She eats well on some days. Patient not homicidal or suicidal."

"Chronic brain syndrome" was the initial diagnosis when she was admitted to the public asylum at Jackson. As I read through the dated entries on her medical chart, I remembered that, though by then conditions at Jackson were improved over those described by the counselor as existing in "the old days," an undercover journalistic exposé in the early seventies had disclosed continuing atrocious deficiencies at the hospital during the years Dorothy was there. One entry made it clear that her records had been confused at least once with those of the other patient who shared her name: "Dorothy Phillips is a 41-year-old Negro female. . . . She is combative to other patients and is an agitator." Other entries suggested that she and the other Dorothy Phillips were sometimes confined to the same ward, a circumstance that must have been a trial for her.

In July 1967, she was transferred back to Charity in New Orleans for two days because she had suffered a broken leg. After her return to Jackson, her condition apparently became more stable. Her records included the pharmaceutical treatment of her blood pressure and diabetes and the regular prescription of Valium and Thorazine.

On May 4, 1969, she was released, her chart concluding with these remarks: "Nonpsychotic organic brain syndrome, chronic, secondary to cerebral arteriosclerosis with spastic condition. Findings—Spastic gait and impaired speech after a diabetic coma. Treatment—Chemotherapy and custodial care. Pt. has been on pass several times and has done well. Her husband wants her home and it is felt she will do well if she takes medication and attends aftercare and diabetic clinic. Prognosis—Guarded. Considered competent at this time."

Jerry Phillips signed the release certificate. She lived for about five years longer in the apartment on St. Bernard that she and Collis had first moved to about thirty years before.

Other than the counselor who showed me around, I met no one at the hospital who had any memory of her. But in Collis's drawer of scraps, I found one letter, the only words of hers I saw.

Jackson La.
Dec 6, 1968

Dear Collis

I recved your letter and was glad to hear from you
I am getting along pretty good
I got to letters from Gloria she send me couple dollars.
You told me something about Farris Don't help him Because I love him I will always love him he was the only one help me when I came home I don't understand a the check. We will talk about it when I get home
You can come and get me any time you want. It will

have to be Sunday because Jerry will be off. Everything is ready Bring me a new sweater And my good dress

And stop worrying about Farris You have enough of trouble of your own. Tell Farris to clean the house for me.

I will be looking for you Sunday. And you don't worry about nothing Smile

From your wife
Dorothy Phillips

6

□

"Testing . . . (Let's just let it run for a minute.) Testing . . . August 2, 1983 . . . 'The Coliseum'—"

"Yeh. When we was boxin' at the Coliseum. Well, that was back in the thirties, y' know. In the early thirties back there."

"I know it. Th-this that I've brought with me is the beginning about you. It comes after the parts bringing in your children and Miss Dorothy and tells about your early life. It goes back past when you were born—before it comes on up through the years when you boxed at the Coliseum. And from there up to the sixties when you were shot."

"*Now*. Uh, you don' want me to go back to the River Oaks Country Club, where I started out to come up?"

"Not today. We'll get to that, but for now I just want you to think back about this I have here and cut in and set me straight about anything important I've left out or gotten wrong."

"Whatsonever you say. Pro-ceed."

" ' "The Coliseum."

" 'He was born on July 27, 1909, in Mansfield, Louisiana, the first child of Addie Belle Owens and the Reverend Alvin Phillips. His parents had three more children, all girls, the last born during the First World War.

" 'His father, Alvin Phillips, stood over six feet and weighed two hundred. He was someone who knew how to fix things;

he worked hard with his hands. A succession of jobs drew him to Louisiana from his birthplace in Lufkin, Texas. In Mansfield he earned a living as a concrete finisher, then as the man who ran the furnace in a foundry that turned out dragline buckets and other earthmoving equipment.' "

"Soun' pretty good."

" 'Because of the wealth of cheap black labor on the south side of Mansfield, the foundry had been built there. It still dominates the crossroads where Highway 84 intersects 171. The Phillipses rented a small shotgun house on the corner adjacent to the foundry. 701 Jenkins—' "

"Right! That was my first address."

" '701 Jenkins Street: Collis might forget certain details more important to his life, but he always remembered his first address. The house stood where Jenkins lost its name and became 171.

" 'Addie Belle Phillips gave birth to her son and her first daughter, Elma, in that house. The younger girls, Fanny and Eloise, were also born on Jenkins—but after the family had moved into a larger dwelling next door. Both houses are now gone—' "

"Well, I 'spec' they is."

" '—replaced by a gas station and garage.

" 'Collis first told me his father impressed people as a mild man, one who didn't like to argue and fuss. Later he told me his father once went to jail for wounding someone after a gambling dispute. One of his earliest memories was of his mother and father quarreling in their first house on Jenkins just before the shooting. She stood barring the door to the closet that held the hunting guns, but her husband wrested his pistol from her, and ran out.

" 'Collis remembered too that, because his father "always pulled good with the white folks at the foundry," he had to stay "locked up" for only one night due to the shooting. From Collis's sisters, though, I gathered that their father—after he became religious—was generally peaceable and, in home matters at least, prone to give in to his wife.' "

"He had to. My mother was a war-hoss. *Hot fire!*"

I used recording devices with no one but Collis, and then not until 1982 when I was satisfied that he wouldn't mind it. At that point I had taken a tape recorder with me when I visited him because I wanted to see if the telling of his life could be exclusively in his words. He paid no special attention to the machine and talked neither more nor less openly than he usually did, but during that visit I realized my plan wouldn't work. Although I tried to guide him away from the fact of us there talking in his room, he almost always spoke directly to me, and all the story threads he started eventually broke down into conversation. And that was on days when I found him feeling good. Because of his health, it soon became apparent that it was out of the question to put him through the sessions I would have needed to produce a narrative in his voice alone.

So I began writing a draft in my own language and phrasing, though including his words wherever I could. Working in this way eventually left me wondering what he would think of this growing document that purported to show *him*. As his notations on my Galindez-Rossman piece had made evident, it was an unaccustomed strain for him to have to read more than a few pages on his own; once, when he slowly read me a letter that had just come from Connie, he seemed to have difficulty with some of the words. As an alternative, I decided to try reading him installments of what I had written and to record the process. I hoped his unplanned responses would deepen the portrait.

" 'As a Baptist minister, Alvin Phillips preached Christian gospel on Sundays, urging his congregations to shoulder their burdens gaily and accept the healing consolations of "Doctor Jesus." The Reverend Phillips was skillful in guiding the passion of those assembled so that it dissolved into the calm of his major themes: sympathy and forgiveness. These long Sunday sessions were trying for his restless young son,

but his father's humility and power struck Collis as wondrous
to behold.' "

"Well . . . Maybe it gits a little tied up along in there . . .
But I did listen at him preach."

On this day in August I had topped the stairs to find him
alertly sitting up in bed with an unopened morning newspaper across his thighs. When I came in, the first thing he
did was throw back the sheet to show me his paralyzed leg.
It had been amputated below the knee two months earlier
in the summer.

In fact, I hadn't talked with him since that June afternoon
when he was wheeled, drugged and smiling, from the
recovery room in Charity. His ward had been crowded with
badly hurt men—most of them black and comatose—but
within the scrim around his bed the atmosphere was different,
at times nearly festive. Gloria was there, as were Farris and
Farris's girlfriend, Velma Whittey.

In May, Farris had been released from Angola, where he
had spent the past eight years. Although, beyond bars, he
gave the impression of being a brooding man who was
troubled by casual eye contact, he was the one who convinced
Collis to have the operation that various young residents at
Charity had recommended. From Gloria and others in the
family, I had learned that the purpose of the proposed
amputation was to eliminate the weight Collis dragged and
reduce the strain on his heart. I had heard from others, and
inferred from Collis himself, that he regarded his limbs
mystically and felt he would be "less a man" if he lost his
useless leg. Persuasion fell to Farris, who was described by
people acquainted with both as being the only one in the
family as strong-willed as Collis. Farris had come home from
Angola to be the first to detect that the tan toes on his
father's left foot were gangrenous and tinged with green-
black.

———

" 'Because her mother and sisters lived nearby and helped
care for her children, Addie Belle ran a cafe that Alvin had
leased across the street from their house on Jenkins.' "

"How *you* know? I musta tol' you that, huh?"

" 'The cafe prospered in a small way, specializing in hot
meals on workdays for the men from the foundry. Alvin
kept up with his co-workers' tabs, opened the place at dawn
and closed it in the evening; Addie Belle did the rest,
including the cooking, except shortly before and after the
births of Elma and Fanny. She had problems during her
fourth pregnancy, but she went on working. Even though
the family's personable young Jewish doctor, Shalahum,
came to the house to perform the delivery, the complications
increased. The baby survived. Her mother did not. Pneumonia. Addie Belle never rose from the bed she had lain
down on in labor. Collis was eight—' "

"I was . . . what?"

"Eight. I think, the last time we talked about it, that's how
old you told me you were."

"Oh, my *age*, you mean. Yeh, I was small. Close to that,
I'd say. 'Bout seven or eight. Somewhere along in there."

"So . . . can I leave it at . . . eight?"

"Aw, yeh, that's good! Eight."

Kevin Phillips, one of his grandsons, and a young woman
named Debra, Kevin's girlfriend, were also by the bed on
the day in June 1983 when Collis came back from amputation
surgery in Charity. Kevin and Debra had taken the Southern
Crescent down from New York to spend a week in New
Orleans so Kevin could visit his father, Alvin, whom he
hadn't seen since he was a boy. Earlier in the day, I had
driven Kevin the hundred or so miles north of the city to
Angola. Although he grew up in the most hardening sections
of Harlem and still scrambles for his living there, Kevin was
shaken by the hour we spent with his father. I had offered
to stay in the visitors' waiting room near the gates so they
could have more privacy, but for that particular visit it was

necessary to board a bus and go out into the sprawling agrarian prison and Kevin said he would be more comfortable if I went with him. I felt complimented when he said the same thing the next day as we tried to gain permission for him to visit his brother Alvin Jr. in Parish Prison; but, on reflection, I realized that Kevin's comment involved no special approval of me: just as I would much rather be with him than alone on certain stretches of, say, 115th Street, he preferred to be with someone who could be mistaken for a lawyer when bars were locked behind him.

He was still visibly depressed while we searched for his grandfather's ward at Charity and when we finally joined the others waiting around the bed. If, when a nurse rolled him in, Collis noticed Kevin's mood, he didn't show it. Instead, he made much of the navel oranges I had brought him and drew me around to the left side of the bed for a closer view of his thickly bandaged stump. Being the center of attention seemed to raise his spirits. Whenever his smile displayed his strong white teeth, he looked as healthy as or healthier than any of his visitors, not to mention the other patients.

Feeling that my presence made the visit too social, I left soon afterwards. I assumed I would see him the next day. But I was wrong. He was asleep when I came back the following evening, and on the evenings after that I couldn't find him. My writing schedule caused me to arrive toward the end of visiting hours, when I came to Charity anyway to drive Sally home from her work in the emergency room. On each of these evenings I learned that, because of improvements in his condition, he had been moved to a different floor of the huge warrenlike hospital. Since felonies occurred in the stairwells, visitors weren't allowed to use the steps, and the elevators were always overfull and exceedingly slow. On the ground floor, the harried, indifferent clericals, who handed out the visiting passes and whom I stood in long lines to consult, lacked current information about him and could be of no help to anyone in skirting the bureaucracy. No more than could Sally, who—to gain experience—nursed there under conditions that brought on something close to battle fatigue.

So for most of the rest of the summer, I had kept up with him thirdhand. Gloria's phone had been disconnected in the spring, but I could leave messages and ask her daughter Trina about his health because Trina had a phone and lived across the courtyard on the same end of the project. "He aw right," Trina invariably answered, not inviting conversation, and I usually left it at that. I continued writing about the first part of his life and reading for courses I would teach in the fall. I could reach none of the family by phone around the time of his birthday, so I mailed a card and kept on with what I was doing until the first week in August, when I went to show him what I had done.

" 'His knowledge of the origins of his family was largely from Addie Belle's mother, Fanny Robinson Owens, who moved in with them on Jenkins after the death of her daughter. Miss Fanny told about being born into slavery and growing up on the Lookout Mountain plantation near the Alabama-Georgia border. She stressed that *her* work was done, not in the fields but indoors, assisting her mother in waiting on Mrs. Robinson, the mistress of the house. It seemed strange to Collis that she spoke of her mother but not of her father.' "

"Naw, she would not."

" 'He knew nothing about his great-grandfather until one evening when a playmate of Elma's began teasing him about his name ("*Collis!*"), saying it sounded funny, not like the name of anyone they knew. His grandmother silenced the child by announcing that Collis was the namesake of her own father—' "

"That's where my name come from."

" '—a white planter. Collis looked at his grandmother's long, sandy hair and at that moment understood how, whenever she needed to, Miss Fanny passed for white.' "

"That was it . . . You couldn't hardly tell my grandmother *from* a white woman."

" 'While Collis's great-grandfather was a white man, his maternal grandfather, Jack Owens, unquestionably was not.' "

"Was not. He was dark, dark."

" 'Although Jack Owens also worked on the Robinson place, he was never a slave; his father had been allowed to learn a trade and earn his and his wife's freedom before their children were born.

" 'It was after the Emancipation that Collis's grandmother attracted Jack Owens's special notice, but she still lived with the Robinsons and he put in slave's hours as foreman of the workers in the Robinsons' fields.' "

"Good. Soun' real good." (His words covered a cough as he reached down for the plastic urinal bottle that always stood by the bed, the bottle Gloria scalded at least twice a day. He hawked, then spit.)

" 'As long as no one questioned his right to rule, Jack Owens directed the work cheerfully and well. But out directly under the sun, tensions about status came to the surface, and Jack Owens was known at various times to have killed men both with tools and with his bare hands.' "

"Claim he killed six or seven before they arrested him. He went to prison, accordin' to what my grandmother said. An' he was such a tough type of a person they had to keep him chained down."

The message I left with Trina must have reached him, because on this morning in August he seemed to have been expecting me. That he immediately showed me what remained of his leg suggested he had forgotten our June visit in Charity, though. If he now felt unmanned by the surgery, he concealed that from me, portraying himself as the obedient patient of wise, caring doctors. He acted toward the now unbandaged stump as if it were just an object and no longer really a part of him. He passed his finger impersonally along the whiskery stitches and dismissed my concern about the large half-healed cut across his kneecap, a crescent-shaped gash he had caused by accidentally raking his numb leg across something sharp. As I bent forward to look where he pointed, I noticed the odors of stale urine and disinfectant rising faintly from his sheet and the floor. It had stormed earlier in the morning and an unseasonably cool mist jeweled the window screen. He and Gloria had exchanged bedrooms since I was there last. Taking a seat by his bed—in the rocker, which had previously been located downstairs—I saw that he now had a view of the courtyard, which this morning was sodden and deserted.

"How's the family?" This was his formulaic way of concluding our talks about his health. Then he asked about my "secretary," as he called her, our daughter Julia, then seven, who usually answered our telephone and whom he knew from when he used to phone me before Gloria's was disconnected. In turn, I asked him about "the rabbits," his play name for his great-granddaughters, two children who then lived with Gloria much of the time. Since Gloria was away on errands this morning, her granddaughters had let me in. Andrea, nicknamed "Bookie," was eleven, the child of Gloria's older daughter, Pamela; at the time, Pamela, who had had trouble with the law, was missing in Los Angeles. Keyon, aged six, was Trina's oldest child. During the rest of my conversation with their great-grandfather and after I had begun reading to him, I could hear Andrea and Keyon playing pretend games in Gloria's bedroom on the other side of the wall. Later they scurried in and out of the bathroom at the top of the stairs. I thought this was another game until I heard water splattering and a bucket's clank; then I looked up and saw that they were scrubbing the tub. The tape picked up the work instructions they exchanged and also some of their earlier make-believe talk. Played back, their muffled phrases sound choric, like echoes.

———

" 'Jack Owens's boldness led him to challenge the plantation's caste system by courting Miss Fanny, who had been raised in the house and was regarded by the Robinsons as a member of the family—though not in the strict sense that she was.' "

"Right!"

" 'His grandmother told Collis no more about her and Jack Owens's courtship and whatever it was that caused them to leave Lookout Mountain—' "

"She run off. Stole away. Was a white fella that was aw right with my grampaw, Jack. He's the one helped 'em git away. See, the white people *raised* her. She lived in the *house* . . . *with* them. An', quite naturally, she couldn' jus'— See, by my grampaw bein' a black guy, he couldn' jus' come up an' git her. That's why she had to steal away, y' know, to git away with my grampaw . . . In fact, my daddy tol' me this. My mother had to run off too . . . *with* my *father*. Another older fella that was a good friend of my grampaw's helped plotted the plot for my mother to git away from home."

"I thought you told me Jack Owens's oldest daughter, Alice, was the one who ran off. You mean that happened with all his daughters?"

"He was jus' that strict a type a fella. He killed five or six men, y' know. Back in them times, people then wasn't so sociable 'bout lettin' they daughters have big weddin's an' things like that. I don' know, I guess they thought they chil'ren was too good for anybody else's chil'ren. Because any guy who git grown ain' go'n stay wit' you forever. *Yo'* son probably go'n git married too. An' y' daughter—"

"Excuse me, this is something I need to know—I've mentioned it before, but let me ask you again. Why did, when they left the plantation, why did your grandmother and Jack Owens choose to go to Mansfield instead of any other place?"

"What . . . ? Aw, now I couldn' answer that. See, that's a little too deep f' me. You know, 'cause I wasn't there."

7

□

For midday, even on a Friday, the neighborhood was more active than usual. Groups were out on the porchways around the courtyards, and the undercurrent of radios and cassettes had reached a late-afternoon pitch. I guessed it was a day when government checks had come.

As I walked toward Gloria's apartment, a man, moving quickly, knocked open the screen door. It was her youngest son, Theron, the only one of her male children not behind bars. He came out with his back to me and stood gesturing with a chicken leg to people on the neighboring porch. It looked like some kind of continuing joke.

I didn't want to approach him from behind, but the others were looking past him in my direction. I went up the steps and spoke his name. He appeared mildly startled at being seen without seeing, but his greeting was friendly and he told me to walk right in—his grandfather was upstairs.

I could see, though, that I wasn't expected and Trina hadn't told anyone I had called the night before. She always agreed to call back and tell me if it was a time when Collis wasn't up to being visited. There were probably more of these times than I was sure of, but Trina never called me and I never knew beforehand.

As I stepped inside, Gloria sang out from among a group of people around the kitchen table. "How ya doin'! Aw right! Daddy's awake! You can just go right on up!"

I started up the concrete stairs, nodding, as I went, to a

man who was sitting on the living-room sofa, watching TV and eating lunch from a takeout carton. I had never seen him before. He acknowledged me by hefting a quart bottle of beer and tipping it in my direction.

I called out to Collis from the stairwell. He answered me in a normal voice, which gave no hint of what I would find on reaching the landing. At first I couldn't read the situation. He stood by the bed, wearing only a pajama shirt, supporting himself with his hand flat on the dresser. His head was down, and he seemed to be listening for something in the distance. Then I saw. The floor was smeared with what looked like paint. I thought he must have vomited, so, taking him by the shoulders, I helped him to sit on the bed. He held a stiff washcloth loosely between his fingers. His incision was split and he had been dabbing at the floor, trying to wipe up his own blood.

He protested that it was nothing, that he had just bumped his leg trying to rise from the bed. But he probably had been standing there a long time because some of the blood was congealed.

On my way out for water, I met Gloria at the top of the stairs. She looked into the room and suddenly sounded hysterical: "*Daddy!* What happened? Oh, look at this. *Theron!* The mop!"

Although she began to cry, she immediately brought peroxide and cotton from the medicine chest and began cleaning the wound.

Soon Theron was in the room with a bucket of hot water and disinfectant. When I reached for the mop, he deflected my offer, the surprising rasp in his voice as usual making him sound much older than someone twenty-two. "It's aw right, man, I'll catch it, this ain' no work."

As he scrubbed the floor, squeezing orange water from the mop with his fingers, he scolded his grandfather—but in a deferential, joking way, almost under his breath. "Shoot, Grampaw, you should *call* for somebody when you need a li'l help. We rightchere. Ain' no trouble to come see 'bout you."

As I had before, that day I noticed Collis in Theron's broad, open features and build. In the gym clothes he was wearing he resembled an athlete, a compact football player. He was also wearing a billed polyester cap, the kind displayed on wire trees in Time-Saver convenience stores. The cap's up-country slogan—"Eat More Coon!"—fit the quality that most struck me about Theron when I first met him: the ironic light in his watchful eyes.

I stood at the foot of the bed, suspended between trying to help and trying not to be in the way. Theron was backing out with the bucket, playfully looking from Collis to me as he ended his admonishments. "Now, Grampaw, when you need somethin', you call somebody. Hear?" Gloria had finished with the peroxide and was plumping his pillows. Looking annoyed by all the fuss, Collis pulled on his pajama bottoms. While Theron was mopping, I had noticed them draped, apparently to dry, on a coat hanger hooked on the frame of the closet. They weren't damp, so I had handed them to him and became, in the process, the only one he thanked.

Despite what had happened and the foul way he seemed to feel, when I tried to leave he wouldn't hear of it. "*Look*," he said. "We in this thing together. It's not jus' you by y'self. I'm sup*posed* to he'p you. Reach me that sheet there. I know what gas costs. You cain' be comin' down here on blank trips f' nothin'." I set the tape recorder beside him on the bed. "C'mon. Whatcha got?"

" 'Six children were born to his grandparents. Possibly because all were daughters, some of the protectiveness Jack Owens had practiced while overseeing other people's lands carried over into his style of fatherhood. Few suitors had been found acceptable by the time Owens's eldest daughter, Alice, reached her twenties. Alice became interested in an older man named Willie Pinson. Possibly because he understood it too well himself, Jack Owens disapproved of Pinson's disarming way with women. (The situation was aggravated by the fact that a younger daughter, Addie Belle, had run away to marry.) Owens ushered Pinson from the house and forbade his speaking to Alice again.

" 'Miss Fanny told how Willie Pinson continued to see Alice secretly, and how he paid a man older than himself, a mutual friend of his and the Owenses, to smuggle messages into the Owens house.' "

"He did."

" 'Owens found out. Both the go-between and Willie Pinson left town. It seemed to everyone that Owens's anger had cooled by the time, months later, word came that his former friend, the go-between, had stolen home in ill health and taken to his bed.' "

"Right."

" 'Owens appeared uninterested, but a few days later he went to the man's house and, apparently suspecting him of being armed, fired his pistol through the bedroom window six times—' "

"Killed the man in the bed. Shot him in the bed."

" '—then went inside and stomped the corpse.' "

"So as we heard."

" 'Soon Jack Owens was sent away to prison.

" ' "You don' wanna be like your grampaw." Whenever Collis was unruly, his grandmother would remind him of what had become of his grandfather, a man who was born free but who had died "in pen." Collis knew nothing about prisons, so it was like something in a story when his grandmother spoke of her husband drawing his last breaths "in balls and chains." For the rest, Jack Owens was just gone, one of the many whose lives ended in oblivion on the convict-lease chain gangs that worked the Angola cotton plantation, the 8,000 acres, eventually increased to 18,000, which became the state penitentiary.

" 'Collis understood why his grandmother wanted him to beware of Jack Owens. But one effect of her solemn efforts was to make him want to laugh—because he could see that she too was a little like his grandfather. Anyone acquainted with their family knew that Miss Fanny was one old lady you dared not speak to in just any way you might please.' "

"Naw, naw!"

" 'If provoked, she would pick up whatever lay at hand and try to hurt you—' "

"A shoe or anything!" (Laughing.) "Knock hell out you! 'You think you talkin' to some a them kids?!' *Br-ram!* Better git out the way!"

" 'One reason Collis felt close to the grandfather she helped him imagine was that he shared Jack Owens's opinion of Willie Pinson—' "

"Yeh, he was no-'count, a lazy type a guy."

" '—of Willie Pinson, who later migrated to Texas with the family of his wife . . . Aunt Alice.

" 'It also amused Collis that his grandmother teased him about certain of the children he played with, especially some of the girls. After observing from a window or the porch, she might chide him when he came in: "Boy, why you goin' round with that little *black* thing?" Given such an opening, he would counter her teasing; few of her children could take such a liberty: "Guess I takes after you, Grandmother."

" 'He liked to see her smile when she didn't mean to— something she also did whenever she let him open her special box and take out the tin photograph of her husband. To Collis the man in the daguerreotype was the image of the great heavyweight Jack Johnson—except that his grandfather was darker.'

"That's something I threw in. You think that's okay?"

"Course it is. My grandfather *was* a dark man."

"I mean that about Jack Johnson. I was assuming that, as a boy, you would've been interested in Jack Johnson."

"Aw, well, practically at that time, I didn't pay too much attention, y' know, to, uh, to no Jack Johnson. In fact, I was really too young to take an interest in knowin' that I would ever *be* a fighter. It wasn't on my mind. To really be truthful, what was on my mind was I always likeded trains."

"Trains?"

"Yeh. Y' know. Trains."

". . . Why?"

"Aw, well, at that time y' mind is not thoroughly developed an' you don' know jus' what you wanna be. You jus' see sumpum an' you like it. Like a train: 'w-a-a-o, w-a-a-o, *w-a-a-a-a!*' An' the engineer, he would wave to me. You understan' what I mean, you jus' don' know what you want, an' you don' realize what a great responsibility that engineer's got . . . But I always wanted to be sumpum. I usta race, run race, footrace, I usta run pretty good but I always wanted to win all the time. Then I got a baseball team. Usta play a lot a ball—y' know, *sandlot* ball . . . That's right. All my life, I always pushed to be sumpum. I always wanted to be the head."

8

□

October 10, 1983

"He's up!" Gloria said, waving me toward the stairs and at the same time backing against the curtained doorway to the kitchen. "He's lookin' at the paper."

Again Trina hadn't passed on my message. Gloria's face showed surprise when, after my knock, I did what she shouted for me to do and, pushing aside the bedspread behind the screen, stepped in out of the noon light. Through a tear in the cloth she had mistaken me for the insurance man, whom she said she was expecting.

I had continued trying to piece together his earlier years, but it had been two months since I had visited him. I knew from conversations with Gloria and Farris at court that he had been through surgery again—though for this operation he had been in and out of Charity quickly—before I received word of it. A second amputation had been made high on his thigh so that what remained of his leg would be less in his way. As for me, another year of teaching had begun. I was also trying to help Alvin to gain post-conviction relief and Farris to find a job, and I was closely following the predicaments of two of Collis's grandsons, Alvin Jr. and Gloria's oldest son, Lionel Sorina.

Alvin Jr., Lionel, and especially Gloria were often on my mind in those days, as they were on my way upstairs to see Collis in October. I thought about how it was earlier in the week just after the reading of the verdict in Lionel's first-degree-murder trial: Gloria in a dark Sunday dress sitting alone in a hallway of the Criminal District Courts Building, dusk blanking the windows that stretched away down the empty, weakly lit corridor. A moment before, I had glimpsed Lionel being steered into the holding room beside the judge's box. In preparation for returning him to his cell, a guard turned him by the elbow and another began taking him out of the khaki shirt he had worn every day during the trial. I watched the holding-room doorway and tried not to be distracted by the jubilation around me in the rear of the courtroom. This was the first view I had had of Lionel from the front. I saw, beneath an unshaded light bulb, impassive Latin features, a brow graceful like Trina's, and a short, chesty torso in a scarlet singlet. One of the guards held out olive-drab Parish Prison fatigues. Handcuff dangling from one wrist, Lionel started unfastening his khaki trousers as the other guard closed the holding-room door.

As I followed the just-discharged jurors from the courtroom, I saw Gloria seated directly before us. She had said earlier that she was too upset to witness the verdict. For the moment, she was forgotten by the family members and friends who had rushed back inside at the jury's return. I recalled Lionel under the stark light as I looked at his mother in the dim corridor. Her hair was in the glistening ringlets that she usually wore to court. Sunglasses masked the eye she would otherwise have been involuntarily shielding with her hands. A muted pattern of flowers adorned the broad bodice of her dress. She sat expectantly, her shoulders not touching the back of the long wooden pew.

So it happened that I was the one to tell her the jury had decided it couldn't decide, a development I wouldn't necessarily have taken as reason for celebration even if I *had* believed that Lionel was innocent of executing two young white men—who had entered the project seeking women— a block from his mother's back door. As I reported the verdict and then tried to respond to her questions about what I thought it meant, I also thought of something else, something that had happened at court six months earlier.

The prisoners on the docket on that April morning had been brought out through the holding room handcuffed together in a human chain. At the time, Lionel had been in jail awaiting trial for about two years. I didn't yet know him by sight. As had happened frequently before, that morning his trial was routinely continued for another week. Afterwards I stood talking with Gloria, Trina, and one of Lionel's girlfriends, Linda Rome, in the smoky snack-bar area. Primarily I was aware of small things: that Gloria insisted on buying me coffee, that the strong, cheap chicory mix tasted rich despite the Styrofoam cup, and that Trina and Linda fed the cigarette and candy machines a great many coins. My voice sounded false to me as, in answer to their complaints and requests for information, I explained my understanding of the maneuverings of the assistant district attorneys and the court-appointed defense lawyer. I didn't enjoy trying to describe abstract elements of the case to people who were more intimate with its basic facts than I could be. As we talked, I was intermittently aware of Linda's daughter, a child of four or five who had been silent during the long, miscellaneous court proceedings. The little girl now stood at our knees, hopping first on one foot, then on the other. She wore an immaculate pink dress and multicolored plastic ribbons in her tightly parted hair. A potato chip fell from the cellophane bag in her hand. I watched her quickly retrieve it from the dirty tile and throw it into her mouth before her mother could see. Paying more attention, I noticed that she was constantly making a sound. As if so her mother would listen, she patted at Linda's thigh. But, as harried parents often are, Linda was temporarily immune to her own child's familiar touch. A moment later the child touched me. Although she was looking at my eyes, she sang musingly, to herself, of what she had observed in the courtroom. I can't remember climbing the stairs to visit Collis in the week after the October mistrial without simultaneously remembering his first grandson stripping down to red, his first daughter waiting in darkness, and a great-grandchild he couldn't name chanting a single, repeated, just-audible phrase: "I saw my *dad*-dy . . . I saw my *dad*-dy . . ."

Instead of coming on him reading the paper as I expected, I found him deep in the covers, heavily asleep. The newspaper lay unopened on the corner of the bed. I considered leaving, but Gloria bustled up the steps, then around me to shake him. He clung to his sleep and muttered angrily. Then, opening his eyes and glimpsing me, he mugged— "Well, looka here!"—and struggled to hold the groggy surprise smile. Exactly the kind of situation I most wished to avoid. But since I hadn't seen him in so long and didn't know when I would be there again, I did as he said and took a seat in the rocker next to the bed.

Swallowing a yawn, he at once threw back the bedclothes to show me his leg. It seemed to be healing well, and he had little to say about it even though the pajama cuff had been rolled up meticulously to disclose the shortened stump.

After I refilled his water glass in the bathroom—a ruse I volunteered to carry out in order to give him longer to adjust to having to talk—he told me he had been napping because of his medicine. "I jus' taken one a these." He heaved himself to a sitting position and caught up a plastic cylinder of pills from the night table. "They puts me to sleep." To my questions about side effects, he said it wasn't for him to disobey a doctor. He added that he was beginning "to feel pretty good, now I'm woke up."

I couldn't believe it, though. No more than I could believe he felt like attending more pages of mine. Although I held a folder of new manuscript on top of the switched-off tape recorder in my lap, his not mentioning it while we talked confirmed my sense, drawn from earlier visits, that though he liked the attention, he wasn't really interested in hearing my approximations of what he had already lived through. Despite his considerate manner with me, I think he much preferred being listened to to listening.

"Just one a the spooks," he said later. "That's how I look at it."

We had been talking about changes Gloria had made in his room. The velveteen portraits of Martin Luther King and the Kennedys were now there over the bed, which faced in a different direction. The program photo of Alvin was gone, but new things were taped to the dresser mirror: school snapshots of grandchildren and a glossy of two currently rated fighters being glad-handed by the promoter of a past Superdome card. Commenting on this photograph made him think of other cards and promoters. He mentioned once having met Don King. Feeling that this might be a pleasant memory, I asked him to tell me more about it. He recalled the matter with suddenly harsh honesty: "Don King don' know me. I was just one a the spooks. You know, the guys waved over to shake a big shot's hand."

I knew Gloria tried to shield him from family trouble such as Lionel's. "He grieves for his chil'ren. He lay up in that bed and he grieves." So for the rest of the visit I kept the conversation on boxing, and we talked about Eddie Futch, a successful trainer, who, I remembered from the scrapbook fragments I had seen, did know Collis and sometimes had worked with him. Eddie Futch is still a force in the game.

Gloria was watching *General Hospital*, her favorite soap, when I came down the stairs. As I was about to leave, she turned and began telling me about her brother Alvin. She said he was having new problems in the prison, though as usual she had few details about exactly what they were. She had heard of them in a general way from her sons Dwight and Andre, who were also in Angola. Dwight and Andre had been moved to a less restricted camp up there, and they could call her collect. This had led, she now informed me, to a hundred-dollar long-distance bill she was still trying to pay off.

Speaking over the TV's high volume, she also told me her older daughter Pamela would probably be home from Los Angeles before long. A detective out there had written that they were going to put Pamela on a plane and see that she came. Gloria said she would be glad for some help in raising Andrea—"A child ought to know her own mother"—but she was afraid Pam might take Andrea out of the city. Then she would miss her too much.

Except for the trophy stand, she had also rearranged the living-room furniture. A plastic-fabric pennant—"New York City"—and the studio photographs I had seen on the tables now covered one wall: Trina and a young man; Trina alone; Andrea and Keyon, each shown from two angles within the one shared frame; a recently blown-up print from the thirties of Gloria's mother, Dorothy, seated in a long coat and wide-brimmed hat. I studied Dorothy's thin, straight nose and Indian high cheekbones as Gloria lowered her voice to speak of her father. She kept her arms modestly folded across the front of her thin shift, and the scent of cleanser reached me from the scoured tile floor. Because of the racket of the TV, I had to strain to hear her.

"I been worried, I been worried," she said, her right hand patting at her cheek and self-consciously obscuring her right eye and her teeth. "Sometimes I can't do nothin' with him. When the time come when he used to leave out, he'll tell me he goin' to that gym. Yesterday I found him up in his room almost all the way dressed. '*Git my hat!*' he told me. '*Where my shoe?*' Watn't a thing Junior or I could say would change his mind. Jesus forgive me, I had to lie. I told him you was comin'. He kept sayin', 'You sure he comin' today? You *sure?*' I finally got him to take his medicine. That puts him *out*. When he woke up, he didn't remember a thing about it. Not a *thing*. He even forgits he been so sick. (A doctor told us he had, like, a enlarged heart, and a murmur.) Sometime you tell him somethin', seem like the next minute—the next *minute!*—he forgit. Then he'll turn around and come up with a correction and explain somethin' so *clear*: 'Now, Gloria Mae, if you would stack them dishes thisaway . . .' And, do you know, most any time he talk to you like that, he be *right!* Oh, you got to watch him, him. I told you, didn't I, about comin' home and findin' he'd hung all the sheets on the line. He's somebody wanna do *for hisself*. But he cain't. Not like he is now. You see it, don't you? How easy he coulda fell off that step. Then we'd be back down to that hospital. I don't know, I just don't know."

9

□

Winter 1983

During the next year, I continued—as I had led him to
expect I would—trying to re-create his past. When I visited
him, I sometimes took the tape recorder; but, though we
invariably talked of his life, I never read to him again and
he never heard what I wrote and never read it himself.

A few weeks before his mother's death he woke in hysterics
from a dream and ran into his parents' room. The family
gathered as he clung to his mother and told what he had
dreamed. "My mama's gone."

To his sister Elma, his dream pointed toward not only the
loss of their mother but also toward the death a year later
of Eloise, the infant whose birth killed her. The two fused
in Elma's memory: her brother's dream and her aunt's
putting the feverish infant in her arms and then leaving the
bedroom. Eloise died in Elma's lap there in the nursing
rocker. When I first spoke with her, Elma Walker, who was
then in her mid-seventies, still vividly recalled experiencing
her mother's presence in the room; she said she felt the
baby's spirit rise from her arms as her mother returned and
took Eloise away.

The children's aunt, Hattie Owens Peoples, had come to
help care for them during her sister's fourth pregnancy.
Though she suffered from pellagra, Hattie Peoples had been
working for a white family named Law in the neighboring
community of New Church, Louisiana. On the night of
Collis's nightmare, Addie Belle called her sister and her

mother into the room—Alvin and the children were already by the bed. She asked that they all kneel, join hands, and promise to stay together as a family. Everyone promised. "That was it." Collis told me. "That was our family."

Hattie Peoples did at least as much as anyone to honor the vow. She never went back to the Laws. When Alvin decided to leave Mansfield and move west in pursuit of a better life, she went with him and became a second mother to Collis and his sisters.

In 1919, a Texas real estate concern, the Wright Land Company, initiated a development program selling parcels of inexpensive land in outlying areas north of Houston. The program's targeted customers were blacks. With $250 saved from his and his wife's labors in the cafe, Alvin bought two 25-by-120-foot lots and the materials for a house. This was in Houston's East Independent Heights, which at first was an almost treeless community. A decade passed before indoor plumbing and electric lights were available there, and it would be longer than that before the residents could afford them.

Alvin first moved the girls and Aunt Hattie to New Avery, Texas, to stay with his relatives. He took Collis ahead with him to Houston for the help he could be in building the house. Collis said, "I thought I was doin' a big job, I thought I was a man."

For the first few weeks, he and his father lived in a rented room in Houston proper. During the days Alvin worked as a repairman for Western Union and Collis whiled away slow hours alone in the room. Evenings and weekends they took the streetcar out toward the Heights and then walked two miles the rest of the way. Before long, they were digging the foundation.

To curtail renting, they pitched a tent at the work site. On clear nights they spread out their ground cloth and blankets under the low sky. Collis's days were crowded with the many tasks that Alvin laid out to be done while he was at his job in town. From the nights he retained memories of himself and his father making their dinner outdoors. After these meals, Collis sometimes drifted into sleep while gazing at the bronze margin of the empty horizon and his father reading his Bible in the light from their cook fire.

They finished the well and the cesspool, and Alvin paid various handymen to help with the carpentry on weekends. Once the kitchen and a second room were done, he sent word to New Avery. Aunt Hattie and Collis's sisters arrived on the train. Miss Fanny accompanied them, it having been decided that she would live with her daughter Cora and her husband, who also had built a house in Independent Heights.

Shortly after Alvin finished the remaining rooms of the house, he took a job laying underground telephone cable in Iowa. For some time after that, he was a transient presence in the home he had made. He returned periodically, and he supported them by sending his sister-in-law part of his paycheck each month, but for the next several years he preferred to work in the North, where, he said, a man had a better chance of earning his worth: "Cain't make no money down South, son."

That fall Collis and his sisters started school. There the challenges Collis took seriously weren't the ones he might have found in his books. Physical self-reliance was already an absolute with him. Once he had won the respect of his classmates, he had to fight older boys, some of them truants years behind their own classes. After reaching the top of the pecking order among boys in the Heights, he spent many of his recesses staging sparring bouts of a sort between others, bouts that his sisters Fanny McGlory and Elma Walker remembered as being somehow technical, almost comic, showing their brother at his most vocal. He would name and announce each of the principals—"Hammerhead!" "Black Samson!" "Knockout Charlie!"—then step in between them if someone was about to be seriously hurt.

"Well, them boys, they wouldn' revoke against me, because they knew . . ." (The smack of limp fist against palm, then laughter.) "If they didn' do like I tell 'em. An' they was glad to git on the team. 'Collis, put me on the team, put me on the team!' 'Well aw right, if you wanna be on the team, you got do like I tell y'.' So most any name I give 'em, they'd go for. I'd put the ring, put up the ring—we had a li'l rope ring—an' the gloves."

As I had seen in the gym, being in charge in such a way was one of his special pleasures. His father indirectly supported him in this role of leader and big shot ("I wouldn' lie to you; my daddy was good to me") by telling Hattie to give the children allowances out of the checks he sent. This money Collis squandered at the Lincoln Theater on Preston Avenue on admissions and refreshments for impressed friends who were mesmerized, as he was, by the flickering serialized performances of Bill Hart, Hoot Gibson, Buck Jones, and Jack Hoxie, names he remembered exactly and listed for me as belonging to "top screen outlaws, terrible fellas" who were always taking "differ'nt territories from the Indians."

Fortunately, a willingness to work hard countered his grander tendencies. He inherited his parents' resourcefulness and slept under a roof that reminded him of his father's refusal to go slack on a hard job. In order to keep money in his pocket as his father did, he hired himself out to do chores around the Heights. When he didn't have work, he was looking for it: "I'd be out there."

He was twelve when he had his first opportunity for a steady job. A man named J. C. Neal owned considerable property in Independent Heights. Neal had developed part of his land into a profitable dairy farm. He also drove a delivery wagon, hauling firewood and ice in addition to milk. Neal had a lock on these businesses in Independent Heights and also in Sunset Heights, the adjoining white neighborhood. At about the time that J. C. Neal's enterprises grew beyond his ability to manage them alone, he noticed Collis working here and there and leading others on the schoolyard. Shortly afterward, while putting Hattie Peoples's order of ice into her cooling box, he mentioned that he might be needing some help. Early the next morning, Collis was in his yard waiting to speak to him: "I'm right at the do'."

The first duty Mr. Neal gave him was to learn to ride his personal horse, a spirited pacer named Dan. Nothing could have pleased Collis more. For a dollar a week, he was to use Dan to herd the cows into various pastures each morning before school and to bring them back to the barn at dusk. "Gaited from his heart!" is how he remembered Dan, an animal that could "single-foot or fox-trot. He wasn't lazy; you didn' never have to beat him. In fact, he wouldn't 'cept no beatin'." To the responsibility for his horse, Mr. Neal added the stabling and care of the mules that pulled his delivery wagon. Before long he began going with Mr. Neal on the ice routes. Although at first it taxed him to handle "the small ice," the twenty-five-pound blocks, he was eager to struggle with the fifties and hundreds: "I didn' know I was so young, I jus' wanted to be a man."

Mr. Neal showed him how to collect and keep accounts. Soon he was handling Mr. Neal's money. Then Mr. Neal gave him routes of his own: ice in summer; firewood in winter—plus trips several miles north to the nearest stands of timber on undeveloped land known as Acre Homes.

Once Mr. Neal had satisfied himself concerning Collis's character he invited him to stay for dinner. The invitation was repeated and accepted several times a week. Mr. and Mrs. Neal had no children. They eventually told Collis they wanted to adopt him.

His father refused: "My daddy had a fit." But Collis continued to work for Mr. Neal and to eat well at his table, pleased that in unspoken ways his boss and he were like father and son.

"Practically raised me. I was *with him* more'n I was at home. Go to work in the mawnin' an' I'd eat breakfast." (Whispering:) "His wife, boy, boy, she could cook some good biscuits. I don' know whether you know 'bout them homemade country biscuits. Aw, man, you catch one a them women can cook them homemade biscuits . . . ! Not these women now, you don' find women can cook too much now. But them older women, 'bout twen'y-five years back, that can make

biscuits! An' that country butter, boy! An' some a that
molasses! An' stick in there a good piece a that, that hog-
poke bacon . . . !" (Groaning, laughing.)

Not long after he started working for Mr. Neal, another
opportunity came his way. One of his duties with Mr. Neal
was to take Dan and the mules to the blacksmith, a white
man named Watchter, who had his shop in his backyard in
Sunset Heights. Collis took careful notice of Mr. Neal's
cheerful, deferential way of doing business with white people.
Then, around the blacksmith and his wife, he tried "to do
like" Mr. Neal.

Mrs. Watchter distributed the afternoon paper in Sunset
Heights and other outlying areas north of the city. When
she lost her paper carrier in Independent Heights, she
remembered the courteous boy who worked for the wood-
and-ice man. She spoke to Mr. Neal about it and negotiated
times during afternoons and weekends when Collis could be
free to come to her.

He was glad for the work. He proved his honesty and
pleased the customers so well that Mrs. Watchter gave him
a second delivery route, this one in Sunset Heights itself.
With these paper routes plus raises Mr. Neal had given him,
he now found himself with plenty of money in his pocket,
usually enough to give some to Aunt Hattie and still have
change for his friends and the movies. His new Sunset route
also put him in contact with some white people who were
happy to rely on someone so personable and competent.

"Here's the thing of it: some guys throwin' papers would
miss a day. I went *ev'ry* day on my route. If I threw it, you
could depend on y' paper. That means a lot, 'cause you got
a lot a white fellas reads close behind things, an' they don'
wanna miss a paper. They miss one an' . . . *who-o-o!* You
laugh, but that's true, I'm tellin' you. I dealt wit' 'em, I *know*.
If they miss a important colyum, aw, man, they go to pieces.
An' they payin' you too."

With Mr. Neal as his model, he became accomplished at

staying on good terms with even his orneriest customers: "I learnt this: you git along with people that can help *you*. I come up like that." Even so early in his life, Collis thought of customers and the people he served as being "the public," a generality he felt compelled to please. As a result, it was hard for him to say no, and he found he had almost more work than he could handle. To catch up, he sometimes went on a job over in Sunset instead of going to school. This arrangement suited him because, to his mind, his teachers taught nothing so valuable as how to hit it off with all sorts of people and how to make money in the process. "Mr. Neal taught me this: you makin' a *dolla'*—understan' me good now—you don' git bigheaded, they could git somebody else. You always the underdog, but you makin' that dolla'. (When I pull y' finger like that I mean *that dolla'*.) That dolla's what talks."

Aunt Hattie disapproved of his hooky-playing, but she was proud he was self-sufficient and in such demand. She was also grateful for the extra money he brought in. Such windfalls helped make it possible for them to live better than most of their neighbors.

It was owing to her gratitude and, no less, to the practical side of her nature that she secretly began making payments on a young mare to a man who owned a horse ranch bordering the woods out in Acre Homes. Aunt Hattie was right in expecting the mare, Nellie, would increase his earning power, but the first time he ran his hand along its mane, he was thinking not about wages but about the fact that now he would ride where he went.

From the ages of twelve to fifteen, regardless of the various other jobs that he had and of the pride he took in owning a horse, he hauled ice and wood for Mr. Neal, drove his cows out in the morning and, after riding his paper routes in the afternoon, drove them in at night. On days when he ran short of time, Elma or Fanny would take the mare and deliver his papers. In 1982, both women sharply recalled Sunday mornings back then and being waked in the dark by the tink and rumble of a wagon and team and then a battery of thuds as bound stacks of newsprint were pitched down on their swept yard. In the dark they sat alongside their brother on the floor of the front room, the three of them rolling the newspapers. They said their aunt would feed him before the others, a big breakfast. Then, his pommel slung with sacks—or at least so I envisioned it—he would canter out in the dawn to throw the *The Houston Chronicle* before church.

10

☐

Winter 1983–84

As he grew older, the expansion of his paper routes
prompted him to buy a wagon, a one-horse gig. His increased
income enabled him later to outfit his own baseball team
and, eventually, to race his own horse, the mare's first foal.
Next to boxing, baseball was his sport. His own team grew
out of the boxing group he had formed on the schoolyard.
The equipment he bought wasn't simply generosity on his
part: "Most a them boys didn' have nothin' to play with, but
that watn't it. You know I had to be in the front." He named
the team the Magnolia Sports, and on occasional summer
Sundays for the rest of his time in Houston, they played
challenge games around the city. He claimed that, through
the side bets, he won back most of his investment.

Once, while hunting opposition for the Sports, he happened on a crowd of men who were staging quarter-horse
match races in a field out toward Acre Homes. After that,
he began showing up at these races, in which most of the
riders were boys. Although he was already too heavy to be
a regular, he was sometimes hired to ride "handicap." He
said he bartered his jockey's pay and other earnings to breed
the mare—only an average runner—to a coal-black stallion
from the winningest string at the races. One of his pleasures
during the next few years was raising the foal and training
it after it grew into a colt. Like its sire, it had speed. He
named the colt after Mr. Neal's horse and rode it in its races.
He said Dan and he won many more than they lost.

At around this time Mrs. Watchter gave him a puppy from a litter her mixed spaniel had birthed. It was black and brown except for a white streak encircling its neck. Because of this marking, he called the dog Ring.

Acre Homes teemed with small game. When he had time, he liked to steal off with Ring and the Remington 12-gauge his father had left in his care. The dog also helped drive Mr. Neal's cows, and in hot weather when he swam in the creek, Ring would protect the clothes he left folded on the bank.

Riding in his gig or on one of his horses with Ring trotting behind, he attracted notice in the Heights. By the time he reached sixteen, he felt he was where he wanted to be, moving toward the front.

His next several years included large changes. In ninth grade, he stopped going to school altogether. I don't know at exactly what point he left Mr. Neal. But before he was seventeen he gave up his paper routes and took more of an interest in working away from the Heights where he could be even more independent.

For a while he helped two young Italian brothers in a moonshine operation out in Acre Homes. This work led to a job shining shoes and selling bootleg whiskey in the basement of the Bender Hotel in downtown Houston. "I'm shinin' his shoes, man would say, 'Say, boy, you know where I can get somethin' to drink?' I'd say, 'I'll see can I catch the fella.' I would never tell him I *had* it, you understan', I always let him think I was doin' the thing *for* him. Then I'd slip off to my locker. I kept fo', five fifths locked up, an' some pints. I'd make a profit on the bottle—plus, most times, a good tip!"

He left the Bender after only a short while. His aunt had learned about it. She told his father, who by then had returned permanently from Iowa, and that ended it: "My pa was dead set against *that*. I think I told y', he was a ordained Baptist ministry."

When his father saw that he was beginning to pull away from home, he proposed that he learn a trade. Because of Alvin's status at the time as furnace operator at the Houston Car Wheel Foundry, he was able to have Collis taken on temporarily for an "easy ride" as a molder's helper in the "soft shop" where cast iron was made. It was in the soft shop, he remembered, that his father's furnace "melted that scrap iron like water." The strength he had developed hauling Mr. Neal's fifties and hundreds was useful in the foundry, and after a few weeks he was promoted to the "hard iron," or steel, shop where the boxcar wheels were completed. In the steel shop he was the lone assistant to a white steelworker named Keeler: "Mr. Keeler was a man now!" The two of them worked well together in meeting their daily quota of twenty-five wheels. This connection to the railroad was very different from his boyhood fascination with trains, but he didn't mind the work.

One evening at the movies a friend introduced him to a pretty, light-skinned schoolgirl named Lily Mae Stewart. Because her family had strict ideas about courtship, the only way he and Lily Mae could meet during the next several months was in the company of friends at one of the movie houses—when not at the Lincoln, at the Ideal or the Darling: "Sometimes I practically lived in the show."

It pleased Alvin that his son was following him in his present work. But this satisfaction didn't last. The fledgling trucking industry had begun to make inroads in the freight business. Orders for boxcar wheels declined. As a result, after about a year at the foundry, Collis was laid off.

He drifted for a while, picking up pocket money through jobs over in Sunset. He now found himself with more leisure than at any point since childhood—more time for his other enthusiasms and, as he called it, for "skylarking" with his friends. It was like a vacation, and had it ended then, he might have gone back with Mr. Neal or caught on again at the foundry. Had he done either, he eventually might have inherited or otherwise acquired some of the Heights. As it was, his skylarking didn't exactly stop, and one warm winter night he took part in an event that nudged him toward a different sort of life.

A carnival then touring black neighborhoods in the South offered fifty dollars to anyone who could last two rounds with Lobo Jones, an ex-boxer making a living as a carny fighter. Collis's friends put it to him boisterously: " *'Collis! Man!* They payin' fifty dollas. *Collis!* You can knock this bum out!' "

Outside the performance tent a white barker gestured from a wagon bed above the heads of the crowd. Next to him stood a large black man in fighting tights who "looked like he hadn't bathed in a week" and who seemed to Collis too pleased with "his big stinkin' self." He and his friends listened to the barker: " 'Anybody stay two rounds—! Two two-minute rounds—! Lobo—! Lobo Jones—!' "

"Fifty dollas for two rounds, man, that was a *heap* a money back in them times. Nobody went up, I went up." As the crowd paid to enter, the barker took him aside and said he wanted him to have a few dollars whether he lasted the distance or not. He understood then he might not see the whole fifty. He also had the satisfaction of knowing that, no matter what he won, he would be conning the con man, who failed to see that he would have fought Jones for nothing.

He laughed remembering it and spanked my knee. "Shee! I knocked the fool out the guy. Guy couldn' fight!" He became solemn. "But that was a big show—to the *public.*"

When I asked if the man gave him what he had promised, he hooted again. "Naw, wanted to gimme a job! Workin wit' the show!" Though he might spend time skylarking there, he felt that "that dirty type a life" was beneath him. It ended with the barker finally throwing him a bill; once he said it was a twenty, another time he said it was more.

However much he won, he said he kept back a part to give to his aunt on the side. His friends helped him spend the rest that night in a cafe on desserts and sweet drinks— "monkey food, that's what I call it." The party apparently included the curious or hungry who came in off the street. As he would later say about celebration-night tabs paid with purses he earned over the years, "I didn' have to know you."

After that night, his reputation for his fists spread to other parts of Houston and led to an invitation to fight on the undercard of one of the black professional boxing shows that, during those years, were staged by white men at the Odd Fellows Temple. The promoters tried to persuade him to be part of one of the battle royals, but he said he valued himself too highly for that. He held out and finally was matched against Dynamite Davis, a journeyman middle-weight from Galveston.

For the scheduled four rounds, his pay was much less than he had won at the carnival, but he didn't object: "I didn' know nothin', watn't really interested in no money, all I wanted to do was fight."

He said "naw" when I asked if he had second thoughts or butterflies the night of the fight—which he described as a close decision victory that left him with a swollen face and caused him for several days to avoid his father. The soreness in his body took longer to heal, but he "didn' give a damn —when you're young you think you can do anything."

A few days after the fight, Bradis Flowers, the boxer who had headlined the card, came out to the Heights to see him. This visit from Flowers, also a middleweight, destroyed any notion Collis may have had of becoming an ordinary workingman.

Flowers had been sent by his manager, who worked at the River Oaks Country Club on the opulent south side of Houston. The manager's job title was "club sheriff"—he patrolled the fairways on a palomino to ensure that no undesirable loitered on the lush private acres. Young men in the Heights knew that carrying golf bags and scraping for tips at the River Oaks was one way of making money. Less well known about the club was the fact that on its grounds was a special gym, an extension of the caddy house.

An entertainment for club members, Bradis Flowers and a few others trained there. The club sheriff and friends of his who owned fighters made use of this gym and culled prospects and sparring partners from among the caddies.

The club's business manager and caddy master, a red-headed—"He had hair 'bout yo' color"—young bachelor, had been at the fights with his pal the club sheriff when Collis decisioned Dynamite Davis. The caddy master lived a fast life and fancied he was clever with his fists. He admired the sheriff's success with Bradis Flowers and wanted a top fighter of his own. Collis's showing against so game a veteran as Davis convinced him he was witnessing the debut of a natural.

Flowers brought him to the club to talk business with the caddy master, and Collis was pleased with the arrangement they struck. The caddy master turned him over to an ex-fighter named Mickey McGuire, "the first white man to put a glove on me." He liked McGuire and learned fast.

Except for the length of the trip in from the Heights and the punishment he suffered sparring with Flowers, the days he spent at the country club were some of his most pleasant to recall. Favored caddies were expected to arrive early in the morning and, so they would be knowledgeable about golf, play the course themselves—"shootin' the coast," he called it—and finish before the first golfing parties were to tee off. Collis already had some skill at the game as a result of "two-hole golf"—a pastime he and his friends had devised on the prairies of the Heights with a secondhand iron. A waiter would deliver his and Flowers's lunches to the caddy house, and he had "a whatchacall, a okay"—which meant that, so long as he stayed fresh enough to train, he could caddy when he felt like it and, unlike most of the other caddies, didn't have to take a number and wait for a turn. This made it easier for him to cultivate members who would tip big and use him regularly. He said there were "important people" who sent to the caddy house for "Collis the fighter." The wife of the club pro was one. He eagerly gave extra service—"wash all the balls, wipe down her clubs, clean up the shoes"—to Mrs. Jack Burke, Sr.

He had a standard strategy for handling most of the golfers: "Big oil people that all the time had to be right up to the minute. You gotta know how to stand. Always give the golfer the control. If he don' ask nothin', don' say nothin'. If he does, then you talk on the edge. 'Now, if it was me, I might try a six iron.' Keep a smile on y' face, you git more that way."

When he spoke of how the caddy master "was quick to git rid" of certain caddies, "them raggedy-type guys wit' no control to they mouth," I asked if the ways of the golfers ever annoyed him. He said he "never had no trouble with nobody on the coast." As I prodded him further, he added, "Anybody should know you couldn' go out there wit' y' feelin's in y' hands. You ain' nothin' but a servant . . . But, in them times, how else you go'n come through?"

The late-afternoon action in the caddy-house gym fit in with other patterns at the club. Golfers would be coming in off the course during hours when the gym was active. The men could have their drinks served at ringside and decide how they might bet at the next show at the Odd Fellows.

These sessions were further apprenticeship for Collis. Club members liked to talk to him while he trained because of his knack for answering out brightly even as leather flew. He saw the River Oaks wealthy as "the public" at its shrewdest and most powerful, and it pleased him to charm them at the same time that he won physical respect from the likes of Bradis Flowers.

After he had a few fights at the Odd Fellows for the caddy master, his involvement with Lily Mae Stewart developed into courtship. She was the only child of relatively prosperous parents. They wanted their daughter to have everything she wanted, but they were wary of letting her marry a prizefighter and golf caddy. Collis was strongly attracted to Lily Mae and impressed by the fact that her family were "pretty good livers"—they even owned a car—but he hated to give up his arrangement at the club and the hold that boxing now had on him: "Naw, I did not ever lie to my trainer, to Mickey, about my roadwork, I didn' have to. For this reason. He was so good to me an' took such an inte-rest in me, an' I loveded what I was doin'. So I'd run an' train more than I was supposed to."

The pressure mounted on him to make a decision: give up the club or Lily Mae. Then an unexpected change in the caddy master's fortunes spared him this hard choice.

His benefactor took him aside one day and confessed he suddenly had problems. He would be leaving town soon, but he encouraged Collis in his boxing. "He told me, 'Don' quit.' " They parted on fond terms and never saw one another again. As the caddy master must have expected, a scandal followed. It concerned his handling of country-club monies.

The caddy master's leaving "cut my pull, I couldn' jus' go out like I used to an' git a good bag an' a meal anytime I got ready." Though he tried to continue training, it became necessary to look for other work. This pleased the Stewarts.

He found a regular job in an area of warehouses at Pinkoff's Cottonseed Cake Mill. When he was younger, he had worked at Pinkoff's when extra hands were needed to throw the hundred-pound sacks of cottonseed meal. His past experience at Pinkoff's and his new reputation as a boxer put him "to the front" there too, and he was placed in charge of the scale, one of the better-paying jobs in the warehouse. He volunteered an explanation of the mechanics of this work: "Them scales is like a hopper, she weighs the meal automatically an' dump it automatically. You gotta be just on time where you don' let that"—laughing—"tump out on the flo'! 'Cause if you had dump it on the flo', you don' git no *sacks*. You know that don' help the company. I was about the only guy could operate the scale . . ."

He worked the seven-to-seven night shift at Pinkoff's. By this time, Lily Mae's father, "Mr. Charley," had decided he approved of him. Sometimes at seven in the morning Lily

Mae and her father would be there with the car to drive him to their house for breakfast. Lily Mae and her mother began making wedding plans, and Collis began making payments to have a house built on a lot owned by the Stewarts. By the time they were married their house was ready.

I disbelieved that his pay at Pinkoff's could have financed the construction of a house. Yet family members I met in Houston told me he had paid for it all. It still stands at 739 West Cavalcade, where Cavalcade, now a four-lane thoroughfare, meets Airline. On that corner in 1982 I saw pink roses blooming around the small turquoise structure, and I was told that Mr. Charley, then a very old widower in precarious health, lived alone inside.

About ten months after the wedding, Lily Mae gave birth to a daughter. They named the baby Josephine after Lily Mae's mother, Miss Jo. Soon Lily Mae was pregnant again, and it may have looked as if Collis had settled on being simply a hardworking family man. Anyone who thought that didn't know how intensely he saw himself as "Collis the fighter" or how much he liked impressing "the public." On weekends and on some afternoons he continued to go to the club and to work out with Bradis Flowers, and when the Magnolia Sports had a game he still took pride in dramatically "handlin' " the team and the betting.

But friction developed between him and Miss Jo, who held strict ideas about how a family should be run. His view of the relation between husband and wife was also strict, and patently sexist: "I'm a man," he said he told Lily Mae. "I make the livin', you at home." Miss Jo disapproved of the freedom he enjoyed. He and Lily Mae quarreled about it; then they quarreled about Miss Jo. One night he and Miss Jo quarreled. I never learned all the details of the argument—at one point he charged that Lily Mae "didn' keep her house clean"—but it apparently ended with him bursting out the back screen door on West Cavalcade and Miss Jo firing at him with a pistol. After that, he moved his few personal things back out to the Heights and left the house and the rest to Lily Mae and her mother. He explained it to me curtly as a matter of being able to live with one but not the other: "We separated, I'd say."

April 25, 1982

I don't know if he left before or after the birth of his second daughter, Joyce. Sitting in Joyce Stafford's formal living room in a densely shaded section of Houston, I tried to envision how she and her sister Josephine felt as, cooperatively answering questions of mine, they tactfully balanced their allegiances between a deceased protective mother and a father they had infrequently seen. Josephine and Joyce had married brothers from Houston, and my visit had occasioned a large family gathering. Nieces, cousins, and children beyond my recall were present—along with the Stafford brothers, Ralph and Eldridge (in whose handsome house we all were), Collis's sisters Fanny McGlory and Elma Walker, and Elma's husband, the Reverend Walker. A sumptuous Sunday buffet awaited us in the dining room. The many well-dressed people there had come from church to eat and, it seemed, politely to scrutinize the white stranger engaged in a project about one of its members.

Part of my family was there too. I had brought my son with me from New Orleans. Richard's current Little League successes had given both of us improbable hopes of his one day pitching professionally, and we had spent the previous evening watching baseball in the Astrodome. I also had counted on his presence to strengthen my credibility on Sunday, but now my throat tightened as the room grew quiet. One of the adults, on learning in solicitous conversation of Richard's effort and training in music, had handed him the acoustic guitar that had been displayed on a stand near the piano. My qualms for Richard were greater than his own. Without fanfare or hesitation, he familiarized himself with the guitar and began to play.

I glanced around the thickly carpeted room while everyone

attended Richard's workmanlike rendering of the classical piece he knew best. The Victorian furnishings and gilt-framed prints of British portraiture and pastoral scenes supported my sense that Miss Jo had been successful in her hopes for her daughters. Their husbands had done well in real estate and other business; and Josephine, I had just learned, was formerly a registered nurse and now held a secure place in the postal service. Joyce had been a registered nurse too; but now, having earned a master's degree and a Ph.D. in education from the University of Houston, she taught junior high school. Looking at her pale complexion and delicate features—petite beauty I would otherwise have guessed to be Mediterranean—I thought of Lookout Mountain Plantation, Miss Fanny's mother, and the planter named Collis.

After Richard finished his number and, handing back the guitar, would not be indulged into another, we all stood and went in to the generous meal.

Winter 1983–84

For Collis, back out on the Heights in the summer of 1929, very little about even the appearance of life approached the serenity of Joyce's eventual residence. He came home to his father's and Aunt Hattie's continuing displeasure with the fact of his marriage: "My people never liked the match no way." He also found that he had lost his horse and his dog.

There was pavement in the Heights now, and a highway had been cut through, bringing with it the abrasive new presence of cars. His cousin Nathan, his aunt Cora's son, had left a gate unlatched. Running free, Dan had been killed on the highway. Nathan also was responsible for the death of the dog. Skylarking in a borrowed car, he had hit Ring.

The family kept Collis away from his cousin until his anger cooled. Meanwhile he found himself drifting again. Pinkoff's shut down for the summer, and the Odd Fellows had scheduled no fight cards. He wanted to strike out on his own, but in Houston he could see no way to be more independent than he already had been. He hired himself out in Sunset for odd jobs and felt stifled and restless.

A violent incident near the end of the summer simplified his dilemma. Nathan played a part in this too, but now Collis's anger burned in his cousin's defense.

Gloria and Collis Jr. told me they learned from their mother that he left Houston because he hit a man from there with an ax. They said their mother brought up this event during the few serious arguments she had with him. His version, clarified over the course of several conversations and supported by his sisters, was different.

According to their telling, it involved the Magnolia Sports. One late-summer day, when he planned to train at the club, he turned the baseball equipment over to Nathan so the team could practice. That afternoon someone taunted the players, then roughed up Nathan when he tried to intervene.

"This boy," he said, "that had jumped on my cousin, he never did participate along in no sports or nothin'. He was one a these smart alecs. Next Sunday, I didn' go to the country club, I went out there to catch him. 'Cause I knew he was go'n come out there. He'd already cut up one a my baseball gloves. I was angry, real angry about it. So when all the boys was gangin' around—you know how a gang a guys be around home plate, throwin', catchin', call it warmin' up —I jus' grabbed—I had coupla bats—I jus' grabbed one a them . . . *Pow!* Bust him up side the head. Then . . . I jus' took on off."

When I pressed him for details, he said, "Aw, he would be with a coupla other guys an' they . . . wouldn' let the boys play, take the bats, run all off, delay the game. These smaller kids—an' some guys is very easygoin'—they wouldn', well they couldn', well it wasn't theirs, it was *mine* anyway."

His voice became almost inaudible when I asked why he used a bat rather than his bare hands. "G-g-g, I knock him out . . . I was just that much against him. He was larger than me. See, Horace was—"

This was the only time I heard anyone mention the name. "—was older than me too. I know him from goin' to school, all of us went to school together. He was kind of a tough-type kid. Not too easygoin'. Kind of a bully, I'd say. He'd *take* things! Take kids' money."

Horace lay in a coma for days, and it was weeks before he left the hospital. Collis's sister Fanny McGlory told me this part of it. She was the one who, once he had written to tell her where he was, sent him messages about Horace's condition.

After he put down the bat, he ran from the Heights to the freight yard. When the next freight pulled in, bound eastward it so happened, he slipped inside a boxcar. He had nothing with him but the little money he always kept in his pocket. The rest he left behind: his people in the Heights, his small daughters and the house on Cavalcade, Mr. Neal, the Sports, first youth, first love. I don't know if he in some way realized, when he raised the bat, that his departure would be final. If he had regret, felt remorse—and he must have—he wouldn't express it to me. That night finally he was on a train, on his own.

11

□

Winter 1984

"Hoboin'." This was how he described the days following his departure. "That brakeman sets up in the booth up there. You hafta let him check to see if you's aw right, talks aw-right conversation. 'I'm tryin' to git to the next stop. Think you could help me? Gotta coupla bucks or so . . .' I tol' him I could give him that. 'See, I'm kinda shawt, I gotta scarf, y' know.' He laughed. *Nice* ol' fella he was. He ain' outta nothin'. He sets up there, watches out that window to see where that engine puts them cars, to see that she switches 'em in the proper places. That's all he do, he don' hardly git out, come down. Got another brakeman do the runnin'."

Eventually he hoboed to Chicago, where he heard fights were plentiful. He had been told that one of the arenas there, "the Marigold Gardens, goes *every* week."

In Chicago's West Street Gym he struck up a friendship with a more experienced fighter named Roland Dixon. Dixon was training for a fight just a few days away. He helped Collis land a spot, a four-round prelim, on the card at Amerigo Gardens.

Dixon was from New Orleans, and he was homesick. He preferred having a traveling partner and convinced Collis that there were good boxing opportunities in New Orleans. Shortly after the two of them reached the New Orleans freight yard, they went to a black gym on Rampart Street. "I shadowboxed, loosened up, punched the bags a few.

Dixon didn' work out. An', uh, we *left* . . . But I knew the way to the gym then."

Dixon left him on his own after that day. For the time being, Collis "hoboed around downtown" and trained when he could. "I got me a room. I stayed with a guy. 'Bout a week. Tol' him I didn' have no money. Tol' him I'd pay him first fight I made." He fed himself by shining shoes in the Central Business District and by working at a bar at the corner of Canal and Camp streets.

His first fights in New Orleans were staged at the San Jacinto Center, a black boxing club on Dumaine near Claiborne. He recounted these on an afternoon when he showed little energy and for a long while spoke haltingly, scarcely above a whisper. "First fight I made here I boxed a boy by the name a Lloyd Pinion . . . I beat him . . . In fact, they stopped the fight. I beat him so bad he"—suddenly almost laughing—"he never did fight no mo'. He quit. Messed him up." (Now somberly:) "Kinda cuckoo. I beat him bad, bad . . ."

I asked how he felt at having severely hurt an opponent. His answer was practical. "I wanted to beat y', not kill y'. But he was the champion a the club, I was outta-town. So I couldn' take no chances, you understan' that—I had to know if I didn' win big, I probably wouldn' git it . . .

"Then I fought another boy by the name a— What was that boy's name? Kinda shawt, *stocky!* Guy was a good puncher, I can tell y' that. Anyway, I fought him. Knock him out. That gimme two straight wins.

"Then I fought this boy, Young Wills, that taken the name behind Harry Wills, who was a original heavyweight one time, *from* this town. I fought *him*. 'Nother knockout. Three in a row." (Laughing.)

"So that put me in the action. *Ev'*body wanted to see what Collis was go'n do: 'What Collis go'n do?' So then I went from there to ten rounds, an' I was on my way. I was a ten-round fighter."

During this period, in 1930 or 1931, when he was building a reputation at the San Jacinto Center, he paid off the friend who had put him up and moved in with another friend, who had a room in a residential neighborhood—uptown on Saratoga between First and Second streets. A large Creole family named Simon lived across the street. The Simons were from the upriver community of Vacherie in rural St. James Parish. One afternoon as he left for his workout, he noticed one of the Simon girls, Dorothy, a young woman in her late teens, outside on the sidewalk. This situation repeated itself, and on the second day he blew her a kiss, thus starting a flirtation that led to a forty-year marriage.

Boxing was also a factor in the unfolding of their courtship. Dorothy took an interest in the goings and comings across the street and "was far enough into my business to want to know where was I 'goin' every evenin' wit' a . . . *bag!*' I tol' her girlfriend, I say, 'Tell Dorothy I have to go train at the gym.' Well . . . she didn' think she believed it so much . . .

"But then her *cousin*, he went wi' me when I went to the gym to train one evenin'. An' that turnt the whole thing around! He went back an' tol' her all about the gym 'cause"—lowering his voice dismissively—" 'cause she didn', had never had no opportunity, I guess, to go in a gym an' see a fighter train, an' I guess they's lotsa people don' know a fighter have to work very, very hard . . ."

The "gym" he was then most often training in was no more than a roped-off section of the Bulls' Club, a neighborhood males' social establishment located on Eighth Street between Dryades and Daneel. Dorothy's cousin's visit there provoked the curiosity of others in her family. "Her eldest brother was settin' out one evenin' an' he called t' me. So I walked over to see what he had to say. Say, 'Tell me you're a prizefighter?' I say, 'Yeah, I box.' 'When you go'n fight again?' Differ'nt questions, things like that. 'I like t' see y'.' Sho' 'nuff, next fight I had, he took Dorothy, he took Dorothy's mother, he took his wife. All of 'em went to the fight." Afterwards, to celebrate his victory, Collis treated the Simons to "whatsonever they wanted to eat and drink" at a restaurant in the neighborhood. He hadn't yet won the blessing of Dorothy's mother, but he had become a hit with the rest of the family.

His opponent that night was Josh Willis, an experienced fighter he would meet in a sequence of rematches. Willis was also new in town, and he happened to be living in the neighborhood also, a circumstance that caused both him and Collis to take special care in preparing for the fight. "See, Willis, he likeded Dorothy. He usta come around the drugsto' in the next block from her house, tryin' to see if he couldn' find sumpum on the QT. But Dorothy tol' him she already had a boyfriend. So he tol' her, 'Well, I'm from Califownia. He ain' never fought nobody, he's fought bums. I'm off the West Coast, ain' nothin' but good boys out there. I'm go'n knock y' boyfriend out.' You know, shootin' a lot a bull off. So Dorothy tol' me, 'I don' think you oughta fight that boy, that boy might knock you out.' Aw, Willis, he— You know, you do got some *bad* boys on that West Coast, got them Mexicans, them Spanions out there, shoot, they *come* to fight. If you cain' fight, you better not git in the ring wit' them. Boy, I know! So that's how that . . . Dorothy tol' me about Willis's talk. I tol' her, 'I don' worry 'bout it, wait till the night a the fight.' I was in wonderful condition, an' I had fought some good boys, worked with quite a few heavy-weights outta my class, an' that's why I always thought I had a chance."

The fight "didn' go the limit." He laughed, describing Willis's eye as "so swoll up he couldn' hardly see the next day" when he made his customary stop at the neighborhood drugstore.

June 7, 1983

The older section of Parish Prison shares a city block with the Criminal District Courts Building, to which it is connected by a hive of passageways. Since Kevin Phillips, Alvin Jr.'s brother, was from out of state and hadn't gone through the application process and waiting period necessary to become one of his brother's three approved visitors, it was necessary for us to go to the courts building to try for a special pass. There, in a small office fronting a barred corridor, Kevin fell mute and left the explaining to me. He stood behind my shoulder, his back inches from the wall, slim, wiry, the least bulky of the Phillips men of his generation. The studied neutrality of his stance and the blankness of his expression gave him the bearing of someone who might have been there to make a delivery or perform a similar errand—except that his clothes were too fresh: stiff Yankees baseball cap, starched jeans, spotless leather basketball shoes.

The bailiff, a small, sturdy man in his late fifties, listened to me patiently but without apparent interest. Then he told me that the captain we needed to see would be back sometime the next day. I sensed Kevin's smothered rage, but I didn't know what else I could say other than, uselessly, that the would-be visitor needed to return very soon to New York. "Just out of curiosity," the bailiff wondered, since we had established I wasn't a lawyer, what business of mine was anything pertaining to the Phillips brothers?

When I mentioned my relation to their grandfather, Collis Phillips, the bailiff's gray-green eyes suddenly teared over and he came around the counter. "Collis Phillips," he said. "I've known Collis from a boy."

Without prompting, he started telling us about the drug-store and the neighborhood in the thirties. Kevin maintained his invisibility, and soon the man spoke only to me. He was Wellington Dejoie, the youngest of eight brothers. Dejoie's Drugstore, his family's business, for decades was a focal point of the neighborhood in which Collis and Dorothy met. It had only recently been sold.

The ethnic emphases in Wellington Dejoie's explanations showed that, despite his olive skin and fine strands of thinning hair, he proudly considered himself to be black. When I brought the subject back around to Collis, his eyes moistened again. "He wouldn't know me," he said. "I was just a kid then. But he knew some of my brothers." Dejoie remembered standing in a doorway or corner at the Bulls' Club and watching Collis and Josh Willis train. He said there was great excitement in the place whenever they were present; they were like fierce young princes in the neighborhood, and both of them were nice to him and other young boys. Dejoie looked unexpectedly at Kevin and said, "Your grandmother was a beautiful young woman."

While Wellington Dejoie talked, another bailiff had emerged from the prison corridor. He moved about us with a straddling step that suggested failing health. I sensed I knew him, but I couldn't identify his chalky features above the black uniform. Then, with a small shock, I recognized Lou Messina—a promoter whom I once met when I was at ringside with Collis; this had been during one of Messina's attempts to revive boxing at the Municipal Auditorium near the edge of the French Quarter. A fast-talking Italian, depicted in local sports columns as a Runyonesque character, Messina was one of the first boxing people I consulted when I began gathering background in 1981. Over the phone he had praised Collis, then advised me to "think twice before stickin' your neck out" to try to help his son Alvin. He said Alvin "never liked whites too much. Almost anything would set him off. Him and his daddy were two different people, you understand." Worst of all in Messina's view, Alvin "argued with his father in the gym."

Wellington Dejoie now drew me toward Lou Messina and explained I was connected to Collis. Messina hesitated, but after I mentioned our telephone conversation, he said with uncertain conviction, sure, he remembered me, and he shook my hand vigorously. When I introduced Kevin, stressing he was one of Alvin's sons, Messina paused, as if stirred and perplexed to be unexpectedly beholding both the past and the present. When he spoke, he enthusiastically recalled knowing Kevin from when the children's mother used to bring them to Alvin's fights in the Auditorium. He felt sure Kevin had sharp memories of that.

Kevin answered, yes, he was aware of those fights, but because he had fallen from a second-floor porch when he was very young, he couldn't really remember his childhood.

Messina didn't seem to register what he had just been told, saying he would bet Kevin remembered the fight posters, how he paid Kevin and his brothers to tape them to light poles on Orleans Avenue.

Kevin's answer was very general. And again he referred to the injury to his head. His voice was free of regional accent, and there was no tact in it.

"You remember *me*, don't you?"

Kevin hesitated—during the embarrassing pause, I wanted to press between them and somehow smooth over the awkwardness—then he shook his head; no, he didn't think so.

Messina had stopped looking at him and now dug in his pocket past coins and keys. He drew forth a glittering money clip as he asked after Collis, then murmured sympathetically when I told him Collis's leg had been amputated. Before I could explain the reason for the surgery, the promoter turned the thick clip over—it was decorated with jewels or rhinestones and, I guessed, padded with ones—and peeled off a twenty. "Tell him Lou Messina sent him that," he said, extending the bill between two fingers to Kevin and already beginning to move away.

As we parted, I wondered if Messina knew as surely as I felt I did that Collis would never see that money. It occurred to me later that he probably knew this very well.

By then Wellington Dejoie was on his way out too. But, eyes drying, he gave me his phone number. Now that so many of the Dejoies were gone and he lived by himself, he said, he had time enough to tell me more about the neighborhood.

It had grown so late that, for the day, we gave up trying to gain permission for Kevin to visit Alvin Jr. As we left the building, Kevin tried to hand me Lou Messina's twenty-dollar bill, for safekeeping, but I suggested he pass it along to his grandfather himself when we saw him that evening at Charity. In the hospital room I gave Collis Lou Messina's regards, but if Kevin handed over the money while we were there, I didn't see it. The next day Kevin delayed his departure for New York. We returned to the courts building and he was approved to visit his brother—who would eventually serve time for a crime committed, I feel sure, by someone else in the family.

Winter 1984

The strictness of Dorothy Simon's family and her mother's wariness of Collis limited their courtship. Since the Bulls' Club was considered inappropriate for Dorothy by her brothers and by Collis, secret Sunday-night meetings at the movies constituted their only social outings.

Until the early sixties, in New Orleans blacks could sit only in the balconies of theaters that were also patronized by whites. The Granada, at the edge of Dorothy and Collis's neighborhood, was integrated in this way. Situated closer to them, the Lincoln Theater was exclusively black. He would meet her at either the Granada or the Lincoln, and he remembered these Sundays as especially sweet.

Also pleasant for him to recall was his favorite screen star, Bing Crosby. He liked Crosby's agreeable film personality and always referred to him as "Bing," inflecting the word as if it named an old friend. He said he admired Crosby because he "gave blacks parts" and headlined marquees that included Louis Armstrong, Cab Calloway, and the Mills Brothers.

Busyness, hustle, and the rigor of training crowded his weekdays at this time. Even though the owners of the bar where he first worked in New Orleans began to rely on him, he soon gave up that job. He could do better cultivating high-tipping customers in various shine parlors. His first regular shine job was at a newsstand on St. Charles just above Canal Street. Befriending a man named Keystone, who worked at the stand as a delivery boy, enabled him to catch on there. It was a likely spot for him because the sports crowd came in for racing forms and other betting information and next door stood the Whitney Bank, the city's most venerable. As a result he gained useful acquaintanceships among gamblers and investors and had chances to "catch those fellas that had to be up to the minute" and to "handle 'em nice."

Not long after he left his job at the bar and started working entire days at the newsstand, a white man named Izzy, who had seen him sparring in one of the city's gyms, told him about a better shine job working for Nick Bouzin, a Greek who ran a hat shop a block away on the streetcar line on the corner of Carondolet and Common. Izzy walked him over and introduced him to Bouzin, and soon he was shining shoes in the hat shop and delivering hats. "You couldn' find no nicer guy than Mista Nick," he told me, echoing his generous descriptions of others he had worked for or served.

The hat shop adjoined Rubenstein's, a prosperous men's-clothing store, which eventually absorbed Nick Bouzin's place and now occupies most of that side of Carondolet between Common and Canal. But in the thirties, "Rubenstein's wasn't that large. Rubenstein had one li'l sto' there, an' I usta shine Mista Ru— I don't know if he's livin' now or not, but I usta shine his shoes. Yeh, Rubenstein's shoes. He would always gi' me half a dolla. Wanted to know when the next fight was!"

To the tips he made hustling from his base at the hat shop, he added whatever he could earn sparring at a white gym called Kelly's, usually stopping there after business hours to see if any of the white fighters wanted to pay him to spar with them. It was probably in Kelly's that he met his manager, Tom Brooks, a white man who "held the contract on Kill White," a regionally fabled black middleweight then ending his career in New Orleans. He felt it was a big break that "Mista Brooks picked me up. (I tol' y' 'bout him, *To*emmy Brooks, I sees his son round town now, lives out there in Metry.)"

In his first fight for Tom Brooks, he traveled west "to a place called Crowley. A small town." (Whispering, and slowly, as if very tired.) "Rice town, I call it. I boxed a boy up there by the name a Kid Clarence.

"Fight was pretty close. An' Clarence up there— Them white people up there, they thought there was nuttin' like him. White fella up there, he owned him—handled him anyway.

"An' so we boxed up there . . . an' I lost the decision to him. I never did complain, y' know, or have a lot a gripes if I lose a fight. I jus' say, 'Well, it was a bad night f' me.' "

His next fight was one he felt he shouldn't have taken, "but the Depression was on an', y' know, *you was black*: you took whatsonever you could git." His opponent was Fast Black, a larger man than he was: "At the West Side, over the river, usta have a arena, I don' know if it's still there. I fought him on a Sunday evenin'. That was a heavyweight. If I'd a had the sense I have now, I never woulda fought him. Too much weight. But I was young. Cocky. Crazy, that was the main thing. I lost the decision to him. I had him on the flo' coupla times. But too much weight, too much strength. I think he had me down fo' times. Good fight, aw right! But . . . but he licked me. Yeh, he licked me. Too much—I shouldn't—but work was kinda hard to git."

The Crowley fight wouldn't have been reported in the New Orleans paper, and since his knockout record at home was still intact, he was paid, he said, seventy-five dollars for his loss to Fast Black. To my questioning how he felt about the purse, he answered, "Well, you thought you had some money."

He saved little of this or his other ring earnings, spending his small purses in the openhanded manner typical of many fighters. With this fight he began a certain ritual extravagance that he repeated before most of his others. "I buy a suit a clothes off the stick now," he told me, but then while in training for a fight for which he had enough notice, he would visit Bell's Tailors on Rampart and have himself measured for something personalized that he would wear after his night's work when he "walked the street *down*."

The money he made fighting scarcely lasted longer than the night. Soon after each of these fights, which usually were staged in the Coliseum now, he would be back shining shoes on Carondolet. He scraped by in this way until he was offered a job as a porter at the General Finance Company.

This prospering business, which specialized in industrial and automobile loans, was a few doors from the hat shop. There, for his first regular wage in New Orleans, he worked as a runner—a messenger and deliveryman—during business hours. Then in the early evening, he cleaned the offices, the lavatories, and the toilets.

A white building engineer with whom he was friendly, Bill Bezant, put him onto this opportunity, which also led to better connections. "Bill took me over there, introduced me to the people. They signed them papers f' me, bought my uniforms. 'General Finance' on 'em. They took care a havin' 'em laundered. Three uniforms, so I could change twice a week, wouldn' be walkin' round the office with a smell. See, I have to go to the bank, make deposits. I worked there a good long time."

Even though he now had steady work, Dorothy's mother steadfastly withheld her approval of him—possibly because he continued to spend time in gyms and, though he never drank, in places like the Bulls' Club. Without her mother's blessing, he and Dorothy crossed the river and were married by a justice of the peace on the West Bank. In preparation for living with Dorothy, he had moved out of the room he shared with a friend and rented another on his own. Although their new address, like his old one, was near the Simons' house, Dorothy was able to keep out of sight until her mother reluctantly accepted the marriage.

Despite his new mother-in-law's resentment, this was one of the better periods in his life: he had married a woman he loved, and unlike many of his black acquaintances, he earned a regular salary plus windfalls from his fights and his sparring sessions with whites at Kelly's. There was time yet before Dorothy would begin pressing him to move to one of the housing projects soon to be built at sites around the city—clean, new neighborhoods intensely desired by the majority of the people they knew.

12

□

Spring 1984

Scraps.

I forget what he intended to fish for the morning he jerked open his cardboard dresser drawer and we saw, in a shiny jumble, what had become of keepsakes and the scrapbook he thought lost.

Though the drawer contained fragments of some of the accounts of his fights, their sequence is unclear. Yet the newsprint reports, each dateless and fragile to the touch as dried lepidoptera, preserve a sense of both time and its absence.

NEGRO FI*****

COLISEUM ARENA

COME EARLY TO AVOID THE RU**

32 ROUNDS OF BATTLING

A REAL TREAT FOR FIGHT F***

FRIDAY, 8:30 P.*

12 ROUNDS

AL JACKSON VS. CORLOS PHILLIPS

SAVANNAH, GA.   10TH WARD

JACKSON FOUGHT 3 TIMES IN

MADISON SQUARE G*****

WHITE TO MEET VARGAS IN MAIN NEGRO CON-
TEST. Collins Phillips, who was slated to meet Joss
Willis in the headline event of Matchmaker Ovalisiti's
negro boxing show Friday night, injured his hand in
training Monday and Ovalisiti was forced to pit Kayo
White in the top number Friday night at the Coliseum . . .

This clipping suggests circumstances very different from
those surrounding his and Josh Willis's first fight, which was
little more than a neighborhood affair. He described New
Orleans's black boxing scene in this way: "Fights wasn't that
regular when I first come to New Orleans. Boxin' was bad,
bad when I came here with Dixon. In fact, we didn't have
any black professional fights at the Coliseum at all. We had
fights at the club, the San Jacinto Center on Dumaine Street.
I won about fo', five fights down there. Knockouts. That put
black boxin' back in the socket, an' the Coliseum come back
in swing. An' this Italian fella Lou Ovalasti—*hell*uva nice
guy!—he started promotin' at the Coliseum, started promotin' black fights. The black fights started goin' so big that
that's when Martin Burke fell back in swing. He was a big-
time promoter. Before that Martin Burke never did promote
nothin' but white fights. They had some outstandin' houses
at the Coliseum."

The Coliseum was a large arena with a seating capacity of
several thousand. It stood in a black neighborhood where
Conti crosses North Roman. The neighborhood included a
public elementary school, which is still there and which
whites still do not attend.

At intervals in the thirties and forties, promoters such as
Ovalisiti and Burke staged twice-weekly boxing shows at the
Coliseum. Whites fought on Mondays, blacks on Fridays.
Admission for local cards ranged from fifty cents for ringside
to about a quarter for upstairs. Though seating was
segregated—whites and blacks sat on opposite sides of the
ring—a good view was available to anyone who could pay
for it. For a time, Collis received top local billing, and after

one of his fights with Josh Willis he was named Southern (Negro) middleweight and light heavyweight champion. He also fought preliminaries on the cards featuring well-known out-of-towners. Though his purses were small, there was usually more than enough to finance a ritual visit to Bell's Tailors.

ALL NEGRO BOUTS RESULT IN KAYOS. Every bout on the negro boxing card Friday night at the Coliseum ended in a knockout. The show drew a large crowd and the fans saw some lively action.

In the top 10-round bout, Corlos Phillips stopped Jess Willis in the fourth round . . .

The battle royal, in which five battlers participated, was the outstanding event of the night. All the fighters threw punches from all angles and the fans were in an uproar. One of the fighters lost his glove during the scramble and before it could be put on again he kept throwing punches with his bare fist.

Phillips put Willis away in the fourth round with an uppercut . . .

His best paydays were for two meetings with a main-event fighter from Miami.

FEATURE BOUT AT COLISEUM MARKED BY BAD DECISION. Headed by a feature bout that was one of the best seen at the local arena in a long while, the weekly boxing show Friday night furnished some very interesting action which was marred only by a bad decision in the main event.

This bout found Carlos Phillips seemingly winning a point decision over P. G. Carson of Florida in the 12-round feature, but getting only a draw. Phillips appeared to have an edge in seven rounds with Carson winning four and one even . . .

The questionable upset decision apparently generated much interest, and he told me more than once that the rematch "drew a packed house."

CARLOS PHILLIPS LOSES BY KAYO TO P. G. CARSON . . . the kayo punch proper was a strange one. As the fighters broke from a clinch, Carson brought both hands up to each side of Phillips' face and Carlos dropped like a log and was counted out.

He described Carson's decisive weapon as "the crab punch," an illegal tactic—evidently tolerated at the Friday fights—of delivering a blow simultaneously to each eardrum. He said that night he lost his title, and some of his hearing.

Dorothy was apparently more disturbed by the fight than he was. Not so much because of the controversial manner of the loss as because Carson's crab punch caused his left ear to blossom into a fighter's cauliflower.

After they married, she feared he would be permanently injured in the ring, and she urged him to quit. When he reminded her the money he sometimes made fighting was more than he could earn in any other way, she told him, " 'I'm satisfied if you make fifty cents a week. Why can't you be satisfied?' "

Yet even though they now had an infant of their own and another on the way, there was more boxing.

BOXING!   BOXING!   BOXING!
COLISEUM ARENA
NORTH ROMAN AND CONTI STREETS
FRIDAY, MAY 10, 8:30 P.M.

BOB MANUELS
vs.
COLLINS PHILLIPS
10 ROUNDS

$.27 GALLERY, $.42 RINGSIDE
(ALL TAX INCLUDED)

This fight, a knockout of Bob Manuel, was his final win. Shortly afterwards his boxing career ended, as the careers of the large majority of fighters do—in defeat.

The Ring Record Book reports that lightweight and welterweight great Barney Ross fought in New Orleans on June 27, 1937, in Pelican Stadium. Collis was on the black part of the card.

Moyse Howard, 178, knocked Carlos Phillips, 161, out of the ring into the laps of several fans and knocked him down several other times, but the game Phillips was still in there pitching at the final gong, although Howard received the decision.

As we looked at this clipping, he tried unsuccessfully to remember the names of "the important white men" whom he knew from the Central Business District and on whom he had fallen. He said that when they passed each other on the streets during working hours, they would all share a laugh over how they had pushed him back into the ring and made it possible for him to go the distance—in the last bout for which he would be paid.

I assumed his fondest memories concerned boxing, and one day I said as much. He corrected me at once, saying that his happiest moment by far was the birth of his and Dorothy's first child, Collis Phillips, Jr. This statement confused me because I knew Collis Jr. was younger than Gloria. Then he matter-of-factly explained that his first namesake died in infancy. Pneumonia was more often fatal then, and "Dorothy was a young mother." I know nothing else about this misfortune other than that he was also a young father and that many buildings in their neighborhood—and all over town—are vulnerable to New Orleans's damp winters. The same day he told me of the death of his first son, I learned that another child of theirs, Jean, had died of pneumonia in her eighteenth month. Their first child, Gloria, was born in 1933—and the surviving Collis Jr. in 1940.

In speaking of the thirties, when he and Dorothy were young parents and he worked at General Finance and boxed the likes of P. G. Carson and Josh Willis, he dwelt far more on the good times than the bad. He showed pleasure in talking about what a fine dancer Dorothy had been and how they "would wear a hole in the flo' " on the nights Lou Messina "brought in top bands from up the line" to perform at the Coliseum. The bands, he recalled, would set up in the ring, and the crowd would swing and wheel in the spaces cleared of the rows of folding seats. He said Dorothy could dance the whole night to "the Count's 'One O'Clock Jump' and Duke's 'Take the A-Train.' " Other nights when he and she were still "bummin' "—before their other babies were born—they would go to the Roof Garden, an open-air club atop a building on Tulane Avenue and Saratoga, for "Dancing under the Stars."

Later, as constant responsibility for children began to change Dorothy's life, he would go to dances alone—but not to be entertained. He went then to make extra money to support their growing family. Lou Messina also promoted local dance music—at the Gypsy Tea Room, a night spot at St. Ann near Basin—and he needed someone reliable and physically formidable to work the door, which Collis did, using his personalized hand stamp: "Dance Pass/C. B. Phillips."

His and Dorothy's social life survived their first few children at least, and as long as she was well enough they continued to go out together from time to time. Party invitations from various organizations are among the few dated items from his drawer. The local Boxer's Guild was another organization that involved them socially. For a while after he retired from competing, he was its president and worked organizing dances and suppers to raise money for amateur programs and destitute ex-fighters. He hoped the Guild could persuade promoters to increase the pay especially for fighters in prelims, but there is no evidence his effort succeeded.

He hoped also to earn other money at the Coliseum as a referee. Two of the regular referees for the Friday cards were black. But after he worked a few fights, he found himself in conflict with the white referees. Rather than dramatize the futility of his racial position and lose favor among people who might help him in other situations, he withdrew, kept his grievance to himself, and never refereed again.

When General Finance closed its offices in around 1937, its president, W. D. Troyer, made certain Collis had another job—just as he had sometimes made unclaimed vehicles available for his personal use. Troyer had opened a new enterprise in the 300 block of Carondolet—a New Orleans branch of the White System, Inc., a loan company based in Jackson, Mississippi—and he hired Collis to be night porter in these offices. Soon a friend named Newsboy Brown—"a fo'-round fighter"—had "brought me in behind him" at Woodward, Wight & Co. LTD., a large wholesale concern that handled construction materials. At first his labor here, in the warehouse district, was alongside Brown running the machine that cut lengths of steel used to reinforce concrete, but soon he was taken into the business offices to do the sort of work he had performed at General Finance.

While at General Finance he had become a personal helper to one of the stockholders, a childless executive named Ballix, and his wife. It was arranged for Collis to acquire a chauffeur's license and, wearing his dark General Finance uniform and cap, to drive them. On Sundays he washed the Ballixes' Oldsmobile and tended their yard. He held other side jobs in the late thirties and the forties, among them responsibility for cleaning the Whitney Bank and the offices of an office supply company on Carondolet. In addition, he continued to frequent various gyms and began "trainin' prospects," young whites at Kelly's and young blacks at the San Jacinto and uptown at the Bulls' Club. Dorothy helped him when his interest in his fighters conflicted with his night jobs. With Gloria, and later Collis Jr. and Alvin in tow, Dorothy would take a bus or a streetcar to the Central Business District in the evening. There, while one or more of the children slept on a blanket or lay strapped in a chair, she cleaned—or helped him clean—the offices of the White System, the Whitney, and Seiffert and Sons Office Supply.

Gloria told me about helping her mother with this work as she and I waited in the corridor during the parts of her son's trials that she chose not to witness. She remembered emptying spittoons and dusting desktops with a feather duster she wished she could keep, and Collis Jr. trying to bag trash and making a mess. Her main duty was to keep him and Alvin out of Dorothy's way. Then her father would be coming, she said. She could see him on his way crossing from the Whitney or from the direction of the gym. But "he wouldn't be walkin'. Honey, he *ran!* My daddy ran where he went. He'd be runnin'. Oh, he was fine!"

Over the years Collis's most valuable connection was his friendship with Mike Cusimano, who was a former successful pro lightweight and a self-made businessman. "I usta handle money for Mike, lot a money. An' we never had a minute's confusion 'bout so much as a nickel. In my book, you couldn't find no better guy than Mike. White *or* black."

They first met in one of the gyms where Collis, as a favored black, sometimes sparred with whites. "That was a long time back there . . . back there in the thirties . . . where I first met Mike . . . Weaver had a gym, I b'lieve that was on Galvez Street. I was up there an' I happened to see Mike. I watched him train. Looked to see how he look. He looked good enough. An' they was talkin' 'bout goin' to Califownia. Mista Weaver. Irvin' Bourrier. Mike. A coupla more boys. I don't remember the boys' names, but it was two more boys. An' they went to Califownia. But they didn' do so hot out there. So Mista Whatchacallum brought 'em back. You see I talk a lot. You know *that* by bein' rightchere! An' I was talkin', talkin' to Mike, aksin' him all about the fights out there on the West Coast. Was the pay any good? That's the main thing a fighter wanna know 'bout, the pay. An' from that, me an' Mike, we started, you know, communicatin' wit' each other. Talk—*just* as friends, you know—talkin'. Mike watn't married then.

"Well, after that, see, Mike was coatin' his wife, an' I usta see 'em all the time because I was runnin' a gym right there on Rampart an' they usta come walkin' down the street—I don' know where they went, but they'd go down that way—an' we'd always wave to each other. An' Mike had that grocery, so I started goin' by there. Mike an' them usta sell them samiches in there, them po-boy samiches. They'd put *two* meats in there. I think it was a quarter, no, fifteen cents we usta pay for 'em. So I started buyin' groceries from Mike, an' from then on we got closer an' closer an' I got where I could go there an' his mother would let me git groceries an' didn't have no money! Till payday."

On the day in 1982 that he agreed to meet me in the empty offices of the Louisiana State Boxing Commission, Mike Cusimano answered my questions with good-humored candor. A slimly fit, prosperous white man in his sixties, his face bearing no sign of his years in the ring, Mike downplayed his own accomplishments and spoke dismissively of various past favors I knew he had done for Collis—in particular, bond help for Jerry after each of a pair of arrests. He volunteered instead that Collis was that rare trainer who would give as much attention to a diligent beginner as he would to a contender.

Mike retired from boxing in 1938, the year he graduated from Tulane University. But he continued to help his mother run the French Quarter grocery store their family had lived above since his childhood. The Cusimanos had moved their personal residence out of the Quarter, but Mike's mother continued to keep the store open late. Someone was needed there for her protection on Saturday nights. Mike asked Collis to stay with her. This was their first business association: "I'd come round there 'bout five-thirty, six o'clock in the evenin'. Before night. I'd always stay with her till she closed up. Sit behind the curtain."

I asked if he ever had to protect her.

"No-o-o, we never did have no trouble. Never did. We were *very* fortunate. Nobody never came in to—to . . . Well, I was right where I could see everything went on at the counter. All I had to do was git up an' take the pistol off the shelf an' I'm right *in* the do'. But we never did have no— Well, see, Miz Cusimano was so *nice* to everybody. Blacks round there likeded her a lots. See, she helped a lot a po' people didn't have no money. They'd pick groceries, she'd let 'em have it. *Trust* 'em, things like that. She had a lot a white trade too."

More than once, he told me about the extra groceries she gave him—staples that helped feed his young family. On one of my first visits to him in Gloria's apartment, he mentioned that he still sometimes telephoned Mike's mother "just to say hello and ask how she feel. You know, when you git old and out the action, people'll f'git you, quick."

In 1940 Mike left the family business and went to work as personnel manager at the Lehde Shipyard, where oceango-ing vessels for the war effort were being built. Collis might have stayed at Woodward, Wight & Co. indefinitely had conscription laws not required men his age to serve in the military or hold a defense job. He would just as soon have volunteered—"I was young, it didn't make me no differ'nce." But his first duty was to make a living for Dorothy, Gloria, and Collis Jr. Through Mike's influence, Collis was hired to work in the yard at Lehde, an opportunity that enabled him to stay home and support his family.

Before he left Woodward, Wight, though, he came out of retirement to appear in a large War Bond drive boxing show at the Coliseum. A fragment from a Woodward, Wight photo publication shows him in street clothes standing before a sun-dappled warehouse door, his wide smile in shadow: "***lis Phillips One Time Champ— *** All Proceeds *** Fifth War Bond Drive ****** offered his services **** This is a splendid spirit, and *** to give Collis a big hand."

The fight, his finale, was a second try against the light heavyweight Maurice Howard: "***** Moise Howard, 175, knocked out Carlos Phillips, 161¾, in the third *****."

13

□

Summer 1984

Despite the international situation and the disappointment of his last fight, this period held bright moments for him. The people he worked for continued to demonstrate their fondness in terms of periodic windfalls: for example, a card from his scrapbook—"Xmas/39, White System, Best Wishes to Collis, $600"—bears sixteen signatures, though in one secretarial hand. And shortly after he started work at the shipyard in 1940, Mike brought him in off the yard to serve as chauffeur to Pendleton Lehde, the president of the company.

Lehde was an exacting man who had gone through a number of chauffeurs. Collis immediately recognized that "you couldn't play with him too much." As a result, he was able to drive for Lehde throughout the forties. The extra pay was relatively good, and Lehde was so pleased with him that on a trip to Washington, he saw to it that Collis received a permanent deferment from military service.

When not driving one of Pendleton Lehde's sequence of black Cadillacs, he operated the mail truck at the shipyard. As at General Finance, he was bonded, a fact of which he was exceedingly proud. He handled much of the company's banking. He also co-signed notes for other workers—"blacks *and* whites," he reminded me. A worn pocket notepad shows that he had further means of income: scrawled columns from 1944 and 1945 itemize his practice of lending small weekly sums to men on the yard—at a rate of two bits on the dollar.

With the birth of Alvin in 1942, their small residence became too crowded. Dorothy had visited friends in the new housing projects, and she was impressed by the roomier apartments. She kept after him until he had their name put on waiting lists for the projects near them uptown—the Magnolia and the Lafitte. But the lists were long. Dorothy was restless to move. He made inquiries at another project, one still under construction, the St. Bernard, which is on the downtown side of the Central Business District. It was still not completely finished when they moved in late in 1942. For fourteen dollars a month they had five rooms in which everything was bright and unused by anyone else. They were one of the St. Bernard project's original families.

Collis's increasing extra work and moneymaking arrangements left too little of his time for Dorothy and the children. Connie and Farris told me Dorothy sometimes had help from family and friends, but it was never enough. She remained a pressured young mother with too many domestic responsibilities even though they continued to live better than most of their neighbors.

The late forties and the fifties repeated the pattern of their lives. Connie was born in 1946, Jerry in 1948, and Farris in 1950. Collis went on working evenings and weekends, compulsively pulling in every dollar he could earn; but though his main source of income changed, his labor, like Dorothy's, remained fundamentally the same.

With defense contracts depleted, the Lehde Shipyard closed in 1948. When Mike moved over to become personnel manager at the Standard Fruit & Steamship Company, a large produce and shipping concern, he took Collis with him to work in the mail room and to drive a three-wheel delivery scooter. During lunch hours, Collis earned a second wage and free meals by working the cash register in the company cafeteria. As at the shipyard, Mike also arranged for him to be personal chauffeur to one of the executives, Blaise D'Antoni.

D'Antoni was "a li'l shawt, stocky man" in his fifties, someone who impressed Collis with his sure sense of his own authority: "He didn' take no shit off nobody. Man, wit' Mist' Blaise, I'd park that Cadillac anyplace he felt like. 'Pull over rightchere at the curb.' Cop'd come up, then step back, 'Oh, yessir, Mister D'Antoni, good afternoon, how are you, sir? No, no, sir, it's all right, your driver can keep it right there.' She-e, nobody messed wit' *him*."

His new boss's keen interest in boxing was one reason Collis was able to please him. In the early fifties Blaise D'Antoni had a gym built at the corner of St. Charles and Poydras on property bordering the Central Business District. Collis described the layout as "right up to the minute, showers, a sweat box, new ring, everything you need to make a fighter." The gym was called Curley's—after a popular bald boxing man, Curley Gagliano, whom Blaise D'Antoni put in charge. Collis was one of Curley's main evening helpers.

It was in the fifties at Curley's that he had his first monetary success as a trainer. During his comings and goings about town, he looked for "good boys" to bring into the gym from off the streets. And late in the morning on Saturdays he went back to his old uptown neighborhood and worked with amateurs in the Dryades Street YMCA. In this way he developed Larry "Monk" Armstead and Andrew "Boodie" Brown, who both became competitive pro fighters for him.

Eventually Andrew Brown served time in Angola. While there, he wrote to Collis for help. Collis turned to Mike, who was the manager of almost every pro he trained. Shortly before Brown's successful parole hearing, Collis wrote his fighter the only letter of his I saw.

Dear Son,
    Only a few lines to let you hear from me, I am well & hope when these lines reach your hands it will find you the same.

You will be call back before the board on June 3. When you are released the lawyer said he would bring you back in his car. So take every thing easy.

Charles is fighting a return match with Al Williams. He needs this win. He is 8 rating in ring magazine. We had plan to fight Rory Calhoun in Pel Stadium. Since Calhoun lost the other night we will work on something else.

This is only a few words to easy your mine and set you right do as I am telling you if you want to get out.

I come to a close.

> Yours truly
> Collis B. Phillips, Sr.

The "Charles" mentioned in the letter was Charley Joseph, the most successful fighter Collis ever handled. Joseph is now a stalwart leader in the Stevedores' Union and a regular referee of local fights. Collis "found" him in the Milne Boys' Home, a rehabilitation institution for delinquent boys, where he helped develop an amateur program. Charles Joseph was a very young teenager separated from his parents when Collis began bringing him home on weekends. Gloria remembered Joseph as "just a raggedy little boy then; he couldn't raise his arms for all the holes and tears under 'em." With Collis guiding him, Joseph compiled an outstanding amateur record. For a time, he lived with Collis and Dorothy. In 1951 he turned pro. During the decade, he developed into a top middleweight contender, and Collis accompanied him on bus trips to Miami and on plane rides to Boston, Las Vegas, Chicago, Los Angeles, and New York. Charley Joseph almost always won, so most of these trips became flush occasions. Mimicking her father, Connie told me he "always went first-class!" and when he was in " 'New Yawk!' " he would stay nowhere but in midtown at the Sheraton.

Although these years were profitable and in some ways personally satisfying to him, they were very hard on Dorothy. There were obstetrical complications when Farris was born, and she remained very weak for months after the delivery. Forgoing Charity, Collis took her to Flint-Goodridge, the city's only hospital staffed exclusively by blacks. In order to pay for an operation and other medical fees, he incurred $2,500 in debts. Dorothy had difficulty standing in the weeks following her return from the hospital. At first she used a walker; afterwards a wheelchair.

The family's domestic life was further complicated by Gloria's early marriage, in 1949 at the age of sixteen, to Lionel Sorina, a young neighbor soon to show symptoms of mental illness. Collis disapproved of the marriage, but at that age Gloria was headstrong. There were violent quarrels. I heard rumors, which he denied, that he sometimes beat her. Gloria's version to me was that she was "mischievous" and deserved every beating she received. There were nights when she found herself locked out both from her parents' apartment and from the one she shared with Sorina in the Desire project, a considerable walking distance away.

With Dorothy now a near-invalid, much of the housework and child care fell to the other children. Collis Jr. wasn't much domestic help, and Connie was still too young. It was Alvin who mostly took charge of it. More than once Gloria told me how she loved him at that time: "Alvin was a good chile. Quiet. Never caught a whippin'!"

Soon Gloria had children of her own and wasn't often able to cook for the family as she previously had done. She spoke of going by the apartment and finding Alvin preparing meals even though he was still just a boy. As Dorothy's condition worsened, Alvin would stay home from school to sit with her and to clean the apartment. Connie said that, more so than the rest of his brothers and sisters, Alvin liked solitude and that, in this, he was similar to his mother. He stayed home more often after the first appearance of Dorothy's hallucinations.

Despite pressures, there were Saturday mornings, early. This was the one time during the week when their father almost always was home. There would be a big breakfast, which they helped him cook. Afterwards they would "make groceries," usually with Gloria and Connie inside doing the shopping under his instructions while he read the newspaper or talked to acquaintances as he waited in the parking lot, sometimes in a company car he had use of for the weekend.

On those Saturdays on which he didn't have to hurry in order to open a gym, he would give them his full attention during breakfast, quizzing them on arithmetic or current events and measuring their heights on the doorframe next to the kitchen table. Connie was usually the quickest to answer; she was the most successful in school, and they all understood that she was his favorite. When she grew older she cooked for him and ironed his clothes, and both he and she frankly told me he always gave more pocket money to her than he did to his others. They both believed she would go on to college and pursue a profession.

She distinguished herself in another way when he brought out the training gloves and supervised sparring sessions among his children. He made up play names and elaborate ring announcements. Connie told me the names, but, neglecting to note them, I remember only that Jerry's name ended in "-head" and the first three words of Connie's were "Little Miss Brown . . ." Until their younger brothers began to mature physically, Gloria and Connie boxed them as equals.

Like so many other Americans, Collis and Dorothy yearned to live in a house of their own. He made a start toward realizing this dream by buying two lots of the land that was being developed just on the other side of Senate Street, the northern boundary of the project. He planned to build a house on one lot and a gym on the other. With his gym in the neighborhood, he would have less trouble attracting prospects from around there to come in off the street; and having his house next door would give him more time for his family. But as Dorothy's health bills mounted, this dream became less and less probable. She had undergone a second operation, and she was now constantly on medication for

her nerves. He had to sell his lots. He described them to me
one cool afternoon when I found him outside in his lawn
chair. As we looked across Senate at jammed-together houses
and small yards, a clutter of development that spreads with
increasing opulence from the project toward Lake Ponchartrain, he spoke of his hopes for the lots, their previous
purchase and sale price, and his estimate of their current
worth. Although he mentioned the lots to me only on that
day, they were a subject that must have recurred often in
family talk, for, except for Alvin, each of his children brought
them up at least once soon after we met.

Through the fifties Charley Joseph's continuing success
kept Collis "toward the front" of the New Orleans boxing
scene. In 1955 during a trip to the Northeast, when Joseph
was 27–1, Collis felt that he and prominent promoter Sam
Silverman had reached a verbal agreement that guaranteed
a title fight. But the match fell through.

Joseph remained highly ranked for the next three years.
He started 1959 by decisioning Henry Hank, a fearsome-
punching light heavyweight, in New Orleans in March. Even
though this was Joseph's sixty-third fight, he was still only
twenty-six years old. He had been loyal to Collis, but he also
apparently believed that, under different direction, he would
have a better chance to go all the way. A group of businessmen had been talking to him, and Joseph gave them permission to talk to Collis. More than twenty years afterward,
his hurt still evident, he had little to say to me about their
meeting: "I jus' tol' 'em, 'I'll take five thousand for his
contrac'.' We did it that way." But after I thought we had
moved on to another subject, he added, "You know, a fighter
you gits from a young amateur is lots differ'nt than these
guys that comes to you grown and already turned pro. Most
a them, you cain' do too much wit' 'em. A young fighter
now, you nurse him like you would a baby."

Each time the subject came up, he seemed to prefer not
to speak of the rest of Charles Joseph's career. Under new

Collis's father, Alvin Phillips, in Houston with his second daughter, Josephine

Collis's sister Fannie McGlory, circa 1925   Collis's sister Elma Walker, circa 1925

Collis, age twenty-two

Collis at work in the mail room, circa 1938

Dorothy Simon Phillips, Collis's wife of more than forty years (circa 1935)

Collis's oldest daughter, Joyce Stafford, in Houston

Collis's second daughter, Josephine Stafford, in Houston

THE dream trainer

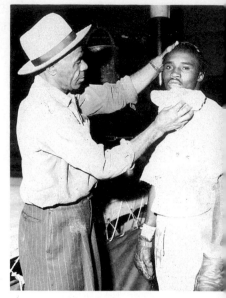

Collis with welterweight contender Percy Pugh

Collis with his stable

Collis, circa 1977

Stanley "Kitten" Hayward vs. Alvin, left, at the New Orleans Municipal Auditorium in March 1971. Alvin wins by an unanimous decision. PHOTO COURTESY OF THE NEW ORLEANS *Times-Picayune*

Collis and Alvin

Elma Walker with Collis, Jr., her son McElroy, Alvin, Gloria Sorina, and an unidentified child

Collis, Jr., in infancy: "I guess it's an antique now"

Farris before entering Angola

Jerry, age ten, on porch of St. Bernar project apartment

Alvin in Angola. PHOTO COURTESY OF THE NEW ORLEANS *Times-Picayune*

onnie in mink coat bought for
er by her family, Christmas Day,
988

Gloria Sorina with her five-day-old granddaughter China

Some of the family gathered in Collis's bedroom at the celebration of his seventy-ninth birthday, the evening following the burial of Collis, Jr.

Collis with great-grandchildren Keyon Blakes and William Farris Brooks

Alvin with his sons Farris and Alvin, Jr., and his nephew Theson Sorina on the morning of Collis's burial

handling, Joseph fought but twice—being knocked out in a rematch with Henry Hank in April, then retiring in July after a decision loss to a journeyman opponent.

The early sixties introduced another large change into Collis's life. In 1961, Standard Fruit & Steamship moved its operation to California. Mike had an offer to go, but he wouldn't leave New Orleans, choosing to continue his work with the Boxing Commission and to become an administrator in Municipal Traffic Court. Collis took a job at the Pelican Ice Company, near the vacated Standard Fruit location. There he worked as a mechanic's helper and operated machinery that loaded refrigeration cars with smoking 300-pound blocks. Just as his first job, as a boy in Houston, involved handling ice, so did his last one—at least the last he would hold as a fully able-bodied man.

Three of the children talked with me about the shooting —the three who were involved.

Of that night, when he was eleven, Farris admitted to recalling only some shouting in the apartment, then himself running in the courtyards, racing other boys. When someone caught up to him and said, "Yo' daddy got shot," he ran home and witnessed the confusion of policemen and medics streaming through the apartment. He saw Connie arrested, then released, and his father placed on a litter and carried "out to the crash truck."

Connie's version started with Gloria. She said there was hostility between her father and Gloria when Gloria was young: "She talked back to him." Apparently her reason for mentioning this distance between him and his first daughter was to explain the unusual intimacy that he shared with his second. She extended her explanation from Gloria to Farris. She said it sometimes seemed her father "almost hated Farris"—I'm not sure why this would be unless it was that Farris was hard to discipline and his birth helped bring on Dorothy's disablement. The sibling closest to Farris in age and the one most intimate with him, Jerry, was also born after Dorothy's nurturing energies were eroded. This may have been why Jerry tended to be dependent and hungry for affection. But, except for Jerry, it was to his fighters and to Connie that Collis gave most of himself. "Connie and my daddy were like *that*," Farris said to me at Angola, pressing two crossed fingers against the screen. "Umn-huh, just alike." They were so close, Connie said, that he seemed jealous of schoolboys and young men who showed an interest in her as she began to grow up. After what he felt was Gloria's disastrous marriage, he would let Connie have few dates, and she said he interrogated and intimidated most of the males who tried to see her. She was familiar with the story he had told me about a banished married suitor being the cause of the shooting. She overheard him telling a facet of this story to the policemen and medics who attended him immediately afterwards: his daughter shot him because he wouldn't let her go to a dance.

The actual immediate cause of the shooting was something quite different. It was a beating—one given by her father to his namesake, Collis Jr.

In Connie's account the catalyst was an argument between her parents about Farris. At its height, Junior came in with liquor on his breath and told his father to let his mother alone. His father hit him then, knocking him down and half under the bed. When his father tried to grind his son under his heel, Dorothy, who had long been unable to stand without help, pulled herself up between the bedposts and screamed for Connie to stop it.

Connie said she first grabbed a toilet plunger from the bathroom. She hit him with that—to no effect. Then she ran into the other bedroom and swept up the .38, which happened to be on the bed along with some bills from his cashbox.

She rushed back into her parents' room.

And, without aiming, she fired.

Then she ran out, looking for Alvin.

Across from the project everyone in the Star Lounge dropped to the floor when she burst through the doors with the pistol in her hand. It seemed to her a long time before Alvin rushed in and she could finally surrender the gun.

She was now terrified of her father, afraid to look at him when Alvin led her back home and they overheard him describing to litter-bearers the dance she had been forbidden to attend.

Though more matter-of-fact, Collis Jr.'s telling of it was essentially the same.

"He's my daddy," he said, "and I love him. But you probably already know, he's quick-tempered. He'll hurt you."

Speaking as if there were nothing unusual in his subject, Collis Jr. said he came home one night, a Saturday, to find his father shouting at Farris upstairs in their mother's room. She was already in bed, so he told his father, " 'Why don't you take Farris downstairs and fuss at him down there?' "

" 'Are you Farris's father?' " his father shouted, advancing toward him.

When he was close enough to smell the whiskey on Collis Jr.'s breath, he hit him. "Busted my mouth. Chin was all bloody. If he hit you, hit *anybody* like that, you goin' *down*. I musta said somethin' about it," because then his father began kicking him. He put up his feet to fend off the kicks that were driving him under his mother's bed.

Then he heard "just a pop," and suddenly his father writhered beside him on the floor.

He glimpsed Connie run down the stairs and out into the night, but when the police and the crash truck arrived and his mother had been sedated, he was still angry and tried to take the blame.

" 'I did it,' " he said. " 'I shot him.' "

By then, though, Alvin had led Connie back, and his brother talked him out of the false confession.

That was all there was to it, he said, though there had been times when his father still hit him, times as recent as 1981 when he came home after a few drinks and "the old man said, 'Been drinkin' again?' and I said, 'What the fuck you talkin' about? I ain' drunk. I'm movin' out.' " He went upstairs to the room they were then sharing. Collis III,

Mookie—the eventual father of Collis IV—was on the bed reading a comic book. Collis Jr. heard his father's crutch on the step. When he turned his father hit him, again knocking him down. Then his father picked up a staple gun—"what they use to stick up fight posters, a heavy little steel thing" —but apparently was held back from striking him also with that because Mookie said, "Grampaw, don't hit my daddy again."

For Connie it was impossible to remain in his presence. She didn't go to the hospital following the shooting, and before he was discharged, she traveled to Texas to live with her aunts. Later, she moved to New York—with a man who *had* been in the background all along. Rarely after that did she return home to New Orleans, and having heard he had bought another .38 and talked of using it on her for "taking his manhood," she never again slept under the same roof with him. Even more than the guilt, she felt relief at leaving New Orleans and his dominance behind. One reason for this was her belief that he actually might shoot her: she said she had seen, when he was beating her brother, that "my father could kill."

14

□

September 6, 1984

On this date, fleetingly, I first understood that my marriage would end before my life would. It's hard to speak of this, and hard to go against a folk axiom that warns, "Don't put your business in the street." But though the particulars of my marital grief needn't be expressed, because of the nature of my relation to the Phillipses and because of my disclosures about them, one dimension of these particulars belongs here.

While we talked on September 6, I watched her brush out her curtains of honey-brown hair. Her words and manner told just enough to invite me to question them, and in this I remember her as more kind than otherwise. As I stood in the doorway to our room, for an instant I saw. Saw a protracted anguish such as neither of us had yet lived. The moments that followed served to make me aware of the young man whose troubled involvement with her would figure in our parting.

As my awareness grew, I also recognized the spectral stereotype of the paranoid white Southern male beginning to stir within me. For in the years to come I had no consistent sense of which made me feel worse: that she went on to give most of her considerable love to someone else; that he happened to be black; or that I couldn't quite stop caring that he happened to be black.

As of that evening I had a better grasp of the feelings of

those who have suffered personally because of race. But this valuable new knowledge was pale consolation; rarely would it temper my internalized rage; nor did it alter the fact that I felt virtually stopped, for the next four years almost dispossessed of my passion for my subject.

THREE

The Auditorium and the Rivergate

□

1

☐

November 6, 1984

Today I am thinking about photographs made available to me in 1981 by Alvin's friend Johnny Powell. Johnny handled him during the last year of his career, six fights, after Alvin broke with Collis and Mike. Johnny trained for Malcolm Faber, the fight manager who owns the sporting goods and trophy store Collis referred me to the first day we met.

Johnny lent me the photographs a week after I looked him up in the gym on Magazine, which he had been hired to run after Collis fell sick. He, or sometimes Alvin, took most of the pictures in June 1973 on the Riviera in Monaco and in San Remo, Italy, the setting surrounding Alvin's last professional fight. Three years ago I made these notes:

"Green sea viewed from high beyond the red tiled roofs of a whitewashed village. No people. This scene in half a dozen variations—I think Alvin took them."

"An enclosed patio, its half-ceiling and walls paneled in balsa. Marble-topped tables, wicker chairs. Wine bottles and empty glasses on the marble. Gil Clancy, handsome retired champ Nino Benvenuti, hangers-on, and other fight people in the chairs."

"Carlos Monzon and Emile Griffith, far away in the ring, seen through smoke above the crowd, Griffith leaning away from Monzon's snake jab. Main event, the middleweight title. Alvin and Bouttier fought the semifinal."

"European maids in a quaint hotel room. Self-conscious

camera smiles. Blue uniforms, white aprons. Making a bed."

"Johnny Powell posed in black velvet trunks and white ring shoes, blond training gloves on his fists, laces dangling. The monogram 'AP' is sewn in glitter on the left leg of the trunks. (These were handmade by Rita Diaz, who lives with Diane's aunt in New Orleans.)"

"Johnny, seated alone at a marble-topped table on the balsa patio. Powder-blue suit, open collar. A wide flat-brimmed blue hat balanced on his crossed knee. Sharp."

"From within an empty training ring: cocktail tables and velvet chairs seen stretching away into shadow in a chande-liered ballroom. All the chairs empty except for two attractive young European women."

"Johnny and one of the women, a rampart behind them, and beyond that the sea."

These were the photographs I gave back, though Johnny said I could keep any of them, all if I liked. He is in none of those I kept: four—in addition to the two of Marguerite with Jerry and with Alvin—taken in New York in 1972, and four more from Europe.

"Subway. 'Times Square' in ceramic wall tiles, Alvin stand-ing beneath them, left hand on his hip, platform shoes, pocket-length coat, a bad leather. Bad dude."

"Clancy's gym in Manhattan. Alvin in a T-shirt, black half-tights and black training shoes, gold laces, white socks. Dancer's knee, thigh, and calf pivoted forward to left-hook a tape-circled bag, lips gone, mouthed in between his teeth. Just a posed shot for Johnny's camera, hands not yet wrapped."

"Weigh-in. Alvin and Bougaloo Watts. Watts on the scale, boyish, lanky, meekly looking down on the Toledos. Alvin, heavy-muscled, staring off into a corner. Four white men, four suits, all making notations on paper in their hands. Wall clock: 11:25."

"Warm-up. Institutional dressing room, Madison Square Garden. Alvin high on the toes of his white ring shoes, prancing, to break a sweat, in red velvet half-robe, hands readied in unsullied gauze and new tape."

"Balsa patio, Italy. Clancy and others at their ease around bottle-strewn marble, Alvin standing behind them, half in shadow, gazing to the left of the camera."

"He stands in a garden, a palm tree behind him, a profusion of roses climbing its trunk. In brogans from roadwork, sweat pants, black pullover, white cardigan sweater. Expression neutral, best fist raised, as in victory, but no higher than his left shoulder."

"Street scene. In front of a shop that looks as if made from candy. Clancy at his back, talking, left hand palm-up, rib high, index finger extended, appearing to be making a point in a casual dispute with someone not in the frame. Next to Clancy another white man, in a jogging suit and glasses, pudgy, a cigarette loosely between his lips. Male passersby gathered in the background, all looking only at him as he stands on display, head back and proud-chested, shoulders squared, tasteful in white slacks and polka-dotted silk shirt, a filled shopping bag—'Kodak'—hanging from his left hand."

"Hotel room. Alone in bed, perhaps sleeping, fetal, sheet pulled high, clasped to his face."

2

□

September 29, 1981

Malcolm Faber offered me a Budweiser seconds after we shook hands. Sipping from a can, he stepped behind his desk and put his palm on a small refrigerator standing alongside a row of file cabinets. He had "a full box," but I declined, thinking of my evening's run.

I had waited in the cluttered, glassed-in executive office of Malcolm Faber Sporting Goods & Trophy Manufacturers for about twenty minutes before he came in. High on the wall was a large blowup of a child in boxing gloves. I learned that this child was his son, now the blue-jeaned young man who had shown me in.

"Golden Gloves." Malcolm Faber spoke quickly even with the present pride in his voice. "Not long, though. And he was never a pro. I can tell you, baby, that's a hard business."

Faber looked to be around sixty, slight of build and with a few strands of dark hair combed across his skull. A big ring, a V-shaped cluster of sparkling stones, decorated the third finger of his right hand. He moved brusquely, in the same way that he talked.

He said he never allowed himself to become personally close to his fighters—"none of 'em"—because fighters were a "hold" on you; once they had your support, they would always be after you, for this, for that, behind in their rent, their car payments . . . He swore he had lost money on every fighter he had owned.

On Alvin too: Alvin, who was "difficult, quiet, a hard

person to know." Five hundred dollars he had paid for Alvin's contract. Not his idea; he took Alvin because Johnny Powell said Alvin wanted to come with him. Yet even though he was able to sign Alvin for better purses than he was used to—fifteen hundred in the Garden, forty-eight for the rematch with Tony Licata, "about three skins" from San Remo—Alvin didn't seem to appreciate it, and his own cut as manager was rarely enough to cover his full expenses.

He was definite in making no apology for "washing" his "hands" of Alvin after Alvin began "fooling with that *stuff*." This was a special shame, Faber said, because it came at a time when he had started Alvin's career moving again. Glancing at the photograph above us, he said he would disown his own kin if any of them became involved with anything like what Alvin had. He raised his beer, a trace of defensiveness in his laugh. "This stuff here messes the mind up enough."

Before I left, we spoke of Collis. "I don't care whether he's black or white," he said, lowering his voice, "that guy's one fine fella." He told me that Collis recently had come into the store to borrow fifteen dollars and that there never had been hard feelings between them over Alvin's defection: Collis understood that it was what Alvin wanted.

"They were building up Licata then," Faber added, conclusively referring to the fight crowd and, I suppose, to Alvin's frustration with the fights that had been available to him. "They're building up somebody else now."

3

□

October 5, 1981

I had spent much of the previous week in the records room in the basement of the Criminal District Courts Building. There I studied files devoted to Alvin, Farris, Jerry, and several of Collis's grandchildren. Now, on a hot, humid day in October, I had traced the transcript of Alvin's 1975 trial to the library of the Louisiana Supreme Court Building.

I had already learned that his short criminal record went back to 1964, when, at twenty-two, he and an older man were convicted of simple robbery. They had approached the victim, a black man in his twenties, and asked for a cigarette, then for a dime. Then Alvin hit him in the face, knocking him down. He and his accomplice beat the man and robbed him of a watch and a wallet containing two dollars. A passerby called the police, who soon caught them in a nearby alley still carrying the watch. Alvin's accomplice, a parole violator, was sent to Angola. On the advice of a lawyer, whom I think Mike may have retained for Collis, Alvin pled guilty to simple robbery, the assault charge being dropped, and was sentenced to six months in Parish Prison. His only other conviction was the life sentence he received in 1975.

In the eleven years between these two convictions, his record showed three arrests. In September 1973, three months after his trip to Europe, he was arrested while sitting in a car in the St. Bernard project and charged with possession of heroin with intent to distribute. The arrest record reported that he had "sold heroin to an undercover agent" and described him as "a heroin addict, who will go into withdrawals during the night."

The evidence that may have prompted the police to look for him in the first place was a note written to him on August 22, 1973, by his brother Farris, who was then in Parish Prison awaiting trial on an armed-robbery charge:

DIG ALVIN

I HAVE 31 DOLLARS THIS IS ALL I HAVE SO GIVE MY MAN "3 BAGS" FOR ME I TRYING TO DO SOMETHING "YOU DIG" I WILL PAY YOU THE 6 DOLLAR'S AS SOON AS I GET IT. "FARRIS"

"My man" was a prison deputy, one evidently not a dope peddler or as easily bought as Farris thought he could be; the deputy turned the note over to higher-ups, and it eventually reached the DA.

Alvin was out on $5,000 bond on the date of his next arrest, February 15, 1974. He and an accomplice were charged with simple burglary for allegedly breaking into a house in a middle-class neighborhood not far from the project. Again he was released on bond—only to be arrested in March, this time for an offense that took place exactly a week after his release on the burglary charge: on February 22, he and another man, a longtime addict, allegedly went into a jewelry store in the French Quarter. Alvin asked to see a ring for his wife. When the owner brought out a display tray, Alvin diverted his attention, and the other man snatched a diamond ring valued at $800; then both ran. After their subsequent arrest, Johnny Powell put up the necessary 10 percent of Alvin's second $5,000 bond, and a friend of Johnny's friend put up his house as collateral.

It was surprising to me that Alvin would be allowed back on the street after each of these arrests. But the street is exactly where the Drug Enforcement Administration wanted him because Operation Checkmate, a large undercover drug investigation, was then underway. A second undercover

agent alleged he had bought heroin from Alvin twice in
January 1974. Afterwards Alvin was kept under surveillance
in the hope that his daily movements would expose his
supplier. This never happened, though; the agents were
unable to watch him closely enough. When, in late summer
of 1974, they began their sweep of the streets—having issued
a warrant for his arrest on August 14, the day Dorothy
Phillips died—Alvin was gone.

It wasn't until the spring of 1975 that the state of Louisiana
had the opportunity to begin making its case against him.
At that time he had already been in jail on Rikers Island for
several months because of petty drug-related offenses committed in Manhattan. Lawyers have told me he might have
successfully fought extradition and served his time in New
York, where the penalties for his kinds of crime were more
lenient. Strangely, he chose not to resist efforts to return
him to Louisiana. When I met her with Connie, Diane
described the judge who granted his extradition as repeatedly
asking him, " 'Mr. Phillips, are you sure you know what
you're doing? Are you *sure?*' " His reasons still are not fully
clear to me—though I believe they involved his feelings
toward Diane, his grief for his mother, his deep depression
in general, and his assumption that his previous status at
home would count for something: he might be looking at a
stretch of time, maybe fifteen years brought down to seven
and a half or less for good behavior, but surely not true
"natural life." No doubt a residue of bravado—why not just
fight the charge—also influenced him to accept the path that
landed him back in Parish Prison, where, during the summer
of 1975, he waited through a string of continuances requested by his lawyer. This was the same summer in which,
in Madison Square Garden, Tony Licata challenged Carlos
Monzon for the middleweight title.

During these months Farris was still in Parish Prison, also
awaiting trial. By coincidence, he and Alvin were tried in
different sections of the Criminal District Courts Building
on the same sequence of days in August 1975. Whenever
one of my conversations with Gloria included both Alvin

and Farris, at some point she usually would mention the last hours of their trials and herself, the only family member present, shuttling between the two courtrooms, which were on different floors. This coincidence forced her to miss parts of each trial. Because of the emotional strain of the experience, she felt it was just as well, "a blessing in fact," that she could witness only fragments of each, and she was glad she had been able to forget much of what she had seen. There was one incident, occurring during the trials, which she invariably recalled, though. Late in the afternoon, when each trial was near an end, an electrical storm put out all the lights in the windowless courtrooms. The indeterminate stretch of darkness that followed became an omen in her whole impression of the ordeal. On each of the various times that she described the trials to me, she spoke of the sudden darkness as if it had happened concurrently with Farris "about to come out that chair" in a rage while a one-armed armed-robbery accomplice gave plea-bargain testimony against him and while Alvin—allowed to embrace her across a pocket-high partition as the discharged jury filed out—wept into her hair, whispering, " 'I been railroaded, sis. I been railroaded.' "

4

□

The trial lasted several days. Much later, after viewing other criminal trials, I would understand that it was not an unusual one: the costs considerable, the incriminating evidence weighty, and the defendant guilty of the crime in general if not the particular charge.

The state's case rested on the testimony of an undercover agent, Bernard Harry, and two informants, Calvin Clark and Emmanuel Stewart, addicted transvestite felons from the neighborhood who had cooperated with the police in several investigations. According to the opening statement of the prosecution, Clark and Stewart accompanied Harry to the St. Bernard project on January 4, 1974. There they went to 3919 Jumonville, the center of a courtyard and the location of the apartment in which, two blocks from Collis and Gloria, Alvin and Diane had lived for years. In the doorway of the apartment, Alvin was said to have sold the three men "five foils of heroin," receiving in return sixty dollars in marked bills. The three returned on January 7 and bought "eight foils" more with ninety-six marked dollars.

Alvin's lawyer waived his right to an opening statement and rested on "the presumption of innocence." Alvin had come in contact with his lawyer through a friend who had cultivated acquaintances with legal people in the course of his work parking cars in a lot near the Criminal District Courts Building. The lawyer had represented Alvin on the previous charges that had resulted in his releases on bond.

He also had represented Diane after her arrest for possession of barbiturates the weekend Alvin fought in Madison Square Garden. After a long string of continuances—granted because Diane reportedly had health problems during her pregnancy with twins, her last children by Alvin—the lawyer maneuvered her charge through a mistrial and then a plea bargain to a suspended eighteen-month sentence and five years' probation—which she violated soon after her sentencing in July 1973 by fleeing to New York with her surviving infant and five older children, a circumstance that ultimately may have led Alvin to jump bond and also flee to New York.

The first significant prosecution witness, Drug Enforcement Administration agent John Phillips, granted under questioning by the defense that the informants had long police records. He also admitted that the DEA paid Clark and Stewart and gave them "psychological incentives," but he denied that they had cooperated in order to stay out of jail and away from others they had informed on. The money was "only to meet expenses," he said, and "only doled out in tens, twenties, and five-dollar bills." Both were in methadone programs, and they informed because they were "trying to make New Orleans a better place to live in . . . These people are junkies . . . and motivation for people like that to live is to get rid of some of the heroin traffickers. It is not the only reason, but certainly one."

Bernard Harry's testimony described Alvin as having appeared in the screened doorway of the apartment in "an orange T-shirt and orange shorts, boxer type," and he repeatedly referred to Clark and Stewart as "corporate individuals." Alvin's lawyer's first questions of Harry appeared exploratory: did he go to the project armed with a gun ("Yes"), had he ever seen Alvin box ("No"), did he know Stewart's street name ("Sticks")? The lawyer then interrogated him more pointedly about details of the first sale, establishing that on January 4 the screen door was not opened, that the money and narcotics were "passed . . . through a hole cut in the door," that Harry couldn't recall whether it was a fair or a cloudy day ("I was not paying too much attention to the weather, sir"), and that Harry remembered the base of the screen as being level with the porch which he stood on and that the man the informants called Alvin looked to him to be about the same height as he was. As nearly as I could determine it, Alvin's lawyer's purpose was to suggest that, since the screened doorway actually was elevated by one step above the porch, which would have made Alvin appear taller than Harry, the drugs in fact were sold by someone else. This suggestion was later challenged by the prosecution, which tried to prove that the flooring beyond the doorway had been broken, causing a recessed standing elevation behind the screen that placed Harry at eye level with the man who handed him the drugs. I believe that, in light of the other testimony and evidence, this densely argued point would have been moot even had Alvin not taken the stand as the only witness for the defense—and given the testimony that struck me as more useful to the prosecution than anything else in the trial.

Gloria described him as sitting hunched forward in a blue shirt with his hands together and speaking so softly that neither she nor many other spectators could hear all that he said.

BY THE COURT:
    Call your first witness.

ALVIN PHILLIPS, DIRECT BY DEFENSE

BY THE DEFENSE:
Q. You are Alvin Phillips?
A. Yes.
Q. Did you on January 4, 1974, distribute or sell dope to anybody?
A. Not that I know of, not to my knowledge.
Q. Do you ever sell dope?
A. No. I get depressed at different times but I never sold dope.
Q. What do you do for a living?
A. Professional boxer and working at Blue Plate [Mayon-

naise] as automatic captain [of a jar-capping machine].

Q. You are a professional boxer?

A. Except I have not been doing nothing in the last three years.

Q. How many professional fights did you have?

A. Approximately forty, I have not counted them.

Q. Were you successful, how many did you win?

BY THE PROSECUTION:

Objection—

BY THE COURT:

Overruled.

BY THE DEFENSE:

Q. How many did you win?

A. I have never counted or kept track, I was fighting at least once a month, I would make— I lost maybe eight to ten out of thirty or forty.

Q. You are used to fighting in front of a large group of people?

A. A pretty decent crowd.

Q. Three or four thousand people?

A. I would say more than that.

Q. You made money out of that?

A. I made a fairly decent living with the fighting and the job.

Q. Were you Southern champion at one time?

A. Yes.

Q. Did you fight Tony Licata?

A. Yes, twice.

BY THE PROSECUTION:

Objection—irrelevant.

BY THE COURT:

Sustained.

BY THE DEFENSE:

Q. What size crowds did you have when you fought Tony Licata?

A. When I fought him at the Rivergate, I don't know the maximum. But it was a packed house at the Auditorium, it was a packed house.

Q.   How much money did you make out of that fight?
A.   Both times roughly about forty-seven hundred, some-
     thing like that, forty-five hundred.
Q.   You fought other places in this country, didn't you?
A.   In the U.S., yes.
Q.   Where?
A.   Kansas City, New York, Alabama . . .
Q.   Where in New York?
A.   Madison Square Garden.
Q.   Have you fought in foreign countries?
A.   France.
Q.   You are married?
A.   Yes.
Q.   You have children?
A.   Yes, I do, six.
Q.   How old are you?
A.   Thirty-three.
Q.   Do you know Emmanuel Stewart and Calvin Clark?
A.   No, I know them by seeing them, but personally I would
     never hang with them.
Q.   Have you ever been in their company?
A.   Once or twice.
Q.   Do you recall anything that happened between you and
     them?
A.   Emmanuel Clark, I know most of them by nicknames,
     Clark and Sticks, I would say they had approached me
     a couple of times, more or less, you know, it was like
     for sex acts, things like this.
Q.   What did you do when they approached you in that
     fashion?
A.   Sticks, I told him to get out, I was a married man and
     this was not my bag, not my thing, the second time they
     talked about getting out again I disassociated myself
     from homosexuals.
Q.   Did you ever sell them any dope?
A.   Not to Clark or Sticks, I merely popped a couple of
     times, but never sold them anything.

5

□

Q. When they approached you for what you call unnatural sex acts, did that make you angry?

A. Yes, it did, the first time they approached me it made me very angry, I came close to hurting Sticks and Calvin Clark.

Q. Did they fear you?

A. They knew I was capable of hurting them with my hands.

Q. Did you use strong language with them?

A. I talked to them plenty foul when they approached me.

Q. You did live on Jumonville Street for a period of time?

A. Yes.

Q. Who lived there with you?

A. My wife and six children.

Q. Did you have people visit you there?

A. Quite a few fight friends.

Q. Did you have friends that were approximately your size?

A. Yes. I had a couple of friends approximately my size.

Q. Were there any dope transactions in your apartment where your wife and children lived?

A. No.

Q. Did you ever shoot up there or do anything with a friend in your apartment there?

A. No.

Q. Alvin, your apartment on Jumonville Street has a screen door?
A. Yes.
Q. It has a porch in front of it?
A. A porch.
Q. Is there a step in front of the porch to the screen door?
A. There are four steps you come up to the bottom floor when you walk up and when you get on the porch. There is a step as tall as this one step, if I was standing in my house he would be standing there and you would have to look up to me, if I was in my house I would be six-two or three and he would be on a lower level, he would have to look up to me.
Q. Have you ever seen that man who took the witness stand against you?
A. I don't know him.
Q. Do you recall Sticks and Clark coming there sometime in January of 1974?
A. No, I don't, I met Calvin and Sticks, I went to jail once for a knife or a theft charge, simple robbery brought down to theft, I think I met him once in jail, I heard about him in jail, when I first heard about Sticks, this was the only time I knew him.
Q. You were charged with simple robbery and you pled guilty to theft?
A. Yes.
Q. You got a sentence in Parish Prison?
A. Six months. I went on work release and stayed three months.
Q. When was this?
A. 1973 or 1974.

[*Alvin served these months in Parish Prison in 1964. I wondered if this was a simple slip or if his awareness of time was already dislocated or if it was an error made by the court reporter.*]

Q. Another time you had a knife on you and paid a fine?
A. I had a knife, it was over three inches, five inches I believe, it was a pocketknife.

Q. You paid a fine for having it on your person?
A. Yes.
Q. The knife was when?
A. Maybe '62 or '60.
Q. From 1963 until today's date you have never been convicted of anything?
A. No.
Q. Before 1962 or 1963 you were never convicted of anything?
A. No traffic record or anything.
Q. When did you begin your boxing career?
A. After I got in trouble in 1962 with the theft charge, I came out of Parish Prison doing three months, I got a job on Tchoupitoulas Street and the gym was maybe five or six blocks away on my way from work and I stopped to watch the fellows work out and I started boxing, I did not intend to keep on boxing, just keep physically fit, then I started boxing, I been around it all my life.
Q. You are on trial for a very serious charge. I want you to tell the jury if you have ever done anything with dope, distributed dope to anybody or gave anything to anybody like that.
A. No, I never gave anybody dope or sold them dope, I got depressed after the last Licata fight and used it a couple of times, that was the most.
Q. Why did you get so depressed after that fight?
A. After the fight and at the time I was pressed for money. I needed a certain amount of cash for my family and I had a bad hand, I should have gotten out of the fighting game, I went through fighting.
Q. What would that fight have meant to you if you had won?
A. The promoter had guaranteed if I would have beaten, it would have been a possibly— I would have gotten a title shot.
Q. The reason you were so depressed is you had a shot for the middleweight championship of the world and you fought with a broken hand and you lost?

A. Right.

Q. That is all.

Cross-Examination, by State

By the Prosecution:

Q. Mr. Phillips, you never use heroin?

By the Defense:

Objection—

By the Court:

Overruled. Answer the question.

A. I chipped.

Q. That means once in a while?

A. Yes.

Q. When did you quit fighting?

A. 1973. I think that was my last fight.

Q. Who was your manager?

A. Malcolm Favor.

Q. You mentioned you made four to five thousand dollars on several fights, on one fight each?

A. Yes.

Q. That entire four thousand dollars did not go to you, did it?

A. No, my manager had a certain percentage and my trainer also.

Q. What was his percentage amount?

A. Usually working like I get two-thirds of my purse, he would work for a third.

Q. Roughly thirteen hundred dollars?

A. Yes.

Q. When was that fight?

A. In 1973. That was the Licata fight.

Q. You have six children?

A. Yes.

Q. When did you start living in the St. Bernard project?

A. I was born in the St. Bernard project.

6

□

Q. Were you living there when you were fighting?
A. Yes.
Q. Were you married at the time you were fighting?
A. Yes, been married since I was seventeen.
Q. And you were bringing home all this money up until 1973?
A. I would not say all of this, I started fighting when I was twenty-five, it was late, I had to start off at four rounds for fifteen dollars, I moved up to six, eight, then ten—
Q. You made ten thousand dollars or fifteen hundred and your manager gets a third of that?
A. I did not make no big money—forty-seven hundred with Licata, maybe a thousand in France, the rest of the twelve hundred, fifteen hundred, with my manager getting a third and expenses coming off the top.
Q. You were not making so much money?
A. No, it depends on what you call big money, I would say I was making a fairly decent living, I needed a job three to four years when I started fighting.
Q. You filed income tax?
A. I filed one or two. I did not have an attorney taking care of my business at the time. I was training and working. I was leaving in the morning at four, getting to work, coming back at five, running an hour for four miles, getting up at six o'clock and going to work.
Q. You said you filed two tax returns?

A. Maybe two, not exactly.

Q. You recall how much you filed for?

A. No, I could not.

Q. Did you put any of this money aside, like savings accounts?

A. I started a couple of bank accounts and wound up using that as time went on— I have a father who is crippled and a mother who is sick twenty years or so in bed.

    [*On this day—August 20, 1975—he knew, though he may have buried the knowledge, that his mother died in August 1974.*]

Q. Where were you living on the 4th and 7th of January 1974?

A. Jumonville.

Q. With your wife and six children?

A. Right.

Q. You never saw Agent Harry on the 4th and 7th of January 1974?

A. No.

Q. Where are your wife and children living today?

A. Now they are living in New York.

Q. Were you using drugs around the 4th or 7th of January 1974?

A. Not that I know of. I don't know if I did or not.

Q. What was the time you fought Licata?

A. Once right before Christmas and I think this was at the Rivergate, it might have been November, something like that.

Q. Was this when you got depressed and when you started using drugs?

A. No, the last fight was at the Auditorium. I figure the first fight was a draw, I did not take much time off, I took maybe a week or two off to rest and went back in training. We rescheduled the fight and I lost this time.

Q. After this fight in 1973 was when you started using drugs and got depressed and you were pressed for money?

A. Yes.

BY THE PROSECUTION:
   No further questions.
BY THE COURT:
   Step down. Call your next witness.

CALVIN CLARK, DIRECT BY DEFENSE

BY THE DEFENSE:
Q.   State your name.
A.   Calvin Clark.
Q.   Do you know this man sitting next to me?
A.   No, just a drug addict.
Q.   Do you know his name?
A.   Alvin Phillips.
Q.   How long have you known him?
A.   Not really, it has been just running back and forth, not
     really knowing him, like you come in contact with drug
     addicts, it is not a solid thing.

Although I continued reading, I stopped copying the
transcript at this point. Clark and Stewart were the only
other witnesses, and their appearances were brief. The
defense put them on the stand in an effort to discredit them.
I learned later from the court reporter who recorded the
trial that the closing arguments—which I very much wanted
to read—hadn't been taken down, a money-saving practice
that recently had become standard.

On August 22, 1975, a brief notice near the end of the
sports page in *The Times-Picayune* reported that the jury in
the trial of former contender Alvin Phillips deliberated "only
15 minutes" before returning a verdict of "guilty as charged."
The same sports section featured news of an upcoming
middleweight fight promoted by Malcolm Faber. The lead
story on the front page concerned two would-be escapees
from Angola who were killed by a posse that had tracked
them with bloodhounds through the unpopulated terrain
surrounding the prison.

Because of the extremity of the sentence, Alvin was entitled
to appeal his conviction before the state's highest court. This

is why the transcript of his trial was stored in the Louisiana Supreme Court Building. His lawyer filed a motion for this appeal; then in March 1976 he withdrew as counsel of record on the ground that his client was "legally indigent." The trial judge then appointed a lawyer in the Indigent Defender Program to handle the appeal and to argue the case before the Louisiana Supreme Court.

That argument was never made. According to the assigned indigent-defender, a man who impressed me as well intentioned but overworked, it is common in indigent cases for the argument to be waived and for the appeal to be judged solely on the merit of the Assignments of Error, challenges of the conduct of the trial made during the trial and later briefed by defense counsel.

Alvin's first lawyer had briefed two Assignments of Error before withdrawing from the case. The Supreme Court rejected the first Assignment, an insignificant one, because "the record is silent as to any such request . . ." Second, the defense asked for a new trial on the ground that the judge did not permit defense counsel to tell the jury that a conviction required that Alvin automatically be sentenced to prison for the rest of his natural life—without possibility of parole. The Supreme Court rejected this Assignment for the same reason: "The record is silent as to any such request."

On October 26, 1976—after Alvin had lived 413 days in Angola, after he had served 75 of these days in isolation, after he had mutilated himself three times and been written up for these and ten other prison conduct infractions, and after he recently had been transferred to the disciplinary unit, Camp J—the Louisiana Supreme Court, in a two-page opinion, denied the routine appeal mailed in by the indigent-defender representing him, and affirmed his conviction and sentence.

On November 4, he took the bleach to his eyes.

7

□

October 10, 1981

Quiet in the gym. Not yet late afternoon: no fighters had come in. We sat in the small school desks. Johnny's large hands lay immobile on the desktop before him, his gestures and movement minimal while we talked. There was no discernible physical difference between him now and the image of him I would soon study in eight-year-old photographs: trim, tall but still a middleweight, firm mouth, small eyes, scar tissue on his left brow, a crescent cut on the broad bridge of his nose. He was about Alvin's color—medium brown. He attended our conversation from the side, without often looking at my face. Mister Arthur was the only other person there; and Mister Arthur fidgeted, sometimes grumbling to himself, away from us over by the lockers, then back in the kitchen.

"He wasn't no dope fiend," Johnny declared with conviction, idly watching Arthur. "He didn't get into that stuff until after the first fight with Licata." He explained that Alvin was a family man, that he was loyal to Diane even though there was a pretty neighbor named Betty who stayed interested in him and even though Diane "had a chest flat as mine, no nice hips, no pretty legs, and hair 'bout long as that." Using his thumb, he measured off two joints on his finger. According to Johnny, it was Diane who was addicted; that was what started Alvin.

"And I didn't steal him from under his daddy, like ol' man Phillips probably told you. Alvin *asked* me to take over his contract." This was in the summer of 1972; they had bumped into each other at Charity on a Sunday when they both were there to visit a hurt friend. Johnny then ran a gym in mid-city for Malcolm Faber. Alvin's contract was due for renewal that month, and Johnny said Alvin told him he didn't want to fight anymore for Mike. Whenever Alvin had brought this up with Collis, Collis would hear none of it. Through Johnny, an old neighborhood acquaintance, Alvin made his own arrangement with Malcolm Faber, who had owned many fighters and went a long way back in the fight game in New Orleans.

Speaking quietly and evenly, Johnny explained that Collis and Mike "stayed in a pout" after Alvin came over to him and Malcolm. He acknowledged that he himself had never been comfortable with Collis "no way" because of Collis's treatment of whites. "*You* might call him a son of a bitch, and he'd make like it was a joke. If *I* did that, that old man would try to kill me." He nodded conclusively toward the kitchen, where Mister Arthur had retreated with the blue long-cord telephone. As an example, he said Collis once had threatened to hit him with a staple gun because he was on the phone, Collis wanted to use it, and he didn't end his conversation right away. "He's somebody who'll hit—to hurt you—if you do any little thing he don't like. Long as you ain't white."

But even after the bitterness that followed Alvin's signing with Malcolm, Johnny still felt sure Alvin gave part of his purses to his father. And, Johnny said, this was even though Alvin didn't like the ring and fighting. "Not him, not like some guys do. He was just in it for the money."

He had nothing further to say about Alvin's trouble with drugs—except again to blame it on Diane. Before his third fight for Malcolm—against Bougaloo Watts in Madison Square Garden on October 20, 1972—Johnny said Alvin "got away from me and messed up," going up to Harlem to see Diane. I didn't know it then, but Diane couldn't have been in New York on that date because on the same weekend she was arrested in New Orleans for possession of barbiturates during a visit to one of Gloria's sons at Central Lockup in Parish Prison. But I did remember Collis's frequently repeated tale about Johnny—a profane narration, which I never tried to substantiate—in which Johnny, strung out on drugs and childishly distraught " 'bout some woman," had to be restrained by Greater New Orleans bridge police from leaping to his death in the river. I didn't want to bring this up with Johnny now. Instead I listened quietly to his account of how he fell out with Alvin after they came back from Europe and Alvin began "to run behind it."

As I knew from the police record, Alvin's then active habit led to a robbery arrest. Johnny said he felt there would have been talk if he hadn't helped him, even though his father wouldn't, so he "called in a favor" from someone in local political office. They arranged a two-year probation for Alvin, to take effect following an imminent election. Meanwhile Alvin was out on bond thanks to money from Johnny and the friend of Johnny's who put up his house as collateral. Johnny said all Alvin had to do was wait a few weeks for the trial, take his probation, and then stay in New Orleans and stay out of trouble. Instead, without telling Johnny, Alvin jumped bail and went to New York, where, by then, Diane was. Johnny said he even sent Alvin three hundred dollars more, but he never heard from him or saw him again.

He paused. Several fighters in a loosely connected group sauntered in from the street. "Just another waste," Johnny muttered, and went on to tell how there was serious talk of a title shot for Alvin—$75,000 or 25 percent of the gate—against the winner between Monzon and Griffith if he won his fight on the undercard. Johnny said he still couldn't understand why, in that fight with Bouttier, a dangerous long-range puncher, Alvin fought as he did. For three rounds he pressed Bouttier according to plan, and for three rounds he was winning on points, working hard and staying busy inside. Before the start of the fourth, he told Johnny he figured he could box this man. Then over Johnny's outraged protest, he moved outside. Bouttier reached him almost at once, and in the fifth Bouttier knocked him down, something only two other fighters had done. Neither Johnny nor the wire-service stringer whose report was carried in the New Orleans paper thought this knockdown or the one that quickly followed it left Alvin badly hurt, but still he failed by a split second to beat the second count. The stringer wrote that he was on his feet as the referee turned to wave Bouttier away. Reportedly, there was a squabble from Alvin's corner, but it was too late.

Johnny shook his head when I asked if Alvin had been out of shape. No, he didn't think so. He did acknowledge that they had had to inject cortisone into his left hand, which he injured two months earlier in training before the rematch with Tony Licata. But as far as he knew, Johnny said, Alvin had been free of all other painkillers and any kind of drug since the Licata fight. He felt sure Alvin's physical condition wasn't the cause of the loss—for which he had no explanation.

By then more fighters were loudly coming in, and we talked only a little longer—mostly about Johnny. He conceded that, despite the bitter loss, he and Alvin had had a splendid time on the Riviera. This wasn't as much because of the beautiful surroundings as because of the way they were treated there: "right, in fact." Concerning Johnny's career, afterwards I remembered best his description of his first pro loss in his seventeenth fight. It was to a white fighter, named Ronnie Wilson, from Detroit. "No reflection," Johnny said, "but before then, I didn't believe white boys could fight." He elaborated on how Wilson gave him a surprise beating in their first fight and then how he, Johnny Powell, knocked the same fighter silly a month later in the rematch.

The next day I stopped by the gym again and, as he had said he would, Johnny handed me a packet of snapshots he had brought from home.

8

□

October 20, 1981

In the Supreme Court file on Alvin's appeal, I had found
a reply to a letter which he had written but which was now
missing from the folder.

Mr. Alvin Phillips, 80293C
Angola, Louisiana 70712

Dear Sir:
I have received your letter of July 4, 1976, but am
unable to assist you in any way since you are within the
care, custody and control of the Department of Correc-
tions at Angola.
However, I am sending your letter, together with a copy
of this letter, to your attorney.

Very truly yours,
Alvin V. Oser,
Judge, Section "J"

I thought a letter written on the Bicentennial might be
important in itself, and I was eager to see what Alvin's writing
revealed about him. I also wanted to meet his lawyer. I
reached him by phone, and he agreed to see me.

Alvin's former lawyer then worked out of an office in his
house, a low dwelling in a suburb on the West Bank of the
river. I went carrying a list of legal questions and hoping to

learn if there was relief available to Alvin. A new trial?
Reliable psychiatric treatment?

"Alvin Phillips is a victim." This unsolicited statement
stood out among the lawyer's responses. I sat between his
and his secretary's desks. His secretary, a thin, pallid young
woman, was suffering from a severe cold and coughed
rakingly as we talked. Alvin, he said, had been exploited in
the fight game, in court, and, now, in prison. The secretary
parted a layer of haze—they both smoked heavily—when
she stepped to the file cabinet to look for Alvin's Independence Day letter.

She could find almost nothing concerning Alvin, neither
the letter nor the closing argument I also hoped to see.
Insufficient evidence was the focus of his defense of Alvin,
the lawyer said. Beyond that, he could remember little of
the case, which had been closed for six years, except the
probability that he had been paid for only a fraction of his
work. A pardon by the governor, he told me, that was the
best chance Alvin now had.

9

□

February 3, 1982

Tony Licata sounded as if he were speaking from behind a mask—the halting speech of a man just waked from a deep, dreamful sleep. He had the strangled voice of an old ex-fighter—except on the day we spoke on the phone I knew he was twenty-nine and had only been retired for a year.

"I really want to talk about Alvin," he said in a whisper after I had explained myself. "He taught me a lot. You know, I fought him twice."

"Yes. You're probably a big part of his life."

"I don't know . . . if I'd go . . . that far." His replies came slowly. "I may have caused the end of his career, though . . . and where he is now."

When we met late in the afternoon a few days later, it became clear that he knew little more of Alvin's present circumstances than the physical location of where he was now. "How long's he in for?" was the first and only question he asked about Alvin after we had begun to speak of him.

He had suggested we meet at a new gym farther down Magazine, one renovated and reopened by Vince Arnona, a longtime New Orleans fight figure. When I told him my reason for being there, Arnona welcomed me and my son Richard inside and proudly showed off the many changes he had made to the place, which was above the pool hall where Collis had once bought me a sandwich.

Evidently one of the last fighters there that day, Cheetah stood alone in the training area working an accuracy bag suspended at chin level between elasticized cables hooked to the ceiling and floor. We looked at each other without recognition.

"I don't have any love for Collis," Vince Arnona was saying, "even if he is crippled." When he had a gym on Tchoupitoulas Street, he continued, Collis ran it for him for thirty-five dollars a week and ended up "stealing" his fighters, taking them with him when he moved to a gym that Mike opened in mid-city. Arnona claimed he had arranged four fights for Alvin, all of which he won, and still Collis wouldn't give him a piece of his contract.

In the locker room we passed Freddie Johnson. He scarcely noticed me, but after I spoke to him, he acted as if we had been well acquainted. He said he was "goin' *good* now!" and asked about Collis, whom he praised, declaring that what Collis had taught him made it impossible for fighters in this gym to touch him. Not knowing then that they had had a falling-out, I gave him Collis's number and urged him to visit him. Johnson said he would.

In his glassed-in office, Vince Arnona told me he had been offered $3,500 to match Freddie Johnson with Tony Ayala, at the time arguably the most formidable junior middleweight in boxing. Arnona said he wouldn't consider such a fight for less than $10,000 because Johnson was "no kid." He said he wasn't going to let a fighter take a beating for next to nothing, then added, "But the money's the main thing. After all, this is a business."

By then Tony Licata had arrived. After ribbing Freddie Johnson and Cheetah from the doorway to the office, he swept in, thirty minutes late. There was bluff openness and theatrical warmth in his greeting of Arnona, then Richard and me. He took our hands in a soft double clasp. He was now the size of a light heavyweight, but even in his street clothes—open silk shirt, bell-bottoms, platform shoes worn carelessly with no socks—he appeared still in good shape.

Vince Arnona went out, and right away Tony Licata began describing his fights with Alvin. Before we had even sat on Arnona's vinyl sofa and chair, he dipped in, demonstrating the left hook he had landed "all night" on Alvin in the second fight. This brought him a forearm's length from me with his right cocked near his dramatic jawline. For an instant it felt as if there was a force field around him. Then he went slack, stepped back, and dropped to the sofa, and I sensed he had resisted an impulse to hit me. Not me personally, but any man who happened to be standing that close to him when the talk was of fighting.

"He crowded you." This was his first description of Alvin. "But he could be hit. Bossman Pace hit Alvin a lot."

Others had also brought up the bout with Eddie Pace, a fight that came at midpoint in Alvin's career. Pace, a large middleweight with a large punch, was an often avoided contender at the time. The way one friend of Alvin's heard it, they were supposed to go easy, but because of his "big heart" Alvin tried for a win and Pace "put a terrible whippin' on him" for the full ten rounds.

"He dropped dead . . . in a gym in California," Tony Licata remembered. "Bossman Pace was a hitter . . ."

Though he wanted to be helpful, Tony actually hadn't very much to say about Alvin, and soon he digressed. When I had mentioned earlier that Alvin's mind now had a tendency to wander, he laughed and said, "That happens to me too!"

He admitted that Alvin could have deserved the decision in their first fight and that the officials might have scored it a draw in order to fatten the gate for the rematch. "I had to lose too much weight, though," he reminded me, before again granting—as others also told me—that Alvin had taught him a lot in the gym when they were both "just babies." Apprentice days in the gym reminded him of one thing more: that he "always had a lot a respect for Mister Collis because he was always good to young kids in the gym. The reason he's crippled, you know, is because his daughter shot him because"—the same story Collis first told me—"he wouldn't let her go out with a guy that was married."

For the rest we talked about Tony, not Alvin: his shot at the title, how he "lived the life of a fighter" instead of saving his money, and how he "could never sleep—not just because I stayed out, because I was so keyed up." Soon he was standing again, demonstrating a ring tactic he had learned, the hard way, from Carlos Monzon.

Eventually he reminisced about when he was thirteen and beginning to train at St. Mary's gym—where he proved to be a natural. Now his back gave him trouble. Immediately after he retired, he was hired as a sheriff's deputy, but he had left that job, which involved helping with the Parish Prison boxing program. He and his brother-in-law were talking of opening a bar in the Quarter. Till then he was supporting himself and his wife by "working nights on the river" as a deckhand on a tugboat. This could be "dangerous work," but sometimes things were so slow that he had time to work out right there on a barge.

He walked Richard and me through the gym and down the steps as if he had been our host. He parted from us warmly. I noticed his bitten-down nails as he again took our right hands in both of his. "If I make a comeback," he said, "maybe I'll see you again." He started toward his bronze Ford Torino coupe, battered along the passenger's door, its outside right mirror frame glassless and dangling. Then abruptly he stopped. His keys, he explained, he must have put them down somewhere upstairs—where he had already said his goodbyes.

As he jauntily skip-trotted up the stairs, a wave of sorrow swept over me. I wanted to ask him another question, any question, so long as I could believe it would help him leave there feeling good. I hoped he had children.

10

□

March 2, 1982

Alvin's friend Pete: Junius Pierre Cole III, a large, tall man with a gregarious air. Graying temples, round face, and a paunch. I might have mistaken him for a professional person or someone in business if it hadn't been for the scuffling character of his street clothes and the shiny welt of a scar on his brown cheek. He wore a visor with "Florida" across the front, canvas basketball shoes, and a satiny, long-sleeved shirt unbuttoned over a T-shirt. Yet, in a sense, a businessman is what he was. He freely admitted that he had drawn his survival for more than twenty years from the fast calculations and transactions he made as a small-scale dope dealer.

Talk seemed to come easily to him, and he laughed in a complete way that made it hard not to join him. After we had talked for only a few minutes, it seemed he couldn't be the same person Gloria had described to me as "a terrible man, a outlaw, honey, he's a outlaw! I walk on the other side of the court to keep from passin' by *that man*."

It was by coincidence that I even knew about Pete. Johnell Fernandez, the mother of one of Richard's classmates, had grown up in the St. Bernard project and known Alvin. When I learned this, I telephoned her, and she agreed to meet me a few days later. Since she was more than ten years younger than Alvin, it turned out that they actually had been only acquaintances and I had heard most of what she could tell me over the phone: that she remembered waiting in crowds which gathered about him at bus stops and that, even before he began boxing, he was regarded as a very important person in the project. She also remembered that his family shared in this neighborhood prestige because they always ate and seemed to live better than most.

A solemn man was with Johnell Fernandez when we met in a coffee shop the following Saturday morning. He wore a Muslim cap, and appeared to have suffered permanent damage to one of his eyes. She introduced him as Walid, the man she lived with. He seemed hesitant and suspicious. After a few minutes of halting conversation as we ordered coffee and he bought cigarettes, I gathered that he knew Alvin better than she had. He questioned me about my purposes, and we talked for a while about some of his scrapes at Clark High School, which Alvin also attended. He described Alvin as a "good brother." He remembered in particular how, when he went into the projects to distribute leaflets for Muslim causes, Alvin was always decent and receptive to him, even though others weren't. Then he told me about a cousin of his, Pete, Alvin's "fall podnah," and how Pete and Alvin used to "run behind it"—drugs—"all day, every day" in the year before Alvin fled to New York. He said Pete still "hangs on the corners" around the project: he was the one I really should see. Before we parted that morning he explained to me how to reach Pete.

So a few weeks later, in early March, I met Pete on a corner, then drove him to a coffee shop. Two policemen were eating at the counter. They made him nervous, he said, so we left and went to the levee, where I parked in a public area overlooking the river.

Before this day I had checked for Pete's name in the records section in the basement of the Criminal District Courts Building and been surprised to find but three entries, each at least twenty years old, that may have referred to him.

He laughed when I wondered aloud why there were no recent arrests. He said he was smarter "and less greedy" now that he was old. As though delivering a punch line, he added that his having lived off and on in "D.C." and New York for the past ten years might also have had something to do with his recently clean record in Louisiana.

At this mention of New York he took out a borrower's card from the New York Public Library—where he said he spent many of his days "up North." We talked a little about books and authors he had read there: *Roots, Manchild in the Promised Land*, Lorraine Hansberry, Richard Wright, Ralph Ellison. These were writers you could believe, he said, because they had lived what they wrote. Then he mentioned another book, a book both he and Alvin had read in their teens, as being responsible for some of the later turns in their lives. This was a popular account of the life of the gangster Lucky Luciano. A movie version followed. What struck them most strongly—he couldn't remember if the indelible scene was in the book, the movie, or both—was Luciano's choosing to be nailed to a tree rather than give up information or his dope, then his not uttering a sound throughout the ordeal.

Warming to the subject of Alvin, he stretched back in the seat, rested his arm out fat through the open window, and scanned the river. They went back a long way, he said, having been friends as children even though they lived "on different ends" of the project. They went to elementary school together and then junior high, where boys from their part of town, the Seventh Ward, had to hang together against gangs from the Ninth Ward and the Sixth. He said he didn't like to go to Alvin's "house," though, because he believed his father was crazy: "The man had a temper, an ex-fighter, you couldn't tell what he'd do."

He and Alvin started high school together and more and more frequently played hooky together. In those years they accepted the attitude that books were "for sissies." They shined shoes on Rampart Street to earn money to put down on pants and fancy shirts in French Quarter tailor shops. He smiled at my worn denims: "We *had* to wear blue jeans, so we didn't like 'em." They didn't want to go to school "all raggedy." It was important to look "real clean" at all times.

Before eleventh grade they had dropped out altogether and begun to spend time at the corner of Rampart and Esplanade selling goof balls as some of their older friends did.

The drug they themselves started on was a cough syrup containing codeine that sold for a dollar a bottle at Waterbury's Drugs on Canal Street. They drank this medicine regularly until it was banned over the counter. From there Pete went to heroin, which then cost four dollars a fix. Alvin sometimes joined him.

"But Alvin wasn't never no *jonk*ie," Pete insisted, "least not till after he got to New York. I always prided myself on not showing it when I was loaded. Alvin, when he copped, everybody would know. They'd say, 'Here come Alvin loaded!' He was so *fresh*, he'd be scratchin' an' sniffin'." By himself, Alvin "never could even *catch*," penetrate a vein, so Pete put the needle in for him whenever he "joy-popped" on weekends.

Alvin stayed "fresh" for as long as he did because of the conditioning that boxing required. But even before he began fighting professionally at the late age of twenty-five, he had kept himself in shape. Pete said one reason for this was that, whatever his father's flaws in temperament might be, Mr. Collis was a trained athlete. Another was the fact that, when they were in their teens, Alvin had married Diane after she had become pregnant. Since that time, again following his father's example, Alvin had worked to support her, Alvin Jr., and the five other children who followed. He went to work first in the warehouse at Woodward, Wight & Co., filling a place Collis had vacated for him. Later he caught on at the Blue Plate Mayonnaise factory. Pete called this the kind of steady job that many men from the neighborhood envied. Alvin held on to it for several years, staying at Blue Plate until he began to earn his better purses.

His becoming a ranked middleweight had no effect on his close friendships and contacts with "homies" in the neighborhood where he had always lived. He and Diane talked incessantly of buying a house in Ponchartrain Park. But nothing came of it. Gloria blamed this on Diane, saying she liked the project life and the gossip and "lookin' out in the mornin' to see who was robbed and who shot who." But Pete said it was hard to know if one of them was the more responsible for their staying on in their apartment on Jumonville. At the peak of Alvin's prosperity, both were around thirty. Diane always had attracted plenty of friends. "You couldn't just like her," Pete said, trying to find words for her appeal. And Alvin, when he came home from training, would, in Gloria's words, "put on that new leather and walk this project *down*." On these gratifying tours, he would often see Pete, who "carried a heavy habit" at the time. " 'Hey, bruh, do somethin' for me, bruh,' " Pete said he would ask him. Alvin, who already had the beginnings of a lived understanding of his friend's need, usually did do something for him—like his father, fingering into his pocket and handing out a five, a twenty, whatever he could spare.

Pete told me that, except for pocket money, Alvin even in flush times gave the rest of his checks to Diane, who managed the family expenses. Some months they quarreled when she didn't have enough left over or when he felt he needed something extra. During the period when his fight income was greatest, Alvin's friends—Pete wouldn't say who—led Diane into more than casual use of drugs. Although Alvin loved her, Pete said he had wronged her. Then she wronged him.

I thought about the hurtful cycle of married infidelity and the specter of drugs framing Alvin as he made his bid for big money and the middleweight title. While we watched a Norwegian tanker slicing upriver, I tried to say what I was thinking.

"There you go," Pete answered with a formulaic phrase of agreement that was like a refrain with him. "That's it. Man listenin' to his wife screamin' and hollerin' upstairs in the bedroom. It was a long time before he even knew what she was cryin', actin' crazy for. But I knew."

Diane had started with pills. Soon after, she was on heroin, which she couldn't use openly at home or often enough.

"The woman cried because she was sick."

As I drove back to Pete's corner, he added to the practical information he had interspersed throughout the conversation: "basic things" that he said would "hip" me to the drug scene, things such as "Never carry more than you can swallow" and "Two on the corner is conspiracy . . ." He said Alvin couldn't possibly have sold the caps of heroin he was convicted of selling because he and Pete never violated a common peddlers' system: neither ever handled both money and drugs; if Alvin was collecting the money, Pete, in charge of passing the drugs, would be somewhere else, "watchin' his back." Calvin Clark and Emmanuel Stewart, he said, were "sissies" they had known since late childhood when Clark and Stewart had been "turned out" at the Milne Boys' Home, the institution in which Collis found Charles Joseph and other prospects—and in which the young Louis Armstrong once lived.

I don't remember how the subject of track marks came up, but when I stopped the car he unbuttoned his sleeve. Craning toward him, I expected there would be crisscrossed scratches in the fleshy crook of his arm. Instead the rolled-back sleeve disclosed raised purple scars, each vertical and about the length and thickness of a small child's finger.

Before he opened the door, he took a photograph from his pocket. It showed him, in a tuxedo that made him look like a diplomat, standing with a large attractive woman in an evening gown; before them stood a budlike girl in her late teens, who was dressed formally like her mother. He said the woman had had a baby for him when they were in high school and didn't tell him of it until much later, after one of his trips North. Now they were sometimes together. The girl in the picture was their daughter, on the evening of her graduation from one of the city's most respected Catholic girls' schools. He now sometimes attended mass himself, he told me. He said he felt most at peace when the service ended and he left to go home. He asked me to send the photograph to Alvin—which I did. As he was about to step from the car, I took out some money. I would have felt awkward offering a hundred, or anything—and all I could then spare was much less. But he quickly put my discomfort aside by slapping his hand across mine and coming away with the bill. "I'll take it," he said, laughing at my embarrassment as he shut the door. "I don't mind. I'll take it."

11

□

March 18, 1982

One night I happened to see Walid—while waiting in line
for parent-teacher conferences at our children's school. As
we waited, he told me a tale about Pete: how he once was
warned by a tavern owner not to shoot up in the men's
room. Pete gave himself the fix anyway, and the man came
in and caught him. Walid spread his hands, establishing the
context: "A small place, see?" The proprietor then "took a
pool cue to Pete" and beat him "till that cue broke down to
just this much," Walid whispered, measuring off the length
of his forearm. "But Pete didn't drop one issue of his fix!"
It was the first time I had seen Walid smile, yet I gathered
that his story also had a serious point and was meant to
caution me that Pete might never kick his habit even though
he told me he had.

This concern was on my mind when I stopped for Pete
on a different corner a few weeks after our first meeting. As
it turned out, my worry was unnecessary. He talked more
freely than he had before, and he seemed even friendlier,
and more reflective.

About two weeks after the first fight with Tony Licata,
Alvin left Diane for the night and went with Pete to a Stevie
Wonder concert at the Auditorium. "We had us a time that
night." Pete grinned, shaking his head. "Everybody knew he
whipped Licata. The whole place was glad to see him, us."
In the course of the evening Alvin "got loaded" on heroin.
They stayed up all night. Toward dawn, back in the project,

they decided to go in together and sell drugs. It seemed smarter than just buying. With Pete's experience and connections and Alvin's intimidating reputation, they felt they couldn't miss: sell a little, make a little money, and always have enough wholesale, high-quality product to keep them feeling good.

They took as a third partner someone called Quiet Man. Pete claimed he "never knew Quiet's real name." But later I learned it—because Quiet Man, who still worked the streets, shot Gloria's son Lionel as the climax to a drug feud with members of a younger generation.

Pete became fond, remembering the money they made and how, on Sundays, they would sit down together to count and divide it. Sometimes there were several thousand dollars to be shared.

His memories of the period also included horrors. A woman they were hesitant to share drugs with insisted she knew what she was doing: " 'I was shootin' dope when you was still shittin' yella.' " She proceeded to overdose—then die in the speeding car Alvin drove to the Charity emergency room. They felt they had no choice but to pretend she had passed out and then to slip away as soon as they could. Pete said Alvin, even more than he, was haunted by this death. The woman had been one of their classmates in grade school. Alvin wanted to quit the drug scene. But by then it was too late.

Despite the tragic nature of Pete's reminiscences, he told them almost like jokes, smiling at the memory of Alvin's consternation when, with medics approaching the car, he discovered for himself what Pete had been insisting from the back seat—that the woman slumped against him in the front wasn't merely unconscious.

Pete continued to smile when I told him about the word "Rock" printed in nail polish across Alvin's back in Angola. "That's him!" he said firmly. "That li'l rock ain' never go'n crack. I never saw him lose." He held up his fists. "With these." He shook his head and seemed moved. "He couldn't be no thief, though. I never run across such a sad thief. I

couldn't trust him with that. He just wasn't no good at it."
Mimicking Alvin, he said he was " 'standin' tall,' though"
after his fight in Europe and his association with Emile
Griffith. "He'd tell you in a minute he was 'a universal citizen!'
Told me, say, 'Bruh, they don't care nothin' for color over
there. Over there, they give you respect.'

"Yeh," he said, allowing himself a rare instance of direct
seriousness as I pulled up again back at the corner. "Alvin
was always a thousand."

After I passed him a bill and we said our goodbyes, he
leaned back into the car. Heroin was a drug he said "you
have to go lookin' for," trying to suggest, I guessed, that the
corruption of innocent youth was foreign to his purposes.
It was as close to self-justification as he came. There was an
odd half-smile on his face as he abruptly declared he was
"almost glad they brought the chair back." Executions made
it known that "that's what I'd git if I kept on." Raising his
hand, he began to turn away. "That chair was for me!"

Through the rearview mirror I saw him adjust his Florida
visor, then stroll around the corner as if nothing in this
world was on his mind.

12

□

I'm thinking this morning of Alvin's career: it began almost by accident in the mid-sixties.

His father, who had adjusted to his crutches and physically recovered from the shooting as much as he ever would, was then running Vince Arnona's gym in the warehouse district on Tchoupitoulas Street. Alvin worked not far away at Woodward, Wight & Co. Afternoons after work Alvin would stop by the gym to wait, unless Collis had a ride, to go home with him on the bus.

The star of the Tchoupitoulas gym was Jerry Pellegrini, a white welterweight and middleweight contender whose training Collis supervised for Arnona. Pellegrini hit hard, and it was difficult to keep him in sparring partners. One afternoon, when no one else was available, Collis asked Alvin to go up into the ring and give Pellegrini some work. Alvin took off his shoes and, in his first formal sparring session, boxed in jeans and bare feet.

In "A Champ at Ringside," a story and interview, which appeared in *The Times-Picayune* the morning of Alvin's second fight with Tony Licata, New Orleans sports journalist Waddell Summers quoted Collis's description of his son's start, an account that was similar to others I had heard from various people who had known Alvin. " 'Well, Alvin used to come by the gym to see me,' " Collis told Summers. " 'So one day Alvin got in the ring and we just told him to move a lot. Alvin was fast but didn't know anything about boxing.

Jerry didn't try to hurt him. Actually, Jerry taught him a lot. Jerry is a good kid, a fine young man . . . Alvin learned fast. Jerry gave him ideas and pretty soon there was Alvin, starting to box pro in his first four-rounder.

" 'It really surprised me when Alvin decided to be a boxer. He could have been boxing at fifteen or sixteen. But I never enticed any of my sons to be fighters. It's such hard work and such a long road to travel. I advised all my kids to get an education. I don't want to stand in the way of my kids. I told Alvin if he wanted to fight, I would help him. I didn't ask him to be a fighter, but I would never try to stop my son from doing what he's doing. Two of my sons, Collis Jr. and Jerry, fought some amateur, but Alvin never did. I guess Alvin has natural talent—that's the only thing I can call it.' "

In his first fight, at the age of twenty-five, Alvin didn't look so much like a natural. He fought on the undercard of a Jerry Pellegrini show and lost a four-round decision to an opponent named Preston Price. Collis told me he "looked like he had a little stage fright" that night; he "didn't stay busy enough" and "let the decision git away from him." Collis said he "got on him heavy" about it afterwards.

After that, Alvin won fifteen straight, all at the Municipal Auditorium, a streak that included a payback defeat of Preston Price. Interest in boxing was high in New Orleans in those days, and Alvin had the kind of mix-it-up style that most fight fans prefer. By 1968, he was a ten-round fighter and a favorite with the large fight crowds that then came regularly to the Auditorium.

His second loss came in his first fight on the road, a decision to a tough veteran, Willie Crosby of Mobile. Although Crosby had beaten Alvin decisively, in his next outing Mike arranged a good opportunity for him as a late substitute in a main event in Kansas City against well-known New Yorker Bobby Harrington. "WILL ACCEPT FIGHT WITH HARRINGTON," Mike wired the promoter. "YOUR CLUB NOVEMBER 12, 1968 165 POUNDS $350 FLAT TWO EXCURSION RATE ROUND TRIP PLANE TICKETS

AND HOTEL ACCOMMODATIONS SEND CON-
TRACT." Mike accompanied Alvin to Kansas City, where
he fought well, but was denied the decision in a ten-round
draw.

His visibility as a boxer now made it possible for him to
move from Woodward, Wight to a better-paying job in the
mayonnaise plant beneath the huge neon "B-l-u-e P-l-a-t-e"
that still sparkles every night in the middle of town on Jeff
Davis Parkway.

At Blue Plate he worked his way up to operating the
steam-capping machine, which stamped lids on jars of pre-
serves. His supervisor there, John Lincks, remembered him
to me as "a very good worker." He said Alvin sometimes
brought boxing posters to tape up around the plant and
often the day after a fight he would come to work "all beat
up."

Alvin's most active year in the ring was 1969. In that year,
in which he still worked at Blue Plate, he fought eight times,
seventy-seven rounds, headlining five cards at the Auditorium and winning twice out of town—in Baton Rouge and
Corpus Christi. In July he took on Eddie Pace, whom top
middleweights and many light heavies were ducking. Just
two weeks after absorbing this beating, he fought again,
winning a ten-round decision at the Auditorium. A month
later, in his biggest win to that point, he decisioned Charlie
Shipes, a ranked fighter. In an ambitious move near the end
of the year, Mike matched him against the formidable Ralph
Palladin in Baltimore. Alvin lost the decision, but the fight
so pleased the crowd that the Maryland promoter offered
him another fight early in 1970. His opponent, southpaw
Philadelphian Billy Lloyd, had a style Alvin never quite
solved. Lloyd won a questionable split decision, but the bout
was so hard-fought they were rematched a month later in
Louisiana.

Lou Messina staged it on April 21 at the St. Bernard Civic
Auditorium in a neighboring parish, the first of Alvin's only
two local fights not at the Auditorium. Although Collis often
told me that he himself had "never been sick a day" in his

life, except for the shooting, Gloria said he was home in bed
with the flu on this night in April. Charley Joseph replaced
him in Alvin's corner alongside Mike. Gloria had a seat in
the front row. The fight was a repeat of Alvin and Lloyd's
first one, a sustained brawl. Both bled freely, but Alvin led
on all cards entering the tenth. He had almost put Lloyd
down in the seventh when, according to the newspaper
reporter in attendance, he hit him with as many as twenty
consecutive rights. But in the tenth Lloyd surged back. Near
the end of the round and the fight, a long left cross dropped
Alvin on his back in a corner. At first it seemed he was too
hurt and fatigued to move; then, using the turnbuckles hand
over hand, he pulled himself to his feet. The wild standing
crowd was divided between those shrieking for more action
and those shouting for the referee to stop it. Lloyd leaped
at Alvin and pounded him with lefts. The referee stepped
in, seeming to call a halt, but Alvin protested. The referee
moved away. Lloyd tagged him flush with another left, and
Alvin went down like sand. Gloria had been beating the
apron, pleading with Mike and Charley to throw in the
towel. She said she couldn't believe they made no move to
end it as the count began again and once more, saggingly,
Alvin commenced arming his way up the ropes. Then,
transported by the frenzy and the blood masking Alvin's
face, she was in the ring, a hysterical fury between the other
man and her brother. At once handlers from both sides
scrambled in followed by small thrown objects, then a chair.
Spectators swarmed toward the steps. In the confusion,
reporters didn't realize that the woman, not the referee, had
stopped the fight. Corroborating Gloria's version of the
ending, Mike said he vaguely recalled that a woman had
intervened at the end of the fight; yes, it could have been
Alvin's sister, but if so she hadn't done her brother any
favor: if he had been allowed to weather the brief remainder
of the round, he would have taken the decision. As it was,
the referee was obliged to declare Billy Lloyd a TKO winner
in 2:47 of the tenth. This was the only knockout Alvin
suffered, until his last fight.

From this low point he again recovered quickly. Within a month he topped another card at the Auditorium, knocking out his journeyman opponent for his twenty-second win. In July he was matched again against Willie Crosby, this time at home. Lou Messina billed the fight for the "Southern middleweight championship." Like Collis's titles in the thirties, this one was purely a promotional device. Although Crosby had knocked him down three times in Mobile, Alvin took charge. Wearing the black velvet trunks a companion of Diane's aunt made for him, he jabbed and moved well. From the second round on he bled from a sliced left eyelid, but he also cut Crosby, who had never been cut before, so badly that the fight had to be stopped in the sixth. In the ring afterwards, Lou Messina presented Alvin with a tall trophy from Malcolm Faber's, the same trophy that—no matter how often or differently she rearranges the furniture—always stands prominently in the first room of Gloria's apartment.

His becoming "middleweight champ of the South" began a period of relative prosperity for Alvin, Collis, and most of the rest of the family, who were boosted by their close connection to his local success. When I met her in New York, Diane told me how, when Alvin fought at home, it seemed that the adult population of the project and many others in the Seventh Ward drove to the Auditorium in noisy cavalcades. Afterwards there would be celebrations lasting until early morning at the Star Lounge facing the project on St. Bernard. Freshly showered and well dressed, Alvin would make an appearance at the Star, set everyone up, and have a beer. Then, just the two of them, he would take Diane to eat at Dooky Chase's, one of the very finest of the city's fine black-owned restaurants. When he and Diane reached home, win or lose he would wake the children and tell them in detail about the fight. Alvin Jr. and Kevin both said they only pretended to sleep, having lain open-eyed in the dark, listening for his step in the courtyard.

13

□

The seventies started so well for Alvin and his family that he was able to leave his job at Blue Plate and devote all his working energy to fighting. He successfully defended his Southern title twice before good houses in the Auditorium. Then in January 1971 Mike arranged for him to fight in Philadelphia against knockout artist Willie "the Worm" Monroe. Monroe brought fifteen straight kayos into the fight. Alvin broke Monroe's knockout streak, but the decision went against him. It was a punishing ten rounds for each of them.

Two months later, back in New Orleans, he decisioned longtime contender Kitten Hayward. But this victory led to no new opportunities. During the next fourteen months, he fought five times more, his last five fights for his father and Mike; two were on the road—in Mobile and Corpus Christi against tough journeymen whose names would do nothing to distinguish his record—and the other three were in the Auditorium. Now that he had had a taste of boxing success, and with his income now based solely on the ring, he was eager for more of the glamorous high life and especially impatient for big-money fights. He became skeptical of Mike's ability to make such fights, and he began to resent Collis's unconditional loyalty to his white friend. Pete described how, before he ripped the pages in half, Alvin would point knowingly to the names of men he had beaten—Charlie Shipes, Kitten Hayward—names printed in boxing magazines, in influential ratings that didn't include him.

The fights he was then fighting were damaging brawls at the Auditorium: a second lost decision to Willie Monroe, and for the third time a loss to his nemesis Billy Lloyd. The crowds loved the action, but Alvin increasingly saw these fights as little more than very painful paydays; even in training for them, he doubted their potential, under Mike and Collis's direction, to move him toward the top.

There was another factor influencing his growing cynicism about boxing: Tony Licata. They had sparred in the same gyms while gaining seasoning, but even very early it was as if they and their handlers sensed they were on a collision course—if not for the middleweight title, then for something more personal. In their first gym meetings Alvin was more advanced than Tony, who was then still a teenager. Alvin may have tried to follow instructions and practice restraint in working with the younger man, but Tony was very aggressive and couldn't easily assume the role of apprentice. Training sessions between them turned into rounds fiercer than some fighters fight. After Tony turned pro, his trainers and Collis decided to keep him and Alvin in different gyms whenever possible. As their skills developed further, it was understood that they were not to work together.

It would have been hard for anyone in Alvin's place not to feel envy at the way influential people were grooming Tony's career. In a sequence of carefully chosen matches, Tony rang up more than twenty wins without a loss. Before he had fought anyone of the caliber of Alvin's toughest opponents, Tony already had replaced Alvin as the top draw at the Auditorium. Like Alvin, he was a crowd-pleaser with undeniable courage, but some of his other ring assets differed from Alvin's: he was a photogenic, very young white man who moved gracefully and possessed dazzling hand speed. His star rose as Alvin's seemed to stall. Soon his name appeared in various rating systems that had never given Alvin much ink.

Even though promoters and fans spoke eagerly of a Licata-Phillips fight as a natural, Tony's people had no intention of matching them until Tony was more than ready. It was no coincidence that Alvin's Southern title wasn't always on the line in fights following his winning of it; the belt was being saved as added spice for his eventual meeting with Tony. So, in the spring of 1972, it must have seemed to Alvin that his only certain prospect was to continue a pattern of hard, not very profitable fighting while being denied the one good payday available to him.

"Left me lookin' like a stupid monkey, me an' Mike," was Collis's description of what happened. "Come to me, aksed for his contrac'. What I'm go'n do? That was my son." The break with Mike and his father came about a month after Alvin decisioned veteran Ernie Burns in early May in Mobile. In buying the contract, Malcolm Faber gave assurances that his next opponent would be a contender. There was also talk of a date in Madison Square Garden before Christmas.

He first fought for Malcolm and Johnny two months later, on August 21. Malcolm had brought in seventh-ranked welterweight Ronnie Harris to face him at the Auditorium. Alvin came in several pounds under his usual weight and, fighting with new vigor, convincingly won almost every round. "I felt in better shape than usual," he told reporters afterwards. "I'm ready for Licata. This fight was to ensure that."

Within three weeks Faber had him fighting again, again at the Auditorium and for a third time against Willie Monroe, whom many top middleweights avoided. This was a popular, profitable pairing since fans vividly remembered their second fight, which had taken place at the Auditorium in January. This time Alvin stayed more on top of "the Worm," and they fought the close, feverish rounds almost entirely along the ropes. Both were punched out and near collapse at the end as the crowd stood to cheer. The split decision went to Alvin. His busy hook, and possibly the location of the fight, had made the difference and finally earned him a win over Willie Monroe.

The fight in New York came a month later. Malcolm Faber made good on his word: he had booked Alvin as a late substitute in Madison Square Garden. His opponent, Bobby

Watts, a coming young fighter, trained, as Monroe did, in Philadelphia, which has the roughest gyms in the country. Watts had had just sixteen pro fights then, but, though he had won them all, Johnny felt he could intimidate him and his manager—"It was a woman, the li'l dude had a chick for a manager!"—by telling her that he was sorry to have made the match and that he feared Alvin would hurt "her boy." In Johnny's pre-fight photos, both Watts and Alvin, who looked old and hard enough to be Watts's father, were noticeably subdued; and Watts, in fact, did look frightened. The cause of Alvin's distraction seemed less clear.

The nervousness Watts showed at the weigh-in was either a psych job of his own or something he put behind him at the opening bell. He used his greater height and reach to keep his listless opponent off balance throughout the fight, mixing flurries to the body with his steady jab and long crosses. Alvin outpunched him for about thirty seconds in the seventh. Otherwise, it was all Bobby Bougaloo Watts, who came back in the eighth to stagger Alvin and knock out his mouthpiece. This was the same Bougaloo Watts who remained a high-ranking contender throughout the seventies after Alvin went to prison and who, during a sparring session in the eighties, broke the ribs of great middleweight champion Marvin Hagler.

Alvin's loss in New York received scant coverage by the New Orleans media and so did little to mute the local clamor for a fight between him and Tony Licata. Tony had been making such impressive progress that the match was agreed on shortly after Alvin and Johnny returned from New York. It took place on November 28, 1972, just after Thanksgiving. In order to accommodate an expected record crowd, the fight was held, not in the Auditorium, but in a larger arena, the Rivergate, a newly constructed convention hall that stands near where Canal Street meets the river.

Possibly because Tony's drawing power was certain, pre-fight publicity touted Alvin. In a feature story published shortly before the fight, Waddell Summers wrote that "Phillips's bouts have been marked by his super condition, his willingness to mix, his courage and his ability to take punishment and come back. He has parlayed the aforementioned assets, plus a good left hook and a great desire to win, into recognition as a foe worthy enough to challenge any top middleweight. Phillips has gained the admiration and respect of the fight crowd by his willingness to battle anyone they sent against him, regardless of reputation."

Gloria had good seats for the fight and enjoyed VIP treatment. She remembered being ushered to Alvin's dressing room during the prelims. Through a distant doorway at the end of a corridor, she saw him "on his back on a table," lying "still, still." As she leaned over to kiss him, he opened his eyes and whispered, " 'This is my last fight, sis.' "

And, in a sense, it was.

When they entered the ring, Tony was twenty years old and undefeated in thirty-two fights. Alvin was thirty, with a record of 30–11–1. That night, both were dead game.

Afterwards, *The Times-Picayune* described it as "an absolutely torrid clash from first bell to last." According to the paper and to spectators I spoke to, Tony's hand speed won the first round, but Alvin stayed busier and also outjabbed him through the middle rounds. Sensing he was behind, Tony pressed Alvin with flurries of punches in rounds nine and ten, but after each attack Alvin fought his way off the ropes.

Racial partisanship throughout the crowd mirrored the narrow advantage that sawed back and forth between the fighters. Blacks and whites alike signified and cheered aggressively each time their man scored. The 3,586 people in attendance stood through the last two rounds. They remained standing after the last bell and gave both fighters an extended ovation. When the decision was announced, an uproar ensued, and altercations between blacks and whites broke out around the arena. The referee voted for Alvin five rounds to four, while scoring one even; but because the two judges scored it five-five, the decision was a majority draw. (The newspaper and the consensus among boxing people at ringside favored Alvin.)

After security forces had escorted the fighters from the ring and extra police finished calming the crowd, Tony's handlers complained of his having a weight problem. Alvin was too dejected to say much to reporters.

In January, a sniper, a young black man firing from the roof of the high-rise downtown Howard Johnson's, killed six people—including three policemen—and wounded nine others before he himself was shot to death by a small army of law enforcement officers eleven hours after the ordeal began. This terrible incident aggravated racial tension in New Orleans, but there was no lessening of enthusiasm for the rematch. The fight, Alvin's final one at home, was set for April 4, 1973—in the Auditorium, which soon sold out.

Alvin damaged one of his hands in training, but it was too late by then to postpone the show. His injury and the cortisone shots he received to blunt the pain were never made public. Pre-fight coverage emphasized international title prospects, the Southern title, and the fight—"a popular 'mixed match,' as they are called today"—as a rare natural pairing of evenly skilled, exciting athletes. There was also the story and interview with Collis, "A Champ at Ringside," in which Waddell Summers portrayed the father-son relation in Alvin's boxing background while maintaining silence about the broken business relationship that had soured it. Typically, Collis's public comments skirted controversy and stressed technical elements of boxing: " 'I don't think there's any hard feelings in this fight. The boys used to work together at one time. Tony's an awfully nice kid. His people, especially his dad, have been nice to me too. He's a fast puncher and is very game. You've got to stay on him. He don't pass up nothing.' "

Except briefly during the first two rounds, Alvin wasn't able to "stay on" his man. Even at the beginning, he appeared fought out. The sports page reported that "Tony consistently got off first and completely outspeeded the game Phillips." Although "both were well applauded at the end," the only similarities between Alvin's performances in April and November were his toughness and courage. Tony drew blood early and several times had him on the verge of a knockdown.

It was rumored Tony could have knocked him out but respected him too much to do it. When I asked Tony about this, he raised his hand as if to block the question. He said that rumor wasn't true. In his dressing room after the fight, Tony praised him routinely: " 'Alvin always comes to fight.' " Pressed for an explanation of his loss, Alvin tossed off an answer that suggested his frustration and a willingness to give up the battle: " 'My legs gave out on me after the third round. It could be age or I over-ran—or didn't run enough.' " He said nothing about his hand—and, naturally, nothing about his habit.

European closes are common to the careers of many once potent American fighters. On June 2 came the end-of-the-road meeting with European champ Jean-Claude Bouttier in Monte Carlo. Ten thousand people paid to enter the Louis II soccer stadium to see Emile Griffith, in his twenty-first title fight, unsuccessfully challenge Carlos Monzon in the main event. Except for his slack effort against Bouttier, Alvin must have had a good time, maybe the time of his life, in Italy and Monaco. He had traveled far, and he had worked with Griffith and would remember him as a friend. Bouttier went on to a title shot, and decision loss, against Monzon in September in Paris. Alvin flew home to the project, a universal citizen.

Two summers later, Tony had his shot at the title, and Monzon praised his bravery after knocking him out in the tenth round in Madison Square Garden. By then, Alvin was in jail, awaiting trial.

14

□

December 11, 1981

Velma Whittey, Farris's girlfriend, startled me by leaning
on the horn of my car and shouting into the empty courtyard
for Alvin Jr. to come on. She and I had had conversations
in the small grocery store she leased, but this was the first
time I would see Alvin's first son. I was driving them to
Angola on this morning so he could visit his father and as
an excuse for me to meet him in an unhurried way. Velma
would visit Farris. Despite my having spent an hour with
each brother in September, today I wouldn't be allowed
inside the prison. In September I had a special pass; now
my mandatory application to be added to Alvin's list of
regular visitors remained stalled in preliminary stages of the
bureaucratic process. Excited by soon to be seeing her man,
Velma wore an appealing dress with a flattering low neckline.
She sassed Alvin Jr. when at last he emerged from a doorway
that appeared to have been scorched. She continued to tease
him as he came on to the car, looking as if he had just
stumbled from bed.

He was stocky like his father was, no more than 5'8" and
about 165. On this almost cold day, he wore a gray vinyl car
coat, a velour shirt, grime-sheened blue jeans, and, oddly,
gray Hush Puppies of a style more typical of settled, much
older men. These clothes concealed the heavy muscles that
would be conspicuous when, months later, he boxed on local
cable television as a member of the inmate team from Parish
Prison. A ring sparkled on his left fourth finger and matched

a medallion suspended from his neck—imitation diamonds. At once he gave the impression, accurate in his present circumstances, of being unable to wash himself and his clothes as often as he would have liked. Viewed in profile, there was a cast to his eyes that could make him seem to be of little account. But seen full-face, beneath thickly curling lashes, his large eyes conveyed a haunting impression of sincerity and woundedness.

Entering a rear door of the car, he greeted me shyly. He had a cold, and it soon became clear that he was hardly awake. Saying no more than the minimum, he responded to Velma's many comments without raising his head. During the first hour of the drive north, he initiated not the sheerest scrap of talk. Not until, when passing through Baton Rouge, one of us mentioned Jerry did he speak with any animation, telling how his uncle Jerry took him in at a time when he was living in the street in New York, surviving by washing cars on Seventh Avenue and 133rd for pimps and pushers, "those cats who has their big cars washed and waxed once a day."

Jerry also taught him to cook—a skill Jerry had developed in the Job Corps—letting him learn by doing. Now he remembered with pleasure how he and Jerry cooked "ribs, shrimps, fish, anything." This helped prepare him for all facets of kitchen work, so that, when he came back to New Orleans, he was able to be employed in several restaurants, including the dining room of the opulent Fairmont Hotel. He had done everything from dishwashing and busing to baking and occasionally cooking main dishes. He described recently losing his best restaurant job because a black manager there had it in for him due to a white chef's taking a liking to him. He still hoped to attend cooking school and earn a chef's license. It was just that this manager was "the type guy no one could get along with, the man would fuss if you so much as put a piece of quiche on a plate backwards. I just left, I wasn't go'n let him fire me."

From recollections of cooking and Jerry he slipped easily into solicited remembrances of his grandfather—of being in the bed with him on St. Bernard and the stinging tickle of having him rub chin stubble across his child's flesh. "Grampaw called me li'l Al-*vee*." Mornings he would cross the courtyard from Jumonville, go into Collis and Dorothy's apartment, and say, "Grampaw, I'm hongry." Collis would tell him, "Go down in the kitchen, tell Farris and Jerry I say fix you sumpum to eat." Velma nodded in agreement as he straightened and declared, "Farris and Jerry could eat now! They used mixin' bowls for their oatmeal." Farris would try to make him stay around after breakfast to help him and Jerry clean the floors—"He'd make 'em shine so you could see your face"—and he would try to slip out with his grandfather. Sometimes, without Collis's knowing of it, Farris would catch him and lock him in the closet under the stairs where he told him bats lived. Al Jr. would scream and fight about that because "it was dark in that closet." I asked if he was really scared. "Yah! You know I was scared! We had us some fun then!"

There were problems in the reception center at Angola, which we entered from the visitors' parking lot. Alvin Jr.'s name wasn't on his father's visitors' list as he had thought. Alvin's other children's names were there, but not that of his namesake. The clerical guards wouldn't discuss it with either of us, and I tried using the pay phone outside to call in to one of the warden's secretaries, whom I had previously talked with long-distance. As I already knew, a Special Visit was now our only hope. She told me there was no one available who could authorize that today; and anyway, she added, Special Visits weren't approved unless preceded—as mine had been in September—by a telephone call or a letter of request at least a week in advance. It didn't matter that the prisoner in question's omission of his first son's name was a trivial mistake, one probably caused by his disorientation. A rule was a rule. People were paid to enforce them. She reminded me that Angola was a prison.

When I reentered the reception center, Velma had already been searched and had finished her commiserations with Alvin Jr. She was now eager to pay her own visit. We watched her trip spiritedly through the guarded turnstile on her way to the bus that would take her to Camp J.

Knowing our wait would last several hours, Alvin and I tried to settle back on the white slat bench. The small room was overheated and the near presence of the guards not conducive to any conversation unconnected to their bored, vocal horsing around. Christmas tinsel hung from tape on various surfaces, and lights blinked on an aluminum tree on the counter by the turnstile. As relief from the heat and the room, several times we went to stand and pace in the chilly parking lot. At first he seemed too downcast for words, and I avoided intruding on his sullen silence. But on one of these short trips, in the process of finally complaining of this treatment, he began to speak of his father. Tacitly I encouraged him.

In summer they would sit outside at evening time and eat frozen orange juice balls, the adults lacing theirs with vodka: "My dad liked those." And on Fridays, a night when their mother sometimes worked, the children would stay up late and watch TV with their father. Everyone's favorites were the old horror movies introduced by a New Orleans actor in the campy role of "Morgus," a mad comic doctor whose weekly purpose was to preserve mankind through bizarre experiments, all of which blew up in his face because of his nitwit assistant, "Chopsley." Their father would "be at the top a the bed," laughing, with the children "all around him and down by the foot."

Other times, when the children were older and Alvin's prestige as a boxer had grown, he would let them pile into his unreliable old Chevy, the one Diane was ever "worryin' him to get rid of," and drive to the lake, to the park, to buy ice cream or cold drinks. These trips would include whatever children from the neighborhood happened to be around. During his first winning streak, he became "like a model" to the boys near Alvin Jr.'s age. They'd say, " 'Al*vin!* Where yo' daddy?' " " 'At the gym,' " he would answer. Then they would want to know, " 'When he comin' home? When he comin' home?' " When Al Jr. or Kevin needed clothes, Alvin, enjoying his own extravagant generosity, would take their friends along and "buy shirts and pants for them too." " 'Man!' " they'd say. " 'Yo' *daddy*, he's aw right!' "

Soon to lapse into bitter quiet, he now gazed at the cold crushed shells at our feet and told me he knew "for a fact" that his father always stuck up for the weak: "He would never stand by and let someone be run over." This was the reason he thought Alvin had been involved in so many fights in prison and had suffered the clubs of the guards.

His mood was milder when Velma returned in high spirits, flushed and faintly exuding the scent of arousal. Back in the car, she had him smiling again, reporting how Farris laughed and slapped the table, startling a guard, when she told him Alvin Jr.'s story about the closet beneath the stairs. Farris had forgotten his game of bats roosting among coat hangers and was amazed that " 'li'l Al,' " whom he hadn't seen in ten years, should remember it so well.

Through dusk, then in darkness, the rhythms of travel and talk became easier and less directed. Under the cover of night, there was a sense of release from the hurry and some of the tension that had accompanied us in the morning. Of the three of us, Alvin seemed to me the most changed. Instead of huddling again in a corner of the back seat, he sat forward in the middle behind us, for all his hard knocks and street smarts, seeming younger than before, a quiet kid earing in on what the adults had to say. Velma mentioned Diane and someone named Ernest, and deftly Alvin changed the subject to include only his mother. He said he saw her not long ago when he was last in New York. It was her birthday. He took her out for a drink. Ernest, I learned later, was the man she lived with and with whom Alvin Jr. several times had fought because Ernest mistreated his mother; the last time—his reason for leaving New York in his mid-teens—he stabbed Ernest so severely the man almost died.

Diane disclosed none of this when we talked in New York. She said her oldest child spent his teenaged years shuttling between New York and New Orleans because he was too easily led and always seemed to "fall in with the wrong crowd." She mentioned Ernest, but only to make the point that she let Ernie know from the first that she had a husband in prison and that she "would want to hook up with him again" if he ever were freed. It would have to be like this, she said, because she had met her husband at a girlfriend's when she was "only nine." She was so surprised when he liked her because all of her girlfriends liked him. She and he grew so close so soon that her mother sent her away in the summers to "stay by" her father's in Providence or Boston. But each time she returned it was impossible for anyone to keep her and Alvin apart. When at fifteen she became pregnant, he took it on himself to marry her, a decision some of his male friends thought foolish. But during their marriage she took much on herself too: she would drive the car for his roadwork early in the morning, then take him to work, then pick him up afterwards and take him to the gym and wait while he trained, then drive him back home. After the dinner she served him, he always smoked part of a cigarette, even when in training for a fight; he would "dench" it out and smoke the rest of the "dench" later when they were in bed and she would talk to him, and while she talked, he would drift off to sleep. Then during the few months they spent together in New York, they would "swing"—that is, share her methadone. Since he wasn't registered in the clinic, only she could stand before the attendant and drink from the paper cup; afterwards she would swing around to kiss him and he would swallow what he needed out of her mouth. Privately she insisted to Connie that Alvin was " 'better off where he is' " because at least in prison there were three meals a day.

Later, rocking home from Angola to the steady motion of the car, Velma aired an old notion: "They say God is for black folks 'cause the white folks got what they want and don't think they need Him." After she attested to the great personal value of worship for her, I tried, in the spirit of sharing, to express such convictions of mine and said something to the effect that I didn't know if I believed in God, but that either way I couldn't not pray. In the mirror I saw Alvin Jr. watching our profiles after it was evident no more would be said.

He was watching me again just before we said good night in New Orleans. Velma had invited me into her store, which was closed to business. We were all tired, but I accepted out of respect for her courtesy. Inside lights burned and maybe a dozen people, most of them male, stood around drinking beer and wine. The males wore a look of men on the edge; warily they appraised me. Yet there was no threat there—my being with Velma and Alvin insured against that—only their uneasy surprise, then formal politeness and general constraint. When, after a passable interval, I thanked Velma and started for the door, Alvin hung back so his would be the last hand I took. Not that intimacy had formed between us. Only the recognition as we parted—I saw it in his eyes and sensed he could see it in mine—that we might be valuable to each other.

On my way home I tried to remember at what point he responded to my question about when he last saw his father. Were we in the car or on the shells at Angola? I had learned he was twelve at the time and in New York just after the extradition hearing, but I had so few other details. What more could he have said?

"We was walking together through the court building. Down underneath, where they keep the cars. Then we stopped. He told me, 'Take care of your mother.' Then he kissed her. Then we had to stay there and he went on with the detectives."

FOUR

The Penitentiary

□

1

□

Fall 1981

To go from New Orleans to Angola, you travel eighty
miles upriver to Baton Rouge, the capital. From there
continue about twenty miles farther on Highway 61 until it
enters St. Francisville. Anyone visiting prisoners should leave
New Orleans early, the time of morning when gassy mist,
the land's poisoned breath, often blankets the green shoulders of the roadbed. Those in haste will miss the chemical
wastes pooled beneath the thick vegetation, but other signs
of the grip of the petroleum industry on southern Louisiana
appear blatantly along 61 and the Great River Road. Haze
radiates from refineries thrumming near plantation houses
ranged along the river.

At picturesque St. Francisville, the route branches west on
state road 66, which splits rolling acres of woods. Smaller
trees stretch for light between oaks, pines, pecans, and kudzu-
shrouded utility poles that crowd the road, wreathing it in
archways of shade. This part of the trip would be bucolic
except for rusting trailer homes that occasionally loom ahead
on bald swatches of earth. Eventually, weathered gray houses
appear against the undergrowth surrounded by chicken
coops, hoe patches, and junked cars.

Ten miles from St. Francisville a smaller road intersects
66, and a sign announcing Hollywood points toward the
northeast. Farther along, 66 crosses another road—
Weyanoke—but nothing is there except woods and the sign.
Before 66 enters Tunica, a village twenty miles from St.

Francisville, it passes a hive of cinder-block sleeping units—
Shirley's Motel—then Tara's Place, a grocery shack plastered
with beer and cigarette posters. From Tunica, named for
the Indians who made it their beautiful burial grounds, 66
sweeps downhill in a long, blind curve. Just beyond the curve
the road ends beneath the gun towers of Angola.

The first morning—a Saturday—that, adding fumes to
the air, I drove this route, some of the light bulbs still burned
in the cord strung up above Shirley's. Passing Tara's I read
"Fresh Fish 4 Sale" on a piece of cardboard tacked among
the posters. A tangle of birds feeding on the roadside
wouldn't scare; they eyed the car out of black-green heads
free of the tics of domestic fowl.

I NO ALL THERE CROSS PLAY I TRUST NO ONE IN HERE
BUT ALVIN THIS IS DOG EAT DOG IF YOU A LIL DOG YOU
WILL BE WALK OVER. I DIE 100 TIME BEFORE I BE WALK
OVER. I DONT THINK ALVIN IS GOING TO MAKE IT OUT
OF HERE. A WEEK AGO I CAME BACK FROM VISITING
VELMA I MUST PASS "CUDA" THIS IS UNIT ALVIN STAY
ON. I MUST PASS THERE TO GET TO "GAR" UNIT. THIS IS
MY HOUSE. "GAR" SOON AS I GOT TO "CUDA" ALVIN
CAME TO MY MIND THEN A "FREE MAN" SAID TO ME
SOME FOOL HUNG HIS SELF ON "CUDA" I NO ALVIN MIND
IS NOT ALL THE WAY RIGHT AT THIS TIME. A WEEK
LATER OR SO I DREAM IN MY DREAM I SEEN ALVIN
HANGING FROM A CELL BAR'S AND I JUST COULD NOT
GET HIM DOWN HE SEEM LIKE HE WAS INJOYING DIEING.
IT WAS SO REAL I ASK A "FREE MAN" TO CALL "CUDA"
TO SEE WAS ALVIN "OK".

A few days after I first returned from Angola, I received
this as part of a three-page letter. It was as if some of the
stifled energy that had gone into Farris's extreme physical
conditioning now spilled out onto the yellow legal sheets,
sheets that were deeply scored with the intensity of his

exclusively uppercase printing and that came to me almost weekly for the next two years and eight months.

I answered most of these letters, our correspondence becoming heavily involved in practical matters: his complaints about the way the state had figured his time; his appeals for parole; his wishes to be transferred either closer to Alvin or elsewhere in the prison; his requests for me to send him canned goods, newspaper subscriptions, and, eventually, books. Although his letters often seemed driven by an impulse to con me about one thing or another, they made it possible for me to know him better than I could have otherwise, and they helped me keep up, if fleetingly, with Alvin.

During that fall, I studied both brothers' cases and began trying to find some just alternative to Alvin's sentence. I also read Farris's description of prison experience, "Living Within a Living Hell," one unrelieved, single-spaced paragraph covering six legal sheets, which had been typed with a very old ribbon by another inmate and passed along to me. Farris's intended exposé recounted what he hated at Angola, harsh conditions that are widely, if often tacitly, understood as facts of daily life in a great many prisons. Yet, while much of his effort might accurately be understood as a predictable attempt to vindicate himself, some of what he wrote also communicated a lived knowledge of particular injustice and outrage.

▶When I arrived here at Angola on that first day one of the security guards told me "You're on your own now old thang, you can be strong by building you a reputation of being a bad ass, or be weak and get yourself an old man who will stand up for you and take care of you, or be an informer and let us know whats going on with other inmates" I knew then I was caught in a world of young guys getting raped, putting dope in their arms, getting stab or beaten by other inmates if they refused to be that inmates prison wife (gal-boy they call them) . . . When I was here at Camp J in 1977, a security officer told me to my face when he put a young inmate in the cell with me "here is some young meat you can take his manhood away and make him your wife" he then came back later and ask was it good, and I told him it was okay, and the reason I had to lie is because if I would have told him I didn't do him anything he would have simply moved this inmate to a cell with some one who was going to actually rape him, this situation has always been this way in Angola, it's not just out in the open because most inmates are afraid to tell the truth, I've been all over Angola prison grounds, and I've seen the truth . . .◀

Not that his portrayal of this truth was ever completely free of his own bias.

▶During my stay in Orleans Parish Jail from 1974 to 1976 I experienced a great deal of acts of violences, such as rape, stabbing, and most emphatically police brutlity, I myself was stab in the back by another inmate, class "A" drugs (of all type) was always in my personal possession, one of the officers would bring it in to me and the deal was that I split the money that I make from the sale down the middle with him . . .◀

I remembered the dually incriminating note he tried to pass to Alvin from Parish Prison. That was in August 1973 after Farris had been extradited from New York, where he had been arrested on suspicion of armed robbery. I was unable to learn why he was released on this charge and others pending against him in 1973. In 1968, when he was seventeen, Collis and Mike had spoken in his behalf after his first two arrests in New Orleans (for simple burglary and armed robbery), and Mike had posted bond. But in the summer of 1974, when he was arrested again in New Orleans for armed robbery, the bond was higher and Collis was no longer willing to ask Mike to help.

After spending fourteen months in Parish Prison awaiting

trial, Farris was convicted in August 1975 and sentenced to Angola for forty-five years. In 1978 the legal clinic of the law school of Loyola University appealed his case. During this retrial, Leslie Bonano, the chief of security at Parish Prison and incidentally also New Orleans's most prominent boxing manager in the eighties, testified that "any time Farris Phillips was around, he was a risk to other inmates and personnel employed at Parish Prison." Parish Prison was designed to house 450 inmates; at the time of which Bonano spoke, its population was 1,300. Describing Farris as a "vital security risk," Bonano said he had been involved in five fights, had "led a rebellion of the inmates," and was "apprehended for possession of weapons, selling food to other inmates, insubordination, manipulating the inmates assigned to tiers he was on, leading to one occasion where he was the victim of a serious stabbing incident and had to receive medical attention."

Arguing that there were procedural errors in Farris's first trial, the young Loyola lawyers won a reduction of his initial sentence from forty-five to fifteen years. Because of Louisiana's "good time" policy (a one-day sentence reduction for each two days of not uncooperative behavior) and because of the credit he received for the period already served in New Orleans, his time remaining after the 1978 appeal was less than five years. Leslie Bonano's testimony, though, did prompt the judge to stipulate that these years be served not in Parish Prison but in Angola.

▶It is now June 26, 1981, at 5:30 am., an inmate at this camp, which is J, life was taken, he hung hisself, they found him in his cell with his neck pop, it wasn't going to be long before he was discharge, and the strange thing about it was he had never made an attempt on his life before . . . It is now a new day 6 am. 6/27/81 I can hear the security officers useing foul language out front, saying that some inmates should be put in cells with the strong and be raped and be misused in any way necessary, it seem as if they are going to have a bad conversation about inmates before they decide to bring us our breakfast which has been sitting out side since 5:30 this morning but I must not allow that to bother me, I'll just keep on writting this and avoid their insanity . . . Saturday/june/28/81, here's what taken place with 12 inmates as witness right here on this tier at Camp J, a security officer came on the tier turn off the television set and made a statement, "we're putting an inmate on this tier, this inmate is a rat so anything you all do to him is alright with us" he than turn the television set back on and left, now that's playing with this inmate's life, and it's no surprise to me because they do this number everyday, they careless . . .◀

The 1974 crime that sent Farris to Angola was both sinister and ludicrous. According to testimony of the main prosecution witness, career criminal Jesse Holmes, alias "Wing Ding," Farris planned and led the June 3 robbery of a French Quarter bar, the Pirate's Den. It was the practice of the bar's owner on Monday mornings for a fee to cash the paychecks of employees of the Marriott Hotel, which stands nearby on Canal Street. Holmes said Farris and Louis Sutfield, who worked at the Marriott and drove the getaway car, reckoned there would be between five and six thousand dollars in cash on hand in the Pirate's Den that morning.

Holmes said he had "been knowing" Farris since childhood, but "it wasn't much of a close friendship. He stayed at one end [of the project] and I stayed on the other end." Jesse Holmes testified that he happened to see Farris in the project on Sunday afternoon, the day before the crime. "We had did time in jail together, so I went over there and we just started talking. We shot some stuff together, we shot some dope—" At this point Farris's court-appointed lawyer moved for a mistrial. The judge overruled the motion.

After sharing drugs, Holmes said, he and Farris walked to Louis Sutfield's apartment in the project. There Farris and Sutfield, who usually cashed his check at the bar, laid out their robbery plans and cut Holmes in. Sutfield, the only one with a car, would drive and receive a fifth of the money. Because one of his arms was disfigured and made him more easily identifiable than the rest, Holmes, for a fifth of the money, would stand out of the way and guard the door. Two other men from the project, Larry Gabriel and Thomas Marquez, Farris would recruit later. They were to accompany him inside the bar. Holmes said Farris would give them whatever portion he wanted them to have. After leaving Sutfield, Holmes and Farris "went across the street, where they was shooting drugs, across the street, you know, everybody be there, you know."

The next morning "early," between eight-thirty and nine, Sutfield and Farris picked up Holmes and their other accomplices in Sutfield's green-and-white '71 Monte Carlo. Holmes said the original plan was "to ice the man," but "I stopped this . . ." because "I didn't want to kill a man for nothing."

As Sutfield drove slowly along narrow Iberville Street, the location of the bar, they happened to see the owner, Harry Armstrong, "a real settled age man," on his way into his business place with a money bag. Holmes said Farris directed Sutfield to stop two blocks away. There they took two pistols and a blank check from the trunk.

The four of them—Holmes, Gabriel, Marquez, and Phillips—approached the Pirate's Den twice. The first time "we peeped in the place," then "made a block." The second time they went inside—Holmes said Farris and Gabriel each "had a .38 on his side"—and stood near two white men who were playing pool. Another man sat drinking beer. A fourth tended bar. Armstrong, the owner, was also behind the bar, using the private telephone.

The place was less empty than they had counted on and, when Gabriel joined the pool game, Holmes said Farris lost patience and told him, " 'We going to do it *now!*' " He then asked for a drink, and when the bartender turned for a bottle, he jumped onto the counter and put his hand on the owner. Gabriel sprang behind the bar, and Marquez went for the money.

"The guys with the pool sticks left out" past Holmes, and when he turned from them back toward the bar, he saw Harry Armstrong dropping the telephone receiver. Farris "had him in the collar with the pistol in his face." Gabriel told the solitary drinker and the bartender—"a small, small guy"—to lie on the floor behind the bar. Farris made Armstrong do the same—but not before "he snatched the man by the pocket, and his pocket came off, and the money fell out on the floor. About a hundred fifty dollars, balled up tens, fives, and twenties."

At about this point, Farris "flew out" in rage against Holmes because an unaware patron tried to enter the bar and Holmes couldn't turn him away. Farris "came back and grabbed" this startled man and made him "lay on the floor" with the others. Then "he went to kicking some of 'em."

Holmes said he was by then "disgusted how things was going." He told Farris, " 'Don't kill him,' " and started to leave. That was when Farris held him at the door with his voice by calling out his street name—" 'Wing Ding!' "—the information that led the police to Holmes and then the rest of them.

The prosecutor questioned Holmes about his alias, asking if his damaged arm was "something you've had from birth." "About eighteen years," Jesse Holmes said. "Eighteen years." This would have been when he was eight. "I got shot playing with a shotgun when I was young."

Holmes said Marquez went out first with the money "in something like a toolbox." Gabriel went second. He himself was third, "and Farris came out last." Before the prosecutor cut him off, for no evident reason Holmes began filling out the scene by starting to describe the bar: "A black door, it was a black door . . ."

Holmes said Marquez broke into a trot. Gabriel was "stepping fast." Less than a block from the bar, all four began running. "Then the man come out and fired a shot and Thomas Marquez dropped the money and we started running faster."

Here the DA asked Holmes, "What kind of money fell

out?" and I remembered hearing how their losing the stolen money at the last moment was soon hootingly known on the corners around the project as a great joke and a mark of incompetence.

I imagined a pause preceding Holmes's answer and the involuntary courtroom laughter that probably followed it. "Well . . . I didn't look back . . . to see how the money was looking," he said. "When I heard the shot, I just went to running fast."

A similar pause perhaps was caused by the DA's questioning him about where he was when he heard the shot. "Where were I?" This line of questioning, though not very relevant, led, I feel sure, to a statement as fully truthful as any that appeared in Holmes's entire testimony: he granted that it was he who reached the car first.

The position of the car confused them. Sutfield had it idling, pointed in the direction of Canal Street; it was supposed to be turned the other way, toward downtown, "because we lived in that direction; we didn't live the way we went." Once they were back inside the car there was further agitation: "We were arguing; everybody was sweating. Everybody wanted to kill one another about the [dropped] money. Farris was mad about Marquez about the money, and he wanted to kill him. I had to talk him out of killing him, I had to talk him out of killing him."

After they crossed Canal, "Gabriel and Marquez got out and caught a bus, and later me and Farris got out by the precinct uptown," and with the money Farris had ripped from Harry Armstrong's pocket and then picked off the floor, "caught us a cab and went and bought some drugs."

"Wing Ding" Holmes was arrested on June 20, seventeen days after the botched crime. One of the arresting officers was Patrick Branighan, an ex-amateur heavyweight whom Collis had trained and with whom he remained on mutually fond terms. To Branighan and others, Holmes made a statement of guilt for which, along with his testimony, he was promised he would be convicted of simple robbery (zero to five years) rather than armed robbery (five to ninety-nine years). He also had assurances that he would serve his time in Parish Prison, away from his main accomplice, who, for a much longer term, would be away in the state penitentiary.

▶I came here to Angola in 1976, I was sent to the main prison, big yard as they call it, you have 500 to 700 inmates on the big yard, and most of them are from 25 on up, and they put a 17 or 18 year old kid down there around these old convicts who has been off the streets for 20 to 30 years without having a woman, it's obvious what will happen to them, or to someone trying to protect them but they still say it's all in rehabilitation. I appeared before the disciplinary board and was transferred to camp-A and went to work in the cellblock farm line, doing everything there is to be done in farm work where you must put up with for four hours in the morning and three to four hours in the afternoon a guard on a horse wearing a 357 magnum while another carrying a shotgun is saying things like "Your mammy should have cut your throat when you was born ol thang" and that's not half the things they be saying to you out there, and sometimes it 95 to 98 degrees in the summertime, and the guard be running all over your back . . . Later I got a job as a hall man, which was to keep the tier clean and serve the other inmates in the cellblock their meals, the hall man cell stays open all of the time, the rest of the inmates cell door are locked, the hall man has what we call a lay out job, he's consider cool with security, the hall man can get a inmate moved into another inmates cell . . . he can have a knife and the security officer would be fully aware of this, I myself had two or three . . . I've even had one officer come to me in 1980 and say "Farris, would you go to cell block D," which is the hole, isolation, he said they had a bad inmate over there who didn't want anyone in his cell with him "and we know if we put you in the cell you will take care of him for us" and he promise I could beat this inmate or anything I wanted to do with him.

I was hall man in cellblock A from 1979 to 1981 and I will tell about the young guys I seen get raped, stab, beat up, get introduced to drugs by older convicts and security officers, and there were no one there trying to help them unless they wanted something in return, therefore most young inmates who turn to another inmate for help end up being a gal boy, now they do not want to live this type of life but they know they have to live it or go around proving themselves as to be a man, if they don't they a gal boy and anything their man tell them to do they do it and in return they get protection from their man, and when that man leaves they will be given to another man and that go on and on until that young inmate leave to go home or until he stab a few inmates just to prove he is sick of living that life and want to be a man, some young inmates come here and be given to older inmates by security, and mainly when a inmate arrive here in Angola and the security officers learn that their charge was violent and the victim was a white person then he will never have a peacefull day as long as he's here, that is the reason that so many young guys end up back in prison or being killed once they get out, it is because of the mental affect that prison has, they feel they have to fight back at some one when they get back to the streets . . .◀

The owner of the Pirate's Den testified that on the morning in question he was interrupted while talking on the phone by a voice saying, " 'Give me your money!' "

"Man, get away," Harry Armstrong said he replied. "Can't you see I'm making a telephone call?" Then he turned and found himself inches from "a black male, late twenties, approximately a hundred fifty-five to a hundred sixty pounds, about five-eight, five-nine, thick lips, thick nose, hair plaited . . . and on the back of his head, and the eyes appeared to me as if he had been drinking, pardon me, under the influence of something." Armstrong said the person he described then grabbed him by his shirt, put a pistol against his face, and said, " 'You honky, white motherfucker, this is a stickup, hang up the phone!' "

As the robber was ripping away his back pocket, Armstrong said, he heard someone else say to the men who had been shooting pool, " 'Get out of here, brothers. We don't want you.' " After the robbers left, he took up his own pistol and followed them outside on Iberville Street, where, he said, because of traffic, he fired one shot overhead into the sky.

Like the bartender and a passerby who witnessed "three or four Negro males" come out of the bar pursued by an older white man with a gun, Harry Armstrong failed to identify Farris in a police lineup. The bar owner volunteered that he always liked to sit in the back during lineups, evidently having been to several. He did recognize Farris in a photograph lineup, though. The prosecution stressed that the reason for this less than fully convincing identification was the hair of the man who led the robbery: on June 3, it was braided and covered by a bandanna; in custody, Farris wore his hair in a tall Afro.

When the prosecutor asked him if he was afraid during the robbery, Armstrong said, "I went through two campaigns in World War II, and I never was afraid as I was at that time."

Because of his vulnerability as a previously convicted felon, Farris did not testify in his own behalf. As was typical of many similar cases, a woman—in this instance his girlfriend Velma—was the only witness for the defense. She testified that he was with her on June 3, "in bed by himself until ten or eleven because I get up and do my work. Later he woke up and I fixed breakfast. About twelve or twelve-thirty we left to go by his mother's. And when we left from there, it was dark. We came home, and he left to go to New York about nine-thirty or ten." She said she remembered the date so well because he had promised to take her to Manhattan with him "to visit his sister Connie . . . It would have been my first opportunity to leave New Orleans, and I looked forward to this here. I never will forget June 3."

Cross-examination established that he returned from New York on June 15, four days before his arrest, and that when he left on the night of June 3, "two guys came and picked him up in a car." Velma could be drawn out to say little more on this subject: "I seen him leave out my door, whose car, what color it was, I didn't see this . . . No, I didn't ask him who he was going with. I know I wasn't going. I locked my door."

Lengthy interrogation about Farris's ways of wearing his hair established only that "I would braid his hair mostly at night going to sleep. He mostly sleeps with his hair braided. He wears his hair mostly in the street combed out."

Persistent personal questions caused her to admit that "I'm on the County, on Welfare," that "Farris was more or less staying with me," and "Well, yes, I care for Farris," and "Sure, I care enough to testify for him."

The jury's prompt 11–1 verdict was "Guilty."

▶I've seen so much of this until I had to write about it the way it is, this is something that a man can't just hold inside and live in it, I couldn't hold this any longer because I felt I was about to explode, this is one black man who refuse to play the part of one of their good little nigger boys and keep my mouth shut, no matter what happen I am going to let people know whats going here, there are some inmates here will tell the truth but they just don't know who to tell it to, so they just go off to themselves and try to stay out the way but some times they just can't stay out of the way because things have a way of coming to a person here . . . heroin, homosexuality, how to kill and how to do the things that older convicts has done and passed on down . . . I have seen officials cross young inmates out of their manhood and their freedom, it all make me sick, all these things that go on here at Angola, you will never read about them in the prison magazine they so proud of, drugs in cellblock A (and other cell blocks too) is always in an inmate hands because security bring this in to them just like bringing candy to a baby . . . this place suppose to be for rebilitation, no way, I will never forget all the cold acts that I have seen go down here and all the things that they try to cover up, there's no amount of time can make me forget what this prison has instilled within me◄

2

□

Winter 1981–82

1/28/82

I HOPE MY LETTER FINE YOU DOING WELL I AM NOT SO
COOL IF I SAY I AM I BE LIEING TO YOU "RANDY" I BEAT
A DUDE WITH A "PIP" HE HAD A KNIFE I AM NOT HURT
AT ALL BUT THE DUDE STAY IN THE HOSPITAL 13 DAY'S
I BE BACK HERE IN J SOME TIME BUT I BEEN MOVE ME
AND ALVIN IS NOW ON THE SAME TIER TOGETHER CUDA
GOD MUST HAVE DID THAT PUT US TOGETHER ANYWAY
ALVIN IS IN 12 CELL I AM IN 8 WE TALK A LOT I GIVE
HIM SLIPPER AND A LOT OF THINGS I NO HE NEED I
REALLY FEEL SORRY FOR ALVIN I JUST TOOK A LONG
LOOK AT HIM IN THAT CELL IT HURT ME "DEEPLY" BUT
I DID NOT SHOW IT I MUST SHOW ALVIN I AM STRONG.

In fall and winter, Farris had made requests of me. He
had insisted, for instance, that calls and letters from me to
the warden could cause him and Alvin to be housed on the
same tier. Then he could "SEE ABOUT" his older brother "AND
MAKE HIM STRONG STRONG."

Despite my initial success with the bureaucracy in September, I was regularly unable to reach the warden (and now
there was a new warden) by phone in the following months;
but even though I had reservations about Farris and about
such questionable intervention from me, I wrote letters.

These weren't acknowledged either, and I never learned if they played any part in Farris's transfer, which evidently had taken place immediately after he had spent ten or so days in isolation as penalty for the pipe-and-knife fight.

Like the transfer itself, the difficulty of now being around his older brother was also a surprise to him.

2/18/82

. . . BELEAVE ME I AM VERY GLAD YOU SENTING THE NEWSPAPER I MAY CAN GET ALVIN TO READ IT ALL HE DO IS TALK ABOUT DIANN I GET SICK OF HERING DIANN. ALL ALVIN DO IS LAY IN BED HE DON'T WANT MUCH OF ANYTHING I GOT HIM TO EAT A ICE CREAM I HAD 4 OF THEM HE AN'T WANT TO EAT THAT. HE WAS CALLING THEM PIG'S 4 DAYS AGO ASKING THEM CAN HE GO HOME TO HIS WIFE AND KID'S. "RANDY" THINK HOW I WAS FEELING. ALVIN DON'T WANT ME ON THIS TIER HE DON'T FEEL COMFORTABLE AT ALL. I FACT WITH HIM HE ACT LIKE HE GOING ALL THE WAY "CRAZY" HOW CAN ANY MAN LET HIMSELF GO THAT WAY. IT IMPOSSIBLE FOR ANY THING TO HAPPEN TO ME LIKE THAT I AM THE "BABY" OF MY FAMILY BUT BELEAVE ME I WILL BE STRONG UNTIL "DEATH". I HAVE THE PAPER'S YOU SENT ON PARDON BUT ALVIN IS FUCK UP MIND AND "BODY".

3/3/82

. . . YES I AM UNDER MORE PRESSURE ON CUDA A LOT MORE BUT I TAKE PRESSURE AND USE IT LIKE I WANT TO. I STAY UNDER PRESSURE I AM USE OF IT. THEY PUT ME ON CUDA BECAUSE THEY NO I WAS NOT GOING TO BE COOL UNTIL I SEE ALVIN SEE HOW HE DOING HIS TIME WHAT GOT HIS MIND AND BODY ALL DOWN AND OUT. I SEE "NOW". HE IS ON THOREZINE PILL'S. THESE'S FOOL ASS DOCTOR PUT HIM ON IT. ALVIN LOOK BAD

DON'T WANT TO EAT. SLEEP MOST ALL DAY ALL MOST
ALL NIGHT I TRY TO TELL HIM IT IS NO GOOD FOR HIM
ALL HE TALK ABOUT DIANN. WE ALL GET ONE HOUR ON
THE HALL WHEN HE DO GET UP ALVIN COME OUT WALK
VERY SLOW AND GO BACK IN HIS SELL. THOSE PILL'S
FUCK HIM UP BADER THEN HE ALL READY IS. WHAT CAN
I SAY GET A WRITE UP LOW COURT BIG COURT TAKE MY
GOOD TIME KEEP ME HERE LONGER. THEY WOULD LOVE
THAT TRYING TO HELP MY BROTHER. EVERY BODY NO
THOSE'S CRAZY PILL'S IS NO GOOD FOR NO BODY. THEY
PUT ALVIN ON THEM PILL SO HE CAN'T THINK AND ACT.
ON TOP OF THAT THEY GIVE IT TO HIM 3 TIME A DAY.
KEEP HIM OUT. I NO ALL THEY LOW DOWN MOVE AND
THEY NO I DO.

Then, as if inexplicably and despite the Thorazine, word
came of another surprise.

3/15/82

I CAN'T BELEAVE IT BUT I MUST I SEE IT ALL I CAN SAY
IS "GOD" MADE A MIRACLE HAPPEN. IF YOU SEE ALVIN
HE IS NOT THE SAME ALVIN ANY LONGER HE DON'T TALK
FAST ANY MORE YOU CAN UNDERSTAND EVERY WORD HE
SAY. THE FREE MAN BRING HIM HIS PILL'S BUT HE PLAY
LIKE HE TAKE THIM BUT HE DON'T. "GOD" MADE IT
HAPPEN I LEARN FROM THAT YOU CAN'T NEVER GIVE UP
NO MATTER WHAT. "GOD" SENT ME TO CUDA I BEAT A
DUDE WITH A "PIPE" IT ALL HAPPEN FOR A REASON FOR
ME TO COME TO ALVIN. I GOT A FEW DUDE'S ON THE
"TIER" TO PLAY A LIL GAME IT CALL "EGNORE SOMEONE"
WE WILL TALK ABOUT WOMAN-FIGHTING-SEX-BLACK-
WHITE EVERYTHING WE WILL DO THIS EVERY DAY PLAY
LIKE ALVIN IS NOT THERE. I WILL TALK ABOUT HOW
STRONG MY "MIND AND BODY" IS AND HOW WEAK ALVIN
IS "RANDY" IT WORK. BUT "GOD" DID IT NOT ME. I PRAY

IT STAY THAT WAY ALVIN GOT MY MIND MOVING FAST
FAST HE TOLD ME HE WILL BEAT ME IN 10 ROUNDS I
TOLD HIM HE MAY CAN IF HE WORK OUT HE HAVE WORK
OUT 2 TIME'S ALL READY. DUDE'S ON THE TIER TOLD ME
ALVIN NEVER DID THIS BEFORE. EVERY BODY IS VERY
HAPPY FOR HIM. NOW IF YOU WANT TO TALK TO HIM
THIS IS YOUR BEST TIME TO DO IT. HE ASK ABOUT YOU
7 TIME I TOLD HIM YOU GOOD PEOPLE HE SAY HE WOULD
WRITE TO YOU SOON. I CAN'T BELEAVE WHAT I SEE AND
HERE COMING OUT OF HIS MOUTH HE GOT CONFIDENCE
NOW HOW HE GOT IT? HE PICK HIS BLACK ASS UP AND
SAID THIS AN'T ME I GOT TO BE STRONG NOT WEAK AND
CRAZY. I AM WRITING SO FAST UNTIL I CAN'T BELEAVE
HOW FAST MY HAND MOVING I AM HAPPY.

I wanted to share such optimism, but these letters left me wondering further about Alvin's condition.

3/18/82

. . . ALVIN IS EATING MATTER OF FACT EATING ALL MY
COOKIE AND POTATOE CHIP'S . . . WHEN YOU GET THIS
LETTER I WILL BE IN ISOLATION JUST FOR 10 DAY'S YOU
CAN STILL WRITE TO ME I WILL GET IT.

Spring 1982

Alvin wrote in a small, slanting script, the penciled characters faint—like his whispery voice—and in places barely decipherable, as if the yellow legal sheets were tissue. Although he dated it "4/19-82," his first letter was postmarked on March 16.

Mr. Bates
Writting you concerning your visit & interest in me, first I hope you're in the best of health. At the same

time your interest in *My Father*. I'll tell you something of me with this time at the same time I know little of you.

I'm doing time which is confusing at the present and which you can be of some help. I think I have a life sentence, which has to be determine into yrs before I can get some help. At the present I've been lock up 8 yrs. I don't know how long I'll be up here.

I'm married + 6 children, at the same time I don't no three of them. When ever I get my freedom I have a date with the cemetary for my *Mother* who died while I was doing this time.

I've been addicted to drugs for the past 20 yrs and they has been a problem to me. Would appreciate any help you can be at this time. Excuse me for taking so long to write, I've been going through some mental changes.

P.S. Excuse my penmanship.

There was no signature.

I answered the letter at once, urging him to sign and return the clemency petition I had sent earlier. A spate of letters from him, sometimes two a day, followed during the next two months. The recurrent elements in what he wrote communicated grief and guilt concerning Diane and their children. His tone alternated among fair-mindedness, resentment, tenacity, and hopelessness. Toward me, he expressed a mixture of gratitude and mistrust. There was also a perplexing obsession with "water."

3/23-82

. . . I'm very indebted to the fact that someone is trying to help me. I do feel throwed away here in the penitentiary for show . . . This time been like a night mare and horror to me, and . . . I'm still not adjusted to it. At the same time it's been a lot of water because it really has gotten to my head.

I guess our relationship . . . is mainly the book.

Because I was wondering with my head down, why
would any one be interested in me. So I thought I'm
an ex pro fighter & my hooks on those drugs.

3/24-82

I feel forward writting to you . . . at the same time
indebted . . . that someone has shown concern . . . I'm
even surprise with Farris because we do live seperate
lives, since was both addicted to drugs.

I'm really lost where my wife & children are concern,
but still holding on & will try to help myself if possible.
I've been trying to keep up with the newspaper & society
on a small basis so I won't feel so lost. Politics from
home & Washington D.C. at the same time I do have
children.

Where I come from I have seen a lot of people die,
I'm trying to feel myself as a person. I feel like a dog a
car run over . . .

I know a lot of people one way or other take a dive
on life where as they might have to do some time. I've
been around it so much I can't believe I'm doing time.
I think of my nephews. I have two of them is addicted
plus they're on the penal cycle.

Sincerely,
Al

To his repeated questions concerning the whereabouts of
his family, I had given basically truthful, direct answers that
were probably unwise. I wrote that Connie didn't have
Diane's address but that they saw each other and I thought
his sons Kevin and Troy lived with Diane. I said his son
Farris lived with Connie and his daughter Leslie lived with
Diane's aunt in New Jersey. But I did suppress one recent
hurtful change by untruthfully telling him that Alvin Jr. still
lived with Diane's aunt, Helen Cheno, in New Orleans.

4/2-82

. . . I must say your letter throwed me way off because of reasons that I have no control over. My wife and children seem as if they are all split up. That's really down to me because ever sense they were young that's been the problem. I hoped I could keep them together with their mother.

I signed the papers to the board of Pardons which have some markings on the back which I wrote when my mentality was off. Excuse my feeling so negative. The way my wife & children is spread out I can't help feeling the way I feel. I received a letter from *Pete* who said you had been in contact with each other. I'm writting the classification officer to try put your name on my visiting list. Be careful driving and getting around these days. I been reading newspaper on a lot of accidents. Well, that's all for now, words getting short.

On the back of the clemency petition he had drawn and redrawn, unerasably in ink, the outline of a plot of real estate. Within the rectangular diagram, along with the words "bungalo" and "home," was a repeatedly retraced name and address: "Mrs. Diane Phillips, 1227 Prospect Place, Ponchartrain Park." (Ponchartrain Park is a middle-class subdivision in New Orleans.) Adjacent to the other words, he had inscribed "Solid American Stile." I decided against encrusting what he had done in white-out and went ahead and mailed the petition.

A few months later I learned that his clemency appeal had been summarily denied and that it would be another year before he would be eligible to apply again.

4/15/82

I CAN'T LIE TO YOU I AM A LIL MAD IT IS 7 AM. A DUDE JUST BEAT ON MY WALL AND GOT ME UP THE NEWS I GOT I DID NOT LIKE IT AT ALL THE DUDE TOLD ME ALVIN

BEEN MOVED I NO FOR A FACT ALVIN DID NOT DO
ANYTHING AT ALL ALVIN BEEN ON CUDA-12-R FOR 18
"MONTH" THEN ALL OF A SUDDEN THEY MOVE HIM FROM
A ROUND ME FOR NO REASON AND I DON'T KNOW WARE
ALVIN AT OR NOTHING ANY ONE CAN SEE THEY NO I GOT
ALVIN MIND TO WORKING RIGHT AND HIS BODY TO THEY
IS AFRAID OF POWER I WOULD LIKE YOU TO CALL THE
WARDEN . . .

Although I never reached the warden, I did call the prison.
A number of times. Eventually I learned Alvin was now on
the maximum-security isolation tier of the psychiatric camp.
I could find out nothing about either the reasoning behind
the transfer or what treatment, if any, he would receive as
a result. None of the several psychiatric personnel whom I
spoke with would tell me anything. It seemed possible that
Alvin had requested the move himself, preferring to be away
from Farris's pressuring—for later he wrote, "My brother I
heard he was going home this year, and doing time around
him do fool with my head." In fairness to Farris, though,
Alvin's letters from the psychiatric camp seemed more
scattered than the ones he had written on Cuda.

4/21-82
. . . the way you do your time mean a lot . . . I really
can't believe you're serious on doing a book where as
my Dad & myself is concern. You ask do I need money.
I do have some small I.O.U. where as cigarette is
concern. I tell you if you were to send me any thing, I
would have to refuse.
    In my letters I jump from one subject to another, it's
only because I don't talk to no one where as some
personal things in my life is involved . . . I'll tell you
some of my confusion is my wife. I know she is still
hooked and I know how hard it is on her. When I was
out there I would look out for her being hooked, with

those children. I didn't have anything to do with her being hooked. What she was around such as invironment she would have volunteered. A lot of this might be hard for you to understand. That is why I really would like to have a long talk. May be I can clean up some of the confusion I have in my mind.

-82

. . . completely lost without my wife & children, my wife it's been close to 30 yrs. involvement & that's hard on me. I'm eating & doing a lil exercize, trying to help myself. I'm still employable & if I can get any help I can go to work.

I'm very sorry about my attitude toward you in the past. I think I was very arrogant, but laying in these cells you go through changes in your head. I do turn feeling of compassion off & on. I have put them on the side at times because if I don't it will eat every one up I come in contact with.

I have scars I live with such as some of my friends died violently this effects me. Political assasination also effect me heavy, three that really do is Abraham Lincoln & John & Bobby Kennedy. I'm familiar with each case & know the effects it had on immediate family & on the American People.

4/28-82

Randy,

I'm still trying to add you to my visiting list, at the same time things are a mess. In order to add you I have to know whether you are married & your date of birth . . .

It would be two months more before I had passed through all of the procedural tangles and was finally able to visit him. Meanwhile his paranoia, and his struggle against it, became more pronounced in his letters.

5/5-82

. . . in '73 a Universal Crisis things were down. Every human being were faced with it up until '78 and I got a lion share.

Which on my part is small thinking. I'm sure some where there's some one worst off than I. I know there are people with more responsibility than I.

. . . I've been addicted to more than a Million dollars worth of hard drugs if you wish to put money on it. I will add you on my visit list & am happy you are married with children. I relate better with married people. Although you didn't mention your wife or children names. I feel like a kidnapped person. Excuse me how I jump from one subject to another, but that is how things are.

Apparently one of my letters had referred to the fact that I perceived race to be a pervasive dimension of what I had undertaken.

. . . You mention race to me it's water from your feet to your head. It's not real if I ever come out of this penitentiary, I've died about three times. The book it's deep if it concern My Dad in Louisiana & Texas. To much for me to relate on, plus you said you visit my people in Texas.

You know there is an accident goes around my head, but believe me I know I saved 30 or 50 people lives one way or another. Don't go out of your way to visit me I appreciate what youre doing . . .

I feel I've been put in a show which involved Politics let me know if I'm wrong or right. Any way I can only say I'm in it over my head, which has been in it all my life from feet on up . . . I'm still interested in living.

Elements of his letters were personally disconcerting—"I think I may have worked for some of your relatives in N.O. Star Sales that deals with stationary business." I had never heard of Star Sales and had no family in New Orleans except wife and children. It seemed to be disconcerting to him when I encouraged his criticism of what I was doing, especially his criticism of anything he might sense as exploitive.

5/24-82

Now the Book, man you take care of that, it's to deep for me. If you write concerning my Dad that will get around. When it comes to me I say that's to down . . . to down even for America especially where children is involved. Now unless you write and make it look like something, it's to far off for people to accept.

At the same time on exploitation that's one to a hundred all type way's. There has to be exploitation in order to produce or be creative . . . is it just for a book store, what about the financial side of it. I mean a book don't get over unless it's a movie or a televison script. Man my head is messed up right now, this is madness the reflection I get when I think . . .

6/5-82

I'm about to blow in the hood where it's my wife & children . . .

6/15-82

. . . I'll sure be glad when you & I can sit down & have a long talk . . .

3

□

December 15, 1981

The ring of the phone and Alvin Jr.'s dejected voice brought me awake in the darkest hour of morning. He was arrested, he said, "for nothin'," and now he was being held in Central Lockup. The charge—he described it as beyond belief—was attempted car theft.

Hurrying, he told me he and two friends were talking in the parking lot of a disco and a stranger asked them to help him start his car. While they were gathered near the car, one of them with his hands under the dash, the police happened by and the stranger "ran off."

Dislocatedly, I listened to the alibi, not yet registering its apparent transparency. The name of the disco? I asked him to repeat it.

". . . New York, New York," he said impatiently, then interrupted my next question with a quick one of his own. Would I help him?

Well, yes, I began, hoping a break now would render him less prone to crime in the future. Why, tomorrow I—

He made a low, unreplicable sound that caused me to realize he meant would I help him within that hour, before dawn. We discussed the amount of his bond; he believed it had been set at "around five thousand," but I would have to put up only a tenth of that. It depressed me to have to explain that I lacked the cash to meet his request. Oh, he said at once, it was okay then, he understood, I shouldn't worry about it. A voice ordered him to hang up the phone.

At the beginning of business hours I telephoned the office of the lawyer who, I knew from reading Alvin Jr.'s record, had represented him during his first conviction—for a petty burglary in June 1980. The lawyer advised Alvin to plead guilty, filed the plea, and appeared with him in court. In lieu of the $1,500 bond, which was not posted, Alvin was remanded to Parish Prison to await sentencing. Four months later, in October 1980, he was given a suspended three-year sentence and placed on active probation for five years. I didn't know specifically what this lawyer's counsel did for Alvin, and I wouldn't learn what his fee was, but I already subscribed to the belief, an impassioned consensus in the project, that the first step toward a successful defense was to hire a "pay lawyer"—as opposed to relying on a legal-aid defender. Since this lawyer defended Alvin once—and no sentence resulted—it seemed wise to have his defense again, especially since now the stakes were higher: If Alvin were convicted of this charge, he would be "double-billed" as a second offender—that is, given double the maximum time due for the second crime alone, in this case twenty-four years for attempted theft, auto.

In the afternoon, when the lawyer was free to receive my call, he entered the conversation in a minimal way, offering me a few moments to describe the case. He had no recollection of defending Alvin over a year ago, but granted that probably he had. When I began to go into detail, he interjected his fee. For $500, he would "look into it."

Would he take a portion of this now and the rest later? Possibly Alvin could work to pay off the balance. His reply was perfunctory: "The way to do it is to bring in the fee." Hoping it would make the case more attractive to him, I volunteered something of Alvin's background: "His father, for example—" The lawyer had already learned that I was writing about the family, and "just out of curiosity" he interrupted me now "to ask something." Did I hear in his even question a tone of assumed privilege and easy self-acceptance—the jocular yet reserved manner of speaking of much of New Orleans's white elite? "What can be so interesting about these people?"

As I floundered to articulate intriguing evidence that would satisfy him, he again mentioned the fee and curtly signed off.

December 22–23, 1981

We peered at each other through hazy panes of plastic inches from our faces and spoke into gummy receivers. Beyond the static on the line, Alvin Jr.'s voice seemed more reticent than usual. He still wore the only clothes I had seen him in. Now the velour pullover and jeans were dirtier and—like the plastic enclosing us and in our hands, and like other surfaces in the visiting area of the House of Detention in Parish Prison—they seemed coated by a film of grime.

He tersely answered my brief questions about his mother and his aunt Connie and about the logistics of visiting them, but he was far more interested in repeatedly vowing that the charge against him was "wrong." When, as his aunt Helen asked me to, I told him that, since he had been in jail, the tape deck had been stolen from the old car he had been repairing and restoring, he said nothing but looked down, long lashes veiling his eyes. Not long after I had taken a seat, a guard signaled me out with an assured wiggle of his finger. Alvin lowered his eyes again, and I heard his murmur in the static. "I was hopin' I wouldn' be in here for Christmas . . ."

The next day, his probation officer telephoned me in response to messages I had left for her. She already knew about the new charge against him, and, yes, she acknowledged, he had always been a cooperative assignment. But she was noncommittal about his chances for dismissal or, at the least, for a reduction of his bond. She took pains to determine my connection to him. Then she listened to my description of elements of his background that had been unknown to her.

January 1982

"Well, they got him again." This was how Helen Cheno greeted me when I answered the phone. She was the unmarried sister of Diane Phillips's mother and for years had been principal mother to Diane and, later, to Alvin Jr. During his periods of return from New York, he usually slept in the small house she shared with her longtime companion, Rita Diaz, and it was their address that appeared on all his official "papers." She and I had talked several times before, usually as a result of family misfortune. Earlier in the month I had learned from her that, for once, a wish of Alvin Jr.'s had been granted: the House of Detention had released him on Christmas Eve. He and other family members had said this was a good sign, meaning the DA's office didn't feel the case was strong and would probably drop the charge. This was enough for me, and during the next few weeks I more or less forgot about Alvin Jr.'s immediate trouble and largely devoted myself to writing about Collis.

Now Helen Cheno told me her nephew had been "re-arrested." She couldn't tell me the charge, stressing that in her fifty-eight years she had "never had one minute's trouble with the law" and that she didn't "understand all that jailhouse stuff." All she knew was that several weeks earlier he had been driving his prized possession, the old car he had rejuvenated. A police detail pulled him over and impounded the car, telling him only that it was suspected of having been used in a crime. Yesterday evening, when he made the last of several trips to the precinct station, trying to regain his car, he was taken into custody. "Now they holdin' both him *and* the car." Would I please look into it and let her know? She already suffered from "pressure and nerves," but she had to find out "what they doin' " to Alvin because he was "the closest to a son" she would ever have and because, as she said he often told her, " 'You all I got left, Aun-*tee*.' "

Over the next few weeks I pieced together many of the facts of a crime.

On January 6, at about 6:50 p.m., which is long after dark at that time of year in New Orleans, a Hispanic working woman came out of a supermarket at the intersection of Gentilly Boulevard and Elysian Fields in a plain section of the city known as Gentilly. Stopping her loaded shopping cart, she turned to call a taxi from the pay phone near the entrance to the store. Her purse, containing about sixty dollars and her dead husband's wallet (an object of senti-mental value), lay in the portion of the basket designed to carry small items or children. The purse was actually a blue British Airways flight bag her husband had given her from a trip he made to England shortly before his death in October. As the woman turned, a slender young black male stepped quickly past the unattended basket and snatched the bag. He then ran along the side of the building toward another slender male who stood at its corner, a position from which he could signal to the parking area behind the store. This was all the victim could see. From the first, she knew she lacked a view that was direct enough to enable her to identify the thief.

The testimony of another witness, I learned later, served to reconstruct the rest of the crime for the prosecution. This witness was a deputy in the Orleans Parish sheriff's office, a deputy who happened to be off duty and on his way home from work. This deputy said he was stopped in traffic at a red light on Gentilly at Elysian Fields. He said he observed a car swerve out of the supermarket's back parking lot. He said the driver, who unlike the two passengers was thick and wide of shoulder, looked at him to make certain he would stay put, then pulled out in front of him, ran the light, turned left, and sped away on Elysian Fields. The deputy said he noticed a blue shoulder bag held by one of the passengers. Attributing his systematic behavior to his training in law enforcement, the deputy said he then trailed the car long enough to record the license number on the back of a medical prescription slip he had in his pocket. He described the getaway car as "a nice-lookin' vehicle, a candy-apple red Javelin." A registration check revealed its owner to be Alvin Phillips, Jr., and investigators reported that about ten days later the deputy identified him in a photograph lineup.

Winter 1982

At some point during this period, unbeknownst to Helen Cheno or me, Alvin Jr.'s case was processed with unexpected promptness, and tried—a proceeding that resulted in a mistrial. The day after I learned this, I determined on the phone that his court-appointed lawyer, a man named Vernon Thomas, was young, effectively plainspoken, and black. Once I explained my connection to his client, Thomas talked with me openly and without professional haste. Despite the youthfulness of his voice, he expressed himself with the authority of someone who had seen many cases such as Alvin's. Too often, he said, such young men wanted to fight the charges rather than accept a plea bargain even though their chances of acquittal were slim—it was as if the matter were some kind of street challenge. The DA's office had already offered Alvin six and two-thirds years for a guilty plea. "Their manhood thing destroys 'em," Vernon Thomas said of this type of defendant before going on to talk of Alvin in particular.

He didn't think much of Alvin's story, an insistence that he was at his cousin Trina Sorina's at the time of the crime and also that on January 6 his car was being repaired for damage a tow truck had done to it. Thomas had made a hasty attempt to check the second part of the alibi, but since he was overworked, with no funded investigative resources, it had been impossible for him to track down the claim, which was of a kind common among the people he often

defended. He was frank about the small pride he derived
from the first trial having resulted in a hung jury, though:
he had called no witnesses—not even Alvin, because to put
him on the stand would have allowed the prosecution to
bring up his prior record—instead attacking the deputy's
testimony and the dubious coincidence of someone in law
enforcement just happening along as the only real witness.

But neither did Thomas think the mistrial necessarily
improved Alvin's chances in a second trial. If anything, it
would cause the DA's office to sharpen its case, and he felt
that Alvin's guilt was suggested by the fact that no one in
his family initially came forth to support him. After I told
him about most of Alvin's close relatives being in New York
or in jail and about other problems consuming the family,
Vernon Thomas was no more or less sympathetic to his
client than he had been before. But he said that, as long as
Alvin wanted to make a fight of it in court, he would do his
best, as before.

April 14, 1982

I met Vernon Thomas on the morning Alvin's retrial was
scheduled to begin. Judge Thomas C. Braniff fierily presided.
Appearing to be past seventy and with a customary scowl
creased into the folds of his face, he ran his court with a
firmness equaled by his bluster in shouting impatiently at
defense and prosecution alike. On this morning one of the
state's witnesses—I think it was the deputy—couldn't be
located, and the trial date had to be reset—but not before
Braniff boomed out at a table of young assistant DAs: "Don't
you people know how to prepare a case! Next time your
witnesses don't show, I'll jail them *and you* for contempt.
You'll learn, buster!"

The young prosecutors nodded in attentive compliance
while not quite stifling grins that broadened when the judge

turned his head to scrutinize Vernon Thomas, who stood beside Alvin. With mock solicitousness, Braniff, who seemed to like a chastened playfulness from all respondents, asked the whereabouts of the witnesses for the defense. Demonstrating a studied refusal to be cowed, Thomas played it almost straight and answered naturally but with terse respect. "Like last time, it's just him and I, your honor. That's it."

In contrast to his tall lawyer, Alvin stood a head shorter but seemed half a foot wider, now visibly wider than he had ever appeared to me. He wore olive-drab inmate fatigues, hugely stamped in several places with "OPP" (Orleans Parish Prison). A cast sheathed his left hand, which I knew he had broken while making it clear to other inmates that he wouldn't "BE WALK OVER."

Braniff's taking no exception to Thomas's reply showed that it had been deemed acceptable. The judge brought down the flat of his hand rather than the gavel and growled about proceeding to the next case. "Well, c'mon!" he bellowed at the bailiff. "Let's *move* this docket!"

Afterwards, the AC roaring softly in his new GM sedan as I rode with him on a legal errand, Vernon Thomas talked about Judge Braniff. Starting at the heart of the portrait, he described Braniff's service as a bomber pilot during World War II. He said that, after being shot down and badly wounded, Braniff continued to volunteer for the fighting. Now an essentially recovered alcoholic, he had been known sometimes to show leniency toward certain kinds of drug offenders, though plain robbers and thieves could always expect maximum time from him. And, without exception, he refused to discuss the exact length of bargained sentences with defense lawyers until the pleas had officially been made.

Thomas's restrained admiration for Braniff tacitly entered his conversation, as did his own stern attitude toward the families of many of his appointive clients. He felt that too often these relatives came forward in anguish only after no time and means were left to do anything more for their sons or husbands. Although we parted on good terms and I was aware of having been impressed, I didn't yet fully enough appreciate how much worse Alvin Jr. could do than have Vernon Thomas represent him.

The same day I spoke again with Alvin Jr.'s probation officer. I have no memory of exactly why I called her, but I won't forget the first thing she told me: My sympathetic description of Alvin when he was in the House of Detention in December had persuaded her, against her better judgment, not to put a routine detainer on him. Her supervisor criticized her for this decision. Because of our conversation, she had made it possible for him to be released in time for Christmas.

As we talked further, we found areas of accord that softened the sting of her accusation. But after we hung up, I was well aware that if not for me, Alvin might still have been in jail on January 6.

May 6, 1982

A chaotic situation greeted those entering court on this morning, Alvin's most recent trial date. I arrived early only to find that Judge Braniff had suffered a heart attack the night before. Until his recovery his court would be run by a stand-in, reputedly a more lenient judge. This judge arrived around eleven, and, the docket moving slowly, it wasn't until after the long lunch break that Alvin was called from among the handcuffed black prisoners sitting in a row off to one side. Vernon Thomas, apparently engaged in another courtroom, hadn't appeared since before lunch. The new judge singled out one of the several indigent-defender lawyers who usually were present during docket proceedings. This man was to stand alongside Alvin when he pled innocent or guilty. The temporary switch seemed to put added strain on Alvin. The man chosen to stand with him was the most seedy in appearance of all the lawyers in the room.

Vernon Thomas had told Helen Cheno and me that the

DA had again offered a plea bargain and that the new judge had already guaranteed the original maximum of six and two-thirds years for a guilty plea. As we knew, if Alvin went to trial again and lost, he could be double-bill sentenced to as much as forty years (twenty being the maximum in Louisiana for one count of purse-snatching)—and automatically would be if Judge Braniff should recover in time to preside.

The new judge mildly asked the disheveled lawyer how his client wished to plead. Helen Cheno had vacillated throughout the morning between wanting Alvin "to cop the plea and stop doin' this to me" and wanting somehow to hire a lawyer who might be able "to get him off"; and I had already been put out of the court once by an irascible bailiff for trying in signals to impress on Alvin the gravity of again taking this poor case to trial. Now, in an instant, he had to decide.

The lawyer, arching the middle of his long, flaccid body slightly away from Alvin, turned to him and put the judge's question into some even simpler form of English. I could see only Alvin's recently cropped hair and the side of his face. It seemed as if shadows moved on his lips and the planes of his profile. Without looking at the lawyer, he obstinately shook his head. Drawing his rumpled person back to full height, the lawyer reported that the defendant pled not guilty and intended to retain his own attorney.

Immediately there was a small explosion at the prosecutors' table. A young assistant DA slammed his palm down on the hardwood, upsetting a Styrofoam cup. Those of us seated near the front had no trouble hearing him. "What! Okay! All right! Let's bring it to trial right away! This Phillips thing has been dragging on too damn long!" He held up four fingers like a spade and thrust them—once, twice—at Alvin. The judge set a new trial date for the beginning of the next week. As Alvin crossed from the lawyer to the bailiff who would handcuff and lead him away, his eyes passed without expression over the table of prosecutors. The young DA put up his fingers again—a gesture Judge Braniff would never have tolerated—and mouthed words all of us could read: "Forty years, buddy. Forty years."

On our way outside, Helen Cheno sagged against Rita Diaz and began to sob. She said she knew it was a bad day from the beginning when the bailiffs wouldn't pass on to Alvin the clothes she had bought for him to wear in court. She had spent twenty dollars on jeans and forty-seven on "rubbers," the leatherlike basketball shoes he had asked her for. To catch her breath, she sat for a moment on the long stone staircase leading from the building. She mentioned her nerves and her heart. Then, based on no connection that I could see, she was speaking of Jules, of how she cared for him for the first four years of his life. "He couldn't walk and had that tube runnin' under his skin," and finally she "just had to give him up" (to Diane, who was in no state to raise him either) because she—Helen—"just wasn't strong enough" because of her nerves and her heart.

I wondered if this was a way of telling us she would have to give up on Alvin too. "Alvin loved that baby!" she declared as if defiantly, lurching to her feet. "Lord, he loved that baby boy!" And in the small skirmish of helping her down the crowded courthouse steps, I missed learning if she meant Alvin Jr. or his father.

May 9, 1982

Mother's Day, late afternoon. I rode in the back seat of Helen Cheno's old car on a stretch of interstate laid through developed marshland within the eastern sprawl of the city. Rita drove and Helen sat to her right in accustomed near-silence, two small women in late middle age, Rita lightly complexioned, Helen medium dark. Drinking hot wind and road fumes, we were bound for an appointment with a man Rita once worked for. She had described him as "a big shot white pay lawyer," and she and Helen seemed to believe it easily within this man's power to "get li'l Al off." He had asked them to his house, which was also his office, to tell him more about the case and to discuss a fee. I was with them because Helen asked me to be and because I now felt obliged.

Over the noise from the highway, Helen spoke sporadically about Alvin. Her Creole mother, "Grandma," called him "her Popeye" because of "those big eyes he got in his head like his daddy." The darkest of her great-grandchildren, Alvin Jr. was Grandma's favorite, "and *she* was almost white." When I asked if difference caused the attraction, she nodded, but Rita, who had a deceptive way of only feigning inattention, suddenly spoke for her in a bawdy outburst: "Yah! She loved it! She loved it!"

Helen went on praising her nephew, telling how people in her neighborhood were always remarking on how "manly" he was. This trait was the reason for the injury to his hand, which was broken "beatin' a dude to the ground in the jailhouse, a dude that tried to get at his pretty legs." Of homosexuality, he had told her, " 'I'm a man, Aun-tee. I don' play that.' " She said that, while he might "beat a man," he would never "misuse a woman." This was one reason she couldn't believe he was involved in a purse-snatching. His respect for women caused him to stab Ernie, Diane's boyfriend in Harlem, because Ernie was inclined to beat her. And she remembered Alvin Jr., while still a young boy, on the verge of attacking his father because big Al had hit Diane.

As we exited from the interstate, she and Rita began a companionable squabble about directions that lasted until Rita found the lawyer's subdivision and parked before a large, low house built along a murky canal. No one was home, but soon a late-model car appeared on the white-top, then swept around us and into the driveway. "That's him," Rita said. "He was a fine-lookin' man." The lawyer climbed out and waved us toward the door to his house. He was stately and tall, lipless and gray. He wore Western boots beneath his slacks, and beneath his chin, a neck brace. "Flowers," he told us; he had come from placing flowers on his mother's grave.

Inside, he was solicitous toward Rita and marveled that her hair was no longer red—as it had been years ago when she worked for him and he handled her divorce. He gestured out into a spacious den-and-kitchen combination and asked how she liked his "little place." When we settled to business, he had them describe the crime and testimony. He posed only a few questions. He established the time of day of the theft and asked Helen if her nephew was "as dark as you."

"Yes, he's dark," she answered, "but not glossy." The lawyer wanted to know about Alvin's hair, and she told him, "Oh, he got plenty hair on his head," adding that his hair was "passable."

The lawyer nodded knowingly and said he believed there might be something he could do. It had come up right away that, though he no longer tried many criminal cases, he was well acquainted with the judge standing in for Braniff. Trying to hide her relief and eagerness, Helen mentioned money. At pains to make it clear that he wouldn't take on the case just because of the payment involved, he said two thousand would be his necessary charge. But, as if answering Helen's visible disappointment, he offered to accept a couple of hundred right away and the rest in installments. He would have to act swiftly in order to gain a continuance of the trial, which was due to start first thing in the morning, and Helen said she would meet him at court with some money.

Riding home in darkness, she spoke of taking out a loan and selling some of her furniture. Although I ended up giving her half of the down payment, I had misgivings. The unspoken agenda—cronyism—was like the landscape of the afternoon, and none of it felt solid. But I went along with it, telling myself that this was how things were done.

4

☐

June 26, 1982

The air crackled; then there was a deafening crash of thunder. Generators went down, pitching the sparsely windowed compound in near-blackness. After cursing out in alarm, men within the other partitions down the row fell silent, but Alvin's whispery monotone droned on as if we had heard nothing.

I had asked why he didn't resist extradition from New York, and he had been saying he thought he would "get only seven— Or fourteen at the most." At that moment a flash whited the walls, and lightning struck a tree or utility pole nearby. The thunder and darkness that followed sent him down another, even more voluble mental path, and he began talking about his lawyer—in phrases I couldn't catch —before reminding me, "I'm more than sho' he's your relative."

I brought up having visited his father's sisters in Houston, expecting this would be more agreeable to both of us. At once he told me flatly that "Aunt Elma died ten years ago." When I said I had spoken with her the month before last, he insisted she was long dead; it was a "fact, just like this other fact here that you have people at Star Sales, Star Sales and Stationery in New Orleans." I didn't contradict him further when he told me I also looked like someone he had seen on television; "in fact," it occurred to him now, I "could be just that person."

The sky that Saturday morning had been near-cloudless

when I walked, as instructed, along the groomed pathway into the restricted-visiting compound just beyond the front gate. By the path a muscular white trusty tossed feed to several mallard ducks stepping about him in the clipped grass. Seeming compelled to conversation, he asked if I wanted "to take one a these ol' boys home and put him in the pot." I commented on the luxuriant honeydew melons growing along the path. These too were his work, and he proceeded to tell me more about them.

Inside, the visitor at the screened slot nearest to me slept with his head on his arms while waiting for his friend or relative to be brought out. Thunder had begun when, about thirty minutes later, Alvin appeared on the other side of perforated sheet-metal partitioning.

Despite being cuffed in front, he greeted me gracefully, half bowing in an almost courtly way. He wore a new blue chambray shirt that must have been in the box of clothes I remembered Gloria saying she recently had sent him. The short sleeves fit him closely, and he appeared larger and more thickly muscled than he had in September. As we sat down opposite each other, I noticed something I had forgotten from before: a green snake tattooed as if slithering up his right forearm. Then I noticed his eye.

It was swollen nearly shut, a puffed bulb of flesh. Beneath it, in the encircling slit between his lids, dried secretion shone like glue. Then he moved, shattering my focus; because of the diamond-shaped holes in the partition, it was hard to maintain a sense of seeing his whole face.

He dismissed my alarm about his eye, saying it was just "a li'l problem" he lived with, one started not by the bleach he had poured into it but by blows in the ring. Before I could press him on this, he changed the subject to ask incredulously was I "still serious about that book." When I answered, he seemed not to believe or want to hear me and began talking about the Pardons Board. It became clear that he actually had more knowledge about this body than I did. He ticked off the names of board members, several of which I had never heard, and contradicted my speculation that his prison

record could pose a problem. Even such a long list of write-
ups as his counted for little, he said, because members of
the board "understand this environment." But he showed
slight interest in my account of having recently talked with
the judge who had sentenced him and that judge's explanation of how he could apply for a writ of habeas corpus
and possibly be granted a one-time-only hearing in that
judge's court, a hearing that could result in some degree of
post-conviction relief—if the prisoner could demonstrate
rehabilitation. He seemed reluctant to commit himself on
whether he had even received the habeas writ I had sent
him.

As we talked of other wishful solutions to his predicament,
he recognized himself that he "couldn't just be turned loose."
He said that, under some supervised program of release, he
would "snatch a job," vowing that he "wouldn't take no kinda
drug," not even methadone, unless he "had to to stand up."

Soon afterwards, the lights had gone in the storm, and
the darkness seemed to magnify his mistrust and the distance
between us. With the slack time hanging oppressively, I
asked if he had experienced much hate in his life. His answer
involved "hits"; he told me he had once been shot in the leg.
"I don't like hits, people all around gettin' hit." This was
"struggle" rather than "hate," he said, pointedly offering a
corrective of my terms and conception. It was "struggle," he
stressed, "not hate," that you saw especially in young convicts'
eyes; you could see they wouldn't "take any more," wouldn't
let themselves "be touched." Living in the projects and in
prison you grew to know your neighbors well: "who can be
jammed, who can't," the effects of struggle on each and in
what ways each can still be pushed.

When the power returned, a guard came around, announcing that all visits were "terminated." As if to dispel
what he described as "the off feeling" from earlier, Alvin
said his goodbye politely rising from his chair. I told him
that, after leaving Angola, I would drive on to Mansfield,
where I hoped to locate his father's first neighborhood. He
looked down and to the side as if listening with a degree of

pleasure to a voice beyond my voice. I told him of seeing
Collis a few afternoons before, of him sitting in a sunny
swatch of the courtyard in the lawn chair Collis Jr. had set
out for him; although he had claimed he would finish "lookin'
at" the paper when I left him, there were children around
the chair before I reached my car. Alvin looked up. I
mentioned the program photo I had seen above Collis's bed.
"He still got that trophy!" he interjected, the eyeball now
visible, like those of a face within a mask.

July 8, 1982

The word along the stairs and corridors was that Judge
Braniff was back the morning I arrived with Helen Cheno
and Rita Diaz for the beginning of Alvin Jr.'s second trial.
We also heard that different prosecutors would try this one.
Initially, not even Alvin himself seemed more disconcerted
by these changes than did his new lawyer. During the coffee-
drinking, paper-shuffling, and comings and goings that
preceded the actual addressing of the docket, he stepped
around the bench and talked his way past a bailiff into the
judge's chamber.

Helen and Rita nodded and drew in their breath in
anticipation. But he returned quickly. Even in his boots,
white suit, and the neck brace, which allowed him the leisure
of not wearing a tie, he looked confounded if not yet shaken.
He beckoned the three of us outside to explain that he had
been "cut from the case" because Judge Braniff wouldn't let
him advise Vernon Thomas.

Vernon Thomas?

We were dismayed—I more by the possibility that the
lawyer thought he could use Vernon in this way than by the
news that he wouldn't be defending Alvin after all. Before
we could continue that confusing conversation, a bailiff
summoned the lawyer inside.

Just then Vernon Thomas emerged from another courtroom. Stopping among us in the doorway to Braniff's court,

he asked me one question. "Y'all pay this guy anything?"
When I mentioned the down payment, he continued on past
us and, catching up to the other lawyer, walked alongside
him directly to the bench.

Judge Braniff, now robed and in place, looked as if he
might give off steam. After a brief agitated conference
between the judge and the two lawyers, Vernon Thomas
walked out of the courtroom, having been allowed to withdraw from the defense. I heard Braniff say to Alvin's lawyer,
speaking as he would to a prosecutor, defender, witness, or
anyone in his courtroom, "It's yours now, buddy. You're the
counsel of record." He made one concession, though, to the
lawyer's request for further time "to get close to it" and
granted yet another two-week continuance.

Afterwards when I angrily accused the lawyer of trying to
mislead us, he had a quick excuse, knowingly describing his
job in such cases as being "like a plumber's." As he went on
to assure us he would consult closely with Alvin in jail and
be ready for trial, I was already forgetting the terms of his
explanation, all but its metaphor.

In the evening over the phone, Helen Cheno told me she
was so upset on reaching home that she had to take a double
dose of phenobarbital rather than the single one her doctor
prescribed. I had a strong sense of how she felt.

Summer 1982

A few days later I wrote Alvin at Angola, again asking if
he had received the habeas writ and describing some of what
I saw in Mansfield. The day I mailed this letter I received
one from him.

7/7-82

Randy
   Writting hoping every thing is going good for you &
family. My self I'm sitting & holding on where my
Pardon is concern.

The visit we had might have not been the best, but I think it open my mind more to any expectations. When I say expectations, I mean I'm going to live in New Orleans, La. & I know some one name *Randy Bates*.

Plus I had another visit from some one in Concern name *Miss Rempel*. I'm more than show you know her plus, I think it's your relative. She is affiliated with the Southern Prisoner Defense Comittee. She was concern over my incarceration here at Angola. I had a talk with her & your name was a miss, but I'm more than show that she is aware of our relationship.

Yours truly, 'Al'

I puzzled uneasily over "expectations" and the letter's other ambiguities. Then I telephoned Melita Remple. Because of a conversation we had had months back concerning one of Farris's complaints about Angola, I knew she worked with the Louisiana Coalition on Jails and Prisons. Although hoping her visit had encouraged Alvin, I worried that it might have generated new mental confusion or made him more an object of attention among other inmates.

Melita Remple's voice was patient, her inflections considerate—whether these might be accompanied by a too ready theoretical sympathy I could only guess. She told me the Southern Prisoner Defense Committee, a regional organization based in Tennessee, was gathering information for a class-action suit against Angola because of conditions in Camp J. In assisting the committee, she had interviewed Alvin because he had been identified as a long-term resident of the camp, which was designed to house prisoners only for short disciplinary periods. She found it hard to believe when I told her he had been a fighter. She remembered him as being so mild, so polite, so sensitive, and, she searched for the word, so . . . "lovable."

This was my last conversation with Melita Remple. She soon left Louisiana to return to graduate school in another part of the country. Unfortunately, also losing touch with whether the suit was ever argued, I learned nothing more about the Southern Prisoner Defense Committee.

The night before her nephew's latest trial date, Helen Cheno called and told me she "jammed" a friend of Alvin Jr.'s named Charlie, and Charlie confessed that he was the one who snatched the purse and that Alvin wasn't involved. " 'I'm sorry, Auntee, I'm sorry. I didn't know Alvin would get in all this trouble.' "

She also said she had seen Alvin, and so had his lawyer. He had told the lawyer firmly that he wanted " 'to go to court' " and that he wouldn't cop a plea, as the lawyer suggested, for something he didn't do—which he felt is what led to his being on probation in the first place.

The lawyer's advice was to wear a long-sleeved shirt to cover his tattoos.

Helen had taken him the shirt along with the new clothes she had bought, saying, " 'Why you want to put that on your arm anyway?' " D-I-A-N-E now decorated his left forearm above A-L-V-I-N, which named either himself or his father on his left hand.

She described his answer: " 'Nothin' else to do when you're in jail, Auntee.' " Then she said he was " 'sure' " he would " 'go free' " if the lawyer " 'fights' " for him, because he "knows 'that deputy is lying.' "

As soon as she hung up, she said she was going to her church to light a candle for him and to make the Stations of the Cross on her knees.

The next morning the lawyer arrived late. But it didn't matter. Alvin's trial wouldn't be that day either. A burglary case was given precedence, and after this, the judge would be away for six weeks' vacation. The purse-snatching was continued until September.

Near the end of July I wrote to Angola, to tell Alvin I would be away for a month. I also told him about going to the fights with Collis the night before, on his seventy-third birthday, and how it took us a long time to reach our seats because so many people stopped him to shake his hand and talk—and how afterwards, in the course of a meal at Dooky Chase's, the maître d' and son of the owners greeted him warmly and, when we left, personally escorted him out to where I was parked.

Collis was dressed that evening as I had never seen him before, poignantly flamboyant in a checked blue suit and a spread-collar shirt. As we were leaving the apartment, Gloria intervened so she could arrange a silky scarlet handkerchief in his breast pocket; this was fit accompaniment to the flat-brimmed felt hat, almost as large as a sombrero, that he clapped on his head.

I didn't exaggerate to Alvin. Well-wishers converged on him before we even entered the Auditorium. Their inquiries about his health seemed to cause him to concentrate more intently on manipulating his crutches, and he repeatedly answered, "You can see, caincha? I'm still hoppin'." Even after we sat down, ex-fighters and fight people came over, many of them to take a seat themselves and watch part of the card with him.

Toward the end of the show-closer, an elderly white man hesitantly approached. "Mr. Phillips, isn't it? I just wanted to shake your hand. I saw your son fight many times. He was a great fighter."

Collis refrained from his usual response to comments about Alvin: "His head was hard. Now he's gotta pay." Nor did he offer the sort of strict technical qualification he normally used to temper excessive estimates of a boxer's skill: "Now, Alvin did move pretty good, and he *had* a left hand. But—" Instead—and I saw the man's words catch him—he looked away past the ring for an instant before smiling and repaying the compliment. "Most kind of you to say that, sir." He delicately took the man's hand. "Thank you very much."

I didn't describe this in any detail to Alvin, though, since I no longer believed I could tell whether such a scene would make him feel better or worse.

8/5-82

. . . hoping every thing is going good for you. I'm aware of some of your relatives, here at the prison & out in society. I probably don't know all of them but a lot.

I'm suppose to be getting out pretty soon, & probaly will look at you on T.V. one way or other . . .

The weather has been getting around, with some rain, & plenty heat. Want to let you know if there is anything I can do let me know. I appreciate the help you have been while my incarceration. Hope things is getting around for you.

Looking forward to retiring to N.O. La. one day. Wish you health and prosperity . . .

This letter was among my mail near the end of August when I returned from a family trip. Rather than reply right away, I found excuses in other things I had to do: a new job, his son's trial, trying to keep up with others in his family and with writing about them. A more personal reason for the delay was my bewilderment at the strange mental connections he made for me. As it was, I didn't answer his letter until early in October. For months after that, it looked as if I would never hear from him again.

On the last night in August, Helen Cheno called, telling me that, while I was gone, Rita Diaz had spoken to the lawyer on the phone, but evidently he "wasn't in his right mind, or somethin'," because he asked Rita if Alvin Jr. was " 'in jail in some little country town.' " She also told me that Alvin's friend Charlie was arrested for an armed robbery and had already been tried and sentenced—to five years.

5

□

September 23, 1982

Once it began, after three more continuances in September, the trial went quickly; all was done in a day.

In the morning a six-member jury was picked. From a pool of seventeen whites and seven blacks, Alvin Jr.'s lawyer and the chief prosecutor agreed on three white men, two white women, and one black man. Another black, a young man, excused himself, contending he shouldn't serve because he faintly remembered Alvin as a playground acquaintance. Among the half dozen or so black habitual trial-watchers in the otherwise near-empty gallery, there was muttering about the racial makeup of this jury, and someone said the young man should be punched in the mouth. Word from the project was that Alvin was innocent, and spectator sentiment was unusually strong in his favor.

The opening statements were routine, the prosecutor defining the nature of circumstantial evidence, which was the basis of the state's case, and Alvin's lawyer resting on "the presumed innocence" of his client. During the lunch recess, I learned that his lawyer's defense would rest largely on Alvin's claim that on January 6 his car was in a body shop as a result of damage done to it while being towed by a wrecker. The lawyer said there hadn't been "time to check this through completely," though. While he went to lunch and, I supposed, to make final preparations in his defense, I used the pay phone in the corridor and eventually reached someone who worked at the towing company. He remembered a problem with a red car, but he didn't know which body shop had been used and there were no towing records from January. The company had moved its offices since then, and those invoices weren't saved. Not to have maintained such records seemed incredible to me, and I asked to speak with the owner, but the man on the line was the only one in the office and the owner was out of town. Reluctantly, he gave me the number of a driver who might have been handling the wrecker that day. On my next call, despite my careful explanation of my purpose, a suspicious male voice told me the driver, a woman, was "just out" and, no, he didn't know when she would be back.

As I turned from the phone, I felt a presence beside me. It was a young man from the project, someone I knew to be connected to Collis's family by, as he said, "a marriage-type thing" and with whom I had spoken before. Each time it had been the same as today: he would be standing quietly interested nearby before I would see him. Now he murmured, "This charge, it ain't Alvin." I pressed him for reasons why not, expecting the standard of public silence that he lived by to end the exchange. But on this day, after some usual indirection, he told me he had "heard" that on the 6th of January Alvin's car "was lent" to someone in his family and that, as Alvin had contended all along, Alvin was with his girlfriend at his cousin Trina's that entire afternoon and evening. Without mentioning names, the young man made certain I understood exactly who this relative was who had borrowed Alvin's car. Then, without transition, he was exchanging pleasantries with someone walking by and receded toward his place against the wall.

When he returned from lunch, Alvin's lawyer truly had much on his mind and time only to go on with the defense he had planned. So I wasn't insistent when I told him what I had learned, knowing Alvin had long since chosen not to "rat" on his own blood, a circumstance that probably would have been harder anyway on the family as a whole. (Much later, when I confronted the actual driver of the car, his denials became almost abusive; it was a conversation that, on future meetings, we each chose to pretend never happened.)

The state's case proceeded briskly to its key witness, the deputy, who pointed out Alvin in the courtroom.

Cross-examination established that the deputy was currently unemployed. Alvin's lawyer tried to capitalize on the fact that the man wrote the license number on an envelope containing medication. The deputy insisted that the pills were over-the-counter "muscle relaxers," a "form of Tylenol." Black court-watchers whispered in knowing disgust, believing the defense had discredited the witness, but this detail—like the whole trial—would prove to be beside the point. As would Alvin's lawyer's final question to the deputy, which was to ask if he understood "what it means to transpose a number." The deputy did not.

"It doesn't look good," I heard Alvin's lawyer whisper to him.

Alvin testified in his own behalf as the first witness for the defense, whose presentation I would learn about later because, as the last character witness, I was now required to wait outside. Helen Cheno testified next; and, third, Alvin's lawyer called "Earl Thompson" before correcting himself when it was pointed out to him that he was misreading the name. Earl Thomas was Alvin's immediate supervisor when he "threw cases" on a route truck for Barg's Root Beer. Thomas described him as a good worker and a reliable young man, then became baffled when, on cross-examination, the prosecutor ticked off a lengthy arrest record and disclosed that, according to police reports, Alvin sometimes went by the alias of "Alvin Stone." He asked would having knowledge of these arrests change Earl Thomas's opinion of the defendant. Well . . . yes, Earl Thomas admitted, he supposed it might.

Then it was my turn. I explained my link to the Phillips family, and at the lawyer's cue I gave my opinion of Alvin's character: ". . . a sincere person who wouldn't try to take unfair advantage and who is honest with people who are honest with him."

The prosecutor wanted to know if "a few statistics" would alter this opinion. As he did with Earl Thomas, he then recited a litany of arrests for alias Alvin Stone that included eight for simple burglary in 1978, two for possession of marijuana, and one for attempted auto theft outside the New York, New York disco in 1982. As he intended, I was surprised by much of this information, though I answered, "Not necessarily. I would need to know more about the circumstances." As I tried to add something about the circumstances of Alvin's upbringing, Judge Braniff boomed out above me, "Just answer the questions!" But the prosecutor had no further questions to ask. I stepped down from the stand vexed with myself for not—not that it would have made a difference—thinking quickly enough to point out that, according to our system, guilt is not to be inferred from arrests.

Braniff had already denied the defense permission to call Trina as a last-minute alibi witness, so Alvin's lawyer stepped past me and said, "That's our defense."

Unfortunately for the state, in its long-term intentions at least, the prosecutor then called a rebuttal witness, the arresting detective, who now testified that he had telephoned a repair shop and been told the car was brought in on New Year's Eve or New Year's Day. A shop employee assured him the car was returned to its owner no more than two days later and well before January 6.

I wondered about the means of the police department compared with my lack of success over the phone during the lunch recess. But there was no chance to discuss my misgivings with Alvin's lawyer, for, because of the lateness of the hour, Braniff had already hustled him into his closing argument. To the lawyer's credit, right away he reminded the jury that arrests were not convictions and suggested the police department was trying to act as "judge and jury in this case." Using terms I regretted, though, he also said that "even the best of crooks" would not be "so stupid" as to go to police headquarters to claim his car if he had used it to commit a crime, especially if he was already on probation.

He challenged the credibility of the unemployed deputy and—most important—finished by taking issue with the fact that the information from the repair shop was based solely on a telephone conversation.

The prosecutor began by thanking the jury for its patience and for having "wasted the whole day rather than being at work." He closed by marveling that "it's not easy to get arrested for burglary and then purse-snatching" and describing the defense as "a smoke screen" and Alvin as "either the most unlucky individual in the world or guilty as charged."

The jury entered the jury room at 5:15. Alvin was moved to a holding cell. I sat in the gallery alone with Helen and Rita. Fading light—Judge Braniff's courtroom had a window—striped the false Doric columns that were plastered onto the walls. Rita comforted Helen, and I fretted privately that our testifying had worsened Alvin's chances by allowing, as it did, the prosecution to introduce all those early arrests. I didn't know why his girlfriend hadn't testified, or why Trina hadn't been included as a subpoenaed witness from the beginning. Not that their testimony would necessarily have changed any minds. But these were elements that deserved care. Despite our intentions, Helen and I hadn't done very well by Alvin. The prosecution was correct in calling his defense a smoke screen. Given the incriminating nature of his background, all that could really be done was to attack the heavy-handedness of the prosecution, as Vernon Thomas had. The DA's office was convinced he was guilty, and he was—guilty because of the general circumstances of his life. But although he may well have known in advance about the plans of his relative who drove his car and his friends who committed the crime, he was strictly innocent of what the circumstantial evidence was described as having proved. Three males perpetrated an inexcusable offense against an innocent woman, but it was one absent of violence, a petty crime made grave by the disproportionate sentence, a virtual lifetime, that any convicted second offender could expect to receive in Judge Braniff's court. At 5:30, in time for most of us to be home for dinner, the jury returned with its "Guilty" verdict.

10-17-82

Randy,

I know it's been a while since you've heard from me.

I am troubled about something Alvin Sr. wrote me. He told me that he is slipping again that he once had faith that you gave him he stated now he feel there is no hope. He said he do not see or here from you and that the prison separate him and Farris.

Alvin said he was waiting to see if you were going to let him know if he was to receive pardon.

Now I told him you are not a *lawyer* and that I feel you did what you could. Maybe you can explain this to him better than I can since you are there. Will you please write him or go see him or help him or talk to my father. Maybe he will listen to you as far as Alvin is concern.

I know you can see that he really needs help. Gloria told me Alvin may lose one of his eyes.

I heard the bad news about Lil Alvin. Satun is sure busy. Big Alvin must not know this. It would set him back.

If you have lil Al address please send it to me.

Connie

Later on the same day, as I had at the beginning of the month, I wrote Alvin. And began a futile wait for an answer.

October 29, 1982

I knew Steve Lemoine because of our sons. He and his wife, Helen, had organized a Scout troop at Abe and Richard's school.

Personable, patient, and apparently not much taken with his own good looks, Steve impressed me as being someone who enjoyed listening as much as speaking and who practiced more criminal than civil law because of tacit egalitarian convictions that most of the lawyers I was acquainted with had either never held or abandoned by the time they were Steve's age. He showed interest in Collis's family and always seemed to have time to hear about their problems with the law. Because Steve was both busy and struggling in his practice and because he had already given me a wealth of free legal advice, I was reluctant to take further advantage of his generosity and involve him directly in defending anyone. Concerning Alvin Sr., he thought that the odds were long against helping him in his present mental state and that the legal effort would be costly under any circumstances. But when I told him about Alvin Jr.'s trial, he said he thought something could be done, and he agreed to handle the appeal for no charge if Helen Cheno and I could come up with the money for the transcripts.

Before Alvin's sentencing I had stood for a few minutes in the corridor with Steve and the assistant district attorney who had prosecuted the case, two men very similar in size and dress and both still some years away from middle age. I listened to their comradely bantering and looked from Steve's round glasses and abundant, curling hair to the prosecutor's more cautious grooming and the quick, competent gestures of his hands. Their less evident differences seemed of a kind that are more commonly generational.

Steve slipped in a cajoling jab. "You know this guy doesn't deserve the max."

Despite a sheepish tilt of his head, the prosecutor came right back. "You think he deserves to be back on the street? What can I do?"

"Ask Braniff not to give him the max."

"You know I can't do that. My name'd be all over the building before lunch."

"What? Trying to get promoted?"

Soon Steve was standing with Alvin before the bench. The

sentencing had already been continued once from earlier in the month because the paperwork for revoking Alvin's probation hadn't yet been completed. That day Alvin, his hair severely cropped, wore baggy new fatigues. A muscular white detective, evidently a weight lifter, came in at Braniff's summons, laid out his materials, and fingerprinted Alvin for his permanent prison file. During the procedure Alvin's large eyes were palpably without expression; after the fingerprinting, they looked newly dead. Now, before he finally passed sentence, Judge Braniff asked if Mr. Phillips's new attorney wished to say anything.

Steve did. For the record he told the court that Alvin's father had been sent to prison when Alvin was in his early teens and that his mother was also a convicted offender.

Risibly, the judge interrupted, declaring he "certainly" had no intention of holding "the crimes of the parents against the son."

Steve continued, disclosing that Alvin had left school thereafter and worked, when he could find work, to help support his family. He said, "If it can be argued that Alvin Phillips didn't take advantage of opportunity [the court's first probationary lenience toward him], it can also be argued that there were many opportunities that Alvin Phillips never had."

In response, Judge Braniff, speaking in rare measured tones, patiently explained his policy toward recidivists: he always gave a man a first chance, but almost never a second one, because his long experience on the bench had shown him that, if a second chance was required, time in jail usually was all that stood between the man and a career in crime. He asked Alvin if he had anything to say.

Alvin did: "I didn't try to hurt nobody, and I never will. And I didn't snatch no purse."

Judge Braniff then calmly sentenced him to forty years at hard labor in the state penitentiary. To this he added three years more from the revoked probation, and deducted nine months for time already served.

Alvin turned to Steve and shook his hand.

6

□

February 17, 1983

Reaching out quickly, Alvin caught the little girl as she ran past, and pulled her into his lap. Taking his time, he began telling her about his daughter at her age. The child's mother came over, a strained expression on her face. My pulse thumped.

As if unaware of the smoldering stare of the young convict the woman had been sitting with three tables away, he whispered to the child and peered at her face. It was the child herself who broke the tension, shrinking back and murmuring to her mother about "the man's eye." To my great relief, he set her on her feet then, assuring her mother—as if this explained everything—that he "once *did* have a little girl."

He had been returned to population, and was living in the same dormitory as Gloria's son Dwight by the time Steve Lemoine and I had been able to schedule a day when both of us were free to travel. Steve had a paying client he needed to visit; driving him to Angola was a small favor I could offer. I also had hoped that meeting a concerned lawyer might give Alvin a lift that would lead to something positive.

While Steve saw his client in a room designated for legal consultations, I had waited for Alvin in the general visiting lounge of one of the population camps. It was a large room shuttered with blinds and furnished with institutional tables and chairs. Crude religious murals covered the walls on the snack-bar side of the room. The murals incoherently depicted events drawn from the New Testament.

From this direction Alvin appeared in a doorway and paused, waiting for a guard to uncuff him. He wore jeans, a sweatshirt, and oversized rubber boots that shuddered and plopped when he was given leave to cross the room. He appeared larger and heavier than I had yet seen him. As he walked he nodded to the several other prisoners seated at tables.

He greeted me pleasantly, but soon he was talking low and fast with his head down or to the side, his words manic and testy. "That's aw right, that's aw right," he would say, dismissing subjects he seemed not to want to consider. Right away he challenged me, asking if I hadn't "backed off on that book yet" and acting unable to believe I hadn't "put that thing aside."

In these peopled surroundings, he paid me scant visual attention, watching instead the other prisoners' women and children. He said it felt "good just to see the faces of free people" even though it was "like a fantasy that plays with my head" to be "around" such visitings.

When the mother and little girl returned to their seats, he touched his puffed eye slit and wondered aloud if he should apologize for how he looked. Almost derisively he answered my questions about how his eye felt, insisting that he could see and that it didn't hurt him—except sometimes when he had "headaches." It was the "tissues," he said. "The tissues is damaged." Gazing around the room, he went on speaking in low, trancelike tones of how "the worst thing to do to a ex-fighter is beat him in his head. Men in good condition have already done that." He alluded to being "stomped in the head on Rikers Island" and beaten with "bats" at Angola, but when I pressed him for details he said, "That's aw right," and closed the subject by making a sound between his teeth to attract the attention of a white child at another table.

This little boy hid fearfully behind his chair back. Alvin shrugged and asked me if I had children.

I repeated the names and ages I had written in a letter.

"Yeah?" he said skeptically. "Lemme see your ring."

I put my left hand on the table.

He glanced at it, then away, saying he never wore a wedding band himself, only a small diamond on his little finger, adding that Diane wore a ring with seven stones in it. Those were their wedding rings, but no one else knew it. They didn't travel as married people; "this other," their rings, was a secret that only they shared.

As he was explaining this, an attractive Hispanic woman came in and sat down to wait near us. He watched her closely, saying how pretty she was and how it had been almost ten years since he had had a woman and that he would never have one again.

Abruptly he became apologetic: he hoped I didn't misunderstand or hold it against him that he had been discussing something personal concerning his wife and then allowed himself to become distracted in that way.

Soon afterwards he began to shake. He said he felt cold, felt there were "things like ice" on the ends of his hair. There was "frozen water" on his "hands" too: thinking of the past made it form there. No, he corrected, now speaking more to himself than to me, not ice but "rocks . . . rocks on my hands."

I grew tense again, sensing him on the verge of an outburst. He rubbed at his hands, fretting that they weren't clean enough. They didn't look dirty to me despite the cracked silvery skin scaling around his knuckles. He said he was "no fanatic" about cleanliness, but he didn't like being dirty. He would "never be an individual again," he continued, as if the connection were clear. "The ring, drugs, prison" had "taken that" from him, that and "the rest of it, the things throwed away." But—he seemed unable to cease on his own—what he had lost made him "feel free too."

The Hispanic woman rose and walked to the Coke machine. He fell silent in mid-sentence, watching her. I listened to the clock-clock of her spike heels and feared he would do something irrevocable.

He raised his hand in a muted wave. I stifled an impulse to take hold of his wrist and return it to the table. "It's aw right, man," he said, reading my thought. "That girl goes to St. Raymond's"—his mother's church. "I been knowin' her since she was a child. She's growed up pretty, huh?"

He waved again.

The woman pointedly turned from us and sat down at a table farther away.

Steve now stood over us, to me a welcome diversion. Alvin seemed thrown by having to size up a strange new person. He seized on Steve's name. Oh yes, he told us, he already knew Steve. They had met "back in the sixties, the late sixties back there" when both were "athletes in New Orleans." Steve was "Steve Stonebreaker," once a well-known linebacker for the New Orleans Saints.

Despite Steve's assuring attentiveness, our attempted conversation about particulars of Alvin's situation proved futile. Looking down again and speaking low, Alvin said he had "recycled" his feet "three times," insistent that we learn exactly how a person did this: "You get you a good pair of leather shoes, not the cheap kind, fifty dollars or more, you wear those, and no socks." When Steve brought up questions of law, he asserted that he had known "judges outside that must be a hundred, hundred ten years old by now." But many other people he had known—he also mentioned his mother—were dead; he had had "podnahs that's dead now too." He shook his head, wondering aloud why he himself was still alive.

Looking up and speaking in the same tone, he told me he knew I "work in TV." He couldn't understand why, "since TV gets around so," I was having so little effect on his case. He knew my sister, had heard her on the radio. And my brother—"same name as him," he said, nodding toward Steve Lemoine—my brother Steve was still "back there, locked down" in the psychiatric camp.

During the stutter of leave-takings, Steve repeated my earlier concern about his eye. Already on his feet, Alvin said he had "a son, a son name Jules who had trouble with his eyes," but he "spanked his butt, spanked it good, and took him out to look at the stars."

He left before we did, following a guard toward a garishly painted door that vaguely figured in the narrative of the murals. He turned once for a bluff, abrupt remark—"It's too late to give up now!"—then wheeled back, thumb up, on course toward the door. The misfit rubber boots waffled his stride, giving him the look of a man trying to walk naturally in water.

Spring 1983

I can no longer read the letter he wrote me several weeks after we saw him. Because he was asking for visits from his family, I mailed the faintly penciled original to Connie; possibly she could send one or more of the children, if not persuade Diane to make the trip. The photocopy I kept has faded so that only phrases are still readable: ". . . hoping you can help . . . I'm wishing . . . my wife & children . . . try to find out how much time . . . to look at them all . . . if you can arrange . . . would mean everything in the world to me . . . especially my son Jules and my daughter . . . the rest of my life . . ."

Farris downplayed my inquiries about his brother's delusions: "ALVIN ALL WAY'S SAYING OR THINKING HE SEEN SOME ONE ON 'TV' HE SOMETHING ELSE. BUT HE WAS READY 'DIG' YOU SHOULD HAVE TALK TO HIM WHEN HE WAS A FEW CELL FROM ME."

Gloria's son Dwight, who signed himself "Reno"—and who carried an inoperable bullet lodged in his head, a bullet which gave his mother recurrent anxieties—tried to stress the positive about his uncle and new dormitory mate: "Well man everything is coming along fine, no shit, Al is talking with a lot of sence, I don't no what happen but I can handle

him now! Randy, he rap's with me all so other dude's around
here . . . at first I thought he wasn't going to even come
back to him self, hey, now I don't no! But there's still thing's
that he don't want to hear or except."

"You *know* Alvin's in New Orleans, huh?"

Gloria broke this unexpected news in mid-March. Her
phone was temporarily reconnected and I had been returning one of Collis's then frequent calls. Learning he was
asleep, I had talked for a while with her. Collis's reason for
phoning hadn't concerned Alvin, though; it was just his
periodic keeping in touch, and it seemed Gloria might not
have mentioned Alvin either if we hadn't spoken at some
length. He had been transferred from Angola to Charity.
Though not to the psychiatric ward. To my questions, she
answered that he had been moved, but only temporarily, to
undergo an operation. A doctor thought he had "like a
tumor behind his eye."

Collis Jr. had visited him the day before and, in a slip of
the tongue, had mentioned Jerry's death. Even though Alvin
had been told of his brother's suicide not long after it
happened, he now refused to believe Jerry was dead. Junior
told her he thought Alvin was " 'go'n come off that mattress
and hit me' " despite being handcuffed to the frame of the
bed.

The next morning, my thirty-eighth birthday, I visited
him on the fifth floor of Charity.

He lay perfectly still, flat on his back. Between the taut
sheets, he looked huge, his skin lusterless, oak gray, drier
than I had seen it, making me guess he had just had a
thorough wash. His darkened eye, now shut tight, bulged
like an exaggeration of a fighter's mouse above an oozing
crescent seal. Matter trailed from his lashes toward a crusty
stain on the pillowcase.

Rising from a corner of the half-populated high-security ward, a large coppery-skinned guard blocked my path. "The man's a prisoner."

"It's aw right, man," Alvin told him; ours was "a business connection."

Almost young enough to be a son to either of us, the guard looked from Alvin to me. We were both speaking to him insistently. Raising his fingers to put an end to it, he said, "Three minutes, that's it."

I set several packages of cigarettes on the top sheet as he dismissed my questions about his eye. Yes, there was a tumor, but it was "aw right"—he could "live with it or without it." What he wanted was for me to "see about" his "discharge papers." Speaking in a rush, he asked me to "see Lemoine, Steve; Mista Cusimano; see my first lawyer." Between the four of us, surely we could *do something*.

He would speak of nothing else and showed no interest in hearing me out when I tried to explain some of the difficulties involved.

The snake on the inside of his right forearm, which was cuffed to the special bed rail, seemed curiously sedate and out of place. He now appeared balder than he was, his receded hair brushed severely back, not standing tall on his skull as it usually did. The guard came toward us. Alvin whispered a last confidential instruction about his release. I shook his free left hand and, in turning, saw it move crablike to sweep the cigarettes out of sight between the sheets.

That night I telephoned Collis to ask if he wouldn't let me drive him to Charity to visit his son. Pressured in that way, he spoke to me more fully about Alvin and himself than ever before. "Look, Randy, lemme tell you sumpum you don' understand. Alvin, my son, was number two, the number two contender in the world! I'd brought him all the way from a baby, all the way to the top, to the big money. Then he come to me an' aksed for his contrac'. Dorothy was lyin' sick. Spent all the money we had on hospital bills. Two or three months later, I learned he was foolin' with that *stuff*.

"I'd do what I can to help him now. Send him a few dollas when I have it, sent Gloria to the hospital with five packs a cigarettes. But I don't want to see him all shackled and chained up. That's my son, you understand. I raised him from a baby.

"People come all the time, offer me rides up to Angola. All I gotta do is git in the car. But if I was to go there, I'd break down. I couldn't look at him like he is now."

Sally, who still worked at Charity then, was able to slip in to see him for a moment the day before his transfer back to Angola. His chart showed that, in addition to complicating high blood pressure, he had in fact had a tumor, which surgery now had successfully removed. Like Melita Remple of the Coalition on Jails and Prisons, Sally marveled at his polite mildness. Looking up at her one-eyed, his head swathed in a bandage, he had asked how I was and told her I would " 'always come looking' " at him " 'with wondrous eyes.' "

The following year someone else told me about seeing him during the short while he was in Charity. This was Trina Smith, Collis Jr.'s second-oldest daughter. A gregarious young woman with a beautiful face, Trina was with her girlfriend on the fifth floor looking for another man when a bedridden prisoner said, " 'C'mere, baby.' " She whispered to her girlfriend, " 'Look at that old man talkin' to me.' " Then she wanted to go down on her knees when a sympathetic guard told them who the old man was. The guard uncuffed him so he could rise up in the bed and put out his arms. She saw a tear run from his eye as he told her she couldn't know what it was for him to hold a woman from his family after so long. She told him not to cry because she knew she was emotional and sentimental and she wouldn't be able to handle it.

Since his trial I had regularly heard from Alvin Jr. At Christmas he had sent me a handmade card in an ingeniously folded prisoner-complaint form held together with tiny strips of chewed gum, and there were frequent letters plus messages by way of Helen Cheno. For the time being, his pending appeal postponed his transfer from Parish Prison. The appeal was stalled because Steve still hadn't received a copy of the trial transcript as he had requested. As he explained to Alvin, he was in no hurry, though, because Judge Braniff was due soon to retire, and Steve felt it was better not to file until then.

In the meantime Alvin Jr. had been boxing on the prison team. His coaches, Melvin Paul and Jerome Clouden, pro headliners whom I sometimes saw in passing at the courts building, told me he had "a good pair of hands on him" and he could probably do well as a professional. Helen said Rita had sewn him a pair of green velvet trunks, cut from the same pattern as the black ones she made for his father to wear in Europe, and on March 18 he won a trophy and gave it to them to save for him.

On March 22, he sent me a newsletter clipping that described the prison boxing tournament: "The most impressive victory was scored when Alvin Phillips, Jr., 176, son of former contender Alvin Phillips, delivered a devastating left hook to the head of Barry Cauley, 170, and scored a knockout in 1:30 of the second round. Phillips is described by coach Jerome Clouden as having superior upper-body strength and unlimited potential." His own enthusiasm about his chances was more muted and apparently influenced by larger concerns: ". . . I just had to write you and let you no what's happending on my end. From what these people tell I have ability to go a long way's. Well I hope that's true as they say it is becuse I'am will to go for it . . . so I can help my self and my family . . . Randy we have a lot of good people in our family it just we had our problems coming up. I just hope that some day thing's will change. I really don't know why I'am sitting hear telling you about my family and you no all reddy."

On April 25, I was at court expecting the beginning of the murder trial of Gloria's son Lionel, but it was continued for another month. As I was on my way to meet Steve in another part of the building, the assistant DA who had prosecuted Alvin Jr.'s case stopped me. Ostensibly, he wanted just to talk about Alvin, but it soon became clear that he was fishing for information. He implied there was reason to suspect that Alvin, for safekeeping, had been given a gun used in the crime with which Lionel was charged. When he saw that I didn't know anything, the conversation ended and I continued on my way to catch up to Steve at the end of the long hall.

Steve had just come from an abruptly scheduled nonjury trial before Judge Braniff. The judge had found Alvin guilty of the attempted auto theft outside the New York, New York disco in December of '81 and had added six months to his forty-two years.

In May, I stopped at Helen Cheno's house—for what reason I don't remember. A tiny bald man stood in reverie on her steps. I nodded moving past him, then was startled when he spoke to me in her voice, a voice which broke into weeping when she told me, with tears visibly popping from her eyes, that worry about her nephew had so aggravated her nerves that now her hair, "all of it, I'm tellin' you, all of it, it just fell out."

7

□

June 2, 1983

Kevin did most of the talking. His girlfriend, Debra, sat
in the back and said almost nothing. I drove.

He was explaining why his memory "was always strange."
It was because he had been "a special child," the specialness
being caused by his fall from an unrailed second-story
balcony when he was "small, small." As a result, he still
sometimes had headaches and could remember little of his
childhood before the first year he entered school; this was
in the sixth grade in Cherry Hill, New Jersey.

The moments of his past that were most clear to him were
distant ones before the accident. While watching his father
run a circular course around a playground near the project,
he stepped on the decomposing carcass of a bird—"It looked
like glue"—and became piercingly afraid. In another, he
himself was running, running with his brothers in the
Auditorium during the fights. They had run from the top
of the balcony to ringside, where their grandfather slapped
them for being out of their seats.

From among the years largely lost, he did sharply remember his tenth birthday—January 17. Since before Christmas
that winter he had looked forward to his father's release
from Rikers Island; a lawyer had told his mother it probably
would happen around the 17th. But on January 14—"I
don't forget that date"—when Alvin was "near the front,"
in the last phase of detention, a records double check
disclosed that there was no such living person as a petty

thief named Raymond Whiting and that "Raymond Whiting" was an alias of an ex-fighter wanted on a narcotics charge in Louisiana. That night, "the house was cold. I went to bed with my coat on. Did the same on my birthday."

His happiest moment came "the first time I made a lot a money for myself." This was a year or so after he had left school and moved on to New York. First he worked "for a Jamaican named Sam, a big Rastafarian dude, I liked him a lot." Sam had a job at a grocery store and paid Kevin out of his wages to help him with chores. This, the most conventional work Kevin would do, ended one day when Sam "just stopped coming by" the store. Kevin never saw him again. After that he "started scramblin' " in earnest. For a time he "got by" alongside Alvin Jr. washing cars for pimps. One such person, "a martial-arts dude and ex-convict," gave him "a break—sellin' weed on one stretch of one side of the street because I had told him what went down with my father."

Kevin said you have to realize that "there are trip wires all over the street, you have to be careful, careful on each move out there." To illustrate, he spoke of Buddy and Reverend, two sellers "bigger than I am now." Buddy had been "jealous of Rev's action" and let it be known "he was go'n kill Rev." Buddy's next mistake was "sittin' on a car hood without checkin' his back." Reverend "raised up off the seat with his pistol and shot Buddy in the back of his head, then he shot him in his chest, he shot him eleven times." This was the first "true killin' " Kevin had witnessed "from close up."

Gradually, opportunities had improved for him. He had "moved some" on the ladder of the street. With pride in his voice he told me he could now buy "clothes and things" for Debra. In the rearview mirror I saw her smile. And even though he couldn't yet afford to move from Connie's, it was a satisfaction to him to come in from work early in the morning and "play with" Troy, Farris, and Donny before they would "go on to school"—and a special satisfaction "to maybe lay a few dollars on 'em."

He was talking about his brothers when we reached
Angola.

Rules required Debra to wait in the screening area near
the main entrance while he and I, the only passengers,
sweltered in the prison bus that takes visitors to outlying
compounds. Before a driver ambled out, Kevin wiped sweat
from his face with the heel of his thumb and talked about
Debra. He stuck with her, he said, because she was the only
one he could talk to. They had been through a lot; years.
"She chopped me once with a bottle." He touched his left
shoulder. "Right here." All his friends on the street had
made their girlfriends pregnant and they had been after
him to do the same. And he wanted to do that, it would be
a special intimacy: "Don't they say, 'Jill had a baby for Jack'?"
He felt he would be giving Debra something special and at
the same time giving himself a goal to work for. Supporting
a child would make him save and be more responsible.

As the bus lurched into motion, I mentioned the interests
of the child and the need of each parent first to be self-
sufficient. He nodded, but his eyes followed the passing corn
fields. The healthy stalks glimmered in the bright sunlight,
and I was struck by both the beauty of the corn and the
futility of offering unsolicited values that came from a way
of living alien to his. When I let the subject drop, he filled
the vacuum with a flurry of questions about the prison:
"How many men do they keep here?" "Where does that
fence go?" "Was that a woman up in that perch?"

When finally we stopped at a compound, one new to me,
he was still asking questions, many of which I couldn't
answer. For reasons I would never learn, Alvin was now
kept in yet another camp. As in the last one, the visiting area
here was a large unpartitioned room. But this space also
served recreational purposes. It contained a folded Ping-
Pong table, and, eerily, a knee-level boxing ring dominated
one corner of the room.

As we waited at a round Formica table, Kevin smoked and
glanced tensely at the room's several entrances. "Which way
will he be comin' from?" he wanted to know. Scanning the

doorways, he asked another question, which seemed unrelated. "Them two morphodites, the ones ratted on my father, is it like we heard, was they killed by the cops?" I didn't know, I didn't know. But I could see that his present talkiness grew from accelerating anxieties. The cigarette trembled between his fingers. I expected this visit would be hard for him; but, like him, I hadn't realized how hard.

He was asking me something else when, from the direction his eyes had just quitted, his father strode into the room.

He looked big, much bigger, like a magnification of the man I remembered from earlier visits. Dressed entirely in faded denim, he clumped toward us in heavy brogans, the kind he once wore for roadwork. His arms swelled the cutoff sleeves of his shirt. There was a hint of a gut. He put out his hand toward me; then he turned in surprise to Kevin, who, as I was, was now on his feet. Almost as tall as Alvin's friend Pete, Kevin stood poised, holding himself back, peering down at his father.

"Hey . . . ? Kevin . . . ? It's you? I didn't know you."

They almost shook hands. Then a sound rose in Kevin's throat, and his arms fell limply to his sides. Alvin's hands went up to cup his son's ears and hair. I turned away, hearing as I did the thump of a hard male embrace, and busied myself with the details of leaving a money order from Kevin, then buying hamburgers and fried potatoes.

Carrying over the food, I saw tears shining on Kevin's cheeks. But he seemed vexed with his father. "I *talked* to you on the phone, I *told* you I was comin'!"

Alvin maintained an aggressively cocky attitude—a side of him I had never quite seen—teasing Kevin in low tones about "that water" in his eyes. Asking to see Kevin's teeth, he cautioned him to take special care of them. His hand moved down Kevin's shoulder to his biceps. To me, he said, "His arm does up like mine do." And to Kevin, his hand now proprietorially feeling his ribs, "But how come you so skinny?" The hand moved to browse purposefully among the French fries. "Don't you eat? Don't you know you gotta *eat?*"

Kevin said he couldn't eat just then. "My stomach's a knot."
The room was stuffy, but his parted lips shook as if from a
chill.

Although there was scant sign of surgery, Alvin's eye was
permanently shrouded. His pupil glittered between the half-
closed lids, and he said, "It's aw right," he could see; it was
"just a tumor," he had had other tumors in his body. The
thread of talk skittered, and he told me he had a tumor
where he once was shot in the leg. "That's a tumor, yeah."
Pointedly not looking at it, he gestured toward the low
boxing ring across the room. "And them corners, that's a
tumor too. Yeah, that's a big tumor, plenty tumors there."
He whispered to Kevin, "It's hard, yeah, it's hard. You gotta
fight. You ready to fight?"

Kevin gave him an annoyed look. "I fight!"

His father pushed his shoulder not so lightly and said
jokingly, "Boy! I'll tear you up."

In response, Kevin mentioned "a young lady" who had
come with him from New York. Alvin flinched, and I sensed
he was automatically denying the knowledge that his family
was scattered far from New Orleans and home. Kevin
persisted. "You go'n be a grampaw, Pop! I'm tellin' you. We
go'n make a kid soon."

Alvin dismissed him, "Go on, boy," and I hoped he would
offer fatherly words of caution. Instead they bickered. Alvin
insisted that Kevin, his mother, and siblings still lived on
Jumonville. Exasperated and again near pained tears, Kevin
contradicted him. "I *told* you, Pop. I live in New York, and
I work in a grocery store."

They were interrupted by a heavily tattooed white prisoner
who passed the table and, calling Alvin by name, obsequiously
greeted him. Alvin didn't move his head, watching the man
from the corner of his healthy eye. "Hey, whatcha say . . .
ay . . . ay?" The taunting way he drew out the phrase
contained a nuance of mockery I had never heard him use.

Conversation lulled. As I had said I would do, I passed
along greetings from Pete. Still sullen from their disagree-
ment, Kevin took no notice. Alvin nodded, speaking under

his breath, then louder in talk-patter. Pete was "a friend," but he "liked to call him Jules, Pete liked that better too."

For reasons hard to explain, it was his son Jules I was most curious about, and I hoped they would speak of him. And they did, but not in the detail I wished for. "So how's Troy?" Alvin asked softly. "Leslie?" "Farris?" "How's Jules?" "Is your mother all right?"

Kevin's frustrated facial expression and terse answers suggested that this was ground already covered, largely in this way, while they were alone together. "He all right." "She all right." "All right." "He all right, he's this high now." "She's doin' okay."

Time dragged. Even though I fabricated excuses to leave the table several times more, they both seemed uncomfortable, sitting for long periods in stiff silence, neither seeming to have more to say to the other.

When a guard finally signaled that we had no more time, I took leave of Alvin and went over to the counter by the door. Maybe a minute passed. I glanced back when I heard the guard again mention time and tell Kevin he had to leave. His face was pressed down against his father's shoulder, his back still heaving. Half smiling, Alvin whispered to him playfully, telling him to take heart. "This ain't the worst."

A clerk spoke, requiring my attention to procedural trivia concerning future money orders. The outer door closed behind Kevin. I turned to follow and, as I did, I looked squarely at Alvin, who was waiting in the near-empty room for the guard to finish a conversation with the clerk and come over with the cuffs. Standing there with the ring behind him, his features vacant, and both hands going from the table to his mouth, from the table to his mouth, he gobbled all the meat and potatoes left on his son's paper plate.

July 1983

Toward the end of the month, near his birthday, I was sitting by Collis's bed in the rocker when the mail came.

"Daddy! It's Connie!" Excitedly, Gloria hurried up the steps to give him his letter.

Rather than put it aside for the moment, he surprised me by at once tearing apart the envelope with big-fingered fumbling, then beginning to read aloud at a very slow pace.

Although there was nothing I would have been more interested in hearing, some sense of propriety made me feel that I should go downstairs. But his determined laboring over the words seemed purposeful to the point of fixing me to the chair. Possibly, though a little teasingly, he let me hear the letter because he understood how interested I was. He himself showed slight engagement with the words; it occurred to me later that he may have preferred admitting them to thought in this way rather than later in the greater reflectiveness of silence.

The letter was several small pages. He read haltingly and faintly, sometimes in a fatigued and feeble whisper. The greater part of what Connie wrote described coming home from school to a sick mother and wanting to do well in her classes but not liking them. " 'Fifteen years' " was a phrase that returned like a refrain. " 'Some . . . times,' " he read, " 'I . . . wish . . . it . . . had . . . been . . . me . . . in . . . stead.' " She closed with the words " 'I . . . love . . . you.' "

Finished, he let his hand with the last page in it rest inertly on the sheet. "Now she castin' back over her life," he said. He shook his head conclusively. "It's too late now."

Several times before, I had tried to talk him out of that attitude, and I wanted to try again, but it was too late for that too—particularly then. As he lay back against the propped pillows, weary from his effort, Farris filled the door, then came jarringly into the small room in a towel from the shower. Hunting clean clothes to go out in, he rummaged in the closet he had shared with his father and oldest brother since his parole in May. After he came in, what we talked about was different.

8

□

On March 12, 1981, a Thursday, two young white men, Joseph, twenty-seven, and Stephen (these two names are fictitious), twenty-three, went out for a night of pleasure and daring in New Orleans. The city was new to them; Joseph had worked here for about six months; his friend Stephen was recently down from Michigan for a visit. Toward midnight, they entered a short-lived tourist restaurant on Bourbon Street. There they struck up a mutually exploratory acquaintance with Ferdinand, twenty-five, the young black man who shucked their oysters.

When the oyster bar closed at around two, the three left together. Ferdinand had told them about women they could have in exchange for some of the drugs they reportedly possessed. Joseph then drove them to the residence of his brother-in-law, with whom he had lived since he came to New Orleans. The probable reason for this detour was so Joseph and Stephen could strap shoulder holsters and weapons under their jackets. They had an interest in large handguns. Joseph owned a .357 magnum. Stephen had just bought a .44; the sales receipt was still in the glove box of Joseph's blue 1980 Datsun station wagon. Unluckily for Ferdinand, they made enough noise to wake Joseph's brother-in-law: unluckily because Ferdinand had a criminal record, a circumstance that caused his photograph to be in the files of the police. The brother-in-law didn't like having his sleep interrupted by loud voices and then coming from his bedroom to find a stranger sitting in his den with a beer in his hand. He ordered them all to leave.

Five months later, according to police, Ferdinand made oral statements describing the sequence of events that ended just before dawn that Friday the 13th. According to these statements, he directed Joseph and Stephen to a lounge that faced the housing project on St. Bernard Avenue. Reportedly they saw the brother of Ferdinand's "girlfriend at the time" standing outside the lounge. Ferdinand was said to have confessed that this brother was solely responsible for the rest.

Ferdinand's "girlfriend at the time" was Trina Sorina.

The arrests were made in August 1981, but I heard almost nothing of the case until it began to move toward trial in the spring of 1983. I still didn't know specifically what was alleged to have happened, but by then I understood that Lionel Sorina and an accomplice were charged with, according to a bailiff I questioned, "murder one" and that the state was "after *death*."

When I entered the courtroom on June 15, the trial was already in its second day. Gloria glanced past her daughter Trina's profile and nodded to me as the prosecutor, after a momentary interruption, resumed her questioning of a patrolman who had first answered the call. The patrolman said the car was parked in the long communal alley and driveway that constituted the 4000 block of Jumonville. The passenger, he reported, was wearing a shoulder holster; the contents of his pockets included five live .44 caliber bullets and his wallet, which contained credit cards and about twenty dollars. The driver's money and wallet were in the glove box, along with the receipt for the .44, but the immediate area was strewn with trash from the car's interior (two beer cans, plastic cups, envelopes, a McDonald's bag).

Joseph's brother-in-law, who had identified Ferdinand Matthieu in a photograph lineup, took the stand and testified that Joseph and Stephen told him the man in his den was "going to fix them up with some women." On cross-examination, he conceded that his brother-in-law and Stephen sometimes used marijuana and liked to drink beer.

A ballistics specialist reported that technicians who combed the car found a .38 caliber bullet and a .44 caliber bullet jacket. He identified one of the state's exhibits, a .357 magnum pistol, recovered the following year in an unrelated crime, as being registered in Joseph's name. The .44 was never found.

A well-dressed homicide detective was the last prosecution witness. He testified that Ferdinand had turned himself in shortly after a warrant was issued for his arrest. The warrant resulted from a slip of the tongue, made during interrogation, by his brother Brian, who was then being held on an unrelated charge. The prosecution rested after mentioning that its final witness, Brian Matthieu, could not be located.

The indigent-defender said he had only one witness to call—the defendant, Ferdinand Matthieu. I wouldn't know until the recess that, in a surprise late move, the DA's office had separated the defendants. Lionel would be tried later, by himself. But if only Ferdinand was on trial now, why was Gloria there? (I well knew that going to court was an undertaking she no longer approached lightly.) After I heard Ferdinand testify, I better understood, understood the importance to her of following each word—so she or Trina could pass it on, exactly, to her son.

Speaking in a sincerely soulful voice, Ferdinand said neither Joseph nor Stephen said or showed that they carried guns. He referred to them fondly as "Stephen Boy" and "Joseph T." Describing Lionel, he said, "Everybody's afraid a Sorina, he have a notorious rep in the projec'."

"Say, bruh, you done turned po-lice?" This, he said, was how Lionel greeted him outside the lounge while Joseph and Stephen waited in the Datsun. When Ferdinand told him what Joseph and Stephen wanted, Lionel then called "a middle-aged lady, about twenty-five or twenty-seven," out of the pool hall. (In one of his alleged statements to the police, Ferdinand described the woman as a "junkie-hoolah.") The three rode in the back seat of Joseph's car as they entered the project on Jumonville. The woman went inside to see if her girlfriend would come out. After a wait, Ferdinand followed after her to see what had happened. He was just entering a building when he heard shots. He turned to see Lionel running toward him "in the cut" (the diagonal space between project buildings) carrying the bloody guns. It was because he was so afraid of Lionel that he did as was demanded and took the guns home, washed away the blood, and stashed them for Lionel until the next day. His voice breaking as if with sorrow, he said he couldn't believe Lionel "would kill 'em . . . not Stephen Boy . . . and Joseph T."

Following his lawyer's leading questions, Ferdinand said he turned himself in because the police had put out the word that otherwise he could expect the electric chair. Such threatening had caused him to make the first statement, and he insisted he made the second because he had been deceived and falsely promised a deal.

On cross-examination, the prosecutor lingered on Ferdinand's prior conviction and repeatedly called his attention to exhibits #4 and #5, large photographs of the victims propped on a stand visible to the jury but not to the gallery. Reminding him and the jury that Joseph had been shot behind the left ear and Stephen through the right cheek, she wondered incredulously how one man could accomplish both murders alone—especially since the victims had died from bullets from different guns. Ferdinand shook his bowed head in denial.

In the course of the prosecution's closing argument, I learned the state was trying Ferdinand for murder in the second degree. A first-degree conviction required twelve votes of guilty; second-degree required only ten.

The closing argument for the defense, the whole of its case, rested on a most appealable technicality: its contention that the court was permitting the use of an illegal confession. In fleeting acknowledgment of the crime itself, Ferdinand's lawyer mispronounced "heinous," giving it three syllables. He was bound by the situation to say nothing of the larger heinousness of the complex causal links between the crime and its whole context.

Gloria left the courtroom almost as soon as the jury did. What she could have predicted was still new to my eyes, so I stayed to see it to the end. I didn't have long to wait. The jury returned in thirty minutes. Two women from Ferdinand's family began to scream and curse as the verdict of "Guilty" was rendered. Bailiffs had to restrain them and escort them out. One of the women kicked a panel out of the outer courtroom doors; the other rolled on the floor in the corridor, shrieking. A team of deputies lifted her bodily and half carried both of them down the stairs. I left, thinking that was the last of it. But according to the next morning's *Picayune*, their demonstration continued in front of the building, where they stood in the middle of Tulane Avenue screaming at backed-up traffic.

Lionel was tried for first-degree murder in October, but the prosecution's case fell apart because Ferdinand wouldn't testify against him. Ferdinand was led in in prison attire, but when the bailiff stepped up with the Bible, he began what Trina and Lionel's girlfriend, Linda Rome, later described as "puttin' on a show." He slapped down the gooseneck mike and propped his crossed ankles across the front of the witness box. Waving bailiffs over to hustle him out, the judge said he would be cited for contempt of court. Between the bailiffs, who were shouldering him away, Ferdinand shouted, "You already messed me over once, what else you go'n do? Gi' me another life sentence? Beat me with a strap?"

A large woman in front of me jumped to her feet, also shouting. "You bet' not touch him! You bet' not!" The defense motioned for a mistrial. The judge called a recess.

The case was given to the jury late in the day. Trina and Linda went out for sack food across the intersection of Tulane and Broad. I waited with Gloria. It felt novel, reminiscent of visiting a day school at night, to be alone in that normally cluttered corridor whose usual illumination was pale daylight streaming through its high windows. Gloria said she was "scary" about the dark and, if she had been by herself, she would have had to go back into the empty courtroom even though she already knew she would have nightmares about it. I dreaded how it would be if she had to face, there in that corridor, the news that her first son would be executed. But now the dimness seemed to soothe her, relieving her of some of her self-consciousness about her defective eye and several lost teeth. Talking also seemed to help. Taking off her dark glasses, she shifted to be more in a shadow that fell across the pew in which we sat.

Her nerves were worse now, she said, fluffing the hem of her flowered dress, because they were bad all last night. Sleep had been out of the question. She had ironed until dawn. Once, startled, she heard Collis speak out accusingly from the darkness of his room as if from a dream: " 'Ya'll goin' to court tomorra, I know it, don' nobody tell me nothin', but I know it.' " She kept very still for several minutes, and he said nothing more. This morning when she and Trina left, he was sleeping deeply. She had just phoned Trina's to have a child run and see if Junior was feeding him his dinner. Junior was. They were eating in his room and looking at his little black-and-white TV.

That little TV was a blessing to him. He liked to follow "what he call, the 'latest develop-ments' in all that *fight stuff*." She was referring not to boxing but to news reports of crises in Grenada and Beirut, reports depicting the kinds of violent street scenes that always made her want to leave the room. " 'Girl, don' be scared!' " he would tell her, just as he did when she was hesitant about rolling his wheelchair into crowded elevators in Charity. Heights and tight enclosures had always made her nervous.

I said he was lucky to have her, and she remembered saying to him just the other day, " 'Daddy, we didn't get along so good when I was little, but we gets along good now.' " And his answering, " 'Yeah, we do.' "

Trina and Linda came back with rattling bags and force-fully offered us chicken and fries. Gloria protested that, because of her nerves, she couldn't "think about food." Though I hadn't much appetite either, I took some of the potatoes.

After they finished eating, Trina and Linda went back into the courtroom to wait "where it's light" with the few others who had gone out and come back. These included Joseph's brother and Stephen's father.

It had become clear that, if she could help it, Gloria wouldn't be going back into the courtroom that night. Her agitation compelled her to keep talking, though. Trying to hit on a subject we could share that wasn't related to the trial, I asked if she had heard from Alvin.

"Alvin my brother?" she asked. "You know, I saw him, I saw Alvin. Last month."

I hadn't known.

"Oh yeah, for true." She had caught a ride up with another girl who also had sons there. She had had nice visits with Dwight and Andre. "But now Alvin . . ." The enthusiasm left her voice. "Alvin wasn't so good. No, he wasn't." He was back in Camp J. She had visited him for only thirty minutes. That was as long as she could stand it. He hadn't known her and had called her " 'a hooker—yeh, I know you're nothin' but a old hooker!' " She said she would leave him a money order and then told him goodbye, putting a kiss in her hand and her hand on the screen. Along with everything else just then, he had been too much for her.

I wanted to steer us toward anything that didn't summon more stress. It wasn't easy to do. We had exhausted the subjects of my children and children in general when she mentioned Lionel, meaning her husband, Lionel's father. I wondered aloud if he knew about the trial. Her answer, given as a bailiff came out of the courtroom, tactfully showed me my question was beside the point. She said she ran into Lionel from time to time, usually on the bus, but that was about it. She reminded me that he had been in a mental hospital.

Her eyes instantly teared over when the bailiff told us the jury was back. She shook her head. No, she couldn't go back in there and listen to it, but she wanted me to. Then I could "come quick" and tell her.

I stepped inside to find a dialogue underway between the judge and the foreman of the jury. The foreman insisted they were hopelessly deadlocked at a verdict of 6–6. Faced with those numbers the judge eventually declared it a mistrial. There were whoops in the back of the room. Trina and Linda bounced in each other's arms and were hugged by people I didn't know. Except for the men from Michigan, who had lowered their heads, it seemed everyone was moving swiftly. The discharged jury filed out hurriedly. Two bailiffs hustled Lionel into a holding room. One was handing him his prison fatigues as the other reached to take back the khaki shirt he had worn through the trial. His features were expressionless.

It was after eight. A flashy white juror stepped impatiently past me on spike heels and went through the first set of doors. Remembering Gloria was waiting, I followed the juror toward the outer door. Talking to me or to herself, the woman was annoyed and in a rush and had the idea that someone from the court was responsible for walking her to her car. We pushed open the outer door, and she flinched at the sight of the nearly dark corridor. I have no memory of the complaining juror after that.

She sat leaning forward in her flowered dress, hands in her lap, the light behind me a fractured reflection on her sunglasses.

9

□

[DECEMBER 1982]

"PLEASE" YOU AND YOUR FAMILY DO INJOY CHRISTMAS
IT IS A TIME TO BE *HAPPY EAT SMILE* AND STAY STRONG
MENTALLY AND PHYSICALLY.

"Ye shall find the babe
wrapped in swaddling clothes,
lying in a manger."
Luke 2:12

"GOD" LOVE EVERY ONE I KNOW THIS FOR A FACT.

May the Blessings of Christmas
Bring You Peace and Joy
Throughout the New Year

(FARRIS M. PHILLIPS)

1-4-83

. . . I WAS LOOKING AT MY ALMANAC YOU SENT WHEN
THAT *FOOL* PUT YOUR LETTER IN MY BAR'S I DID NOT

SAY NOT ONE WORD I JUST PICK IT UP AND OPEN IT. 4
STAMP'S WAS INSIDE I REALLY NEED THIM 4 STAMP'S
. . . THIS SHORT TIME I HAVE I NO IT GET NEXT TO ME
EVERY DAY *REASON* IS WHEN YOU GET SHORT YOU MUST
EXCEPT SO MUCH OF *SHIT* YOU WILL EXCEPT IT "OR"
YOU WILL GET *GOOD TIME* TAKING AWAY I *HATE* I REALLY
HATE TAKING *SHIT* IT GET TO ME "SO" DEEP UNTIL I
MUST *SAT* AND GET CONTROL OF MY SELF. "NO" BODY
IS "SAME" WHEN HE LEAVE ANGOLA. NO WAY HE CAN
. . . A LOT BEEN GOING ON AT J PASS FEW MONTH'S.
SOME GOT BURN UP A FEW GOT *SHIT* THROW ON THIM
RIGHT *SHIT* I PRAY I NEVER GET *SHIT* THROW ON ME I
WILL NOT BE RESPOSIBLE FOR MY ACTION AT ALL! I WILL
FORGET ABOUT "FREEDOM" I BEEN TO MY SELF A LOT
WHEN YOU GET *SHORT* TO GO HOME IT IS BEST YOU DO.
THE LIGHT IS OUT I CAN'T SEE TO GOOD I AM USEING
LIGHT OUT OF THE HALL . . .

                                        FARRIS

                                     2-28-83

. . . I RAN INTO A LIL MISUNDERSTANDING HERE AT J. I
HAD TO DO SOME TIME IN ISOLATION BUT I AM OUT
NOW ONE CELL TO ANOTHER "SMILE" THE OUTSIDE IS
A CELL TO BUT A MUCH BIGER CELL THEN WHAT I
AM IN. YOU ALL OUT THERE IS IN MINIMUM SECURITY
AND I AM IN MAXIMUM SECURITY IN HERE . . . I LOSS A
LIL GOOD TIME "SO" IT PUT ME BACK TO 5-25-83. I
REALLY NO WHAT THESE DOG'S WOULD LOVE TO DO
TAKE ME OUT IN THE WOOD'S AND PUT A BULLET IN MY
HEAD "SMILE" WELL IT WAN'T BE LONG NOW . . . I TOLD
YOU I WAS GOING TO LET YOU NO WHEN I GET OUT
ISOLATION I TRY TO KEEP MY WORD IT IS ALL I HAVE
SMILE.

                                        FARRIS

3-14-83

. . . I AM ON THREE FAST'S *A SILENT ONE. NOT EATING. NOT SLEEPING.* I BEEN ON IT 2 DAY'S I WILL COME OF IT TOMORROW MORNING NOTHING IS WRONG I AM ALL WAY'S TESTING MY SELF. "WELL" MY *DATE* TO COME HOME *PASS* IT WAS *3-12-83* I CAN NOT LIE TO YOU I DID FEEL IT NOT 80 PERSENT *BUT* I FELT IT 100 PERSENT. I GOT TO WAIT UNTIL *5-29-83* . . . YOU NO I HERE CRAZY DUDE'S LIE AND SAY PRISON IS NOT NOTHING THAT BULL S—— IF A DUDE SAY THIS HE IS TRYING TO IMPRESS SOMEONE CONFINE-MENT IS HELL AND PAIN . . .

FARRIS

5-16-83

. . . I AM AT CAMP-A NOW . . . A VERY GOOD CAMP FOOD HOT AND GOOD. I AM COOL I DON'T TALK TO MUCH ALL I DO IS WORK OUT AND EAT A LOT AND WATCH HOW THESE'S DUDE'S OPERATE. I FEEL VERY GOOD BUT I FEEL VERY EMOTIONALLY AT TIME YOU DO NO IT IS HARD FOR ME TO BELEAVE I WILL BE FREE ON THE *28* OF THIS *MONTH* I AM TRYING MY BEST TO BE COOL AS ICE AND EVERYBODY NO IT TO.

FARRIS (JIMBO)

1983–84

I met him, for the second time, at Charity early in June —shortly after his parole and immediately after he saw to it that Collis would have surgery for the gangrene in his foot. As Gloria and others gathered about the bed, he hung back, subdued and tentative, even toward his father, his hamlike arms attracting an attention on the ward that seemed only to make him uneasier.

He said he might go to New York for a while, then maybe to California with Velma. She had family there and talked of starting a snowball business. He listened with his head lowered while she enthusiastically explained her hopes and needs. When she stepped down the hall, he told me that what *he* needed was work, "*hard* work, somethin' hard to keep this thing in me down, heavy construction or road repair, I could get into a jackhammer."

Through the summer I tried to help him find such work, discovering that I had acquaintances in the building business—people who had become disaffected with careers in education and now, in their late thirties, were catching up on more lucrative livelihoods. But my acquaintances stiffened and the conversations faltered when I disclosed that armed robbery was the crime of the man I had come to see them about. My not being able to guarantee that the parolee was truly a nonviolent and misunderstood individual added to the problem. No one told me *no*, only that they weren't hiring just then. But they would call me when they were. When I called again instead, stretching the limit of their goodwill, it was the same thing. One contractor did tell me that two brothers we had taught in high school had inherited their father's large construction company. After a sequence of increasingly pained contacts, my former students finally told me they weren't hiring just then either.

With similar results I called agencies and an overburdened organization existing to help ex-convicts find jobs. The problem seemed hopeless until one fall evening I happened on someone willing to offer a solution.

This was Robert Martin, whom I also had known through teaching high school. Then, in the mid-seventies, he had been a ponytailed painter and sculptor who made his living teaching art. He still painted, but now, I learned, he made his living as a carpenter. He was on the levee with four or five other white carpenters about our age or younger. Just having finished work, they were throwing a football and drinking beer within range of low music that came from the bed of one of their trucks. As we talked I gathered that, in organizing this group, Robert had maintained principles I remembered him to hold: each fully skilled carpenter in their concern shared equally in the total of its profits; nothing was scraped from the top for a boss. I held back nothing in describing Farris, and from the watchful expression in Robert's eyes, it was clear that he grasped the possible problems involved. He said he would discuss it with the others and call me.

And he did, agreeing to hire Farris for five dollars an hour as a carpenter's apprentice. His pay would increase as his competence developed. To me the job seemed an incidence of good fortune, one offering marketable skills and very decent co-workers. Eagerly I looked for him at Gloria's and left messages at the various phone numbers he had given me. But no one admitted to having recently seen him. There was an added urgency to my effort to reach him: the last few times we talked, in each conversation discussing his difficulties in finding work, he had said such things as "It wouldn't be nothin' for me to take a gun and go out and stick up somebody," before he relented and added that he knew this would only land him back in prison indefinitely.

Then, in October, suddenly he was standing beside me during a recess in the rear of the courtroom in which Lionel was being tried. Wearing cheap new clothes that had no flash, he muttered about the DA not having a case against Lionel. It was a struggle to divert his attention from that to the good news I thought I had. When I finished describing the job and Robert Martin and his friends, he sniffed and said, "A carpenter. I don't know if I could dig that."

I began to speak insistently, disbelievingly; but, again mentioning New York and maybe California, he was already moving away. I watched him go over to a man from the neighborhood—evidently they had come in together. They moved toward the doors, bitterly denouncing the DA. I stood torn between following to argue for the job and turning

back to the trial, which was about to recommence. The doors
swung closed behind them.

He did go to New York shortly after that day in October
1983 when we were both "at court for Lionel" and he passed
up an opportunity to become a carpenter. He made several
more trips to New York during the next fourteen months.
Now I think of these trips as a restless pacing of the corridor
of the country known to him, a strategy for avoiding creditors
and police until pressure had passed.

Connie said her brother was "hard to be with then" because
he was so tightly strung. She said her children and Alvin's
made him "nervous"; when they were in a room with him,
he would order all of them to "sit down and sit still"; all the
while "his foot would be going, going" in a tense jiggle, and
"if there was so much as a dirty glass or a cigarette out in
an ashtray, he would take it out of the room to wash it."
Kevin said his uncle Farris made him uncomfortable and
seemed bound to stir up unnecessary trouble because he was
"always talkin' about how bad was this, how bad was that,
who was bad, who wasn't—long as it was *bad*, it was cool with
him."

I didn't directly see this side of Farris, but I believed that,
even with Velma's support, he had to be pursuing questionable and precarious means in order to survive. Every several
months or so, he would contact me and describe one scrape
or another that required "a few dollars"—"loans," he called
them. A few times, I gave him the money—small amounts
were all I could manage, a ten here, a twenty there; other
times, I gave him nothing. Each contact left me feeling bad:
either cowardly and easily manipulated or insincere. I lost
even the guarded hopefulness for him that had made me
willing to involve someone else and to take advantage of
such generosity as Robert Martin's.

In the summer of 1984, he called me several times to
make increasingly desperate requests for money. Afterwards
I thought he had gone back to New York, because I heard

nothing more from or of him until the 25th of August. That morning, the phone woke me at 4:30. It was Gloria's Trina. She said he was cornered in an apartment in the project. He had a gun. The SWAT team was there and had cordoned the area. Family members had been permitted to approach the barrier, but the police were talking "nasty" and it was feared they would storm the dwelling. She fell silent. For dazed seconds I listened to fuzz and a faint ringing on the line and felt I might be still asleep.

I asked her what she wanted me to do.

Her voice dipped sullenly. "I don't know."

Already I had disappointed.

Shakily awake, I reached the project at about five. Right away I saw Gloria and Theron crossing a courtyard. With them was Connie and her husband, Walter Sutton. Connie? Why had no one told me she was in town?

In a confusion of voices we went inside Gloria's. She had rearranged the family photographs in a new configuration on the living-room wall. Beneath them sat Trina in curlers and a nightgown, the telephone in her lap. She had been calling the newspaper, TV and radio stations, and various people they knew. I gathered now that the point was to gain publicity or at least attention. They felt this was their only hope for deterring the SWAT team from "just goin' in and wastin' him."

Gradually I was told that Farris had beaten up a woman he had been living with and that she had left and taken her children. Where was Velma? Velma had gone to California. (After waiting eight years.)

Yesterday Trina had seen the woman with "her jaw all swoll up." Theron said the woman just wanted Farris "outta there"; she probably wouldn't press charges, but he thought it was better for Farris to be locked up for a while "till he cool off."

Gloria told me then that, "not twenty minutes before you come," he had given himself up. He had just wanted to be sure family and witnesses were there watching the police when he came out.

Relaxing somewhat, I learned that, in answer to a complaint, a policeman had gone to the woman's apartment and found Farris alone there in the dark. Like the policeman, he held a flashlight in one hand and a pistol in the other. Farris slammed the door in his face, and the policeman called in the SWAT team.

Earlier the family had waked Collis and taken him to the scene as their "last card" to persuade Farris to give himself up. Theron described it as "a good li'l walk for him." On the return walk Theron had carried him—I knew from having seen them manage other distances together—like a bride.

At 7:30, after I had gone back to sleep at home, a call came from Central Lockup. Farris described the incident this way: "I beat up a dude with my hands because the dude insulted my lady friend." No gun was involved, "not to my knowledge." The dude, who was "just a ol' junkie," had "put three assault charges" on him. Now he was in a very bad situation "for a guy like me. These people might decide to put other charges" on him while they were holding him.

He said Gloria had said he should call me.

I didn't pick up on what he was angling toward.

He said he was trying to find the number of a woman he had met on a plane. She "liked" him "a lot." He felt "more than sure" she would want to make his bond.

I said nothing; but, achingly, we stayed longer on the phone. He wouldn't ask, and I wouldn't offer. Sourness infected our long pauses.

The next day I was at Gloria's again, providing Connie and Walter the use of a credit card and a ride so they could rent a car. Before we left I met Collis Jr.'s Trina. Brimming with energy and talk, she was eager for it to be better understood that her uncle Farris wasn't the " 'animal' " she had heard the police describe.

She "*saw* this": in one of the courtyards the husband of the woman Farris had been with had "come at him with a butcher knife." Farris took the knife from him and "beat him, but he didn't kill him," even though the man continued to threaten him when Farris let him up. The woman didn't want to press charges, but the husband was an ex-convict and "a rat" who informed to the police whenever he was in trouble; it was he who had reported Farris in the first place.

Her uncle deserved also to be understood in other ways: for instance, through the eyes of "young boys all around here." They idolized him, and "most any day in the afternoon you could spot gangs" of them trailing him in the courtyards. He would have them "out there doin' this"—she simulated calisthenics.

Although recent events seemed to have left her in a state of mournful dismay, Connie echoed some of her niece's opinion, recalling how, not long before, a seventeen-year-old took up for her brother when she herself had been angrily criticizing him. Both women remembered that he was always warning his young admirers against being sent to prison.

Trina continued to stress the positive, but Connie (who was much older, though in appearance they might have been sisters) shook her head as if no longer able to fathom why her brother "loves this project so." Just a few weeks ago when he was in New York, she had begged him to stay, but he wouldn't listen, insisting "he had to be back here in this project" even though he himself acknowledged it was "no good for him." For the moment Trina was silent and looked closely at her aunt.

With tears in her voice, Connie spoke of how much worse life in the project was now than when she was here, growing up. She was sorry she had come, yet she knew she had "to see about my brother." But "all this"—her hand rose in a gesture intended to include more than the defaced bricks, litter, and racket around us—it was too much.

"Well. I'm out." In October he called to tell me.
I didn't probe for details.

He said that while he was in jail, the husband he had had trouble with was killed, so "that li'l problem's over."

Now he wanted "a sue lawyer" who could file a suit for him against Parish Prison; he had fallen down some steps and been left to lie there "for over an hour" with a hurt back.

After a pause, he said that what he wanted most, though, was to make enough money to leave town. Would I read the classifieds for him? Would I try again to help him find a job?

As it turned out, I did try. But I wouldn't have had much heart for the effort—or success at it either—even if Robert Martin, having decided to risk giving up carpentry for art, hadn't himself already left for New York. Nor if, by then, there hadn't been crisis in my own family.

10

□

Spring–Summer 1984

Nine months passed before the retrial. In March, during an appointment I was able to make with the prosecutor, I asked about the long delay.

She had shown me graciously into the new office building that housed the district attorney's staff. On the way up in the elevator, she said she had checked on what she could discuss with me. Now in her office, she disclosed that the cause of the delay was her appeal to gain permission to use Ferdinand's testimony from his own trial in order to prosecute Lionel. If she lost the appeal, she would then have to try Lionel, like Ferdinand, for second-degree murder rather than first. But if she won, she would "go for death." And that might give me, she added, "a big finish" for my book.

A tall, blondly handsome woman, whom I guessed to be in her forties, she had the disarming ability to smile pleasantly as she looked you hard in the eye and spoke about unpleasant matters. She smiled at me and said I might as well face it: the Sorinas were like "the Ma Barker family." It made you wonder about genes and environment.

I agreed that it did, and for the moment our differences of emphasis concerning the dichotomy remained tacit rather than argued. I ventured that the victims had no business being where they were, especially for their purpose, at that time of night. She countered, and I couldn't deny, that that fault was insignificant compared with the fault of their murderers.

Then we were talking about race, blacks and whites, in terms disquietingly general and worn. She said blacks couldn't "expect us to give them respect" if they wouldn't do for themselves. I suggested that our *giving* anything wasn't the issue. She had a point she wanted to make about industriousness and referred to her own earnest youth as the child of immigrant parents who worked so hard they scarcely knew they were poor. She felt that a great many blacks—unlike the majorities in other ethnic groups—seemed to think they were owed a living. I observed that other ethnic groups weren't brought to this country in chains, and then, without intending it, we were arguing, arguing politely, but arguing. An argument in which neither of us shook the conviction of the other.

I think as a kind of summation, she wondered, just out of curiosity, if, in light of his cold-blooded crime, I could truly care for Lionel Sorina. I wasn't sure how I felt about him, a person to whom I had never even spoken. All I could say for certain was that I cared for his mother. Right away she said she cared far more for the mothers of the victims. I admitted the compelling relevance of this extension as she went on to say she always wished she could make the bereavement of family and loved ones a factor in trial testimony; pictures were never enough. Too late, going down alone in the elevator, it occurred to me to question the necessity of making a fixed distinction about who was most deserving of sympathy. In the face of such suffering as this, wouldn't a sympathy large rather than discriminating ultimately be best for all concerned?

As she walked me to the elevator, she gave me her hand and told me she admired my "inquiring mind." Smiling, she said again that she hoped to have a big finish for me.

The trial was finally set for the 27th of July, Collis's seventy-fifth birthday, a Friday. That morning it was continued over the weekend to the 30th. The big finish apparently had fallen through: the state had reduced the charge to second-degree murder. But there was a rumor, which drove Gloria to intervals of compulsive talk, that the DA had given Ferdinand a deal.

Opening testimony was the same as before—except that this time the details of death were more prominent. Even from where I sat in the back of the room, I could see much red when the prosecutor entered the large photographs of the dead victims into evidence and sweepingly carried them past Lionel from the exhibits table to the jury box. Wearing pink, rose, and white, she guided an assistant coroner through a minute description of how the .38 caliber bullet, which was on exhibit, entered behind Joseph's ear and came out above his eye, destroying his brain. Exacting the same precision, she had the assistant coroner explain how an unrecovered bullet, which couldn't have been fired by a .38 but quite possibly was from Stephen's own gun, the .44, had struck him in the side of his face and, traveling at a downward angle, pierced the carotid artery in his neck. Yes, the coroner confirmed, Stephen probably "drowned in his own blood."

When I returned early from the lunch recess, Gloria was where she would be throughout the trial, in the corridor. I hadn't seen her in the morning. She said she had overslept because it had been "a bad weekend." Collis had felt bad even though she had been able to keep him from knowing of the beginning of the trial and of how upset she was. Early on his birthday he had been in good spirits, and after I visited in the afternoon, "he give me some a that money you left him and said he wanted a plate a fried seafood and a root beer." He had fallen asleep immediately after eating without taking an interest in the cake she had bought and shown to him the night before. "He slept clean through to Sad-dy," when he waked with a headache "and taken some a his medicine" and slept again. But "first thing" when he waked on Sunday he wanted to know, now that she had almost forgotten it, " 'Where my cake!?' " He enjoyed his cake, but his mood soon changed and by nightfall he was "sayin' things like, 'Well, reck'n I'll be seein' Dot soon,' and frownin' like he do when his head hurt." She had given him his medicine—"Honey, that puts him *out*"—but then *she* couldn't sleep. So finally she had taken some of hers—Trival, a sleep-inducing antidepressant, which was prescribed for her at the mental health unit to which she then went for monthly group sessions. Her nerves had been so bad that she felt maybe she had taken too many of her pills, because it wasn't like her to have slept late—even if she hadn't been dreading a trial.

But did I know—she said this proved there was always some reason to hope—that her psychiatrist—"a woman!"—"come up in the Calliope pro-jec'?" It just went to show that you *could* get out.

I went downstairs to the machines for a can of grapefruit juice for her. When I came back some of the investigators, lawyers, and spectators had returned from lunch and were drifting in and out of the courtroom. Drinking the juice, she watched them and spoke again of her husband, Lionel. No, she said, Lionel would never be well. He took no responsibility for his children even though he always admitted that they were his. "He still live right back there in the projec', y' know."

I didn't know.

"Oh yeah, he *been* back there. Sometime he come by to visit. But he don't know how to leave. If I didn't run him off, he'd sit in that kitchen all day drinkin' coffee."

I said it sounded as if he wanted to live with her again.

She agreed that that was true, he sometimes spoke of it, but she had told him, " 'You a patient, I'm a patient. What good would that be?' "

This seemed to end that subject, but she went on speaking of Lionel. It was a few moments more before I realized she was referring to her son. It was February 1981 that she was thinking of now. Collis was on the eighth floor at Charity, Lionel was on the ninth, and she "was runnin' between 'em"—though Lionel's girlfriends helped her considerably by "givin' Lionel his bath and stayin' by the bed." Collis was there because he had collapsed in the gym. Not long after his uncle Jerry's death, Lionel had been shot by Quiet Man while he was out walking with Alvin Jr. ("Quiet." I remembered: the one who had sold drugs with her brother Alvin and Pete.) Alvin Jr. had saved Lionel by pulling out a small gun, which he carried in a pouch, and firing into the air, causing Quiet Man to run.

"Almost blew his arm off, his arm was just hangin'." Doctors at Charity had taken an artery from Lionel's leg to repair his arm. After Lionel came home from Charity late in that February, she urged him to "let it go." But he said no, Quiet had "put him to too much pain." Soon afterwards, Quiet Man had been sentenced to fifteen years on some other charge: "Just fifteen years after all the dirt he's done did people." But at least she thought then that this had ended the violence between him and her son. Now it might just go on in prison.

We knew Ferdinand was scheduled to testify either that afternoon or the following morning. It was about this that she was most upset. She had known him for "so long, from a baby." "Way back" when she was sixteen and she and her husband, Lionel, had first lived together in the Desire project on Pleasure Street, Ferdinand's mother, whom she remembered as selling dope at the time, had lived over them. Later his mother had moved to the St. Bernard project just as she and Lionel had. Like all of her and Lionel's babies, Ferdinand was also born in the St. Bernard. All of these children "come up together." She remembered taking Ferdinand out along with her children, "all of us," on Carnival to watch parades in front of Krauss's department store on Canal Street. And even though Trina had broken up with him, she felt sure that Ferdinand was still in love with her daughter. He had "liked her from a child." Early on she had noticed how he would pull on Trina's braid. How he would leave candy for her, knock on the door, and run.

The next morning Ferdinand took the stand as the first witness on the second day. Photographs of the victims in the car were on display near the jury box; some of their detail was discernible from where I sat in the third row on the side of the aisle away from the prosecution. At first it struck me as a coincidence when I noticed that I was the only white on this side of the aisle and that there were no blacks on the prosecution side. But casting back over other days in court, I was reminded that this unconscious pattern of segregation had been more the rule than the exception and that blacks in attendance usually gravitated away from the prosecutors. On this morning, the people from Joseph's and Stephen's families, including in-laws, were in the front row near the table for the assistant district attorneys.

Ferdinand's testimony was basically the same as in his own trial, although now he often seemed near tears and his inflections left the impression of being even more heartfelt than they had a year before. In this account, he said Joseph and Stephen took Quaaludes in the oyster bar. Another new facet was his more explicit portrayal of Lionel as a pimp. " 'Bruh, why you don't use my women?' " is how the defendant reportedly responded outside the lounge when Ferdinand told him Joseph and Stephen "was lookin' for some ladies." Descending from euphemism to vernacular, Ferdinand hesitantly said, "Sorina . . . Sorina had some fuckin' women." As before, he said Sorina shot both victims, then intimidated him into keeping the guns for him until the next day. This was why his brother Brian and their mother saw Ferdinand washing bloody guns in their bathtub.

On the third day of the increasingly expensive trial, the prosecution called Brian Matthieu, who had been located at the last hour and extradited from out of state. It was his admission, while in jail during the summer of 1981, that had broken the case. Under interrogation, he had conceded to detectives that he recognized photographs of Joseph and Stephen as "the two white boys killed in the pro-jec'." He had seen their pictures on TV. The detectives then pointed out that they had prohibited televised photographs of the victims and scene. I don't know exactly how Ferdinand became implicated, but this interrogation led Brian reportedly to make a graphic statement that extended the story Ferdinand told the two times he testified.

Over protests from the defense, the prosecution then argued for and gained permission to read from Brian Matthieu's alleged statement from three years before. The witness sat shaking his head in denial.

At various points in her reading the prosecutor paused. She looked up significantly just before completing the description of Stephen's death: as his pistol was being lifted out of his shoulder holster, he woke and said, " 'What's this?' " According to the statement, Lionel touched the barrel to his face, and squeezed the trigger. While quoting the statement, the prosecutor looked at Lionel: " 'He shot him with his own gun. It was like his head exploded.' "

Lionel looked back at her with an absolute neutrality, just as he had at Ferdinand and at Brian. This absence of apparent animation, this sustained wordlessness, was his only expression through the course of two trials.

She read on, through descriptions of Lionel running around the car to complete the double murder and of Ferdinand's urgent knock on the door of their mother's apartment and then his ducking in with the bloody pistols wrapped in his oyster-shucking shirt. She looked up from Ferdinand's reported words: " 'Lionel just shot two white boys.' " My ears rang, and I wondered what Lionel was thinking—then and in 1981—and what went through Ferdinand's mind as he washed the blood down the drain; and I wondered most about Joseph and Stephen and the duration in Stephen's mind of the reported instant of recognition before the end.

The last witness for the prosecution was a lawyer for Ferdinand, but not the one appointed by the court to handle his trial. So there would be no challengeable ambiguity about it, the prosecutor had called the lawyer to inform the jury that his client and the district attorney had struck a deal. Ferdinand would receive post-conviction relief amounting to a reduction of his sentence to twenty-one years in exchange for his testimony and a guilty plea to the crime of manslaughter. During questioning of this lawyer, the prosecution clarified and stressed a further stipulation of the agreement: Ferdinand Matthieu was not to be incarcerated in the same prison as Lionel Sorina.

The defense was the same as in October. Trina and Linda Rome testified that Lionel was in their respective apartments throughout the early evening of March 12. The third witness, Anastasia "Stacy" Asmore, with whom he lived at the time and whose apartment was in the same building as Linda's, said he spent the rest of the night with her, "lookin' at television," then sleeping in his bed until about eight in the morning on the 13th. There was an attempt in this trial to have Lionel's ten-year-old daughter by Stacy also testify. But the child was so frightened by the proceedings that she broke down before the public defender could ask her a significant question.

In her closing argument the prosecutor, wearing a black blouse and a black-and-white suit, summarized her case and again passed the ghastly photographs before the jury. Dressed in gray, the appointed defender argued that neither Ferdinand nor Brian was a reliable witness and that Brian's statement had been introduced unethically. He said the trial had convinced him that the state was trying "to lay a dead dog at the defendant's door."

In final rebuttal, the prosecutor replied, "We're not talking about a dead dog, ladies and gentlemen, we're talking about two dead boys, two dead young men." She showed another photograph of the inside of the car; from where I sat, it seemed almost entirely red. "This is what we're talking about—this blood that was spilled." She reached for another photograph.

After the judge charged the jury, almost everyone streamed from the courtroom, as if for better air. In the corridor, where Gloria had been comforting the daughter of Stacy and Lionel, his lawyer spoke apologetically to Stacy about the decision to put the child on the stand. Gloria began to cry and went into the women's room. It was understood among Trina, Linda, and me that she shouldn't stay for the verdict. I said I would drive her home, relieved to be leaving myself.

Outside, in a faint rain, she adjusted her dark glasses and put up her umbrella before we started down the vast staired façade that rose to the building's columned second-story entrance. She mentioned needing to cash her check and said Rosenberg's furniture store cashed welfare checks "for po' people"; she was also making furniture payments there. As we rode down Tulane Avenue, we scarcely spoke of the trial. Around us was the gift of a glistening gray afternoon.

The white people at Rosenberg's seemed in no way threateningly prosperous. They were very polite to her, and she exchanged cheery small talk with a cashier before we went over to look at the mattresses. She wanted to buy a new one for Collis as soon as she finished paying on the living-room furniture. It pained her that he would become severely embarrassed when his pills occasionally caused him to wet his sheets in the night. He had always been so clean and she *knew* he was clean; yet sometimes he acted as if he didn't understand that she knew—this was what hurt. Soon she would "put somethin' down" on one of these mattresses and a set of good box springs because, even though she and Junior had wrapped it in plastic, she couldn't entirely eliminate the smell from the old one.

As we priced various mattresses and springs, she told me how Collis had made gifts to the family with "that money from you"—part of a small windfall I had received the year before and shared with him, hoping most of it would be saved for medical emergencies and taxis to Charity. She said he told her not to " 'git no curtains for the kitchen' " or anything like that but to buy personal things for herself and then "bring him the receipt." She mentioned "a pair a sixty-dollar shoes" from Krauss's and suits he had bought for Collis Jr. and Collis III. He also wanted her to have her teeth fixed, insisting, " 'You could still be a fine-lookin' woman.' " But she told him her nerves were too bad for her "to sit for that."

We drove back up Tulane and turned down Galvez. After we had ridden several blocks, then crossed over to Broad, she said that, even though she appreciated the ride, if it weren't raining today, she might just as soon be walking. She told me that when she was a girl, the land around the project was like country. Sometimes "even now" on her way to the grocery or drugstore, she would "just keep goin' and walk and walk" through the neighborhoods that once were woods in which she used to play. The walking relaxed her and usually brought her back home in a happier mood.

As I turned onto St. Bernard, she seemed startled as if just then recognizing her surroundings and realizing that I was taking her home rather than back to court. I said I would return with her to wait for the jury but only if she felt very certain that that was what she wanted to do. She paused, then shook her head. No, Trina and I were right, this was best: "With my nerves like they is, I don't belong on the streets today." The brown brick apartment buildings rose into view, and though she was still on the subject of walking, now she was evidently thinking of sights she saw returning from her spontaneously extended errands, sights she had had to grow accustomed to "back here" in the project. The day's freight, temporarily deflected, came down hard as I pulled into the alleyway that was Jumonville.

What she feared most, she said, was not dying but dying with her body—as she had seen the bodies of many others —on display at a curbside or "crumbled in the bushes" in one of the courtyards or cuts. She staggered leaving the car and I was out on my side rushing around it to steady her, but there was no way I could have reached her in time. Waving me away, she regained her balance on her own and totteringly started up the wet walkway toward her steps. I watched until she was inside—like her, now thinking of my own death and, as I believe she had been, about Joseph and Stephen.

———

It was no surprise to me when I learned the next morning that at the end of the afternoon the jury of six blacks and six whites—nine women, three men—had returned a unanimous verdict of guilty. Had the DA's office tried it as before as "murder one," the prosecutor probably would have had the finish she spoke of. As it was, she could take pride in having been instrumental in permanently removing a violent man from the streets: Lionel's second-degree sentence was for natural life.

Gloria called a few nights later. She sounded as if she had been drinking or careless with her medication. One of the perpetual trial-watchers from the project had told her of "a big-time appeal lawyer" who was locally celebrated for his successes with unpromising cases. She said she had to fight for her son; she couldn't let him "just be throwed away." Would I contact this lawyer for her? I ventured that he might charge a big fee. She said Linda, Trina, and Theron offered to help; they would pay in installments. I asked her to let me think about it and call her the next day.

She talked on, compulsively, of how she knew now that Lionel had been railroaded. It was just like with Alvin and Farris and little Al and her last child, Andre. It had to have been crooked for the jury to come back 12–0. In this loosened moment she made none of her usual effort to disguise her bitterness, asserting challengingly that "if those boys had a been black, nobody woulda heard a thing about it." She said that recently "a white nurse was found dead back here." It was understood throughout the neighborhood that the woman had been murdered elsewhere and the body dumped there to make it look like another housing project crime. She said that afterwards "the po-lice was all back up in here, throwin' people across cars and kickin' in doors with they guns drawed. I made Theron stay inside for a week." Her voice rising in thwarted rage, she went on, unable to stop: "My son didn't kill them two white boys, I *know* my son didn't kill them white boys! He told me, 'Mama, I ain't crazy. I know better than to do a thing like that to white boys . . .' "

I lay awake through most of the sour night, miserable in my choices. I had no interest in trying to help Lionel in the way she wanted, but I wished I could do something to relieve her pain. That my refusal could only increase it made me feel hypocritical. At this point, no matter what I chose to do, that was how I would feel.

The next afternoon I reached her by phone. She sounded calmer. I told her plainly that I didn't want to do what she asked. Then I began an explanation I had thought over and over, an explanation whose final point would require me to say I believed her son had committed a murder.

She interrupted before I had scarcely begun, shaming me by making my refusal so easy. "Well, you have to do what you think is best. You're human. Like everybody else. It's aw right."

But herself, she would have "to keep fightin.' A mother has to do that. I have to try to help him. I have to know I'm doin' all I can . . . Now you come see us anytime you want. Hear?"

11

□

In November, Farris called and said he had "shot a dude five times" and the SWAT team was looking for him. He would probably be going to New York; his sister Gloria, he said, was trying to raise the money for a bus ticket.

He went into a tale of a grudge left over from Angola— "vibrations." A dude came looking for him with a pistol and found him sitting on a porch. Someone opened a screen door a crack and pitched out a second pistol so he could protect himself. You had to draw a line somewhere, he said; otherwise, people in that environment would push you.

I said I had drawn a line too, but he didn't seem to want to hear about it and continued talking until, sounding self-righteous, I squeezed in what I had to say. "I hope you don't hold it against me, but I won't help with this, especially if you *have* shot somebody."

As his father had had so often to do, he then chose to talk on the edge. Whether his indirection masked anger, I could only imagine. "Randy, Randy. I don't look at things like that. If I see you tomorra, I'll still say, 'How ya doin', what's hap'nin'?'—like that. It's aw right."

The next day Gloria told me she didn't know anything about any shooting, but he had asked her too for money to go to New York. Since he had come home from prison, she said, he was all the time doing that, pressing people for money, and now she didn't know where he was.

That was the last I heard of him until Collis called me late

on the 3rd of January. During the weeks between, I decided
to act as if he *had* left town and to try not to worry about it.

Collis began feebly. " 'Scuse me. This is . . . 866- . . . 52
. . . 24?" I thought I recognized a tactic he often used to
make certain he had me, and not a wrong number, on the
line.

We passed a few minutes in small talk, as we had done
the night before when I called to wish him a happy New
Year. Only he, Gloria, and Theron had been there. The
apartment had sounded much quieter than usual; a bowl
game buzzed softly in the background. It had been a strained
conversation because, I assumed, like me, he felt sheepish
about our not having been in touch since before Christmas.
I asked how he liked the published excerpts about the gym
I had left him during that visit. He said he hadn't finished
reading them, but someone around there had them. He had
seemed more interested in telling me that "when the children
git grown, it changes Christmas." He said my children were
too young for me to understand the changes he spoke of,
but I would find out. Then he talked about how he and
Dorothy "usta run for presents."

Now, on January 3, he came to what I thought was the
point.

"I told you 'bout my son bein' killed, huh?"

"No . . . !" I sat down.

"Yeh, you know him, Alvin, the one usta box."

"Lord, Mister Collis . . ."

"What'd I say? Naw, not Alvin. My youngest son. Farris.
You knew him?"

My impulse was to offer sympathy, to listen to his grief if
he needed to express it. But, at least superficially, he didn't
need that; he talked around the subject.

"You cain' stay out on these streets with these weedheads
an' dope pushers. I never had anything to do with anything
like that. If I went in a bar, it was to see somebody, that was
all. You cain' stay round these weedheads. Dope pushers.
This street is no life . . . How's the family? You go'n run in
that race Sunday?"

Farris had been shot, but not by the SWAT team. I tried to return to that subject and learned he had been dead when we talked the night before—and dead for five days before that.

Then he came to the real point of the call. He said Farris's sister had come down from New York for the wake and the funeral, which would be on the next day and the next. As before, she and her husband needed the use of a credit card (as collateral) so they could rent a car and attend to preparations that had to be made.

Afterwards I rifled the newspapers stacked in the pantry and eventually found a brief account of the crime—it took place on December 27.

MAN FOUND SHOT TO DEATH IN HOUSING PROJECT

The body of a New Orleans man was found in a courtyard of the St. Bernard housing project Thursday evening, authorities said.

He was identified as Farris Phillips, 34, 1427 Foy, Apt. E, police spokesman John Marie said.

Phillips's body was found in the courtyard at 1400 Foy Park at 5:40 p.m., Marie said. He had been shot once in the chest and once in the forearm.

Police found Phillips's body when they investigated a report of gunshots. There are no suspects and no motive.

January 4 was a clear, cold day. Connie's husband, Walter Sutton, was on the steps of Gloria's apartment. A medium-large, well-spoken man, he greeted me in the brisk, cheerful way that I remembered from our previous meeting.

Inside, Gloria appeared drawn, thinner, as if her old housedress were suddenly too large. She was both sad and excited. Crying, she immediately told me Farris had been "on ice" for a week and had now begun "to swell." But she seemed also in a state bordering on joy because someone had given her the idea that, if they could reach the warden at Angola by phone, her brother Alvin would be allowed to come home for the funeral.

Just then her youngest son, Andre, came into the kitchen through the back entrance to the apartment. I had never met him before, but I knew he had very recently been paroled from Angola, where he had spent the past ten years—having been convicted of rape at the age of sixteen. Small and wiry, a true lightweight—with an angular face and a sparkling stone in his ear—he moved quickly through the two rooms to glance out the front door before coming back to shake hands. As I stood trying to adjust simultane- ously to Andre's jittery manner and to Walter's friendliness, Gloria's Trina came down the stairs, a cigarette in her hand and looking more attractive than I had seen her in months in a long, fur-collared brown coat and brown boots that almost reached her knees. I gathered then that we were all, except Gloria, going to the Rent-A-Car together.

On the way there, Walter and I spoke of the weather and the city, and from the back seat Andre commented on changes in climate and neighborhoods, changes he noticed every day. Except for her sneezing, Trina made no sound. In the mirror I glanced at her face, which was still pretty but entirely without expression as she gazed out the window, showing an absence of interest in whatever was passing.

"It was a *con*-flict with a dude." These words of Andre's were all I then learned about the circumstances of Farris's death. Concerned for Collis Jr. and Theron and for the emotional resilience remaining in Gloria and Collis, I won- dered if this killing would exact a cycle of vengeance and more killing. Would one of the Phillipses feel obliged to try to kill Farris's killer? So far as I know, this never happened. I wasn't surprised when I heard later, though, that, years before, Lionel had shot the man who eventually murdered Farris; but I was very surprised when I learned that, soon in the future in an unrelated conflict in New York, Andre —while on drugs—shot and killed Walter's youngest son by a prior marriage, a crime for which he was sent back to prison.

I went to the wake at around eight that evening. The mortuary was on Jackson Avenue near the uptown neighborhood in which Collis and Dorothy met. A kind of neon shooting star lighted the parking lot.

There was no one at the receptionist's station. I made my way past a sequence of well-lit but empty parlors until I came to one with a sign—"Phillips"—on an easel at its threshold. Fifty vacant soft-seated chairs faced the coffin in half-circular rows. I saw none of the family's names among the dozen or so large signatures in the guest book. I knew they planned to bring Collis here rather than to the funeral, and I sensed they would come late so he would be only among family when he looked at his last son for the last time.

Silent on the fluffy carpet, I moved toward the front of the room.

Farris's body had been put into a dark three-piece suit, a blue pinstripe. White shirt and handkerchief, black tie. Because his hair was freshly styled and cut close to his head and because his sideburns, chin beard, and mustache were now conservatively trimmed, I might not have recognized him. I saw scars I had never noticed in his eyebrow and at his hairline. Then I made myself stop looking. Although in life this was what I had done—looked at him, at his family —in death he seemed too vulnerable.

A muffled generator somewhere in the building reinforced and deepened the stillness. Recalling his hard voice, I half remembered certain words he had sent from Angola:

ABOUT WRITING THE BOOK YOU SAID IT IS DIFFICULT FOR YOU. WELL I TELL YOU LIFE IS VERY DIFFICULT FOR ME BUT I LOVE IT ANYTHING HARD FOR ME I LIKE IT

"WHY" I TELL YOU AFTER I DID WHAT EVER IS HARD
AND DIFFICULT FOR ME "I SMILE TO MYSELF". ONE THING
I LOVE ABOUT ME AND I BEEN THIS WAY I THINK I WAS
THIS WAY WHEN I WAS IN SIDE OF MY POOR MOM'S BODY
I DON'T GIVE UP "NO WAY" I TRY ONE WAY IT DON'T
WORK I TRY A NOTHER WAY "OR" I FALL OUT TRYING
"DIG" ANY ONE WHO NO ME WILL TELL YOU THIS. YOU
NO! I NO IT MAY BE CRAZY BUT I THINK IF I GET SHOT
"OR" STAB I WILL NOT FALL "FUNNIE" BUT I FEEL THAT
WAY.

There was a kneeler at the base of the stand for the coffin.
I sat in a chair near the front and thought about him.

After about ten minutes I rose to go, not wanting to be
there, a possibly intrusive presence, when Collis and the
family arrived. At the door I bent forward to sign the book.
It wasn't until then that I actually read the first signature.
"Velma Whittey."

The service the next morning was at Dorothy's church, St.
Raymond's, on Paris Avenue near the other end of the
project. The family came in a limousine, one I had no part
in renting. Among the scattering of mourners, I recognized
only Gloria, Connie, the two Trinas, Theron, Andre, and
Walter. Mistakenly, I hadn't believed Alvin could gain permission to come from Angola for the service, so I hadn't
tried to help make that happen; and it didn't occur to me
until I began recalling this to wonder where Collis Jr. was.

The white priest told us we were there because on December 17, 1950, Farris (he pronounced it like "Forest"), Farris
Michael Phillips, was baptized at St. Raymond's. The priest
said that entitled him to a proper burial and to enter the
kingdom of heaven if God saw fit, for only God knew the
state of his soul at the moment of death.

In his sermon the priest stressed the Christmas season and
the fact that officially it wasn't yet over. He reminded us that

the death of another reminds us of our own deaths, and he wondered were we ready. In a reference to a recent holiday murder in New Orleans, he suggested that our end could come in the form of a fifteen-year-old who didn't like the way someone tried to protect her pocketbook from him or, now tacitly alluding to the Bernhard Goetz shootings, he said we could die in an altercation in the subway or on a streetcar or a bus. He then spoke of a seventy-eight-year-old priest, a dear friend of his, who recently had been beaten almost to death.

A frail Creole acolyte swung the censer.

Gloria and Collis Jr.'s Trina wept openly after the mass ended. But there were no hysterics. I now wonder, would Junior have wept too? Is that why he wasn't there? No— now I realize he was probably with Collis.

At the rear of the short motorcade, I followed the hearse and the limousine to Holt Cemetery (for the indigent) near City Park. The family assembled swiftly around a corner plot. While I was still a short distance away, trying to walk quietly on the crushed shells, the brief burial ceremony began. I stepped past two men not involved in the funeral. Idling, these two smoked and joked behind their hands about money, behavior that contrasted with the sustained dignity of everyone gathered beyond.

I encountered many reminders of Farris following his death, but it was Gloria whom I most often heard speak of him. Especially around Christmas and on the 27th, the anniversary that he and Jerry now shared. She seemed to understand herself that, concerning her youngest brother, she was prone possibly to grieve too much. Yet she didn't apologize for it and would tell anyone that, among her siblings, he was the one most special to her—so special because "when he was comin' up it look like he never had no one, just a li'l boy always had to do for hisself."

While talking about Farris, she once said, "You know, my mother's in Hope too."

"Hope?"

"The name a the cemetery."

She mentioned wanting to save the money for "a stone . . . to go in Hope." Then she described the amount of carving that would be involved. "It's go'n be plenty words, got two names to go on it already—plus Jerry even though he was buried in New York." At that moment I realized something probably immediately obvious to many. I knew the family was very concerned about being buried properly, and in a family plot—this had been the point of the life insurance policies Collis paid on through much of his working life. All the family plots I was personally familiar with contained varying numbers of individual graves. And I had already seen the plot in Holt Cemetery, a plot scarcely wider than one casket. But it wasn't until face-to-face conversation made me think actively about a single stone naming them all that I grasped how it would be.

And still I had to ask. "Everyone will be there in that one, each on top of—?"

That was it, she said. There was their mother, Dorothy—the foundation. Then Jerry's name. Then Farris. Then each in their turn . . . "We will all stay together."

12

□

"I smell good people here!"

Collis Jr.'s voice rose in the stairwell before he came into view at the top of the steps. This was the gruffly flattering way he greeted me the last time I was visiting in Collis's room and he happened to come home. From the early eighties on, it was his room too, and most nights he slept in the double bed next to his father. Sometimes I would see signs of him—cigarettes, his lighter, an ashtray—on the other side of the bed on the windowsill or, if the window was open, on the fire escape.

Not that this meant he was home. He was rarely there during the afternoons or early evenings when I usually visited. Over the years I saw him maybe half a dozen times. But it would always be clear when he had been away or any length of time—recovering in the detox unit at Charity or just temporarily living someplace else—because then his father's cheeks and neck would be covered with a froth of whiskers. Junior shaved him.

In November and December 1984 he was in Charity with pneumonia. This was around the time Lionel was finally transferred to Angola and Farris's behavior gave increasing promise of some imminent catastrophe. Yet in our conversations Gloria spoke as often of Collis Jr. as she did of the other two. Describing the alcoholic seizure that led to the pneumonia, she said, "And after all that, he just look so innocent. Just sittin' there lookin' so innocent." When I mentioned AA, she told me he had gone to meetings in the past, "but look like none a that could stick with him." She made a point of stressing, though, that he was never the kind of drinker who didn't work. He was "a little like his daddy" about work. He had always made "some kinda money," and he would again when he came home from the hospital—even if his only source of income now was "just these li'l no-'count jobs" such as at the pool hall. But she seemed to take pride in his very stubbornness—in his marriages, for instance—and described how, like Farris, he would never be a heedlessly loyal lover as Alvin and Jerry were: "Auhn-*auhn!* Not Junior! Helen, a beautiful, light-skin woman, looked like a movie star. She left them chil'ren with dirty drawers and was next door dancin'. When he come home and saw it, that was it! He never went back to her even after she came beggin' him. Junior ain't never been a fool for no woman!"

Two days before Christmas in 1985, I visited to find Collis asleep and Collis Jr. the only other person at home. After letting me in, he limped on a wrapped ankle back toward the kitchen table, where he was eating beans and rice. Already dishing up another plate, he asked me to join him. "It was a fight," he said, setting the plate across from his and acknowledging his discolored eye socket and blood-marked eyeball. "The other day outside the pool hall." The ankle was more of a worry to him than the eye was. But it didn't matter; both would soon be all right again. And he wouldn't have to bother with revenge: "just last night" someone told him, " 'the dude beat you been jooged up bad with a knife by a woman.' "

As we ate, he talked about other fights, including one of his father's that he would never forget. He had been "just a young kid at the time," and he and Collis were about to board a bus on Canal Street. A large man had accidentally stepped on Collis's heel. Collis turned. " 'Whatsa matter, you cain't even say "excuse me" when you walk on somebody else's foot?' " The man said something like " 'Y' foot's in y' mouf.' " Collis hit the man with a right that broke open his mouth and sent him crashing through a picture window at Krauss's. With Collis Jr. pumping hard beside him, he ran down Basin Street and, in case witnesses were following, cut through the Iberville housing project. They caught another bus on Claiborne; it was a clean escape, one that gave the son evident pleasure in the telling.

He also seemed to take pleasure in telling how a similar pugnacious streak in himself had caused him to lose jobs. His main work skill was driving vehicular machinery—backhoes, forklifts, tractors. One of his jobs had been to ride a mower and cut the grass in all the housing projects in the city. He liked that work because it gave him opportunities to talk to women. But he stressed that he never went in any of their apartments—because he believed many of those women would be married even though they claimed they were separated and it wasn't worth "bein' dead" over. That job ended because the man there—"a black motherfucker, not no white one"—told him to put out a cigarette he was smoking in the office. He had just asked for matches—" 'Baby, gimme a light' "—from one of the female clerical workers the supervisor was sweet on. He told the supervisor he was going into the men's room to finish his smoke, adding, " 'That bathroom has four corners, you can come in and make me put it out if you think you can.' " The supervisor told him to punch out and draw his pay—which he did, with a lighted cigarette in his mouth.

In a similar way he lost his best job, one he had held for ten years, as grounds keeper at City Park. This was when he was married to his second wife, Lillian, and lived on London Avenue, at some distance from the project. He had asked "the big man there" for a few hours off to take care of some personal business, an errand that involved accompanying Lillian to the food stamp office. The man wanted to know exactly why he needed the time. He said that was his business. One thing led to another, a sequence that ended with his telling the man to have all of his money ready—retirement, sick days, everything—when he returned from his errand. That had been a job with benefits.

Early on, such stubbornness helped shape his ways. Throughout Collis Jr.'s youth, his father never ceased to be enraged about his first son's drinking. Once when Junior was in his mid-teens Collis hit him for smelling of liquor, and he had left home. He stayed away for three days, "just livin' in halls, me and my dog." Finally Alvin came to him and told him their father said, if he came back, "he wouldn' do nothin'." Which proved to be true. I heard Collis stirring above us as he said, "I know you know I still drink, still keep a dog too—Poochie. He out there somewhere now."

I didn't see him at home again until April 1987. On that afternoon when I visited, Gloria called for me to let myself in. She was on the sofa in her nightgown, watching TV and bottle-feeding Trina's new infant son. From upstairs, I heard deep male voices in loud conversation. But since Gloria wasn't dressed I went up immediately without lingering to find out who was there. Collis was in the rocker, puffing on but not inhaling a cigar, something I had thought he did only on special occasions. Junior lay on the bed, smoking a cigarette. They were arguing jestfully about a basketball play-off game on the small black-and-white set. Demanding that I sit, Collis scooted from the chair to the bed. We watched the rest of the game, and I was pleased that they didn't pay me much attention and continued to pick at each other's opinions about the players. After the game ended and the evening news from Washington began, Junior turned on his side facing the fire escape and may actually have fallen asleep. As the newscast ran its course and Collis and I exchanged occasional platitudes about the state of the world, he didn't stir. Not even when Collis's great-grand-daughter Andrea came in with a fresh-faced teenaged girl about her age and introduced her to her grandfather as "Farris's daughter" (by a woman I hadn't met).

Although I saw Collis Jr. other times in passing, my only specific memory is of one summer noon on Canal Street. While waiting in my car through a red light, I recognized him two lanes over stepping up onto the median curb while talking to a woman. After I shouted to him, he stared in my direction for several seconds. Then, taking temporary leave of the woman, he strolled back across the pedestrian walkway. Laughing at the novelty of such a meeting and slapping the roof of the car, he greeted me expansively and leaned in the window even though the light had changed. We exchanged only small talk as cars gunned around us in the sparse traffic, but afterwards he once spoke embellishingly of the time we had seen each other on Canal. " 'What's a white dude in a car doin' callin' out *yo'* name?' " he repeated, mimicking the woman's surprise. For such a trivial encounter to take on oral proportions of an incident reminded me of just how tenuous our connection was. It also made me feel he liked me well enough.

In September 1988 when I came home from a summer away, I hadn't seen him since before Christmas when he had flatteringly classed me as good people. On that December day he had also jokingly grumbled about Collis keeping him awake in the night talking. Now, in the heat of September, Gloria sang out "C'mon!" as I raised my hand to knock on the bedspread-shrouded screen.

On stepping in out of the brightness, photographs were my first impressions—more of them than I remembered—and diminishing wall space. The room was also crowded with people. Gloria sat on one section of the newly divided sofa next to Andrea, holding Andrea's newborn daughter, Derreon. Before I left in June, she had told me sadly that Andrea was pregnant. Now, proudly showing her to me, she seemed gladdened by Derreon, who had made her "a great-grandmother at fifty-four." Trina and one of her girlfriends sat facing them on the other section of the sofa. Trina's second child, William Farris Brooks, lay playing on a strip of rug between the four mothers.

Gloria's face suddenly lengthened and without clear transition she was apologizing over the volume of the TV for something I didn't understand. Apparently having forgotten the summer phone numbers and addresses I had left with her in June, she said she had tried to reach me at home in July. She had wanted to let me know about the wake and the funeral. As with first news of other deaths and shocks, particularly the ones that have become the losses that have stayed with me, I felt myself growing still. I could see Gloria's mouth continuing to speak, but I was now listening so hard I had trouble hearing her.

The child William had rolled to his feet and tottered through the kitchen to push open the back screen. Past William I saw him then, his mashed ear, fringe of white hair, and familiar large hand reaching absently toward the boy from where he sat in a kitchen chair facing out on the back porchway. Relief flooded my legs and I wanted to sit down, but there was nowhere to sit.

"It was them ol' DTs," Gloria continued, "that was what killed my brother." He had come in in the evening and gone up to bed. Soon after he lay down, he began to retch, as he sometimes did. But this time it was worse. "He liketa died right up there."

Speaking for the first time, Andrea said he *would* have died there if she hadn't looked in on him. This was what prompted them to call the crash truck. "My uncle was *dy*in'!" Affecting the manner of someone older, Andrea pronounced it absolutely as if to head off probable contradiction.

It was true, Gloria confirmed, he *was* dying in the van on the way to Charity, but "he came back" and lived a few hours longer in the emergency room. The attending doctor told them, " 'He was a fighter.' "

Where was Collis? I wanted to know.

"Where he at now. On the porch." The bearers had carried the litter in and out past him.

"It was the same night as Jerry and Farris," Gloria said, becoming agitated.

My expression must have shown I didn't understand.

"The twenty-seventh, honey, it was the twenty-seventh!"

I realized then that she meant not the month—December—but the *day* of the month. I asked had she told me before that this happened in July.

"That's right," she said, guessing my thought. "On Daddy's birthday. July 27. He died on his daddy's birthday."

I could see William standing against the part of the chair where his left thigh would have been. Lowering my voice, I asked how he had taken it.

"Oh . . . he know it," she said, deliberating, "but sometimes he'll . . . like . . . to put it out his mind, you know . . . he'll forget."

Andrea described how he often asked her and her friends what had happened and how sometimes they told him the truth and sometimes they told him her uncle was in New York.

Gloria put out her hand to signify how he sometimes patted the bed in the dark to determine if he was alone: " 'Glor*ia*. Better leave the door open for Junior. Junior didn't come in yet.' "

With her hand still extended, she gestured for Andrea to bring her the photograph album, which was on top of those stacked, and for me to take Andrea's place on the sofa. She wanted to show me the new pictures. Connie, Walter, and their four children had flown from New York for the funeral. Connie had said she and Walter would just have to bear that expense because her " 'family was dying too fast.' " Gloria had worried about how Walter might act "because a that in-ci-dent with Andre." But he was friendly and helpful "like always and didn' make no trouble." They had celebrated Collis's birthday on August 2, after the funeral, and the pictures were of this. In most, his birthday cake was in the foreground. There was one of him and Gloria, and several of him with family gathered about him. Although he was photogenic in each shot, in each there was an uncharacteristic reserve in his smile. In one, the frame was filled by burning candles and fifteen laughing faces drawn close around him on the bed.

He gave me one of his good smiles when I joined him out back. Except for his light robe and whiskery cheeks he looked in the best of health, sitting with his shoulders evenly against the bricks that framed the kitchen door. There was barely room for two chairs on the two-apartment porchway, but he insisted I bring another from the kitchen and have a seat. As we talked, William squirmed against him while staring at me, his abrupt brown hands clutching or patting absently at his great-grandfather's robe and tan face. Neither took direct notice of the other; Collis alternately looked at me and past me, briefly tracking the movements of neighbors. Suddenly he shouted, startling both me and a heavyset man who had cracked open his screen two porches down. "You know that book I tol' you 'bout!" he continued, addressing the man. Then followed a hollering explanation of me as "the one writin' it." The man and I nodded uneasily before he ducked back inside.

He tried to say the same to a preoccupied young man, one of his next-door neighbors, who kept coming to the screen partly blocked by my chair, but the young man was looking searchingly for something in the distance and Collis couldn't catch his attention. Eventually the young man opened the screen door and came out. I rose to let him pass to the steps, uncomfortable at being in his way on his half of the porch, but with scarcely a glance at me he made the four-foot leap down to the turf and hurried off up the alleyway. "Don' worry 'bout it," Collis said. "These kids, he don' never use the step."

Trina was now—at Gloria's insistence, I knew—serving us "cold drinks," cans of cola, but in this case also with glasses and ice. She had appeared increasingly thin on each of the last several times I had seen her. Today she looked strangely emaciated, as if anorexic, her fine looks gone. For the first time I noticed she was missing some of her teeth.

William followed her into the kitchen, whimpering. "Shut up!" I heard her tell him. "Or I'll give you somethin' to cry about!"

Soon he was back, holding a plastic bottle top, which he threw into the grass. Then he again took hold of Collis. Calling him "Willum" and making a fierce frown, Collis put his big fist against the child's face. William pulled down on his wrist and reached to drink from his glass. "Yeh, Willum,"

Collis said. "Sometime he sleep wit' Grampaw. An' sometime he don't."

"Hello, Mr. Phillips!" Two men who looked to be in their twenties sauntered on a sidewalk in the distance. The one who had greeted him raised a beer bottle. Temporarily wresting his glass from William, Collis lofted it overhead and began another shouted conversation. "Naw, naw! This ain' what you think I'm drinkin' here!"

During this exchange, I looked over to see Andrea now standing on the steps eating the last potato chip in a small cellophane bag. As William reached for the bag, she tossed it out on the grass. William scrambled after it. Discovering the bag empty, he dropped it too, then picked up a small plastic ball. He threw the ball at Collis, who batted it back toward him. During the rest of the time I was there, the ball skipped about generally back and forth between them.

And all the while we were talking—and saying nothing not said before: how's the family; how are you feeling; reminds me a one time in the *Bender Hotel*, corner a Prescott an' . . . As if for the first time, he spoke of facets of his past that I had already recorded and composed.

Gloria came out, now in one of her cheeriest moods. She too said things I had already heard her say. Some of her favorite versions of her father: how he would wash and stack the dishes and take their clothes off the line, how clean he was. "And he'll turn *off* a light now." How sometimes, because she was scary, she had to yell at him for having the upstairs in pitch dark. She wanted to tell it jokingly, but he scowled and began seriously explaining how, because electricity was included in the rents in the project, many residents heedlessly just left things on. Gloria quietly went inside. But he had little more to say, assuming no credit for his practice, as a matter of principle, of strictly using no more than he needed.

While William tumbled after one of his own errant throws, we just sat there, looking at the light. Despite the heat, it was a shimmering blue day, the air much less wet than usual.

I said I was sorry about Junior.

He glanced down the shorter stretch of the alleyway toward

several trees that grew across from the project on the other side of Senate Street, and I could tell that he couldn't or wouldn't ever really speak of this. "Ah, somebody *shot* Junior," he said brusquely, then tipped his thumb to his lips, his dismissive gesture to signify drinking and to explain his son's whole life.

The ball glanced off his shoulder; inattentively he trapped it on his chest.

Before I left, we talked a little, because I wanted to, of two things that kept attracting my eyes the whole while I was there. At the weedy edge of the alleyway, a tall hibiscus stood flowering, its trumpet blossoms nearly perfect. There were no other such shrubs within sight. No, he didn't know when it had come to be there, or if a resident or the city had planted and cared for it. One of the trees I most love, a sycamore, towered over everything that stood across Senate Street. The sun was now below the buildings behind us, but the supplicant crown of that tree remained radiant with pastel New Orleans light. We agreed it was splendid.

13

□

December 23, 1988

There was no answer to my knocks on the day that I now realize was exactly a year from when I had last seen Collis Jr. The screen door hung cracked open. I opened it farther and brushed aside the spread.

Oblivious to a hectic game show on the TV, a skinny old woman lay on the realigned sofa. She wore a halter and shorts, and slept with her neck arched across a bedroom pillow to protect the curlers in her hair. This position caused her to sleep with her mouth open, exposing her remaining teeth. I blinked, trying to adjust my eyes to the inside light, and looked again. I was looking at Trina.

A teenaged girl stepped up into the doorway behind me. I couldn't remember having seen her, but she seemed to know me. She said why didn't I just go on up.

He sat propped against pillows in the bed, smiling fixedly at the doorway. In his open pajama shirt he looked still powerful and as healthy as he had in September. Noticing me just after I entered the room, he laughed and, reaching for my hands, fetched me a smart slap across the shoulder. "I *thought* you was go'n come!

"Now. How long you here for?" he asked as soon as I sat down in the rocker.

"Well—I don't know." The question, which was so uncharacteristic of his manners, puzzled me. "An hour or so? Like usual."

"Oh," he said, nodding. "Thought you might could stay longer. But we gotta go back tomorra anyway."

"Back?" I recognized then that our minds were in different places.

"Yeh. Back home."

"We are home."

His features remained affable, but a wariness came into his eyes.

"Who's traveling with you?" I asked.

"Wuh . . . Gloria an' . . . Willum . . . an' . . . Aks Gloria when—" He fell silent.

Presently he touched a withheld fist to my knee. "Aw, man," he conceded softly.

I laughed along with him about the confusion, but I couldn't resist pressing him to tell me where he had believed we all were.

"Ah, sheee." Laughing harder, he pushed off my knee and into a defensive feint. "Thought we's in Vegas!"

A good enough place to be, I said, for someone in the fight game. Soon we were talking formulaically about the things we usually talked about. As we did, I listened to what sounded like small-caliber gunfire crackling all around outside. I had a disquieting but resigned vision of trying to walk naturally to my car while kids with, at the least, pellet guns targeted things from balconies overlooking the courtyards.

Possibly awakened by the racket, William trudged in torpidly. He had been napping in Gloria's room. With his feet on the floor, he lay across his grandfather's leg on the bed and gazed back over his shoulder at me until he fell asleep again.

Later, as I set about leaving, I said that, as in the fall, it would be probably several months before I saw him again. He nodded. "Well, that's left to you." We hadn't spoken directly of the book in some time. Standing in the doorway, I told him it was almost done. He became enthusiastic about that, and I couldn't help qualifying what I had said by adding that that didn't necessarily mean it would be sold. He shrugged, smiling and sitting free of the pillows. "Well. Then we'd just have us a book."

Gloria had returned from the hardware store while I was there, and I found her downstairs painting over some spots on the wall in the kitchen. I gathered it was part of her preparation for Christmas. Because it was the first such holiday since the death of my own mother, in subtle and unpredictable ways Thanksgiving had been harder than I could have imagined. I thought this now gave me a surer sense of how holidays were for Gloria. Yet she was in a much better mood than I expected. She bustled energetically in the kitchen and seemed intent on putting her house in its best order for the coming celebration. "Doncha think Daddy looks good?" she asked.

I agreed that he did, although I told her about his imagined visit to Las Vegas.

"Oh, he do that," she said. "He go off on his li'l trips, but the doctor said his pressure's better. You know him, he go'n *go* some kinda way." The doctor to see him most recently at Charity had shown concern about his enlarged heart and occasional periods of incontinence, but he also told her that a degree of such symptoms were almost inevitable in a man his age. Today she was disinclined to worry and I thought it a good thing.

She did mention again that Junior had died on the 27th, but she didn't dwell on it and she said nothing of Jerry and Farris. She confided that, because of an increase in crime in the project, she sometimes had fears for me when I came to see them. "It's so dangerous back here now, and worse every day!" But this was something else that was beyond her control, and she kept on with her painting, telling me, "You can't give up. No matter what happen, you can't give up." She had me thinking again of the continuing crackling reports from outside when Trina came in yawning and asked her why there never seemed to be any matches around.

During their brief vexed conversation, I thought of something I had been meaning to bring up, something that was then much on my mind. After they stopped speaking, I asked about Alvin's son Jules. Would she tell me again what she remembered of Jules?

"Jules?" She straightened thoughtfully, leaving off with the brush. "I kep' him, you know, just after he was born. Po' li'l thing." She shook her head. "Watn't no bigger'n what you might keep in a shoe box. You could put him to sleep in that right there."

We looked at the rattling drawer Trina had pulled out. Whatever else Gloria might have said about Jules that day was interrupted by Trina's further rummaging for matches. Not finding any, she dropped to her knees on the scrubbed tiles, her extreme thinness and bare feet now giving her the bodily appearance of a malnourished child rather than an old woman. I thought she was searching for matches under the stove, but she had craned down into the broiler to touch her cigarette to the pilot. Then someone spoke my name.

I looked around to see Collis Jr.'s Trina. Two or three other women were coming in through the screen door behind her. She took my face firmly between her hands—stilling a mannerly impulse that would have caused me to turn directly in to her—and kissed me not on the mouth but just beside it. Except for Collis, she was the only person in the family to have touched me so frankly. It was simply a friendly gesture. She wished me a merry Christmas.

We exchanged the usual other pleasantries, then spoke a little of her father. As the litter-bearers carried him out, he had told her he wouldn't survive this one, but she hadn't believed him. How could she have known? He had been rushed to Charity many times before. I think plain lingering grief caused her to tell me what he said. That and the ageless unconscious wish to compliment the dead by speaking of them.

There was some inconclusive conversation about my returning for gumbo, if Junior's Trina had a chance to make it, around New Year's. Then it seemed time that I leave. The women had evidently gathered for a common undertaking, which I sensed I was delaying.

Gloria walked with me past the groups of photographs to the front door. A bemused smile came to her face and she cast a look up the stairway toward his room. She put out her hand, his hand, as if he were patting the sheets to determine if he was alone in the bed. As she had done for me in September, she repeated his instruction. " 'Gloria. Leave the door open for Junior.' "

"Alvin!" Through the screen I glimpsed a familiar figure, her nephew, striding across the courtyard toward Gloria's. I was so surprised and pleased to see him that I had surprised myself more by shouting out his name. He looked pleased too.

I had meant to find out the date of his final release, but that date had passed without my knowing. I was aware that he had been granted weekends of freedom as part of the Parish Prison work-release program, and two summers before I had stopped to see him at Scottie's, the auto-air-conditioning shop where he then worked as a stipulation of the same program. Every several months for a while he had written me polite, empty letters, but except for an occasional note or small money order, I really hadn't kept up.

Now, though, he was more apologetic than I was, saying he felt bad about not contacting me and Steve Lemoine as soon as he was out for good but right away he had started a second job and since October he had spent almost all of his time working. He had hoped he could save for Christmas presents—for his father and for us—but that hadn't worked out. He hadn't visited his father yet either—he was apologizing to me for this too—but he didn't want to go back up there until he had presents and money to give him.

I didn't take his apology concerning Steve and me very seriously except to regret that he felt he had to make it. I was sorry that he was out of touch with his father, though, and also that I knew so little of specifically how it had been for them during the year they were both in Angola. In the summer of 1985, when Steve's successful appeal for a new trial brought Alvin Jr. back to Parish Prison and a plea-bargain arrangement that required that he serve only three more years, I was out of the country.

Alvin had written me that he and his father had seen each other only a few times in passing at Angola and that he had once thrown Alvin Sr. a package of cigarettes over a fence. I gathered from other reports that his son's presence there caused big Alvin to withdraw further into himself and the isolation of Camp J. I might have tried to learn more about this from Alvin Jr. now. But now I lacked the push to keep trying to know more.

"I didn't tell you he was out?" Gloria called. "I thought I told you!" I had hurried down into the courtyard to meet him, and she stood at the screen watching us. I had never seen him look as well. His starched denim jacket and jeans didn't fully conceal the new prison-born massiveness of his muscles, and it was Friday: he said he had been let off from work early because of the holiday. Even in the fading light it was evident that he had used the extra time to shower and put on conspicuously clean clothes for the evening ahead.

"Ain't he like Farris?" Gloria was saying. "A strong, fine man like Farris."

Trying to act as if he didn't hear, but smiling self-consciously now, an involuntary hand rising to deflect her, he began telling me about his jobs. He was continuing at Scottie's, where his boss, Mr. Lee, was "good people." At night he worked at the Metairie Country Club. He had been hired there as a hand on the custodial staff, but now—and he showed pride in telling it—he was in charge of the night crew. As I congratulated him on this and on not pursuing boxing at twenty-seven, I thought of how intimately he must have understood the attitudes of embittered men who would scorn his jobs as chump labor.

I said he was a hardworking man like his grandfather and, for most of the time, his father. He seemed to consider this; then—I made no effort to draw him out—he talked on about the night job and how it frightened him to walk after dark from the bus stop through opulent neighborhoods to the country club. I found it hard to imagine him being frightened by something I wouldn't have given a second thought. Then I thought I caught his meaning. That country club is in the legislative district that had just elected former Klan leader David Duke as its representative.

We talked on as the small explosions continued around the courtyard and the afternoon passed into the blue hour before night. I knew what the noise was now. Not any kind of gunfire. I had spotted children in the distance tirelessly throwing firecrackers into the twilight. Their efforts had been so constant that, thinking of them now, I realized that for stretches of time I, like possibly everyone else, had been oblivious to their noise.

As we began leave-takings, I thought of his future and took it as a positive sign that he was only visiting in the project. He had told me that, as before, he lived with his aunt Helen—who had regained her hair—and he was maintaining "a steady thing" with one particular "lady friend." It was an open question as to how long he could remain, like his grandfather, satisfied with cultivating the kind of work and on-the-job favor he had found.

Thumb up, he turned toward the apartment's steps and Gloria. It had been good to see him—a lift, in fact. This Christmas anyway he wouldn't feel bad.

14

□

1984–89

Once, during a countering moment of accord in our crescendo of worst days, Sally told me a story about herself, one I hadn't heard. In high school in the American West she had had a friend named Jules. The only black in the school and one of the few blacks in the town, Jules was an excellent student and the most popular person in his class. They weren't romantically involved and had only been close friends for a short time when he graduated and, with his family, moved away. He went on to college in another state, and they lost touch. This wasn't the story. This much she had mentioned in conversation on the single night long ago that had sufficed as our courtship.

Fifteen years later on another outwardly intimate night in New Orleans, I thought of Jules again and mentioned the thought. The newness in the story was her concession there in the music club that, yes, she probably had been attracted to Jules. Then she added that, well, it might not have been so much Jules she was attracted to as her "idea of Jules."

During the less pleasant, solitary nights ahead, I often returned to this statement and found in it confirmation of recently paranoid perceptions of mine that linked her current romantic involvement to politics and stereotypes both sexual and racial. Unfortunately for all of us, my replacement did play to some of the worst aspects of a negative type. But in time their involvement changed. And in time I stopped overlooking the fact that almost all we ever have of others are our ideas of them—ideas that we can let fester toward caricature or that we can nurture toward freedom and approximate accuracy.

"How's the family?" I used to worry whenever I took the time to consider a real answer to Collis's or Gloria's unfailing perfunctory question.

These days she has a good job downtown and a nice apartment in the Quarter. Julia in particular likes to visit there overnight. A while back Richard mentioned that she had a new boyfriend, someone older than she, mature, stable, black. Richard, whose judgment I trust, said he was "a nice guy."

My wife was a diamond.

The rest is her story. And theirs.

FIVE

Saint Jules

□

1

□

March 15, 1989

The years had softened him. I would have missed him in a crowd. He sat, waiting alone in the small dayroom, his face bloated, his good eye now also compressed into a steady squint. His shoulders and chest lacked mass, and he joked about "this li'l penguin stomach," the oval bulge beneath his sweatshirt. Though his dangling chin whiskers were still entirely black, gray and white flecked his mustache and the overlong hair swept back around his bald crown. For the first time I noticed resemblances to Gloria in various expressions that crossed his features.

He knew me at once and spoke my name, but as I sat down with him at the small snack-bar table, he shook his head in astonishment. He said he couldn't imagine who it would be, if not Gloria, when they told him he had a visitor; he hoped most that it was Diane and the children who had never visited him—Jules, Leslie, Farris, and Troy—but seeing me, well, "that was some news" too.

Although he expressed surprise that I hadn't "put that book aside," I sensed none of the suspicion and hostility I remembered from six, seven, and eight years ago. For one thing, he was older. *We* were older. There was an ease, an ordinariness, in the meeting that I sense will make it, even though it happened the day before yesterday, less distinct in memory than were the other times I saw him.

His cuffed wrists were chained to a strap around his waist, and a clean-cut young black guard sat watchfully at the next table. The guard's presence made me uncomfortable, but he sat partly turned away from the guard and seemed unbothered. Like the aging idlers that in a sense we were, we talked at length of his health. He mentioned problems with his bowels and his back and the "tissues" in his eyes. He said he could see, though, and there was no pain in the indentation that the surgery at Charity had left near his eye socket, but he felt he had to avoid being drawn into fights now because "if I get hit in the temple it could kill me."

"That's too old to be behind bars," he said, touching his hands to his eye, the chain lifting the hem of the sweatshirt away from his paunch. "Too old," he said, to have any interest left in "the type a life that put me here." He looked every year of the age he repeatedly attributed to himself—fifty-one, "fifty-one because it's 1991." I didn't contradict him although I was certain he was forty-seven. He knew exactly how long he had been in prison, though—sixteen years, going back to his time on Rikers Island, time that started in 1973.

Nor did I argue when he contradicted me. "Aw, man, you know my dad died," he said with mild assurance after I told him Collis was receiving good care from Gloria.

"Connie died," he said in the same quick way when I mentioned I had spoken with her by phone a few nights before. "Yeah, she died."

I withheld sad tidings and went on with the better news I had learned from Connie. I told him his daughter Leslie was now working in a hospital and going to school. I said his son Farris was reported to be quietly doing well, but I didn't also tell him that Farris now had a child. I had decided beforehand that his having become a grandfather was something probably best learned from family.

Several times he spoke in passing of his "oldest brother" and his "youngest brother," who he said were "still out there." I said nothing of Collis Jr.'s and Farris's deaths, as it occurred to me that Gloria was the only member of his original family who, in ultimate terms, was actually as he thought her to be.

While not knowing he was now an only surviving son, he insisted on giving me siblings, which I have never had—a lack I feel more sharply the older I become. He reminded me that he still sometimes saw my sister Doris on television, and he was aware of my younger sister—I think he said her name was Carolyn. My brother, whom he didn't name, I gathered was still somewhere in Angola.

Since we were talking of me, I mentioned Richard and Julia in order to share something of my actual life. He said he couldn't believe they were seventeen and twelve. This may have caused him to remember that we had once spoken of them years before, for almost clairvoyantly he said, "This time must have been some changes for you too?"

I said yes, the main one being that my wife and I had parted.

He nodded, looking at me closely. "Yeah, that's some changes."

I stressed that there were consolations, though—for instance, that Richard and Julia and I still lived together.

"Man, I can't—" He shook his head, though not in disbelief. "I can't even imagine that."

I said there was much about his life that I couldn't imagine.

Through a plastic window square we gazed beyond the chain-link fence and coils of concertina wire. There a prisoner moved back and forth in the early-afternoon sun, back and forth, cutting a corner of a meadow with a push mower. "Them fields," he said. "That's some water. Snakes out there everywhere. I never saw so many snakes. Moccasins, rattlesnakes . . ." He glanced cajolingly at the blank-faced young guard. "Timber wolves, a bear . . ."

More guards had congregated in the dayroom, and soon I would leave. But I had settled the main question that had brought me back to Angola, having now observed that in the years since we had seen each other, he had neither gone completely mad nor become content to be an institutional man. One of the first things he had said to me concerned his successful effort to interest a jailhouse lawyer in his "case."

I said I would tell Gloria and Alvin Jr. about seeing him; they probably would visit him soon.

"Say li'l Al got him a job?" he said, grinning and echoing what I had mentioned early on.

Although they were trying to be unobtrusive about it, the guards seemed to be waiting for us. He had already told me he still received daily medication: two pills—one for his "pressure," the other Thorazine. I asked if he was being treated all right. He shrugged as if to say sure, well enough, though the consideration was of no consequence: "You ain' nothin' but a con-vict." I asked if this new psychiatric building—at the entrance I had seen a plaque dating its completion in 1984—where he had been kept for the past several months was an improvement over Camp J. He shrugged again. "Each one's different—somethin' new to get used to—but don't matter, it's the same: you still doin' time.

"But this is the worst," he added. Although the guards could have heard us if they wanted to, he spoke now, not complainingly or provocatively, but as if merely stating a fact. "Rikers Island don't compare. Angola's the worst prison to be in in the country."

"Any messages?" I asked him.

"Just that I'd like to see my family. My wife and Jules and—"

Why Jules? I interrupted, drawing him out on it. What was it in particular about Jules?

He spoke of the problem with Jules's eyes and how he had "worked with him" shortly after he was born. He had sprinkled water on his brow and let it trickle into his eye sockets; in his own state of mind at the time he had believed that that might heal him. "I know I wouldn't know him now, but I'd like to see him. And my wife."

He thanked me for coming.

I said I'd be in touch.

"Aw right."

Driving home, I noticed small differences between the twisting road—the "snake road," he had called it—before my eyes and the way I remembered it. For instance, the steep, blind curve leading out of Tunica was much farther from the gate to Angola than I had first pictured it as being; the stretch of blacktop immediately approaching Angola was straight and flat. It was pleasant to note fleeting changes that had occurred along the way.

Back on the interstate, warm wind ruffling into the car, I thought about him. What I felt he needed—truly healing medical care—wasn't, so far as I knew, available to a person in his predicament in Louisiana, a predicament given urgency because he was so apparently less of a threat to himself or anyone now than he had been when I first met him, now that he was sobered and older than his actual age.

Soon the road took over and, intermittently, took my attention from this quandary. Something was finished. For the moment I experienced a deepening sense of release and of what I remember most easily from the trip: river birch, cypress, and sweet gum; oak, pine, and the so many more whose names I don't know. But, uncharacteristically, I didn't bother then about not being able to name them, just as I didn't worry then about the tainted earth or tainted water that all of them stood in. I saw flowering dogwood that, in reverse contrast to the sparse new green of the others, looked erotically and fully naked.

When, subjectless, I used to dream of writing a book, every ending I envisioned included the image of a long-haired young mother coming through the trees with her children in her arms. Gold afternoon light burnished the rolling vistas of treetops surrounding the highway. Like us, they would vanish in phases, or a flash. More keenly grateful for my life than usual, I took my hands from the wheel to scribble a phrase: "their every which way upward reach." I was happy.

2

□

March 16, 1989

Connie said no one spoke of him. Especially not his mother, Diane, or Diane's other children. Ever. If the subject came up, they would stop talking, or speak of something else. She and I were speaking of him now because I had asked her to help or advise me in trying to find him.

Years before, when worrying how to close the story, I had hit on an idea that gave me a sense of a thread and the confidence to continue; the idea concerned him because he was Alvin's last child, and even more so because of the skewed poetry of his name. After I had finished everything else, I would go to New York—to Queens or Harlem, the general locations where I heard his foster family might be —and I would visit him and tell him something of what I knew and admired about his natural family. The finish I wanted was to find him thriving among good people, an inspiration despite the long odds against him, but I intended to recount whatever I found. I trusted that at the least the trip would yield unpredictable elements through which I would recognize the right last words.

After unreturned calls to a machine, I had reached Connie a week before. We had talked for a while about two of her daughters, the oldest, Wendy, who is in her third year at City College, and the next oldest, Michelle, who attends

Hunter College. I told her I was going to Angola to see Alvin. She said she had wanted to do that when she was in New Orleans for Collis Jr.'s funeral, but Gloria had warned her against it, saying that under those circumstances it would be too much of a shock for her; according to troubling recent reports, he sometimes now spat on people. When I mentioned my projected trip and search, she was silent. I told her I had mentioned the same thing to Alvin Jr., who had said he would call me about it but never had. Finally she spoke of the family's understandably guarded feelings about what I wanted. She said Diane would be my main obstacle, and she and Connie were now estranged. There were new problems in Diane's life. One involved city agencies and a child she had had not so long ago; the other problems were related to the current crack epidemic. Despite all this, Connie had said she would look into it and call me back in a few days.

Those days having passed, I called in the morning, afternoon, and evening, and each time I reached the machine. As I sat looking at the red phone on my knee, I suddenly reached an understanding: I wouldn't find him. Without the family's official cooperation, my tracing him would be a cold if not an impossible process, and it was clear enough that the family members most involved had no interest in my pursuing it. If Connie, or someone else, were to call back from New York to support my purpose, I would soon be on the train—I had maneuvered myself into a position from which it would be hard to do otherwise. As it was, I called again and told the machine that I had seen Alvin and he was better than I expected. Then I said that, unless someone there wanted to contact me during the next week about what I had proposed, I wouldn't push the matter further.

As soon as I left the message, I felt both relieved and disappointed, but most of all I felt depleted, drained of the energy and patience that such a search would have required. I also knew that, without the idea of Jules, I wouldn't have been able, already, to have spent what I had.

3

□

March 24, 1989

"Set down! You ain' no stranger. Jus' throw that off if you don' wanna set on it."

"I don't want to sit on your clothes."

"If you wanna set on it, *set* on it, 's aw right. I put it there because since I've been sick, I've lost a lot a" (laughing) "weight behind. When I set on that hard chair" (laughing) "hurts my boodie! How y' been? You look better now than the last time you was— I didn' tell y' but you didn' look so good, I don' know, thin in the face— I didn' say nothin' to y' because I don' like to discourage a person. But you look today—"

"I guess that was right before Christmas that we saw each other—"

"Yeh, I b'lieve it was. Anyway, I even spoke to Dorothy an' Gloria about it. 'Randy didn' look so hot. He gen'ly look better than that.' Look fresher, you know, in the face and all. Like you do now."

"I've been finishing the book."

"Oh, yeh, you workin' on— I told Gloria you was workin' on a book. I said, 'Well, Randy was workin' on a book. I don' know how he doin' wit' it, but he said he *was*.' That's the reason why, you know—"

"Wanna see it?"

"*Yeh!* You gotta duplicate of it?"

During the long near-silences to follow, as I took the manuscript out of the wrapper and he then faintly whispered the words that he read, the tape recorded the talk, shouts, and laughter that rose in the stairwell and were a fitful current of sound throughout the apartment. Girlfriends of Trina's were there along with Trina, Gloria, Andrea, Keyon, Trina's son—his great-grandson, William—and Andrea's infant daughter—his great-great-granddaughter, Derreon.

"You ain' puttin' all that in a book!"

"Why not?"

"Oh, but that's go'n be more'n one book, though— Naw . . . ? '. . . On . . . the Life . . . Collis Phillips . . . Rings, Life a Collis Phillips* by . . . Rudolph . . . *Bates*'!" (Laughing.) "I's talkin' 'bout you th'other day! I said, 'Randy's a regular guy, you couldn' help but—' "

"That's just my address at the bottom."

"I'm go'n hafta go to the doctor, Randy, git my eyes checked, gittin' so I don' see letters too good, hafta git real close. '. . . won't do no mo'.' Who is Eddie Jones?"

"Guitar Slim."

"Aw, yeh, yeh, I understand . . . You typed all that . . . ? Aaugh! Damn! Man!" (Laughing.) "I ain' laugh, but that's a lot a work, man. Shee! No wonder it taken you so *damn* long!" (Laughter.)

"—let some water out, some water off." (Hands braced on the mattress and nightstand, lowering himself to kneel on the floor next to the bed.) "See, since I been sick I always keep my li'l pee cup right side the bed, you know, where I can git at it—"

"So you don't have to go all the way in there."

"Shee!" (Laughing.) "I might cain' git there sometime!

*The original title was *Rings: On the Life and Family of Collis Phillips*.

That's why Gloria bought me this pee can . . . All I do, jus' reach down there side the bed, don' hafta jump up an' run to the lavatory."

"You still move around good with your arms and shoulders."

"Aw, *yeh!*" (Laughing, on his knee, throwing a cross-hook combination.) "Yeh, that ain' gone yet!"

"What are you looking for? Can I bring you something?"

"Naw, here it is here. Knew I had it. Like t' wipe my hands . . . Always keep a wet rag close by the bed." (Pushing up with his arms and swinging himself back to sit at the head of the bed with his back against the window frame.) "Yeh, book, book on my life. That's real nice, Randy, I think, really is . . . My susta in Texas, hafta send off to her. One for her an', uh, one for my auntee's husband, Uncle Fritz. He lives in New Avery, Texas. He's a big farmer out there. He been here to see me. I always kid him 'bout not bein' a heavyweight. He's a big two hunerd an' sumpum. Lives in that li'l country town."

"He was married to, uh—?"

"My auntee, my mother's susta, Aunt Timmy."

"Timmy? I never knew about her."

"I haven' saw her in years, I couldn' say too much about her now. She sent me three pair pajamas. There one a the shirts. On that rack right there . . ."

"Gloria!"

"That's Trina on them steps."

"Trina. Trin*a!*"

"Heuh?"

"W-would you ask your mother to come up for a few minutes? I want to show her something."

"Ma!"

"What!"

"And I want to show you too."

"C'mere!"

(Gloria on the stairs, then entering amiably, Derreon in her arms. Trina following, then sitting quickly at the foot of the mattress, her grandfather and I sitting on the corners at the head, breeze from the window at our backs, the bed, like the furniture downstairs, in a new position. Gloria taking a seat in the rocker, slightly winded, conciliatory, the manuscript and small machine between us on the bed.)

GLORIA: "Aw ri-ight . . ."
COLLIS: "There the book."
GLORIA: "O-o-h! Here, Trina, hold my baby girl. Turn the light on, 'cause you know I can't see too good."
TRINA: "Hey, Derry. Grampaw!"
GLORIA: "All this, Randy?" (Taking the stacked pages onto her knees.)
COLLIS: "Grampaw eat this li'l girl up, eat this li'l girl up."
TRINA: "That's upside down, Ma. Turn it round."
GLORIA: " 'The things that I . . .' "
RANDY: "Collis Jr. said he used to play that—"
COLLIS: "Yep."
GLORIA: "Oh yes. He sho' did. My baby used to play it all the time, I miss him too. 'The things I used to do, Lord, I won't—' "
COLLIS: "Set down, Randy! You ain' gotta stand up—"
GLORIA: "Daddy, you remember that! Usta git in the bed and sing it: 'The things I used to do, Lord, I won't do no more!' "
COLLIS: "—come to my house, you ain' . . . *strang*er! Long as you been comin' round here . . . ! There Grampaw li'l girl."
TRINA: "Wait, Grampaw. Here."
GLORIA: "The Gym, the Coliseum, Auditorium, the Penitentiary. Yeh, the penitentiary . . . St. Jude, yeh, that represent our—"
COLLIS: "See, that's the book a my life, my past life . . . See the paper, you wan' read the paper with Grampaw? 'House votes for a minimum wage of $4.55!' "
TRINA: "Momma goin' one page. You'll be al-l-l day."
GLORIA: "How many years, Randy? 'Bout three, huh? Four?"
RANDY: "Well, you can see from where it starts . . ."
TRINA: "Whoa! You been talkin' to Grampaw for ten—"

GLORIA: "Daddy *been* knowin' Randy."

RANDY: "So, so everything is in it—"

GLORIA: "Yeh, I know that!"

RANDY: "—except, except the last pages . . . Because the last page is . . . right now."

GLORIA: "Oh, eh-hunh, this is the last—"

RANDY: "We're making it now."

GLORIA: "Thing in it 'bout my brother died, huh?"

RANDY: "That's in here, yeah."

TRINA: "Hey, hey, hey, Derry. Derreon."

COLLIS: "Come to Grampaw. Gi' me that li'l red girl."

TRINA: "I didn' know—all them years."

GLORIA: "Eh-hunh, see Randy been knowin' Daddy, oh, for—"

COLLIS: "Knew Randy round the gym! Randy come round the gym when I first met him."

A voice from downstairs: "Trina! You want William on the porch?"

TRINA: "No-o. He's not de-cent . . . Or is he?"

Our fractured sentences ranged still further from the sense of summation I had hoped for. Eventually Trina rejoined her girlfriends, who seemed to be both downstairs and in the other bedroom. The rest of our talking went on after the tape ran out. Listening now, I find myself attending, as much as the words, other cadences of sound: the lift and drop of Gloria's breathful voice, its murmurings and sighs; his percussive interjections, most of them faint but a few that boom; the creak of the rocker after she sets the manuscript aside and takes Derreon back into her lap; and, in the stammering lulls between, like birds, the more and less distant hubbub of everyone else.

RANDY: "What would you like to see come in the future?"

COLLIS: "Well . . . I'd like to see my son come home from prison. I'd like to see that."

GLORIA: "Maybe I could git a house to rent out, and I'd take my brother with me and try to take care of him. Bring

him to a hospital, treatments, show him that his family
is there *for* him, you know. Bring him to a clinic for his
nerves. They got group therapy and— Yeh, maybe a li'l
house— Me and my daddy would have our *own* yard!"

COLLIS: "All I got to do is go back to Texas— You know,
I'm lookin' right at seventy-five."

RANDY: "Excuse me for, for contrad—"

COLLIS: "Anything you wanna say, say it."

RANDY: "I believe you're looking at eighty."

GLORIA: "I don' tell him, I don' tell him, 'cause he git angry."

COLLIS: "I's bawn July 27—"

GLORIA: "My daddy's doin' good. And he is strong too, and
you better git out his way when he git them li'l tan-
trums—" (Laughing.) "He know how to cut up too!"

COLLIS: "Now you subtract that—"

GLORIA: "Daddy, Randy know y' birth date, Randy has been
where you been born, and Randy know what he's talkin'
about. Now, I'm not arguin' but I'm tellin' you, he
know."

COLLIS: "Yeh, yeh, that's right, I give it to him in the book."
(Laughing.) "Now you cain' keep Randy's book, Gloria."

GLORIA: "Oh no, un-unh— Talkin' about Owens in the book
too. Grampaw Owens, the one that died with the balls
and chains."

RANDY: "Jack, uh-huh. You see that part about him?"

GLORIA: "Um-hunh. This just go on and on, it's so *pretty!*
And it took some time! Oh, some toils, huh?"

RANDY: "It has been, yeah. Because I don't want to pretend
to—"

GLORIA: "Oh no, no, it ain't pretendin', this is real, here. It
might seem like a dream, but everything you put there
has actually happened."

COLLIS: "Real life, I'd say. See, some people don' understand
this part but—"

GLORIA: "And you know it happened! You are a *fact* to know
it happened. Every little inci-dent. My brother, my
brother like t' died in that bed right there. Right there
where you are, right in this room . . . Three brothers

in a row. Our family have had so much tragedy, we both is very hurted, sometimes we both be cryin'. And, you know, I've still gotta lot a bitterness inside me, I can't help from bein' like that. Sometimes if you wasn't a strong person you would believe, like, you know, *where is God?* But like our pastor explain us in church, that was unfair to crucify Jesus, right? He didn't do anybody anything. He healed the blind, the sick, the sick people like me, like my daddy. And look what they done *Him!* Right?"

COLLIS: "There's a pi'ture right there to show y'. Him settin' in the middle of it. I bought that pi'ture in Miami, Florida, waitin' for a plane. He tuck two loaves a bread and fed all twelve a them disciples."

RANDY: "Last night—"

GLORIA: "Yeah. That's the Last Supper. Yeh, Daddy—"

COLLIS: "The Lord's Supper. And everybody had enough!"

GLORIA: "But, you know, I think this here. You think about God, He still don't make no differences 'tween people, people in the world does this, right?"

COLLIS: "Why, sho'!"

GLORIA: "He is equally fair. We all die the same way, no matter what color, no matter what graveyard. We can't take nothin' with us. Like you take these, these psychic people, these witchcraft people, if you look at these people, they can't save their own self, they gotta die just like you and me."

COLLIS: "They all die!"

GLORIA: "So it proves that above all unfairness, He's got all power. And He don't make no differences between people."

COLLIS: "That's *man*'s law that makes the differ'nces!"

GLORIA: "You know, Randy, if I sit down with my little granddaughter, she's seventeen years old and she had this baby— And I think, 'Whaow!' You ever think about a woman walkin' round with a big baby in her stomach all day!" (Laughing.) "Just think a that, that's enough to blow your— This girl sits here, seventeen years old, and there's this baby, turnin', and these people watchin' this baby. And God fixes y' body to open up like that. And you bump into chairs, sofa, you go all over! And these babies come out perfect! Eyes wide open, hollerin'. Now that's a miracle there."

COLLIS: "That's through Him, though. Don' f'git. The Almighty."

GLORIA: "But the unfairness, I say, well— I was very bitter, I was a bitter person, umn-hunh, I usta walk around and hate everybody. I jus' hated people, because I was mad with the world about my kids and me and everything. And I felt, 'Where is God that allow this!' But I *changed* and I have a lot more changin' to do. And I, when I came to and started relatin' somethin' about God and church and goin' to church, all that helps me, and all that bitterness is, is kinda bombed outta me. But I'm *glad* because, if you don', it's a terrible feelin'— You might go kill somebody! That's how people gits like that. I believe that! But you can't carry all them bitter feelin's, it's not good, it's not—"

COLLIS: "Some people don't understand, but this world here is supposed to be destroyed. By fire. And every man will be judged, every man and woman will be judged accordin' to their deeds—"

A young woman passing the doorway: "Hello-o!"

COLLIS: "And the righteous will be put on the right—"

GLORIA: "Aw ri-ight, how y' doin?"

COLLIS: "—and the hellcats will be put on the left."

GLORIA: "Yeh, we aw right."

RANDY: "Who was that who just came in?"

GLORIA: "Oh, that's my li'l friend Bobbie D., that used to be D-wight's girlfriend, his li'l heartthrob."

RANDY: "How's Theron? I haven't seen him in a while."

GLORIA: "Theron is doin' good. He's gotta nice wife. Did you know they buyin' their home? They have a beautiful home. Nice house. His wife works. He into church. And he works every day. Oh, but when I see him back here, I go to cuttin' up. I say, 'What you doin' back here?

Why you back here? I don' want you back here!' He
say, 'Momma, my people is back here.' But the minute
I see him back here, I'm quick to think he go'n git with
that old crowd. And I feels to believe I don't want him
with that. But he assure me he's goin' straight home.
And his wife, she's doin' a good job with Theron. She
say he always usta tell her that he like plenty money,
but she always showin' him that he don' want that 'plenty
money,' ehn-ehn!"

COLLIS: "No, you can go wrong wi' that. A *honest dolla*'s
better'n a hunerd you come by the other way."

GLORIA: "How can you enjoy money an' you gotta be hidin'
behind the windows an' all that—?"

COLLIS: "I worked down Carondolet Street. Right up to the
three hunderd block. All them differ'nt offices. Seiffert
and Sons; Wood'ard and Wight; General Finance
Company—"

GLORIA: "You remember Momma usta help y' too, my
momma used to help him—"

COLLIS: "Well, yeh, sho'. Had the key—!"

GLORIA: "She would clean that house and cook, oh, she was
a spotless cleaner! Then for three o'clock or four she
would dress us and help clean them offices. Usta take
and tie Alvin in the chair—Al was a li'l biddy boy—
while she would dust and mop. And my daddy would
come about seven, eight o'clock. And by the time Daddy
would come, Momma would be done cleaned two, three
offices."

RANDY: "You'd be helping her."

GLORIA: "Oh, yeh, I'd empty the, uh, spittoons. And li'l
Junior'd be tryin' to dust off with the li'l feather thing.
We all would help, and we couldn' wait till our daddy
come. Here come Daddy, trottin' 'cross the street. Then
we could go to the Palace Theater. You remember,
Daddy? He would take us to the show. We had a beautiful
life . . ."

COLLIS: "Pardon me for intrude, for inter-rupt, but, *Randy!*
Woncha take a *sanwich*, or *sumpum*—?"

RANDY: "No, thank you, Mister Collis. I ate right before I came."

GLORIA: "Oh, you ate, Randy? 'Cause I didn't cook, but I could send, get you a sandwich, fish dinner—"

RANDY: "No, no, thank you, I have to leave pretty soon—"

COLLIS: " 'Dead man free . . . in teenage shooting . . .' "

GLORIA: "Well . . . So like I was sayin', Randy, we had a happy childhood life. My mother and daddy used to throw big, nice parties."

COLLIS: "House parties—"

GLORIA: "They was good livers, yeah. And my mother was so pretty, she used to dance. They was happy, they seemed like they had such a good life, to start with. But when my mother lost her health. Everything started goin' down— When my mother lost her health, that's what really killed us. That's it, when my mother lost her health . . ."

COLLIS: "Bought that rockin' chair special for Dorothy."

GLORIA: "Yeh, I took care a my mother till the day she died. Put her last underclothes on her. She called to me that mornin' and told me she was go'n die, but I didn' believe people know when they go'n die. She musta dreamt that, huh?"

COLLIS: "Well, Dorothy had been sick so long—"

GLORIA: "She called me that mornin' like Daddy calls me in the mornin'—he be lookin' for his breakfast: 'Y'all gittin' together?' (Laughing.) And she told me she was go'n die—"

COLLIS: "Hey, Willum!"

GLORIA: "—and I didn' believe her."

COLLIS: "Boom!"

WILLIAM, falling across the bed and pretending to shoot a yellow plastic pistol: "Bow! Bow!"

RANDY: "Did she seem to accept it?"

GLORIA: "Well, she jus' tol' me, 'Oh, Gloria, my head hurts so-o bad.' I said, 'Wait, Momma, I'm go'n git you a Anacin.' Well, I turnt, but when I turnt, my momma jus' turnt her head, and died . . ."

RANDY: "You couldn't have done any better."

GLORIA: "No, I took care of 'em when they's on St. Bernard
like that. I usta go every day and clean up, cook, wash,
mop, for both of 'em when they was both crippled in
that house over there. I usta git up early in the mornin'
when my chil'ren was comin' up—"

COLLIS: "Gloria has been very faithful to us. Really."

GLORIA: "I would fix their breakfast, give 'em both their
medicine, after I got through cleanin' and washin', I'd
leave about three and go home to my house."

RANDY: "And work some more?"

GLORIA: "That wouldn' a worried me except all the time I
was doin' these things I was facin' so many other
problems."

COLLIS: "Her own chil'ren."

GLORIA: "And the po-lice was in the house . . . Guns . . .
Runnin' behind chil'ren, wanna shoot— Aw, all
that . . ."

COLLIS: "Well, that's the way life is, Randy. A steep hill."

GLORIA: "I seen the time when my daddy almost couldn'
breathe. And I would put, me and Junior would put him
in the tub. It would be so *hard* for us to do these things,
and he would say, 'I'm go'n help you, I'll help you.'
He'd say, 'I know I gotta be clean.' And he'll git in that
tub, and he'll wash hisself—you know from that time
you came, them times you been here. And I say, 'Daddy,
hold on to me, because if we fall, we both go'n fall.' And
he'll grab that door and grab on to me. And my daddy
git *out* that tub! And dry. Dry him off. Say, 'I'll jus' sit
on this rocker till you put a clean sheet on my bed.' "

WILLIAM, now waving a small photograph: "Gramaw, who
this is?"

GLORIA: "Oh! Randy, here my sister's picture. That's the
mink coat her children bought her." (Holding it so I
can see, a snapshot disclosing an expression both embarrassed and proud.) "I didn' tell you? Bought her a
mink, all of 'em put together and bought her a mink. I
said, 'Well, great, girl! You doin' good, huh?' Now that'll

show you, that's our strength. She lost her son and look how she's strong, workin' every day—"

WILLIAM: "Gramaw, what that is?"

GLORIA: "That's Auntee Connie."

WILLIAM: "I wa' show my grampaw Auntee Connie . . ."

GLORIA: "And then you go and put it back."

COLLIS: "Yeh, Will— See, Randy, if you give up, it's over. Got to keep on. I been knocked down three, four times—"

GLORIA: "I'm like that too. My daddy can tell you I been very sick in this house. Like t' lost my life right in that room. But, you know, all you got to do is *breathe* to feel better—"

COLLIS: "Gotta try, cain't jus' give up—"

GLORIA: "I don't know where it come from, but I'm hard to go down with the bell." (Laughing.) "I'm hard to go down with that bell. I'm hard, I'm right here. I musta got it from Daddy and my mother. 'Cause look how long my mother stood sick. She even stopped walkin'. My mother was in a wheelchair at the age of forty-five."

ANDREA (in the room as if to take her daughter from her grandmother, the doorway now filled by Trina, Keyon, William, Bobbie, and others): "Bobbie thought she was cryin'."

GLORIA: "See, what you shoulda did, you didn' wanna listen to me—"

ANDREA: "I gotta wash her walker today? Who this for?"

GLORIA: "That's for Bobbie." (Handing back pictures of a wedding that earlier had been handed through the doorway to her.) "She coulda been playin' in her walker while you doin' things and I got things to do—"

ANDREA: "What that is, Bobbie?"

BOBBIE: "At my reception."

GLORIA: "What I mean, you don't like to listen."

ANDREA: "This is what you wore for your weddin'?"

GLORIA: "She could play in her li'l walker. She gotta li'l walker she plays in round here. And I got these li'l grandchil'ren here, these li'l biddies . . ."

COLLIS: "Grampaw go'n hit that li'l boy in the nose. Bang."

GLORIA: "Oh, he love William. You cain' touch William. 'What y'all doin' to my baby—?' "

ANDREA: "Gramaw, Keyon took off her shoes and put slippers—"

GLORIA: "That's real nice pictures, Bobbie. 'Don' touch William for nothin'. Don' touch William.' "

TRINA (now also mimicking him): " 'That's not your child. Don't be hittin' on him. C'mon by Grampaw.' Gotta grab William downstairs if you go'n grab him, 'cause if you come in the room his grampaw might knock you in the head."

ANDREA: "Where your reception was?"

BOBBIE: "By Bet' Lee house."

GLORIA: "That's lovely, Bobbie. That's so nice . . . But all in all, Randy, we still got the strength. We still here, right? We still here. We right here—"

TRINA (to William): "Don' be lookin' at me, you didn' want me to hold you."

GLORIA (to Derreon): "Yeh, say, 'My granny got the strength.' Say, 'Yes.' Say, 'When my granny walk out that door, you wouldn' believe that she ever went down by the bell, because she don't never hold her head down, she thinks she's the proudest thing there is.' Here we got another little biddy one, look, a li'l, a li'l trait, another li'l offspring." (Laughs lightly.) "Daddy, after while, she go'n be in y' room too, worryin' you, gittin' in y' bed, look—"

COLLIS: "Pardon me for inter-rupt— Lemme make Randy this point. See, when you been through the storm, you don' worry—that's *out*. You jus' gotta *live*—"

4

□

July–August 1989

He lay forty-two days in Charity. I had planned to be out
of town for most of the summer. Although I spent time
dithering about what Julia would do in my absence, I'm not
sure exactly what caused me, at the last minute, to cancel
those plans. If I had gone on with my trip, I would have
known little of what follows. As it was, I was home in the
heat when word came he was in the hospital, and soon
afterwards I sat with Gloria in a waiting room and listened
to her tell why he was now back in Charity.

It was bedsores, she said, bedsores that had become
infected because he couldn't always control his urine and
bowels. Even though he was "very, very sick," he had been
denied admission after a cursory examination at the hospital
the previous Friday. And after a horrific weekend for both
of them, he had had no choice but to sit on the festering
sores in a wheelchair and wait in a line in a corridor during
the protracted admission process on Monday. By then the
infection had spread internally. She told me doctors there
now had "fears for his life." She was also acutely worried
that his present condition somehow reflected on her physical care of him, and I tried to discourage her from blaming
herself.

When finally we were permitted a short visit with him on

the crowded intensive-care ward, we found him only dimly conscious and penetrated with tubes. Through the transparent oxygen mask covering his lower face, I saw him say my name and attempt a big-mouthed social smile. His hands retained much of their vigor, though, and reminded me of Tommy Hayes, an ex-middleweight of his whom I once met at the Auditorium.

That night while local pros hammered each other, he was the focal point of a fluctuating group of well-wishers—including Tommy Hayes—who came over to pay their respects and to sit with him for a round or two. After drawing me aside and garrulously describing his new career as an actor in California, Tommy Hayes had talked about rubbing. No one else in any gym he had ever worked out in could "rub" like him, Hayes said, gesturing with a flick of his head back toward his former trainer, who at that moment was exchanging loud opinions with younger ex-fighters gathered nearby. "If that man once put his hands on you, if he *rubbed* you," Tommy Hayes continued, "you wouldn't *have* no rubbin' from nobody else." In Charity in mid-July 1989, I felt the pressure of his grip and thought about seeing him massage others in the gym on Magazine—even the white amateur, who had asked him for it—and how, although he often spoke of my sore muscles needing a rubdown, it had somehow just happened that he never rubbed me.

During the next week his large hands grew larger, their fingers and palms, like the rest of his body, swelling and thickening as he retained his fluids and his complexion turned from tan to yellow. Each day when we visited, Gloria would take him brusquely by one of his hands; she would squeeze it and pinch it; with spit on her thumb, she would smooth back his eyebrows, then stroke his forehead and bald crown and pat his cheeks hard and kiss him. Meanwhile she would be whispering, "Daddy, wake up, I'm here, you got to be strong!"

To her extreme relief and, I think, to the surprise of a few of the young residents, antibiotics eventually retarded the infection, the swelling subsided, and he began to shrink.

Surgery was now necessary in order to pare fetid flesh from his buttocks and back.

For several days after this operation, he seemed unable to emerge from the anesthesia. But around the date of his eightieth birthday, for which Gloria had brought a small cake, his older sister and his younger daughter, with whom I had been in contact by phone, arrived from Texas. I think that, after Elma Walker stepped authoritatively onto the ward accompanied by her niece Joyce Stafford, each of them dressed in very expensive good taste, the staff regarded him differently. Not that their treatment of him changed—he invariably received the best professional care they could give—but I sensed they were surprised to learn they had been in charge of a person connected to people of means.

Although it strained him to talk, the visits of Elma Walker and Joyce Stafford during the three days they were in town brought more animation into his expression and strengthened his vital signs. For me, driving them and Elma Walker's teenaged granddaughter, Lady, to and from the airport and around town was both difficult and pleasant. Because of my windy, non-air-conditioned car, I worried even more than I said about their comfort, styled hair, and fine clothes, but I enjoyed their attentiveness to me and their energy, particularly Elma Walker's. One afternoon in a French Quarter shop she saw a hat that pleased her. She was seventy-nine and a wearer of hats, and she bought the sweeping-brimmed thing with such infectious decisiveness that, looking at her laughing face and fierce eyes, I felt I was with him.

After they flew back to Texas, his condition for some days remained weakly stable. He still could scarcely speak, but it usually was evident that he recognized Gloria and me. He was sometimes in the care of an aloof, compactly shaped nurse to whom I, like other males on the floor, was distractingly attracted. On various visits my concern for him was complicated by my efforts not to gaze openly, for instance, at the bleached down whorled in the hollows of her suntanned throat. One morning as she gathered the materials for a sponge bath, his eyes followed mine, and I felt certain he knew what I was thinking before I went on to tease him about his good luck with women.

Many days he was virtually comatose, but one afternoon just before visiting hours ended he began to whisper. Even leaning close, I had trouble making him out, but the subject he attempted to speak of was clear enough. "Junior?" I asked him. "What? What is it about Junior?"

"Yeh, Junior," he breathed and continued in faint, fragmentary whispers I couldn't fully catch.

What he said concerned either our meeting Junior or waiting for him somewhere. There was that and something else, some small thing I eventually lost because I made not the first note about any of this that summer.

I do remember, though, that also on this day he startled me by, with unsuspected life in his arm, raising my hand toward his mouth. Reflexively I resisted; then, realizing his purpose and with our pretty nurse occupied with a patient dying nearby, I moistened some gauze and wiped away the dried secretion caked where his lips met. When, as I had seen her do, I coated these newly cleaned places with Vaseline, he said "Thank you" in a clear voice, then immediately receded into his more usual sleeplike state—before he began whispering.

The hottest days passed in this way. I collected parking tickets—Charity visitors in cars must leave them at short-term meters along the curb—and drove Gloria home in the evenings. Or if not home—and this was as often the case— I left her at the shrine of St. Jude on Rampart Street, where she lighted candles and seemed soothed by the hushed solitude. The residents spoke of another operation and the growing necessity of cutting away more of him. But he began to swell again, so the surgery had to be deferred.

The most urgent problem involved his catheters. Temporarily denied admittance one midday, I waited by the door to the ward and watched a resident examine him at the same time that he instructed a group of interns gathered about the bed. The resident laid back the sheet, and the interns, each clutching a can of Diet Coke, leaned forward. I saw two of them exchange a look, as if this sight was something they might quip about later. Then one shifted his stance in a belated effort to cover an involuntary grimace, and I saw the resident, who had pulled on a rubber glove, fork aside the smaller catheter. Next he began tinkering energetically with the larger one. As he did, he lifted a slack flap of skin. The interns stirred nervously. It hurt me too, and more, yet I couldn't not look—though after an instant, the size of the raw, gaping surgical wound in his groin made me lower my eyes.

Irrationally I felt anger at the interns, the hospital—at the partitionless ward on which most of the many patients, though surrounded by machines, were exposed to plain view. Angry with life, I crossed the floor—an infraction of rules that was remarked by no one, because everyone else in the large room was absorbed by his own suffering or hard work. The resident continued to agitate the bloody tube. All the interns looked on, stilled, in uniform technical concentration. Between two of their white shoulders, I saw his naked old torso. I looked away, then looked again. I looked at his face. Deeply sedated, he apparently felt none of it; according to what I could see, he lay peacefully asleep. My grieving began then; and in waves, over time, it came and it went.

In following days the residents, or the nurses, somehow helped restore him, and his bloatedness gradually subsided, revealing to a clearer extent his actually withered state. He regained a measure of consciousness and thrilled Gloria by faintly saying her name. Then near mid-August, I entered the ward to find another comatose patient in his bed. The pretty nurse was busy, so I had to take from an orderly the information that he had been moved to a ward several floors above, where there was a remarkable bed whose cushioning of circulating air and sand didn't aggravate bedsores.

Now alone in a glassed-in cubicle, he lay semiconscious,

his breathing like rapid hiccups. On this less populated floor, Gloria was allowed freer visits, and she spent herself tirelessly in trying to revive and comfort him. "C'mon, Daddy," she would say, stroking or slapping his cheeks. "C'mon! Hey . . . ! Hey . . . ! You got to wake up." With my occasional help, she assumed some of the tasks of nursing him, and she took it as a miraculous sign that, once as she was about to leave, he startled us by entirely turning his head and accusing her—"Where *you* goin'?"—in his resonant voice of old.

Although he wished not to discourage her, the resident in charge of him couldn't share her hope. More surgery was needed, but—because of the resurgence of the infection and the weakened state of his enlarged heart—anesthesia now probably would kill him. So we waited while the resident tried new drugs against the infection and seemed in mild wonder that he was lasting so long. Gloria kept hoping, and I came numbly to the ward each day, the gravity of the situation sometimes vivid to me, sometimes remote. Sometimes I felt pressure in his hand, but usually it was like the fleeting reflex of a dreaming sleeper. Once, though, as I mused above him, his chin scabbed from nicks made by the orderly who had shaved it, sudden strength in his grip took all my attention. His eyes changed, and I saw recognition come swimming up into them. Then he was there, and very faintly his smile.

"Yeh. Whatcha say?"

Then, almost at once, he passed out from the effort.

After that, I saw only a blind gaze beneath his flickering lids. As my mother had during her last hours, he began to gulp the air, laboring for each breath. This went on for days. In an instance of dejection Gloria fretted that not even our visits were any help to him, that for all he knew we might as well not be there. A weekend nurse urged her not to think of it in this way. This kind woman, whom I had seen him try to bite a week previously when she adjusted the tube in his nose, told Gloria it was very important that we came, that though he couldn't show it, he could hear us. Later, when I was alone with her, the nurse told me hearing is the last sense to go.

A few hours past midnight on Sunday morning, August 27, one month after his eightieth birthday, the phone rang. I was in bed, near sleep, driftingly thinking not about him but about an unpredictable young woman from whom I had been futilely hoping for a call. The voice of a doctor I had never met told me mine was the only telephone listed on his chart. Within the next several hours, someone from the family needed to be at the morgue beneath Charity to identify the body. Well . . . yes, the doctor answered, Mr. Phillips had been alone when it came.

When I reached Gloria's apartment, Alvin Jr. and his girlfriend, Latricia, were among those already there; Helen Cheno's number must also have been, elsewhere, on the chart. The contrast between Gloria's bright windows and the dark courtyards reminded me of the late night I had gone there for Farris. That so many people were gathered in the front room and kitchen at such an hour also reminded me of the same night—except that now, and this was something I had never seen, Gloria was the center of things. Either in shock or beyond grief, she was cheerful. Perhaps enjoying the attention, she talked on and on, frequently repeating the platitude that it was finally a blessing. Later I went with Alvin Jr. on my last trip to Charity.

There are many, many faces in the photographs Connie sent me, the photographs she and Walter took at the Greater Asia Baptist Church the morning of the funeral. From New York, her face and Walter's, and those of Connie's oldest and their youngest, Wendy and Raven, and Connie's nephew Farris. From Texas, more than a dozen—including his sisters, his daughters, and his uncle Shug. And from New Orleans,

Gloria, Theron, Collis Jr.'s daughter Donna, and Alvin Jr. and Latricia, who then carried and would in two months give birth to Alvin III, my godson.

In many of the photographs, the faces, their eyes intent on Alvin—the last son—press forward, hands outstretched to touch him after the guards fell back by the entrance to the tiny church and permitted him—according to prison procedure, one of the last to arrive—to walk by himself up the short aisle to the front. There, in denim and a work shirt, he sat between his sisters within reach of the casket. In several of the photographs of the two of them together at the front of the church, the tears are still shining on the face and in the reddened eyes of his grown son Farris, who hadn't seen him since early childhood. Everyone else closely related to him wept too, as did many old friends, but he shed no tears. As in the distant past, composed in the spotlight, he quietly greeted and remembered them all— including a few by nicknames long out of use. Almost all of the photographs are focused at angles that exclude the manacles on his wrists and the chain and strap that bound them near his waist.

There are no photographs of the moment when Charles Joseph and a surplus of those who happened to be toward the front hefted the casket and bore it from the church. But Connie and Walter used the rest of her film outside on the sidewalk because the guards had orders to take Alvin immediately from the church back to Angola. He remained calm and clear through everything—though, delaying the motorcade to Holt, it took the polite, wary guards quite a while to edge him out to the prison van on the curb because of all those who came up to embrace him.

Back on Senate Street after the funeral, Theron corroborated a sickening suspicion that had deepened in me during the short time we were in Holt: he had been mislaid, the casket lowered into a grave made in the wrong plot. There

had been only one family member—one of his grandchildren—present at the cemetery several days before when
the practical arrangements for burial were made. Under the
influence of a drug at the time, his granddaughter insisted
another unmarked plot was the correct one even though the
man who dug the grave, Theron learned just prior to the
funeral, had challenged her opinion.

Gloria had cooked chicken and other dishes in order to
feed everyone, so we went in and ate while trying to decide
what to do. During the meal, I learned from Ernie Cojoe, a
referee and ex-fighter, that, though Mike hadn't come to
the wake or the funeral, he had been at the church the
previous afternoon and was the first to pay his respects when
the body arrived from the mortuary. And before Theron,
Walter, and I left, Gloria, who was not nearly so calm as
Alvin had been, told me Andrea had suffered a miscarriage
the day before her great-grandfather died—a loss that Gloria
regarded with relief and, now, as another blessing.

Outside, a patrol car pulled up behind me as I walked
toward where I was parked. Theron and the other men
outside, even Walter, receded into the cut at the corner of
the building, and I was conspicuously alone. The special-
duty project patrol had assumed that a white man in a suit
would be there to buy or sell drugs. While the red light
revolved, one of them called in my driver's license number
to determine if I had a criminal record; the other told me
about a drive-by attempted killing that had occurred in
another courtyard that morning. Eventually I checked out
satisfactorily, and the policemen drove off. Theron and
Walter stepped out of the shaded alleyway from which they
and others had been watching. Then they followed me to
Holt in the car Walter had rented.

The custodian at Holt was a young man who took his job
seriously. After Connie that morning had confidentially
questioned the location of the plot he had opened, he
consulted the office of city cemeteries. Now in writing he
had the correct information: "Phillips" was in the same

general area, but two rows away. Looking at the weed-thatched swatch of ground that he pointed to, I then recognized the place Farris had been laid.

The unrelenting late-summer sun drew sweat from all of us. The young gravedigger's bare, surprisingly slight chest was already streaming. He wore a St. Louis Cardinals cap and spoke with an impediment; a name—"Ronnie"—was burned in large characters into the belt that helped hold up his jeans. Stuttering, he allowed that even though the new grave was already covered over, he and his helper could transfer the casket. But it was now Saturday afternoon, a few minutes from the time—on the gate a sign said so—when the custodian left for the weekend. And anyway, it had been the family's mistake.

Theron kicked a hunk of earth, already having begun the muttering, indirect talk that would lead to an oblique reference to the gravedigger's family, and possibly a fight. For reasons not then sorted, I keenly didn't want that. It was a matter of a few dollars—well, more than a few, but still paltry payment for the job that had to be done within the next hour without shelter there in that burning early-afternoon heat.

Ronnie and his sun-blackened helper immediately fell to the work while Walter drove us in maximum air-conditioned cool to the nearest money machine from my bank. On the way back we stopped outside a tavern for another beer for Theron—he had been drinking since the funeral. While Theron was inside, Walter spoke in annoyed amazement. Although, I knew, Walter wasn't a man to gossip or complain, he couldn't help but give some voice to his frustration and impatience with the quality of his Louisiana in-laws' lives and with the way things were being done.

As we walked back through the gate at Holt, Theron tipped his bottle to acknowledge several other young men loitering by the entrance. When they were almost out of earshot, he began to speak profanely of spooky people who robbed graves. It wasn't necessary for me or Walter to shush him about this. We weren't more than half of the way along the shelled lane when something else—something on the air—took care of that. We could see that, up ahead, Ronnie and his glistening helper had just finished opening the plot. Despite the smell, Theron led us on. Apparently oblivious to what repelled us, Ronnie stood in the shallow grave, idly severing clods with the edge of his shovel. He began a laboring explanation of why pine decayed so quickly. Then Theron turned away, having determined with his eyes what we needed to know.

I glimpsed a scrap of plaid cloth and, turning, heard Theron curse plaintively while also saying something about his uncle Junior's burial suit. Before I turned away from him too, I saw Theron raise the bottle and both hands to his eyes and start back toward the gate.

Then it was time for me to drive Joyce Stafford and Elma Walker and her son and niece to the airport in the air-conditioned car I had rented for the purpose. With Ronnie and his helper toiling at a distance in the glare, I left Walter and Theron at the gate, confident that Walter would see the job through.

After the prolonged, sweet fuss at the airport, I returned slowly through the suburbs, then took my favorite route back, the road along the levee.

I parked adjacent to the gate and saw, from that angle, that no one, not even the loiterers, was still there. As I walked on the crunching shells, I could feel that the intense heat of the day had begun to slacken. The light belled high above the horizon and the easy swish of the undergrowth told me this could be no time other than a late Saturday afternoon near summer's end. We were entering a transitional period that, in New Orleans, fosters moments of renewal and calm because, in New Orleans, an easier season comes next.

Farther up the lane, I noticed something I hadn't recognized so strongly before: the beauty of Holt, its intense green and the mature live oaks that stand singly and in groups on its grounds. Choice land—though tucked away from common sight. I remembered that developers had made efforts to gain control and make use of it. Very probably, in the next century if not sooner, they'll have their way.

The work of the florists lay in clumps on the fresh mound. Now there was only the clean scent of newly turned earth. Where a stone would have been, either Theron, Walter, or Ronnie had partly buried a bottle that held a weathered plastic rose.

Birds, grass bugs, the quiet. I looked at the trees and listened.

Acknowledgments

I would like to thank Jonathan Galassi and John A. Glusman of Farrar, Straus and Giroux, and I especially thank their former associate Rick Moody, who thoroughly undertook a formidable editorial task and whose author's skills and sensibility made the surviving pages more soundly tempered and far more readable than I could have done alone. For her effective and considerate representation, I also wish to thank Faith Hornby Hamlin and her assistant Douglas Stallings, of Sanford J. Greenburger Associates. And I appreciate the meticulous copy editing of Jack Lynch and the ample assistance of Jenifer Berman.

I am grateful to the National Endowment for the Arts and the Louisiana Arts Council for supporting fellowships; to Blue Mountain Center, the MacDowell Colony, and the Corporation at Yaddo for residencies that facilitated and encouraged writing; to the editors of *Louisiana Literature*, the *New Delta Review*, and the *New Laurel Review*, in which earlier versions of parts of this work first appeared; and to Anne Bernays and Justin Kaplan, who in 1984 chose five excerpts for a special issue of *Ploughshares* and who made a good suggestion concerning the end of Part One. My gratitude also to Tim O'Brien, who generously read a long early excerpt at the Bread Loaf Writers' Conference and gave me very valuable criticism and encouragement.

I owe personal thanks to Kathleen Hill—whose kindness and sure understanding of what I hoped to do were a constant support. Special thanks, too, to Myron Tuman and Eric Trethewey, who have been my friends for twenty years. At a low point in my experience, without my asking and almost against my will, Myron took charge of an unruly and much longer version of the manuscript, promptly read every word, and, in showing me how I might improve it, gave me the help I needed to continue. And without the daily opportunity, in the seventies, to be closely acquainted with Rick's "rhetoric of balance" and his example as a scholar, poet, and former SAAU light heavyweight champ, I doubt I would have tried to embrace the world of the gym in the first place.

Last, and most, I thank many of the people who appeared in these pages or in other ways helped me toward writing them.

Collis and Dorothy Phillips.

Alvin Phillips; Collis Phillips, Jr.; Connie Phillips; Farris Michael Phillips; Jerry Phillips; Gloria Sorina.

Josephine Stafford; Joyce Stafford.

Fanny McGlory; Elma Walker.

Alvin Phillips, Jr.; Donna Phillips; Farris Phillips; Kevin Phillips; Trina Phillips; Donald Smith; Wendy Smith; Andre Sorina; Dwight Sorina; Theron Sorina; Trina Sorina; Raven Sutton.

Keyon Blakes; Andrea Sorina; Derreon Sorina; William Farris Sorina.

Gloria Anding; Vince Arnona; Frank Blackburn; Thomas C. Braniff; G. Andrew Boyd; Cheetah; Helen Cheno and Rita Diaz; Alan Citron; Junius Pierre Cole III; Michael Cusimano; Salvador M. Cusimano; Debra; Wellington Dejoie; Thomas Dierker; Malcolm Faber; Johnell Fernandez and Walid; Tracy Heinlein; Freddie Johnson; Philip Johnson; Charles Joseph; Steven Lemoine; Tony Licata; John Lincks; Robert Martin; Arnauldo Maura; Howard McCurdy; Lou Messina; Arthur Lew Moskowitz; Philip Motley; Willie Pastrano; Diane Phillips; Latricia Phillips; Cheryl Ponthier; Johnny Powell; Melita Remple; Helen G. Roberts; Linda Rome; Ronnie; Angelo Sinito; Eldridge Stafford; Ralph Stafford; Waddell Summers; Walter Sutton, Jr.; Albert Tate, Jr.; Terrell; Vernon Thomas; Diane Walser; Joe Weber; Velma Whittey; Shirley Williams; Christine Ziegler.

Lavinia and Willie Dozier; Jane Emmons; Ernie Messner; the Mockbees; the Nevilles; Cindy, Ruth, and Richard O'Donnell; the Roses; Carolyn F. and Thomas R. Ward, Sr., and family; the Webbs; the Wolfes; James D. Woodfin.

Kelmie Tacon King and family, Maybelle and Dudley Lang, Esther and Horace Thurber—and families.

Julia Bates; Richard Bates.

And Sally.